tear here

Get Your Papers in Order

Before you leave the U.S., take care of these details:

➤ Update your will and insurance policies.

➤ Leave a copy of your itinerary and power of attorney documentation with a family member or friend.

➤ Find out if your personal property insurance covers you for loss or theft abroad.

➤ Find out the international number your credit card company has to report the loss of a card from abroad (800 numbers don't work when you call from outside the U.S.).

➤ Carry only the documents and credit cards you'll need in a wallet or purse.

➤ Pack your U.S. driver's license with your photo in it, even if you're not driving anywhere.

➤ Get an international driver's license before you leave if you need one.

➤ Make two copies of your credit card numbers, traveler's check numbers, phone numbers to report lost cards, and airline ticket numbers.

The Complete Gift-Giving Checklist

Many countries have strict taboos on certain gifts:

➤ Blue: the color of mourning in many countries.

➤ Black: the color of funerals in many countries.

➤ White: the color of mourning in most of Asia.

➤ Purple: it's bad luck in Italy.

➤ Yellow: a "bad" or "unlucky" color in many countries.

➤ Chrysanthemums: a "funeral flower" in many countries.

➤ Red roses: the color of love (therefore, inappropriate for business purposes).

➤ White lilies: considered a "funeral flower" in many countries, including the United Kingdom.

➤ White asters: another "funeral flower" (especially in Switzerland).

➤ Yellow flowers: "bad" color for flowers (especially in Iran, Mexico, and Peru).

➤ Cheese: a poor choice for Asians (many of whom are lactose intolerant).

➤ Knives or scissors: signifying severing of relationships in many Asian countries and Italy.

➤ Straw sandals: bad luck in Asia.

➤ Green hat: means you're a cuckold in China.

➤ Handkerchief: associated with sadness or mourning in many countries.

➤ Storks and cranes: associated with death in China.

Credit Cards and Traveler's Checks

➤ Write your passport number and the telephone number of the U.S. embassy or consulate in countries you're going to visit.

➤ Write down the type of card, number, and 800 number (in case of loss or theft) of each credit card.

➤ List the number and face value of each traveler's check; cross each off as you cash it.

alpha
books

D0474235

Emergency Information Card

Keep this essential information and several copies in your bag, purse, or wallet, with your important papers:

- ➤ Your name and your family's names
- ➤ Your home address and phone number
- ➤ Your work addresses and phone numbers
- ➤ Your doctor's name, address, and phone number
- ➤ Health insurance carrier and policy/ID numbers
- ➤ Names, addresses, and phone numbers of friends and relatives
- ➤ Any special medical conditions or allergies

Healthy Traveler

It's hard to be polite when your stomach is knotted up and you're spending most of your time in the W.C. (water closet). Contaminated food and water can be a big problem in other parts of the world. The following are some suggestions for how to protect yourself.

Water

In parts of the world where water is a problem:

- ➤ Don't use ice.
- ➤ If you drink directly from a can or bottle, wipe it off so it's clean and dry.
- ➤ Don't brush your teeth (or rinse) with unsafe water.
- ➤ Canned or bottled carbonated beverages are okay to drink.
- ➤ Beer and wine are okay to drink.
- ➤ Boiled water is okay to drink.
- ➤ Hot beverages made with boiling water (such as coffee or tea) are okay to drink.

Food

In parts of the world where contaminated food is a problem:

- ➤ Don't eat peeled fruit.
- ➤ Don't eat raw shellfish.
- ➤ Don't drink unpasteurized milk.
- ➤ Don't eat raw meat (or rare hamburger).
- ➤ Be careful of red snapper, grouper, and sea bass if it was caught on a tropical reef instead of the open sea (highest risk areas: West Indies, tropical Pacific, and Indian Ocean).

Diarrhea

In Latin America, Africa, the Middle East, and Asia, the risk of getting diarrhea is between 20 and 50 percent. To help prevent the "green apple quickstep," try the following:

- ➤ Don't eat contaminated food or drink unsafe water.
- ➤ Take Pepto-Bismol (2 oz. four times a day or 2 tablets four times a day)—but don't take for more than 3 weeks.
- ➤ Ask your doctor for a prescription antibiotic in case you get diarrhea—take it at the FIRST SIGN of a problem.

If you do get sick:

- ➤ Avoid dairy products.
- ➤ Drink plenty of safe liquids.
- ➤ Rest.
- ➤ Take affected children or babies to a doctor right away (dehydration is serious in youngsters).

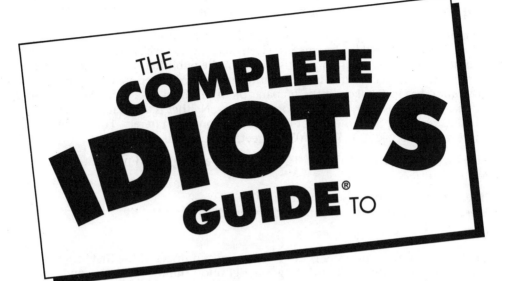

THE COMPLETE IDIOT'S GUIDE® TO

Cultural Etiquette

by Carol Turkington

alpha books

Macmillan USA, Inc.
201 West 103rd Street
Indianapolis, IN 46290

A Pearson Education Company

Contents at a Glance

Part 1: Overview of International Etiquette   **1**

  1 What's Your International "EQ"?   3
*What you absolutely, positively need to know before you
get on that plane to go abroad.*

  2 Officially Speaking   21
*How to act and what to call the international officials
you'll meet along the way.*

  3 Hosting International Visitors   31
*How to welcome foreign friends to the U.S.: everything you
need to know to bridge that cultural chasm.*

Part 2: North America and South America   **41**

  4 Canada   43
*Learning the small cultural differences of our northern
neighbors, and how not to offend.*

  5 Mexico   53
*What you need to know to get along in the culture of our
southern neighbor.*

  6 Latin America   63
Deciphering life in Central and South America.

Part 3: Eastern and Western Europe   **73**

  7 Belgium   75
*More than chocolates and beer: Learn about the cultural
ins and outs of Belgium.*

  8 France   85
*Manners still matter in France, and here's how to handle
yourself with joie de vivre!*

  9 Germany and Austria   99
*Deciphering the right and wrong way to do just about
everything in Germany and Austria.*

  10 Italy   109
*Cutting your way through red tape and business intricacies
in Italy.*

  11 Portugal   121
*What goes on in Spain's tiny neighbor, and how to
flourish here.*

  12 Spain   131
*What's important (and what's not) in this country
of the sun.*

13 Switzerland 141
If it's clean, tidy, and runs on time, odds are it's Switzerland: Learn how not to offend.

14 United Kingdom 151
They may be our cousins, but there's still a lot to learn about cultural etiquette here.

15 Greece 163
Learning how to mind your alphas and omegas in conservative Greece.

16 Scandinavia 175
Deciphering the cultural differences between the five countries of Scandinavia.

17 Eastern Bloc: Czech Republic, Poland, and Hungary 189
Strengthening your understanding of these three eastern Europe countries.

18 Russia and the Commonwealth of Independent States 197
Learning the details of the CIS—and how to handle the newly emerging cultures.

Part 4: Asia and the Pacific Rim **209**

19 Hong Kong and Taiwan 211
As new relations of China, Hong Kong and Taiwan are both ancient lands moving into the modern world.

20 China 223
Recognizing the distant, difficult, and cultural mystery that is China.

21 Indonesia and Malaysia 237
Discovering the similarities and differences in these twin countries.

22 Singapore 249
Learning about the new modern Singapore cloaking the traditional country of its past.

23 Japan 261
Discovering the importance of the group in Japan.

24 South Korea 275
The Land of the Midnight Calm: Discovering the many faces of South Korea.

25 Australia and New Zealand 289
Remembering you're not in the British Isles when you come Down Under.

Part 5: The Middle East   **301**

    26 India   303
        Learning about the vast differences in India, and how to negotiate the cultural minefields that exist here.

    27 Saudi Arabia   315
        Discovering the Muslim taboos and how to survive here (especially if you're a woman).

    28 Egypt   327
        It's big, it's Islamic, and it's easy to put a foot wrong here.

    29 Israel and the Palestinian Territories   337
        Discovering the cultural do's and don'ts of this religious crossroads.

Appendices

    A Glossary   349

    B Further Reading   353

    C Embassies   355

       Index   365

Contents

Part 1: Overview of International Etiquette   **1**

1 How's Your International "EQ"?   **3**

Parlay-Voo Humma Humma?...4
    Silence Is Golden 4
    Avoid Slang 4

My Card 5
The Eyes Have It 5
A Handshake or a Kiss? 5
Bearing Gifts 6
Supping and Sipping 7
Space Out! 7
Gestures 7
Saving Face 7
It's No Joke 8
R.E.S.P.E.C.T. 8
    Age: Not Always a Dirty Word 8
    Other Customs, Other Lands 8

You Want It *When?* 9
You're Wearing *That?* 9
Formality, Please! 9
Joe Camel Goes Abroad 10
Cash In Your Tips 10
    Passport to India and Beyond 10
    Get Your Papers in Order 10
    If You Have Medical Problems 11
    International Health Insurance 12
    Customs: Know Before You Go 12
    Pack with Aplomb 12
    Consular Info Sheets 13

Hotel Safety 13
    Where to Stay 14
    What's Bugging You? 14

Travel Healthy 15
Travel Safe 15
    Train Safety 15
    Rent-a-Safe-Car 16
    Just Say No! 16

Street Smarts 17
Workplace Security 18
Terrorist Attack! 18
Arrested! What Do I Do? 19

2 Officially Speaking   **21**

Royal Addressing 21
    Prince Consorts 22
    Princes and Princesses 22

Dukes and Duchesses	22
Sons of a Duke	23
Daughters of a Duke	24
Marquess/Marchioness	24
Sons and Daughters of a Marquess	25
Earl/Countess	25
Son/Daughter of an Earl	25
Viscount/Viscountess	26
Son/Daughter of a Viscount	26
Baron/Baroness	27
Baronet and Wife	28
Knight and Wife	28
Esquire	29
Dowager	29
Royal Etiquette	29
Royal Has-Beens	30
You Are Excellent!	30

3   Hosting International Visitors   **31**

Bagels and Beer	31
Holy Day Taboos	32
Thanks, but No Thanks	33
Slurping and Burping	33
The Clean Plate Club	33
Gifts That Keep on Giving	33
Colors of the Rainbow	34
Stop and Smell the Flowers	34
Other Objects	35
Wine and Liquor	35
Wrap It Up	35
Not Too Expensive	35
The Envelope, Please	36
Be On Time	36
Up Close and Personal	36
Cover Up!	37
Line Up!	37
Talk Is Cheap	38
Great Job!	38
Eyes Up!	39
Let a Smile Be Your Umbrella	39
Cultural Roundup	40

Part 2:   North America and South America   **41**

4   Canada   **43**

Second Largest Country in the World	44
And the Prime Minister Is…	44
French vs. English	45
En Français!	46
The Religion Mosaic	46

Let's Celebrate 46
Quelle Heure a-t-il? 47
   Open for Business 47
   If It's 2 P.M., It Must Be Quebec 47
Cultural Ins and Outs 48
"Hi There!" 48
Body Talk 49
Gestures 49
Canadian Clothes 50
Sealed with a Kiss 50
Bring On the Cadeaux! 50
Potage to Nuts 51
   Check, Please! 51
   What's for Dinner? 51

5   Mexico   53

It's All North American 53
   El Presidente 54
   Speaking the Lingo 54
   Keeping the Faith 55
Life Is a Holiday 55
On Time, Sometimes 56
   Open and Closed for Business 56
Socially Speaking 56
¡Hasta la Vista! 57
   ¿El Capitán? 57
   Charmed, I'm Sure! 58
Up Close and Personal 58
Señorita Power 59
Suit or Serape? 59
Tactful Time 60
Artful Negotiation 60
To Give or Not To Give 60
   Por La Señorita 61
Entertainment Mexico Style 61
   Mi Casa es Su Casa 61
   Quinceanera 61
Gazpacho to Nuts 61
   Minding Your Mexican Manners 61
   Siesta or Lunch? 62
   Late-Night Dining 62

6   Latin America   63

It's All America 63
Speaking the Lingo 64
Holiday Time 64
Never on Time 64
   Do You Have an Appointment? 64
Getting Down to Business 66

Hello, Goodbye 67
   What's Your Title? 67
   Offer Your Card 68
Group Hug! 68
Gestures That Work 68
Chivalry Lives 69
Stylish but Conservative 69
The Art of Conversation 69
Small Package, Big Heart 70
Zuppa to Nuts 71

Part 3: Eastern and Western Europe   73

7 Belgium   75

Chocolates and Beer 76
   Who's In Charge of the Netherlands? 76
   French, German, Flemish … 77
   Roman Catholic 77
Time for a Break 77
Don't Be Late 78
   9 to 5? 78
   Take This Job … 78
   If It's 2 P.M., It Must Be Brussels … 78
Think Conservative 78
   Privacy, Please 79
   May I Present My Card? 79
How D'You Do? 79
   What's in a Name? 80
Nix on Gestures 80
You've Come a Long Way, Mlle. 80
Dress Up 81
Don't Get Personal 81
Fair and Proud 81
To Give or Not To Give … 81
Guess Who's Coming to Dinner? 82
Pistou to Nuts 82
   Time to Eat 83
   To the Host! 83

8 France   85

Ou Est la France? 85
Who's In Charge of France? 86
Parlez-vous le Francais? 86
Faithfully Yours 87
Let's Go On Holiday 87
Quelle Heure a-t-il? 88
   Wiggling Away 88
   Open Up! 88
   Never on Sunday 89

Formality—*Oui!* 89
  Privacy 89
  What's in a Name? 90
  Shake Your Groove Thing 90
  A Kiss Is Just a Kiss 90
  The Eyes Have It 91
  Let a Smile Be Your Parapluie 91
Doing the Wave 91
Men and Women 92
Wear the Best 92
  In the Business World 93
  And Then There's the Beach 93
Talk Is Cheap 93
Visiting *Chez Nous* 94
  Hostess Gifts 95
Bouillabaisse to Nuts 95
  Garçon, Beware! 95
  Minding Your Ps and Qs 95
  There's a Dog at My Table! 96
  Breaking Your Fast 96
  Take Me to Le Cafe! 96
  Dinner Is Served 97
  Raise a Glass 97

9 Germany and Austria   **99**
Stuff You Should Have Learned in School 99
  Where It's At 100
  Sprechen zie Deutsche? 100
  Half and Half 101
Holidays in Germany and Austria 101
Be There! 101
  Open and Close 102
  Appointment, Please! 102
  If It's 2 P.M., It Must Be Berlin! 102
"Our Kind" 102
Auf Wiedersen! 102
  Who Goes First? 103
  Lots of Titles 103
  Your Card, Sir 104
Stiff and Straight 104
German Gestures 104
Gender in Germany 105
Lederhosen, Nien! 105
Can We *Sprechen?* 105
  Take a Letter 106
  It's No Joke 106
Negotiation Auf Deutsche 106
It Is Better to Give 107
Off to the Biergarten! 107

Souppe to Nuts...108
   Business Lunching 108
   Dinner Is Served 108
   Raising a Glass 108

10 Italy   **109**
   The Boot..109
   Who's Running the Government? 110
   Parlo Lei Italiano? 111
   No Official Religion? 111
Italian Holidays 111
On Time, Pronto! ... .112
   Business Hours 112
What to Expect 113
   Up Close and Personal 113
   Gestures—Yes! 113
   Ciao, Baby! 114
   And Your Name Is ... .114
   Your Card ... .114
   The Art of Conversation 115
No Pinching, Please 115
Armani a Armani 116
The World's Worst Red Tape 116
   The Art of Negotiation 116
   Getting Down to Business 117
Presents, Si! 117
Guess Who's Coming To Dinner? 117
Entertainment, Italian style 118
Zuppa to Nuts 118
   The Most Important Meal of the Day 118
   Luncheon Is Served 119
   Dinner a la Roma 119
   Raise a Glass 120

11 Portugal   **121**
Here or There? 121
Formerly Lusitania 122
Speaking Portuguese 122
Religion 123
How to Have Fun 123
You Be on Time, I'll Be Late ... .124
   Work Week 124
A Handshake Will Do 125
   And Your Title Is ... .125
   Card Me! 125
Stiffly and Straight 125
Equality: Yes or No? 126
Dress Up 126
Can We Talk? 126
Negotiating Portuguese-Style 127
Hold the Gifts 127

Slow and Soulful 127
Home for Dinner 128
Sopas to Nuts 128
    Breakfast 129
    Lunch Is King 129
    Dinner Is Served 129
    Drink a Glass 129
    Tipping 130

12 Spain   **131**

Where It's At 131
    Spanish, Por Favor 132
    Religion 133
Cultural Roundup 133
Life Is a Holiday 133
Laid-Back Spain 133
Daily Business Life 134
Shake, Shake, Shake 134
    Let's Play Cards 135
    ¡Titles, Sí! 135
Can We Talk? 135
Spanish Eyes 136
Señorita Freedoms 136
Neat and Formal 137
Meet the Family 137
Giving a Gift 137
Sopa to Nuts 138
    Breakfast 138
    Lunch Is Served 138
    Tapas Time 139
    Dinner Is Served 139
    Taste the Bubbly 139
    Mind Your Manners 139
    Tips on Tips 140

13 Switzerland   **141**

Where It's At 141
The Big Emmenthaler 142
Four Languages Here 142
Religion 143
Take a Holiday 144
On Time—No Excuses! 144
We're Open! 144
Greetings 145
    Swiss Miss 146
    Card Sharps 146
Give and Take 146
    Age Before Beauty 146
    Molasses in January 147
Sit Up Straight 147
Safe Talk 147

Think Elegant 148
Gifting 148
That's Entertainment 148
In a Swiss Home … 149
Raclette to Nuts 149
    Lunch and Dinner *149*
    Down the Hatch! *150*

14 United Kingdom   **151**

Stuff You Should Have Learned In School 151
    Is the Queen in Charge? *152*
    Real English *152*
    Religion *153*
Vacations..153
Right on Schedule 153
The Daily Grind 154
Ta, Ta!...154
Look, Don't Touch 155
Gestures 155
To Bow or Not to Bow … 155
Gender Gap 156
Saville Row 156
Talk Is Cheap 157
Sealed with a Kiss 157
To Give or Not To Give … 158
Let Me Entertain You … 158
Oxtail Soup to Nuts 158
    Table Manners *158*
    Mealtime *159*
    Tea for Two *159*
    Dinner Is Served! *160*
    Toasts *160*

15 Greece   **163**

The Land of the Greek Gods 164
    Who's Running the Parthenon? *165*
    Say What? *166*
    Religion *166*
Holiday Time 166
What Time Is It? 167
    Open for Business *167*
    Service with a Smile *168*
Greetings 168
    Grin and Bear It...*168*
Pecking Order 169
Suit Yourself 169
It's Greek to Me 170
Basic Business 101 170
Beware of Greeks … 170
Let Me Entertain You 171

Easter Soup to Nuts 171
    Breaking Your Fast 172
    Lunch Is on the Table 172
    Dinner Is Served 172
    Tipping 172

16 Scandinavia   **175**

Stuff You Need to Know 176
Best Time to Visit 177
Who's Who 177
Banking Business 177
Everybody Speaks English 177
What They Believe 178
Painfully Punctual 179
Open for Business 179
On Holiday 179
Formal or Informal? It Depends! 180
Hello, Goodbye 180
    Titles 181
    Business Cards 181
Body of Evidence 181
We're All Equal 182
Conservative Dresser 182
The Art of Conversation 183
Getting Down to Business 184
    Sweden 184
    Norway 184
    Denmark 184
    Finland 184
    Iceland 185
Home in Scandinavia 185
Sauna Rules 185
Suppe to Nuts 186
    Teatime 186
    Dinner Is Served 186
    Skoal! 187
    Tipping Policy 187

17 Eastern Bloc: Czech Republic, Poland, and Hungary   **189**

Who's on First? 189
Learn the Language 190
Religion 191
Holidays: Only a Few 191
Be on Time 191
Handshakes All Around 192
    Card-o-Mania 192
    Titles 192
Body Language 192
Slow and Steady 193
It's a Man's World 193
Suit Up 193

Keep It Pleasant 194
To Give or Not To Give … 194
My House or Yours? 195
Goulash to Nuts 195
   Luncheon *195*
   Dinner Is Served *195*
   Have a Brew *196*
   Tip Your Hat … *196*

18 Russia and the Commonwealth of Independent States   197

Geography and Economy 197
The Native Tongue 199
Religion 200
Holidays! 200
Just Try to Be on Time! 200
   Open Late, Leave Early *201*
   Appointment, Please *201*
Grip and Greet 201
   Take a Card … *201*
   Titles *201*
Talk Tips 202
Space Bubbles 202
Less Equal Than Others 202
Sartorial Swingers 203
Cold War Blues 203
To Gift or Not to Gift 204
Visiting the Locals 204
Entertainment Russian-Style 205
Borscht to Nuts 205
   Breakfast *206*
   Lunch and Dinner *206*
   Tips on Tipping *207*
   Vodka All Around *207*
Don't Leave Home Without It 207

Part 4: Asia and the Pacific Rim   209

19 Hong Kong and Taiwan   211

Best Time to Go 212
Who's on First? 212
What Language Is This? 213
Religion 213
Let's Take a Holiday 213
Early Birds Unite 214
Open Up 214
Slow and Steady 215
Saving Face 215
Hello, Goodbye 216
   Business Cards *216*
   By Any Other Name *217*
No Touching 217

Ancient Attitudes 217
Think Conservative 218
Talk Softly 218
Gifts All Around 218
Let Me Entertain You 219
Changing Money 219
Soto to Nuts 220
 Lunch 220
 Chopstick Tips 220
 Dinner Is Served 220
 Raise a Glass 222
 Tea for Two 222
 Tipping 222

20 China   223

A One-Party State 224
Hong Kong 225
Travelin' Around 226
Chinese Spoken Here 226
Religious Beliefs 227
Local Holidays 228
Arrive Early 228
 Doors Open Early 228
 Timeliness 228
Meet and Greet 229
 What's Your Title? 229
 Don't Be a Card 229
Getting Down to Business 230
 Patience Is a Virtue 230
 No Boasting 230
 Teamwork 230
 Saving Face 231
Hands Off! 231
Speak Softly 231
Gender Gap 232
Suit Yourself 232
Gifts Are Illegal, But 233
Let Me Entertain You 234
Tang to Nuts 234
 Tipping 234
 Lunch Is On 234
 Early Dinner 235
 Banquets 235
 Bars and Clubs 235
 Late-Night Dining 236
 "Here's to You!" 236

21 Indonesia and Malaysia   237

Who's In Charge? 238
Talk the Talk 238
Religion 238

Holiday Time 239
Relax, Be Happy 240
    Take a Number… 240
    Are You Open? 240
Getting Down to Business 241
Limp and Long 242
    Traditional Greetings 242
    Titles 243
    Play Your Cards Right 243
Bite Your Lip 244
Taboos 245
Separate and Unequal 245
Suit Up 245
Presenting a Present 246
On the Town 246
Soto to Nuts 247

22 Singapore   249

Who's In Charge? 249
Speaking the Lingo 250
Holiday List 251
Be On Time 251
Slow and Mellow 251
Don't Lose Face 252
Brief and Businesslike 253
    Here's My Card 254
    By Any Other Name 254
Hands Off 255
Lingo Rules 255
Don't Point 256
Seen, Not Heard 257
Sartorially Speaking 257
Just Say No! 257
Let Me Entertain You 259
Visiting at Home 259
Tipping 260

23 Japan   261

Japanese, Please.. 262
Shinto and Confucianism 262
It's Vacation 262
Don't Ever Be Late 263
Take Your Time 263
Keep Smiling 264
Bowing: They Wrote the Book 264
    What's in a Name? 265
    The Business of Meishi 265
Keep Your Distance 266
Finger Play 266
Kimono or Suit? 267

Talk Is Soft 268
   Accentuate the Negative 268
   Taboo Subjects 268
Artful Negotiation 268
Gifts Are Essential 269
   Not Another Ginsu Knife … 269
   Wrapping Savvy 270
   Hostess Gifts 270
On the Town 270
   Turnabout Is Fair Play 271
   At a Japanese Home 271
Miso to Nuts 272
   Dinner Is Served 272
   Down the Hatch! 273
   Tips 273

24 South Korea   **275**

Who's In Charge? 276
Korean Spoken Here 276
Religion 277
Life Is a Holiday 277
Don't Be Late 278
   Open at Nine 278
   Let's Call a Meeting! 278
   Business Pace 279
   Talk Is Cheap 279
   Nix to Japan! 280
Everyday Life 280
Take a Bow 280
   Let Me Introduce You 281
   Who's on First? 281
   Card Play 281
Body Rules 282
Mind Your Manners 282
Tradition Rules 283
Stow the Flash 283
Driving a Bargain 284
Strictly Business 284
   Age Before Beauty 284
   Sign on the Dotted Line 285
Give and Take 285
Home Sweet Home 285
On the Town 286
Man Too to Nuts 286
   Dinner In Korea 287
   Here's Mud In Your Eye 287

25 Australia and New Zealand   **289**

   Aussies 289
   Kiwis 290

In the Driver's Seat 291
   New Zealand 291
   Australia 292
Where's Your Didgeredoo? 293
Religion 293
When to Visit 293
   Just for Fun 293
Punctuality Plus 294
   Yes, We're Open 294
   Time Zones 294
Informality Rules! 295
Howdy, Mate! 295
   Titles 295
   Where's Your Card? 296
Let's Get Matey 296
Get a Suit 296
Can We Talk? 297
Getting Down to Business 298
Home Sweet Home 299
Soup to Nuts 299
   Tea Time 299
   Check Out the Pub 300
   Tipping 300

Part 5: The Middle East   **301**

26 India   **303**
Tower of Babel 304
Religious Faith 304
Holiday in India 305
Expect Tardiness 305
Greetings 306
Titles 307
Not Everyone Is Equal 307
Watch Your Body 308
"Yes" Means "No" 308
Suit Up 309
   Saris: Not for Everyone 309
   Punjabi Suit 310
   Safari Suit 310
Gifts Are Good 310
Home Entertainment 311
   If It's Bombay, It's Casual 312
A Little Baksheesh (Tip) 312
Pillau to Nuts 312
   Breaking Your Fast 313
   Lunch 313
   Dinner Is Served 313

27 Saudi Arabia   **315**

Al-Saud Is King 316
The Best Time to Visit 316
Arabic Spoken Here 316
Islam Only 317
Say "Cheese!" 318
Small Change 318
  Haggling *318*
  Traveler's Checks *318*
Islamic Holidays 319
  Ramadan *319*
  Islamic Calendar *319*
Slow Down... 320
Doing Business the Saudi Way 320
Greetings 321
  Titles *321*
  Take My Card—Please! *321*
Move In Close 321
The Hands Have It 322
Gender Gap 322
Religious Police 323
Dress for Success 323
Watch Your Language 324
Gifts Are Good 324
On the Town 325
Addas to Nuts 325
  Lunch *325*
  Dinner Is Served *326*
  Raise a Glass *326*
  Tipping *326*

28 Egypt   **327**

Who's In Charge? 327
Speaking the Lingo 328
Islam Is King 328
Life Is a Holiday 328
  Ramadan *329*
  Islamic Calendar *329*
Slow Down 329
Meet and Greet 330
  A Rose by Any Other Name *330*
  Take a Card *331*
Body Talk 331
  Up Close and Personal *331*
  The Eyes Have It *331*
Watch That Hand 331
Women Vs. Men 331
Dress Conservatively 332

Talk Is Cheap 332
   Humor 333
   Saving Face 333
Getting Down to Business 333
The Giving Game 333
Let Me Entertain You 333
Lentil Soup to Nuts 334
   Breakfast 334
   Lunch 334
   Dinner Time 334
   Nix to Alcohol 334
   Tipping 334

29 Israel and the Palestinian Territories   **337**

Country Basics 338
Hebrew and Arabic 338
Religion 339
   Ashkenazi Jews 339
   Sephardic Jews 340
   Other Subgroups 340
A Separate Calendar 340
Money Talks 341
You Be Prompt 342
Business of Confrontation 342
Shalom! 343
   Titles 343
   Take a Card 344
Speak Up 344
Body Wars 344
   Eyes Ahead 345
   Use Your Hands 345
We're All Equal 345
Suit to a Tee 345
To Give or Not To Give … 346
Entertaining Style 346
Matzo to Nuts 346
   Food Taboos 347
   Here's to You 347
   Tipping 347

Appendices

A Glossary   **349**

B Further Reading   **353**

C Embassies   **355**

Index   **365**

Foreword

If business in another country has you packing your bags, *The Complete Idiot's Guide to Cultural Etiquette* will be your helpful companion. It should go right into the luggage with your passport and pants.

The simple fact is, we're all complete idiots about the customs of others until we're taught the rules. The human race shares some rules in common, but etiquette isn't understood by common sense or by merely knowing universal moral guidelines. Your inner compass may tell you not to tote a bomb, but it won't tell you how to avoid insulting the person whose cultural background is completely different from your own.

Americans start out with a handicap in the cultural etiquette department—Americans like Joe, who was discussing a trip to France with friends. The friends recommend planning a couple of years ahead, learning the French language, then visiting the country and being completely at ease. No, says Joe, we'll give the French advance notice that we're coming and they can all learn English!

Getting along with people from different countries has been a challenge for centuries. The Congress of Vienna in post-Napoleon Europe not only included state boundaries to maintain a balance of power, but also helped ambassadors mind their manners by adding rules of precedence. With these non-arbitrary rules in place, carriage races in the streets were no longer needed to ensure a seat of honor for the self-important ambassador. Simple rules of precedence replaced duels and the lopping off of heads—and continue to this day to smooth the way when leaders from different countries meet.

Of course, some can play fast and loose with cultural etiquette—American patriot Ben Franklin got away with informal dress in the court of Louis XVI, for example. But don't assume that casually bending the rules will also work for you. You're probably not the beloved curiosity that Franklin was—and you'll do well to take to heart Carol Turkington's practical advice on how not to stick out like a sore thumb. Not only is it considerate to consider the customs and preferences of others better than your own, it's good business.

The Complete Idiot's Guide to Cultural Etiquette is easy to read and its topics aren't trite. Carol Turkington has done extensive research, and her interesting tips will help you develop an inquiring and generous attitude toward the manners, customs, and languages of others. Though not an official ambassador, anyone who travels abroad represents his country informally.

Remember, breaking the law in a foreign country can get you thrown in the slammer or deported, but breaking the unwritten rules of local culture can get your project canned without your even knowing why. Carol Turkington writes down the unwritten rules you'll need to know so that you don't say the unspeakable in Switzerland or do the unthinkable in Belgium. Bon voyage!

—Sheryl Eberly, *etiquette consultant and former aide to First Lady Nancy Reagan*

Introduction

As we zoom toward the second millennium, we've handed over lots of details to our computers. These desktop marvels can remind you of an upcoming birthday, search cyberspace for the best deal on tickets to Liechtenstein—even turn off your lights and dial your telephone. But your Compaq Presario can't take a prospective business partner out to lunch, participate in a Japanese tea ceremony, or stroll down the Via Venetto with that new Korean Vice President from marketing. Knowing how to handle yourself in today's global village means not just conducting business from your own point of view—you also need to manage not to offend the rest of the world while you're doing it.

As the world's cultural boundaries blend and shift, opportunities for Americans abroad continue to expand—not just in Europe, but in East Asia, the Eastern blocs, and the Middle East. Tiptoeing into this global village, whether for business or pleasure, can be a rude awakening to Americans who believe their country is the center of the universe.

Traveling: A Crash Course

If you don't speak the language—*especially* if you don't speak the language—the least you can do is mind your manners. But whose manners are you minding? A gesture of friendship in one country can be a profound insult in another; a simple peck on the cheek in one land may be interpreted as a marriage proposal in another. It's just not that easy to know when to bow, rub noses, or shake hands. And yet knowing what's right and what's wrong can be critically important, whether you're trying to close an international commodity options deal or you're just looking for that terrific new restaurant you read about back home.

No matter how badly you may want to do the right thing, you'll be at a disadvantage if you don't know what the right thing is. But you won't need to worry if you've got *The Complete Idiot's Guide to Cultural Etiquette*, the guide to international civility. This book includes the do's and don'ts, the tricks and taboos, for all the major countries around the world, together with tips on how to help international visitors feel at home in the U.S.

In the *Complete Idiot's Guide to Cultural Etiquette*, you'll find information on each country (where it is, who's in charge, and when's the best time to visit). You'll discover tips on what to eat and what to wear (and what *not* to wear). You'll learn when it's okay to slurp your soup and when the only thing resting on the table should be your dinner plate. You'll find discussions on what's safe to eat and drink and what's not, how and where to find health care, and tips on everything from tipping to terrorism.

The Complete Idiot's Guide to Cultural Etiquette will do much more than help you become a confident traveler and business globetrotter. Throughout the book, you'll find hundreds of practical tips and easy-to-use strategies that will help you be the most aware cultural ambassador you can possibly be. Because when you leave behind these familiar shores, you're representing not just you and your family—you're also representing your company and even our country. Folks in Kuala Lumpur may not know too many Americans, and if they don't, they're going to form their opinion on an entire culture based on how well you conduct yourself, how sensitive you are to their own society, and how readily you can adapt to another culture. As you grow and develop as a savvy international traveler, *The Complete Idiot's Guide to Cultural Etiquette* will help you grow and develop, too.

How This Book Is Organized

The Complete Idiot's Guide to Cultural Etiquette tries to make polite traveling abroad entertaining, easy, and as gratifying as possible. The book is divided into five parts, four of which roughly divide the globe into easily digestible sections. In each of these four parts, you'll find information on do's, don'ts, and don't-even-think-about-its, covering gestures, lifestyle, eating habits, table manners, religious tips, and more.

In addition, Part 1 addresses issues of special concern that may come up at any time during your traveling career. This part is a sort of overall international etiquette roundup of tips and taboos for surviving in the global village, plus tips on how to entertain international visitors to this country without making a major faux pas.

Part 1, "Overview of International Etiquette," covers the basics: Here's where you'll find the details of international etiquette (such as what to call the wife of an Earl, or how to address an envelope to an ambassador) plus a general overview on international etiquette and hosting foreign visitors.

Part 2, "North America and South America," will include everything you need to know about Mexico, Canada, and Latin America with tips on ancient history and modern leaders. You'll also find details on decoding Latin American names, the Franco-Anglo sensitivities of Canada, and how to dress for success in Mexico.

Part 3, "Eastern and Western Europe," presents the cultural roundup on the other side of the ocean, including tips for Belgium, Germany, Austria, Italy, Portugal, Spain, Switzerland, the United Kingdom, Greece, and Scandinavia. If you've ever wondered how to act in a business sauna, what that head nod means in Greece, or whether to eat or wear a *"weinerbrod"*—you'll find these answers here! In addition, this part tiptoes into revolutionary territory, discussing the countries that used to be called one thing and are now called something else. We refer, of course, to the countries of the Eastern Bloc (from the Czech Republic, Hungary, and Poland, to Mother Russia, and to the newly Independent States).

Part 4, "Asia and the Pacific Rim," offers a guide through the international thicket of etiquette in China, Hong Kong, Taiwan, Singapore, Japan, South Korea, Malaysia, Indonesia, Australia, and New Zealand.

Part 5, "The Middle East," points you to the minefield of manners of this part of the world, including Saudi Arabia, Egypt, Israel, and India.

Extras

The Complete Idiot's Guide to Cultural Etiquette offers you clear, concise information and practical guidance for your trip throughout the world. Throughout the book, you'll notice an abundant supply of tips, words of wisdom, health and safety suggestions, and warnings. You can easily spot these extras by looking for the following icons:

Global Guide

Here's where you'll find brief "bits and bobs" on getting along in international circles—odd sorts of details that can help clarify those sometimes-mystifying actions you'll encounter.

Say What?

When it comes to international travel, there's a world of misinterpretation out there you can fall into if you don't know the lingo of international cultural etiquette.

Faux Pas

These cautionary words on gaffes, taboos, and blunders will alert you to errors that might threaten your cultural savoir faire.

Tip of the Hat

These somewhat longer details or observations may include deeper background to some of the things you'll discover about another country's etiquette.

Acknowledgments

The author would like to thank the many people who provided information or resources for this book, and those of all of the Embassies in Washington, DC who have helped, counseled, and inspired along the way.

Special thanks to Susan Osborne, Evelyn Johann, Barbara Dillon, and Bob Frye for valuable assistance and advice.

Thanks also to the editors at Macmillan, to Nancy Warner and Jessica Faust, and to Mike Thomas. Thanks as always to my long-time agent, Bert Holtje of James Peter Associates.

A final thank you to Michael and Kara, for giving me the time to finish the project.

Dedication

In memory of Randolph "Babe" Merchant, a true gentleman and international traveller, with gratitude and love.

Special Thanks to the Technical Reviewer

The Complete Idiot's Guide to Cultural Etiquette was reviewed by an expert who double-checked the accuracy of what you'll learn here, to help us ensure that this book gives you everything you need to know about cultural etiquette. Special thanks are extended to Robert W. Frye.

As the former Chief of Protocol for AT&T and Lucent Technologies, Frye has over 25 years of experience in marketing and international business protocol. During his career, he has held executive positions in operations, marketing, sales, corporate education, and public relations. Frye is now managing director of his own company, International Business Protocol.

For AT&T and Lucent Technologies, Frye created, developed and managed protocol organizations that served the sales and marketing departments of both companies worldwide since 1981.

Frye has planned and directed well over 4,000 senior level marketing visits to the United States involving chief executive officers, boards of directors, ambassadors, ministers, current and former heads of state, and royalty.

In 1995 Frye was selected to conduct protocol and cross cultural training for the Atlanta Committee for the Olympic Games, The State of Georgia, and the Atlanta City Council in connection with the 1996 Olympic Games.

Frye also conducts International Protocol and Cross Cultural workshops for Saint Joseph's University Executive MBA Program, The American University Business Council for International Understanding, Washington, DC, and the United States Air Force

Air University, Maxwell A.F.B. He also delivers numerous protocol lectures and speeches to corporations and associations including the Los Angeles and Philadelphia World Affairs Councils, The Southern Center for International Studies, as well as multiple engagements for Delta Airlines and Motorola.

Frye, a Certified Meeting Professional, has been featured in articles in the *New York Times* Sunday business magazine, the *American Express Travel and Leisure Magazine*, and *The Philadelphia Inquirer*. He is a member of the board of directors of the Philadelphia International Visitors Council and the New York Council of Protocol Executives.

Contact Information:

> International Business Protocol
> Tel: 610-458-5524
> Fax: 610-321-0541
> Pager: 800-974-5046
> Email: rwfrye@bellatlantic.net

Trademarks

All terms mentioned in this book that are known to be or are suspected of being trademarks or service marks have been appropriately capitalized. Alpha Books and Macmillan USA, Inc. cannot attest to the accuracy of this information. Use of a term in this book should not be regarded as affecting the validity of any trademark or service mark.

Part 1

Overview of International Etiquette

You've got your itinerary, your passport, and a bottle of extra-strength Tylenol—that doesn't mean you're prepared for a trip abroad. When it comes to dealing with the people you're going to meet, you'll need to know something of the culture, the manners, and the do's and don'ts of international etiquette in order to avoid embarrassing yourself abroad. In fact, knowing the right way to act in a variety of situations is especially important if you're representing your company on business—but it's also important if you're just going as a tourist interested in checking out the Eiffel Tower.

So with book in hand, read on and find out the details on how to prepare for your trip (learn some foreign phrases!), discover how to address foreign dignitaries (what do you call the son of an Earl?), and how to make foreign visitors feel right at home.

Chapter 1

How's Your International "EQ"?

> ## In This Chapter
>
> ➤ Find the best places for information about other countries, safety tips, and healthy traveling
>
> ➤ Learn general tips for getting along in other countries
>
> ➤ Discover what to pack and what to leave at home
>
> ➤ Master some phrases in another language
>
> ➤ Remember to watch your eye contact and body language

Before you board that plane for parts unknown, it pays to spend a few hours learning as much as you can about the local laws and customs of the countries you'll be visiting. The world may seem like a global village, but there's a world of difference between Kalamazoo and Kazakhstan.

If you first learn as much as you can about the country you're going to visit—the people and their customs and taboos—you'll be better able to cope with situations in which you find yourself. Bone up on the names of the leaders of the country: the president, prime minister, and royal families. Learn a bit about the local cuisine. The more you can do to distance yourself from that image of the "Ugly American" who doesn't know anything about any country other than the U.S.A., the better.

Far too often Americans figure they can rush into another country without doing their homework and ooze by on personal charm. Since many Americans believe (deep down inside) that the U.S. is the center of the universe, they blithely assume everyone else should follow *their* rules. In fact, the rest of the world doesn't really give a hoot about U.S. customs.

The people of each country tend to mind their own cultural affairs, and usually assumes that their way is the best way. If you're traveling abroad—especially on business—you'll be much more successful if you start looking out a bit for the other guy.

Parlay-Voo Humma Humma?

It doesn't take much to learn a few phrases in the language of your host country, but it's a nice, gracious effort that can speak volumes for your sensitivity and business acumen. We respect those who bother to learn our language, so take the time to learn at least a few words—"please," "thank you," and "good morning" aren't hard. Most toddlers can manage it, after all. While most of your business may well be conducted in English, knowing a few words in the other fellow's lingo will likely earn you points.

Although English is often the second language in most countries, never take that for granted. Your hosts may have only learned English from a textbook but never really spoken it (just as scores of American high school students never really learn to speak the Spanish, French, or German they study).

Faux Pas

If you're not sure if your host speaks English, don't just assume that "somebody over there" knows your language. Arrange for a reliable interpreter.

Make it easy on your foreign hosts: When speaking English, don't mumble or talk too fast—but don't speak at a snail's pace, either, as though your host was a half-wit.

Enunciate. Saying, "gimme" instead of, "give it to me" or, "I dunno" for, "I don't know" will be too hard for many people abroad to understand. Don't speak in monotone: Put some inflection into your words.

If you notice a dazed, blank look stealing over your audience, repeat yourself by using different (simpler) words to say the same thing. Restating what you just said will ensure that you are getting your point across.

Silence Is Golden

Americans often feel nervous in the presence of silence. When there's a pause, we instinctively want to fill it up because we interpret silence as some sort of social faux pas. In many other countries, silence is a good thing. When you feel the urge to burst out with nervous chitchat during negotiations, bite your lip, bite your tongue, and bite your fingernails if you have to, but try to pattern your silences after those of your colleagues.

Avoid Slang

Common colloquial American phrases may not mean much to a person living in Iceland. You may feel "out of the loop" or "out in left field," but odds are if you say so, your foreign contacts won't have the faintest idea what you're talking about. And while you think your puns may be the funniest thing this side of the water cooler, in another country they'll just confuse people. Avoid buzzwords, exaggerated terms, and euphemisms.

My Card ...

Check to be sure you have plenty of your business cards in your attaché before you leave on a trip. They're important because they give valuable information to many status-laden countries about your position and the status of your company. In many countries, how you're treated—even the grammar used to address you—depends on your personal status. Your business cards can supply this information so everyone knows who's on first, who's a rising executive, and who's just a peon from the mailroom.

If English isn't spoken where you're headed (and most of the time it won't be), have one side of your cards printed in the language of the country you're visiting. It's nice if you can have this done before you leave, but if you're the procrastinating sort, ask the concierge at your hotel where you can get your cards printed.

Once you've got those bilingual cards tucked away, be sure you know the correct rules for how and when to present your business cards, and how to accept the cards given to you. Some cultures think it's a good idea to study the card and treat it with respect; others believe you should stuff it in your card case for later viewing. The best rule-of-thumb, no matter where you are, is to present your card formally holding the card between your thumb and index finger. The card should be positioned so the recipient can take the card and read it instantly without turning it around.

Global Guide

It may take up to a week to have your business cards printed in a foreign country so make sure you get them printed before you leave and bring enough.

The Eyes Have It

Not everyone in the world appreciates the direct eye contact so common in America. We think of it as "forthright"—others consider it rude, aggressive, or challenging. On the other hand, some foreign hosts will object if you don't stare them right in the eyes. (In Scandinavia, for example, direct eye contact while tossing back a shot of liquor is absolutely *de rigueur*.) Do your homework to find out the ogling style for the country you're going to visit.

A Handshake or a Kiss?

Americans tend to think that a hearty handshake is the only form of greeting worth initiating. Wrong again! In some countries, the handshake is anything but firm—it's almost limp in its passivity. The best rule-of-thumb is to expect a handshake and match the pressure and enthusiasm extended by the other person.

Some cultures prefer to bypass the handshake altogether in favor of the "air kiss" on both cheeks, while others think it's swell for people of the same sex to walk hand in hand down the street. On the other hand, some cultures find any sort of body contact to be taboo, from patting the back during a greeting to draping an arm on the shoulder. If you're unfamiliar with the culture, you could misinterpret the behavior. In order to do the right thing, study the cultural customs of your destination before you make a significant blunder by kissing when you should have shaken.

Bearing Gifts

Business-related gift giving is an art that differs dramatically from one country to another; what is perfectly acceptable in one place will be taboo in another. To avoid having a business relationship flounder by choosing the wrong gift or giving it at the wrong time, read up on each country's preferences.

Gift giving can be a particular problem for U.S. businesswomen. No matter how liberated you feel personally, it's not always acceptable for a businesswoman to give a business gift to a male colleague from another country. It's a good idea to wait to see what gift he bestows on you (if any); if you do buy a gift, make it something impersonal, such as a pen or a letter opener. Read up on the rules before you make this error.

Faux Pas

In Japan, the wrapping paper rules are so complex it's better to have your hotel concierge take care of this for you. You're sure to get it wrong.

Global Guide

Typical flowers associated with death include gladiolus, chrysanthemums, and white flowers. Avoid these.

You may not have thought much about the wrapping of your business gifts in the past—hey, that's what the mail order folks are for, right? But in many other countries, the wrapping is as important as what's inside. Make sure you follow the rules as to proper color and style.

If you're searching for the right kind of gift, by all means read up on the particular country you're visiting. In general, any gift from the area where you live will be especially favored. American food, gifts with university or sports logos, or local crafts are always popular. Avoid giving a business promotional item as a gift, however, especially if it has more company advertising on it than the Goodyear Blimp.

Be discreet, not ostentatious. Gifts that are obviously outrageously expensive will make you seem too materialistic.

Flowers are always a terrific gift, especially if you're invited to a private home as an honored guest. But in many countries, not all flowers are equal (there may be strict rules about the number of blooms or the color—and many countries avoid certain flowers because of their association with funerals and death). Check with a florist in the country before sending or buying flowers. If your host has children, it's always a nice touch to bring them some sort of American-made toy or game.

Supping and Sipping

The way you handle yourself at the dinner table can have profound implications on how well you impress your foreign hosts. Sheep's eyes and fried scorpions may not be your cup of tea, but be as gracious as you can about accepting and trying foods with which you may not be familiar. Respect others' dietary restrictions as well (don't ask for a cheeseburger in a kosher home, for example, or expect your Hindu hosts to give you steak tartar).

Realize, too, that your capacity for drinking alcohol may be important to your hosts. Some countries don't want to see you drinking at all; others judge your capacity as a business person by whether you can drink them under the table. If you really can't drink or you're a recovering alcoholic, offer a medical excuse for your reluctance to imbibe. (Hepatitis is a good choice.)

Space Out!

Different cultures have very different ideas about how much distance makes a good "personal space cushion" between two people. These beliefs are often unconscious—as children, we absorb many of our strongest cultural norms, and personal space is one of them.

When you stand and talk to other people from other countries, pay attention to their comfort zone. Notice how close or how far apart the natives stand from each other, and try to maintain the same distance. If someone from another country invades your space, try hard not to take a step backward. If you do, odds are they'll follow you to close their cultural gap—and you'll end up dancing all over the room!

Gestures

We're not born with an internal set of automatic gestures—we learn them, just as we learn our language, as part of the culture in which we grow up. This is all fine and dandy as long as we stay within our own culture, but when we venture out into international territory, what we know as commonly acceptable may be interpreted as rude or obscene. Other gestures may not have any meaning at all when taken out of cultural context. Read up on what's acceptable in the gesture department in the country you'll be visiting to avoid making an embarrassing mistake when you're traveling abroad.

Saving Face

Americans tend to be fairly straightforward and blunt, but many people in other countries care deeply about "face"—saving theirs and yours. They may not ask questions for fear of losing face, or they may not want you to lose face if they ask you something and you don't know the answer. Understand the many implications of "saving face" and try to avoid both looking foolish yourself as well as humiliating someone else.

It's No Joke

You may think you're the next best thing to Don Rickles, but humor isn't universal. Someone who doesn't speak your language may not have a clue what you're talking about. Even someone who speaks the same language may not "get" your jokes, especially if there are topical or political comments involved. Puns and sarcasm don't translate well, and in some countries risque jokes are just plain *verboten*.

Tip of the Hat

Even if you think you can get along fairly well in another language, be careful about telling jokes in that language. The humor may not be appropriate, and if you're not fluent, it may come out downright rude.

R.E.S.P.E.C.T.

The Star Spangled Banner isn't the only anthem in the world; when the anthem of another country is played, stand to show your respect. Don't giggle, whisper, make faces, or blow bubble gum during this music. It may not have deep patriotic connotations to you, but it certainly will to your host.

Age: Not Always a Dirty Word

We may think nothing of hustling our elderly relatives off to ignominious retirement, but many other countries revere the wisdom that comes with age. Always treat older people in other countries with respect, rise when they enter the room, and listen to their opinions with reverence.

Other Customs, Other Lands

Maybe you think their president should keep his mitts to himself. Perhaps you suspect their queen needs a new haircut. Or maybe you saw their prime minister in a drunken brawl the night before. No matter what your private opinions are, treat your hosts' government, religion, and local holidays with respect. Even if your hosts criticize their own government, resist the urge to jump in with your own caustic or witty observations. Most likely, they won't appreciate it.

"Treating the culture with respect" doesn't just mean shaking hands with their Minister of Culture. It also means knowing when local holidays take place so that you don't schedule a meeting at the same time. It means having a rudimentary knowledge of the dietary taboos of your host's religion so that you don't offend by serving improper meals. You can show respect not only by your actions but also by your sensitivity. Don't criticize political parties, or compare them with the way they do things "back home."

You Want It *When?*

No matter how laid back you think your foreign hosts may be, strive to be on time (or even a little early) for every meeting or social engagement. So what if they keep you waiting? Many foreign business people know the North American penchant for punctuality and will expect you to be on time, even when they roll in a half-hour late. If you're tardy, they may interpret this as a lack of consideration on your part. Yes, it's a double standard. But that's the way it is.

You're Wearing *That?*

Your best bet when traveling to other countries for business is to adopt conservative, formal business attire—the best you can afford. If the dress styles of the country you're visiting turns out to be more informal once you get there, you can always take off your tie or roll up your sleeves. But if you appear at a business meeting in shorts and a tee shirt when you should have been wearing Armani, there's not much you can do other than crawl under the conference table.

Women in business have other problems. You may think you look absolutely smashing in that slinky slit-to-the-thigh black number, but when you're traveling abroad, you're representing your company. Fashions that work in Marin County may not translate across the Atlantic, especially in Islamic countries. To be on the safe side, aim for a classic, conservative look. If you're too conservative—well, is that a bad thing in the business world? But err too far on the other side and you may well jeopardize your career.

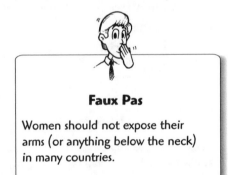

Faux Pas

Women should not expose their arms (or anything below the neck) in many countries.

In general, women traveling abroad should avoid pants, skirts too far above the knee, or see-through anything.

Formality, Please!

Your company may be as informal as the annual picnic at the Elks Club, but other countries often take business far more seriously. Assume that things will be more formal, and don't try to make your business meetings or presentations too casual or friendly.

This also means that you shouldn't immediately call your foreign colleagues by their first names, or start slapping them on the back. Using first names right away, especially in a business situation, is a distinctly American trait. Don't use first names at all unless invited to do so.

Joe Camel Goes Abroad

While cigarette smoking in the United States has become as unpopular as a bug bomb at a flea circus, in other countries they're far more relaxed about the whole thing. When traveling, try not to go on about the hazards of smoking, and don't cough and choke in the presence of smokers if you can help it. Restaurants abroad most likely won't have separate smoking sections, so you'll just have to grin and bear it.

Cash In Your Tips

Estimate in advance how much cash you'll need during a business trip abroad. Then, exchange your American dollars to the currency of the country you're visiting once you arrive (a bank is your best bet for favorable rates). This one-time transaction is a money-saver because a surcharge is placed on each currency exchange no matter what the denomination. Pay attention to the tipping policy. In some countries (such as Scandinavia), most service is automatically added to the bill.

Passport to India and Beyond

Check your passport before you go to make sure you have a signed, valid passport and visa (if required). Make sure your passport will still be valid at least six months from now (you never know what might happen while you're away). Check with your travel agent to see if you'll need a visa in addition to a passport.

Global Guide

Remember—visa and passport application information must be accurate. False information may be grounds for imprisonment.

In the event you find yourself lying in the road after an unfortunate collision with a Parisian minibike, you'll want to make things easier for your rescuers in case of an accident. Remember to complete the information page on the inside of your passport that gives the name, address, and telephone number of someone to be contacted in an emergency. Then make three copies of the page containing your photograph; this will make it easier to replace your passport if it's lost or stolen. Put one copy of the photo

➤ In carry-on bag.

➤ In luggage (not with your passport).

➤ With your office or family member.

Get Your Papers in Order

Before you leave, there are a number of tedious details you need to take care of—and should an emergency occur, you'll be glad you did! Here's your checklist:

➤ Update your will and insurance policies.

➤ Leave a copy of your itinerary and a power of attorney document with a family member or friend.

➤ Find out if your personal property insurance covers you for loss or theft abroad.

➤ Find out how to report the loss of a credit card from abroad (800 numbers don't work when you call from abroad)—your credit card company will have a number that you can call.

➤ Carry only the documents and credit cards you'll need in a wallet or purse (all business documents might be subject to search, seizure, or copying).

➤ Pack your U.S. driver's license (with your photo on it).

➤ Get an international driver's permit before you leave, if you need one.

➤ Make two copies of

  • Credit card numbers.

  • Traveler's checks numbers.

  • Telephone numbers to report lost cards.

  • Airline ticket numbers.

(These items should be stored in separate locations to prevent a simultaneous loss of all of your records.)

Tip of the Hat

Note the credit limit on each credit card that you bring, and don't go over the limit. Americans have been arrested in some countries for innocently exceeding their credit limit.

If You Have Medical Problems

If you have any medical problems, pack a letter from your doctor describing your condition and any prescription medications you need (including the generic name of these drugs). If you think you might need a doctor abroad, check out the Directory of Medical Specialists published for the American Board of Medical Specialists and its 22 certifying member boards. You can find a copy in your local library.

Be sure to pack

- ➤ A copy of your prescriptions.
- ➤ An ample supply of any prescription medications in their original containers (original containers are very important).
- ➤ An extra set of glasses or contact lenses.
- ➤ Your glasses or contact lens prescription in case you need a new pair.
- ➤ An international vaccine record that certifies you've had the appropriate innoculations.
- ➤ A list with your blood type, allergies, medical conditions, and special requirements (medical alert bracelets are a good idea).

International Health Insurance

Check if your health insurance will cover you abroad. If it does, remember to carry both your insurance policy identity card as proof of such insurance, and a claim form. And lest you think Uncle Sam will take care of you no matter how old you are or where you travel, think again! The Social Security/Medicare program doesn't provide coverage for hospital or medical costs outside the U.S. Even if your health insurance will reimburse you for care you pay for abroad, most likely it won't cover medical evacuation from a remote area, or from a country with raunchy healthcare facilities. And zapping you home on a jet can easily cost $10,000 and up, depending on your location and medical condition.

If you don't have comprehensive medical coverage, consider enrolling in an international health program. Hospitals in foreign countries don't take credit cards and most won't honor U.S.-based medical insurance plans. Consider buying one of the short-term health and emergency assistance policies designed for travelers that include medical evacuation in the event of an accident or serious illness.

Customs: Know Before You Go

You can register items of value (such as cameras and laptop computers) with U.S. Customs before you leave the U.S. The embassy of the country you plan to visit can provide details on restrictions or banned materials.

Pack with Aplomb

If you're toting sensitive information into or out of the country, carry it with you by hand. Be sure that your luggage is tagged with covered tags stating your business address and phone number, and put your name and address inside each piece of luggage. Remember, the locks on your luggage aren't secure. For added security, run a strip of nylon filament tape around the suitcase.

Safety begins with your suitcase. To avoid being a target, dress conservatively. A casual wardrobe of Hawaiian shirts and binoculars will brand you as a tourist. Try not to look too rich. Instead, try to travel light so that you can move quickly. This way, you'll be less tired and less likely to set your luggage down somewhere, leaving it unattended.

Avoid handbags, fanny packs, and outside pockets—they're an invitation for thieves. Inside pockets and a sturdy shoulder bag with the strap worn across your chest are somewhat safer. The safest place to carry valuables is just where your mother told you—a pouch or money belt worn under your clothes.

Consular Info Sheets

If it's a simple business trip to London, you probably don't need to spend too much time worrying about your personal safety. But if your company is sending you to Russia, Asia, or the Middle East to scout out possibilities, you may want to spend some time checking out the safety situation. The Department of State issues Consular Information Sheets for every country, describing unusual entry or currency rules, health conditions, the crime and security situation, political problems, areas of instability, and drug penalties. Consular Information Sheets don't give advice (they assume you're a grownup), but rather describe conditions and let you make up your own mind. In some dangerous situations (we're talking war here), the state department does recommend that Americans not travel to a particular country. In these cases, a "Travel Warning" is issued for the country in addition to its Consular Information Sheet. (See Appendix C for contact information.)

Hotel Safety

Your Uncle Maury may have stayed in a nice hotel 30 years ago, but that was then and this is now. It's a good idea to use hotels recommended by your travel agency. If you're traveling to a high-threat area,

➤ Make your own travel reservations.

➤ Consider making reservations using your employer's street address.

➤ Don't identify your company.

➤ Use your personal credit card to pay your bill.

➤ Join frequent travelers' programs, which allow upgrades to executive or concierge floors where security is generally better.

Remember that you're most vulnerable when you're traveling between the airport and your hotel, so get to a lighted hotel entrance as fast as you can. Before getting out of the car, be sure there are no suspicious persons or activities. Don't dawdle unnecessarily in a parking lot, an indoor garage, or the public space around the hotel. Remember that parking garages are difficult to secure, so avoid dimly lit garages that aren't patrolled or that don't have security telephones or intercoms.

Where to Stay

Where you stay in a hotel can mean the difference between a safe stay—and one that isn't. Ask for

➤ A room between the second and seventh floor (most fire departments can't rescue people above the seventh floor level with equipment such as a ladder).

➤ Above-ground-floor rooms without sliding glass doors or easy window access.

➤ A room farther away from the elevator landing and stairwells.

When you get to your room, find the nearest fire stairwell and note the location of fire alarms, extinguishers, and hoses, and read any fire safety information available in your room. Check outside your room window to see if there's a possible escape route. Find the nearest house telephone in case of an emergency. Keep the door closed and use the deadbolt and privacy latch or chain.

You shouldn't have valuables with you, but if you just couldn't leave that tiara at home, keep it in the safe-deposit box at the front desk of the hotel. (Guest room safes are not secure.)

Tip of the Hat

Good security tips: Put a do-not-disturb sign on your hotel room door whenever you leave for an appointment. Ask that your room be made up before you leave the hotel in the morning.

What's Bugging You?

All hotel rooms and telephones aren't bugged, no matter what James Bond says, but your business will be more secure if you act as if they are. Don't say or do anything in your hotel room that you wouldn't want to see plastered all over the front page of the *New York Times*.

Keep your hotel room key with you at all times, and at night, hide your passport and other valuables. Don't share the name of your hotel or room number to all your new foreign friends you just met at the bar down the street.

Travel Healthy

So there you are in Istanbul and you're feeling peaked. All is not lost in the doctor department! If you get sick or hurt, contact the nearest U.S. embassy or consulate for a list of local physicians and medical facilities. Major credit card companies also can provide the names of local doctors and hospitals abroad. If you're seriously ill, consular officers can help you find medical help from this list, and if you wish, they can inform your family or friends back home. Because payment of hospital and other medical expenses is your responsibility, a consul can help with the transfer of funds from the United States if needed.

Global Guide

Senior citizens may wish to contact the American Association of Retired Persons (AARP) for information about foreign medical care coverage with Medicare supplement plans.

Travel Safe

You can avoid becoming a crime statistic as you travel if you keep your wits about you just as you would in any large U.S. city. Be especially cautious in crowded subways, train stations, elevators, tourist sites, market places, festivals, and marginal areas of cities. Don't use short cuts, narrow alleys or poorly-lit streets, and try not to travel alone at night. To stay safe

➤ Don't leave luggage unattended in public areas.

➤ Don't accept packages from strangers.

➤ Don't be a target! Avoid conspicuous clothing and expensive jewelry and don't carry excessive amounts of money or unnecessary credit cards.

➤ Deal only with authorized agents when you exchange money or purchase art or antiques.

➤ Don't publicize your travel plans; discuss your itinerary only with those who need to know.

➤ Inspect any gifts you got from a foreign business contact before you pack to leave.

➤ Never pack your valuables (money or traveler's checks) in your checked luggage.

➤ If you can, get some foreign currency before you leave your home country; criminals may target international travelers getting large amounts of foreign currency at airport banks and currency exchange windows.

Train Safety

Robbing passengers on trains along popular tourists routes is a serious problem. It's more common at night (especially on overnight trains). If your way is blocked by someone and another person is pressing you from behind, move away.

Don't accept even so much as a bag of Oreos from strangers. Criminals can drug passengers by offering them food or drink, or by spraying sleeping gas in train compartments. When possible, lock your compartment. If it can't be locked securely, take turns sleeping in shifts with others in your family or your group. If that's not possible, stay awake. If you must sleep unprotected, tie down your luggage, strap your valuables to you, and sleep on top of them as much as possible.

Tip of the Hat

Don't be afraid to call the police if you feel threatened in any way. Extra police are often assigned to ride trains on routes where crime is a serious problem.

Rent-a-Safe-Car

Carjackers and thieves operate at gas stations, parking lots, in city traffic, and along the highway, and they typically target foreigners in rental cars. Be careful of anyone who tries to get your attention when you're in or near your car.

When you rent a car, choose a common model and try to have the company remove any markings that identify it as a rental car. Choose a car with universal door locks, power windows, and an air conditioner. These are not just luxury items—they're also safety features, allowing you to have more control over your car. Thieves can snatch purses through open windows of moving cars. Follow these tips for safe driving:

➤ Always keep your car doors locked.

➤ Try to avoid driving at night.

➤ Don't leave valuables in the car (if you must carry things with you, keep them out of sight in the trunk).

➤ Don't park your car on the street overnight.

➤ If your hotel doesn't have a parking garage, use a well-lit area.

Just Say No!

More than a third of all the U.S. citizens who are jailed abroad are held on drug charges. Some countries don't distinguish between possession and trafficking; many have mandatory sentences for possession of even a small amount of marijuana or cocaine. Don't carry, use, or purchase any narcotics, marijuana, or other illegal drugs.

Some countries have very strict laws about the import or use of medications; if you use a prescribed medication that contains any narcotics, or a medication that could be abused (such as amphetamines or tranquilizers), carry a copy of your doctor's prescription and check local restrictions and requirements before you leave the U.S. Some countries may require other documentation or certification from your doctor.

No U.S. citizens have been arrested abroad for possession of prescription drugs they've bought in the United States for personal use and carried in original labeled containers. However, some Americans have been arrested for possessing prescription drugs (especially tranquilizers and amphetamines) that they bought legally in certain Asian countries and took to some countries in the Middle East where such drugs are illegal. Other U.S. citizens have been arrested for buying prescription drugs abroad in amounts that local authorities suspected were for selling, not using.

Street Smarts

Get a good map of the city and find your hotel, your embassy, and police stations. Make a mental note of alternative routes to your hotel or local office should your map become lost or stolen. Be aware of your surroundings.

Learn how to place a local telephone call and how to use coin telephones, and make sure you always have extra coins for a call. When you're crammed in a telephone booth, you're vulnerable to pickpockets and thieves, so keep your briefcase or purse in view.

It's not a good idea to jog in unfamiliar cities, but if you must jog, pay attention to the traffic patterns when crossing public streets. (Joggers have been seriously injured by failing to understand local traffic conditions.) Ask your bell captain, concierge or front desk clerks about safe areas around the city.

Be cautious when entering public rest rooms. Purse snatchers and briefcase thieves are known to work hotel bars and restaurants waiting for unknowing guests to drape these items on chairs or under tables. Keep items in view or next to you at all times.

Be alert to scams involving an unknown person spilling a drink or food on your clothing. An accomplice may be preparing to steal your wallet, purse, or briefcase. Pools or beaches are attractive areas for thieves. Leave valuables in the hotel, but carry a token sum to placate violent thieves. Sign for food and beverages on your room bill rather than carry cash.

Faux Pas

Don't leave and return to your hotel at the same time and by the same route every day. Try to vary your habits so no one can learn your *routine*.

Workplace Security

Be careful with sensitive documents—don't leave them lying around in a heap on top of a desk. Guard your conversations so unauthorized people can't eavesdrop. In many countries, local employees are questioned by the country's intelligence agencies or security services to try to learn as much as possible about the activities of American companies. Remember that it's common for telephone, telegraph, and international mail to be monitored in many countries.

Faux Pas

Never accept letters, packages, or anything else from anyone you don't know. It could be contraband or a bomb. You could be arrested.

Intelligence organizations (both ours and theirs) are always on the lookout for sources who are vulnerable to coercion, addictions, or greed. If you want to avoid the special attention of one of these agencies, don't do anything that might be misunderstood, that makes you look stupid, or that would be embarrassing to you or your company. If you wouldn't want to see it in the *National Enquirer*, don't do it. Furthermore, don't gossip about character flaws, financial problems, emotional relationships, or the marital problems of company employees (including yourself). Here's a list of don'ts:

➤ Don't let a friendly ambiance lull you into getting sloshed.

➤ Avoid black-market activities such as the illegal exchange of currency or buying religious icons or other local antiquities.

➤ Don't carry any political or religious brochures or publications that might offend somebody.

➤ Don't photograph anything associated with the military or internal security of the country, including airports, ports, or restricted areas such as military installations, antennae, or government buildings.

➤ Don't buy items that are illegal to import into the United States or other countries (such as endangered species or agricultural products).

Terrorist Attack!

The main terrorist threat you have to worry about is being at the wrong place at the wrong time. Be observant and pay attention to your sixth sense. If you get the funny feeling that something isn't right or that you're being watched, pay attention! Report your suspicions or any information to the general manager of the local affiliate, your embassy, or consulate just in case something does occur. To diminish the risks of becoming a victim of a terrorist attack, remember the following when checking into a transportation hub:

➤ Move in the opposite direction of any disturbance.

➤ Always be aware of where you are in relation to exits. If an incident occurs, you need to know how to avoid it and get out of the area.

➤ Check in early; avoid last minute dashes to the airport.

➤ Go directly to the gate or secure area after checking your luggage.

➤ Avoid waiting rooms and shopping areas outside the secure areas.

➤ At many airports, security personnel will ask you questions about your luggage. Know what items you are carrying and be able to describe all items.

➤ Don't exchange items between bags while waiting for security screening or immigration or customs processing.

➤ Cooperate if a conflict should arise while undergoing the screening process. Discuss the matter with a supervisor from the appropriate air carrier afterwards.

If you're ever in a situation in which somebody starts shooting, follow these guidelines:

➤ Drop to the floor or get down as low as possible.

➤ Don't move until you are sure the danger has passed.

➤ Don't try to help rescuers and don't pick up a weapon.

➤ If possible, shield yourself behind or under a solid object.

➤ If you must move, crawl on your stomach.

Arrested! What Do I Do?

Well, there you are, stuck in the hoosegow. It's all been a misunderstanding—but what do you now? Foreign police and intelligence agencies lock up folks for a variety of reasons—or for no other reason than suspicion or curiosity. Don't panic, use your head, be professional, and remember:

➤ Ask to contact the nearest embassy or consulate representing your country. As a citizen of another country you have this right, but that doesn't mean that your hosts will give you your phone call right away. Continue to pester them until they give in and let you contact your embassy or consulate.

➤ Don't provoke the arresting officer.

➤ Admit nothing; volunteer nothing. (This is the international corollary to "Don't Ask, Don't Tell.")

➤ Sign nothing. They may ask (or tell) you to sign a written report. Decline politely until the document has been examined by an attorney or an embassy or consulate representative.

➤ When the representative from the embassy or consulate arrives, ask for some identification before discussing your situation. You're already in enough trouble.

➤ Don't fall for the old "help us and we'll let you go" ploy. Your captors can be very imaginative in their proposals on how you might help them, but don't sell yourself out by agreeing to anything. If there appears to be no other way out, tell them that you'll think it over and let them know. Once out of their hands, contact the affiliate or your embassy and get out of the country.

The Least You Need to Know

➤ When in doubt, dress conservatively; be polite, formal, and respectful.

➤ Read as much as you can about the country you're going to be visiting before you go.

➤ Stay alert, pay attention, and never let your luggage out of your sight.

➤ Take the time to learn some phrases in your host language.

➤ When you're greeting a foreign national, expect a handshake and match the pressure and enthusiasm of the other person.

ON BEHALF OF THE PRESIDENT...

DIPLOMAT

Chapter 2

Officially Speaking

In This Chapter

➤ Learn the proper way to address royalty, ambassadors, and other officials

➤ Discover what to do (and what not to do) when meeting royalty

➤ Find out the proper way to address correspondence to foreign dignitaries

When you're traveling abroad, it pays to know how to address political officials, royalty, and ambassadors in person and in correspondence.

For example, you should address the king or queen of most European countries as "Your Majesty." Once you've been deep in conversation for some minutes, you can revert to "Sir" or "Ma'am."

When conducting an introduction or referring to the king or queen to someone else, say "His Majesty the King" or "Her Majesty the Queen" (as in, "His Majesty the King would like another buttered roll" or "Her Majesty the Queen would like you to stop feeding her corgis."

Royal Addressing

Should you need to send a short note to a monarch, you would address the envelope thus:

Her Majesty the Queen

Buckingham Palace

London

The salutation would read: "Ma'am" or "Sir," or simply "Your Majesty" together with "Dear" if you were being formal.

When you've finished the note, you'd wind up by saying "Yours very respectfully" or "Yours respectfully."

Prince Consorts

A prince consort to the Queen of England (somebody like Prince Philip, for example, who doesn't get to be King in his own right) is called "His Royal Highness" (there's no "Majesty" involved). You'd address him directly as "Your Royal Highness." He also has to walk a few paces behind the Queen, but that's not your problem.

Princes and Princesses

A royal prince or princess is called Your Royal Highness in conversation (or simply, "Sir" or "Ma'am" after the first "Royal Highness"). If you're introducing a prince or princess to someone else, it would be: "His Royal Highness, Prince Charles" or "Her Royal Highness, Princess Margaret."

Occasionally, the British monarch grants a special title to the eldest princess—called the "Princess Royal." Queen Elizabeth II recently gave this title to her daughter, Princess Anne. In this case, when referring to the Princess Royal, you would say: "Her Royal Highness the Princess Royal."

You would address a letter with one of the following titles:

> Her Royal Highness the Princess Royal

or

> Her Royal Highness Princess Anne

A letter salutation would be addressed as "Madam" and the closing would be "Yours respectfully."

Dukes and Duchesses

In the world of royalty, there are dukes and then there are Dukes. Some are royal, and some are just plain garden variety dukes. If you want to refer to a royal duke or duchess (that is, the son or daughter of the King or Queen), you would say: "Your Royal Highness" (remember, these dukes and duchesses are also princes and princesses). For example, the Prince Andrew is also the Duke of York. (He is called, therefore, Prince Andrew, the Duke of York.)

Addresses on an envelope would be the same for a royal duke or duchess as for a prince or princess.

A plain, non-royal duke or duchess is usually called "Your Grace" in conversation—not "Hello, Duke of Chumley!" and not "Hi there, Duke John!" After prolonged chatting, you can substitute "Sir" Or "Madam." If you are introducing the non-royal duke to someone else, you would call him "The Duke of Chumley."

If you were sending a postcard to a duke or duchess, you'd address it to:

> His Grace, the Duke of Chumley
>
> Her Grace, the Duchess of Chumley.

The letter opening would be "Sir" or "Madam" (for business), or "Dear Duke:" "Dear Madam:" (for social notes).

Tip of the Hat

In England, don't address an envelope of an invitation to both man and wife—it goes to the wife alone. (Christmas cards may be addressed jointly; thus, a card would be addressed: Their Graces, the Duke and Duchess of York.)

Sons of a Duke

The eldest son of a Duke carries the highest family title below his father's (such as a Marquess). The son's wife would then be called the matching spouse title (in this case, Marchioness).

If the Duke has done his duty and produced more than one son, these spare heirs would be called simply "Lord" plus their given name (as in Lord Fauntleroy). If you were writing a business letter to Fauntleroy, you'd call him "Sir" in the salutation (or if it were a social note, "Dear Lord Fauntleroy:"

Envelopes to a younger son would be addressed this way:

> The Lord Peter Whimsey

The letter would open with "Sir" and close with "Yours very truly" (formal) or "Yours sincerely" (social).

The wife of a younger son of a Duke has the title "Lady" accompanied by her husband's full name or Christian name—but not his surname alone. Therefore, if Jane Doe married Lord Fauntleroy Guinness, she would be called "Lady Fauntleroy Guinness." If you met her on the street, you would say: "Oh, how nice to see you, Lady

Fauntleroy!" If you referred to her to someone else, she would be "Lady Fauntleroy Guinness."

You would address a card to her as:

> Lady Fauntleroy Guinness

The letter opening would be "Madam" (formal) or "Dear Lady Fauntleroy" (social). The letter closing would be "Yours very truly" (formal) or "Yours sincerely" (social).

Faux Pas

Don't refer to the aristocracy as "My Lord" or "My Lady" unless you're a serving wench or an upstairs maid—these forms of address are used by servants and tradespeople. Instead, use "Lord James" or "Lady Carol."

Daughters of a Duke

The eldest daughter of a Duke doesn't get any special privileges (women's lib has never penetrated the lofty echelons of the aristocracy). All daughters of a Duke are called "Lady" plus their first name. You would refer to these daughters in conversation as "Lady Carol Spencer."

If you were writing to the daughter of a duke, the envelope would read:

> Lady Carol Spencer

The opening of the note would be "Madam" (formal) or "Dear Lady Carol" (social). The closing would be "Yours very truly" (formal) or "Yours sincerely" (social).

Marquess/Marchioness

Directly beneath "duke" in the aristocratic hierarchy comes "marquess." If you met him on the street, you'd call him "Lord Guinness" to his face; if you were introducing him to your mother, you would refer to him as "The Marquess of Guinness" or "Lord Guinness."

If you were writing him a letter, you'd address the envelope:

> The Most Honourable the Marquess of Guinness

If you two were old school chums, the envelope would be simply:

> The Marquess of Guinness

The letter opening would read "Sir" (formal) or "Dear Lord Guinness" (social); the closing would be "Yours very truly" (formal) or "Yours sincerely" (social).

The wife of a Marquess is a Marchioness. Meeting on the street, you could cry: "Oh, how nice to see you, Lady Guinness!" and introducing her to the Mayor, you would call her "The Marchioness of Guinness" or (less formally) "Lady Guinness."

Her letters would be addressed:

>The Most Honourable the Marchioness of Guinness

or

>The Marchioness of Guinness (less formal)

The letter opening would be "Madam" (formal) or "Dear Lady Guinness" (social); the letter closing would be "Yours very truly" (formal) or "Yours sincerely" (social).

Sons and Daughters of a Marquess

The eldest son of a Marquess takes the next-highest family title below Dad's. The younger sons and daughters are called Lord or Lady. (The wife of the younger son of a Marquess is called Lady combined with her husband's full name, as in Lady Michael Guinness.)

Earl/Countess

Next comes the title of "Earl" in the aristocracy lineup. If you have something to say to an Earl, you call him "Lord Beaverbrook" and if you're referring to him, it's "The Earl of Beaverbrook" or "Lord Beaverbrook." If you were addressing a formal note to him, it would be:

>The Right Honourable the Earl of Beaverbrook

or

>The Earl of Beaverbrook (socially)

The letter opening would read "Sir" (formal(formal) or "Dear Lord Beaverbrook" (social); the closing would be "Yours very truly" (formal) or "Yours sincerely" (social).

His wife is not an Earless, but a Countess (sounds better, anyway). She is addressed face-to-face as "Lady Beaverbrook" and if you're referring to her, it's "The Countess of Beaverbrook" or "Lady Beaverbrook."

Her envelope would look like this:

>The Right Honourable the Countess of Beaverbrook (formal)

or

>The Countess of Beaverbrook (social)

The letter opening would be "Madam" (formal) or "Dear Lady Beaverbrook" (social); the letter closing would be "Yours very truly" (formal) or "Yours sincerely" (social).

Son/Daughter of an Earl

The eldest son of an Earl takes the highest family title below his father's; the younger sons and their wives have the title "Honourable." The daughters of an Earl have the title "Lady" combined with their first and last names.

If you're directly addressing the younger son of an earl or introducing him to someone else, he is called "Mr. Beaverbrook" Correspondence would be addressed to:

> The Honourable Harry Beaverbrook

The letter opening would read "Sir" (formal) or "Dear Mr. Beaverbrook" (social); the closing would be "Yours very truly" (formal) or "Yours sincerely" (social).

Likewise, the wife of the younger sons of an earl would be called Mrs. Beaverbrook and her envelope would be addressed as:

> The Honourable Mrs. Harry Beaverbrook

The letter opening would be "Madam" (formal) or "Dear Mrs. Beaverbrook" (social); the letter closing would be "Yours very truly" (formal) or "Yours sincerely" (social).

Viscount/Viscountess

Next comes the title of Viscount, who is called "Lord Linley" to his face and "Viscount Linley" or "Lord Linley" when talking about him behind his back. If you're writing a letter to a Viscount, address it this way:

> The Right Honourable the Viscount Linley (formal)

or

> The Viscount Linley (social)

The letter opening would read "Sir" (formal) or "Dear Lord Linley" (social); the closing would be "Yours very truly" (formal) or "Yours sincerely" (social).

A Viscountess would be called Lady Linley when you were talking to her, and referred to as Viscountess Linley or Lady Linley otherwise. Her envelope would look like this:

> The Right Honourable the Viscountess Linley (formal)

or

> The Viscountess Linley (social)

The letter opening would be "Madam" (formal) or "Dear Lady Linley" (social); the letter closing would be "Yours very truly" (formal) or "Yours sincerely" (social).

Son/Daughter of a Viscount

The eldest son of a Viscount and also his wife have the title of "Honourable," but you address him personally as "Mr. Linley" and you also refer to him as "Mr. Linley." You would address a letter to him as:

> The Honourable Sam Linley

The letter opening would read "Sir" (formal) or "Dear Mr. Linley" (social); the closing would be "Yours very truly" (formal) or "Yours sincerely" (social).

If you're writing a letter to the wife of the eldest son of a Viscount, you'd address it:

> The Honourable Mrs. Linley

(The fact that you have left out the first name of her husband shows the world that she has married the eldest son of a Viscount, as opposed to a lesser match to a younger son.)

The other sons of a Viscount and their wives also have the title "Honourable." All daughters of a Viscount take the title "Honourable" with their first and last names.

The daughters of a Viscount also take the title Honourable, along with their first and family names. You would refer to the daughter as "Miss Linley" both to her face and to others, and you would address an envelope to her this way:

> The Honourable Sally Linley

The letter opening would be "Madam" (formal) or "Dear Miss Linley" (social); the letter closing would be "Yours very truly" (formal) or "Yours sincerely" (social).

Baron/Baroness

When you're talking to a Baron, you never call him "Baron Littlejohn"—it's always "Lord Littlejohn." You would address a letter to him as:

> The Right Honourable the Lord Littlejohn (formal)

or

> The Lord Littlejohn (social)

The letter opening would read "Sir" (formal) or "Dear Lord Littlejohn" (social); the closing would be "Yours very truly" (formal) or "Yours sincerely" (social).

The title of Baroness is trickier. A Baroness in her own right (in other words, somebody who didn't get to be baroness just by marrying a baron) may be called "Baroness," but she may also be addressed as "Lady." Her envelopes would read:

> The Right Honourable the Baroness Thatcher (formal)

or

> The Baroness Thatcher (social)

or

> The Lady Thatcher (social)

Global Guide

All the children of a baron—both sons and daughters—are called "Honourable" (the eldest doesn't get any special treatment here). The wives of the son of a baron are also given the title "Honourable."

The letter opening would be "Madam" (formal) or "Dear Baroness (or Lady) Thatcher" (social); the letter closing would be "Yours very truly" (formal) or "Yours sincerely" (social).

The wife of a Baron—who isn't a Baroness in her own right—may only be addressed as "Lady," to her face and in referring to her to others. Her envelopes would be:

>   The Right Honourable the Lady Littlejohn (formal)

or

>   The Lady Littlejohn (social)

Her letter opening would be "Madam" (formal) or "Dear Lady Littlejohn" (social); the letter closing would be "Yours very truly" (formal) or "Yours sincerely" (social).

Baronet and Wife

You call a Baronet "Sir" ("Sir Tom, unhand me!") and refer to him to someone else as "Sir Tom Thumb." The abbreviation for Baronet is written "Bart." or "Bt." after the name:

>   Sir Tom Thumb, Bt.

You would write him a letter opening with "Dear Sir" (formal) or "Dear Sir Thumb" (social); the closing would be "Yours very truly" (formal) or "Yours sincerely" (social).

Global Guide

The sons and daughters of a mere Baronet have no title.

The wife of a Baronet is called "Lady" followed by her husband's last name only—so her envelopes would look like this:

>   Lady Thumb

She'd be called "Lady Thumb" to her face as well, and "Lady Thumb" when being introduced to someone else.

Her letter opening would be "Madam" (formal) or "Dear Lady Thumb" (social); the letter closing would be "Yours very truly" (formal) or "Yours sincerely" (social).

Knight and Wife

Knights don't get to go riding over the countryside in chain mail any more, but they do still get to be called "Sir," followed by the initials of his order (or orders) of knighthood. You would refer to him in person as "Sir James" and refer to him to others as "Sir James Wickham." If you were writing to a knight, the envelope should look like this:

>   Sir James Wickham, G.C. M.G.

You would write him a letter opening with "Dear Sir" (formal) or "Dear Sir James" (social); the closing would be "Yours very truly" (formal) or "Yours sincerely" (social).

The wife of a Knight carries the title "Lady" followed by her husband's last name only. You would refer to her as "Lady Wickham" and write her envelope this way:

> Lady Wickham

Her letter opening would be "Dear Madam" (formal) or "Dear Lady Wickham" (social); the letter closing would be "Yours very truly" (formal) or "Yours sincerely" (social).

Esquire

When you don't have any other title, you get to call yourself "Esquire." Originally, the term was used to indicate the eldest son of a knight, and the younger members of a noble house whose title was borne only by the eldest male heir.

Today, professional men and anyone in the arts, letters, music, Members of the House of Commons, and the landed gentry use "Esq." in writing after their names. If you use the title abbreviation "Esq." after the name, don't use any title (not even "Mr.").

Dowager

In the U.S., the title "Dowager" carries quite a few negative connotations, implying an old crone with gray hair, a humpty back, and a cane. In England "Dowager" refers to the earliest surviving widow of a peer, as in the Dowager Duchess of Rothsay. A later surviving widow would be called "Sarah, Duchess of Rothsay"—for life, even if the Dowager dies.

Royal Etiquette

Most of us will never come face to face with royalty, so we don't need to worry about the little niceties. But for those of you who will, keep this in mind:

➤ Don't touch a member of the Royal Family first

➤ Don't extend a hand to shake hands first; wait until the Royal extends a hand.

➤ Don't speak to a member of the Royal Family until he or she speaks to you.

➤ No kissing of the Royal cheek or lips, no matter how thrilled you are to meet the person (President Jimmy Carter did this to Britain's Queen Mum, and she's still fuming).

➤ Subjects must curtsy or bow in the presence of their country's royal family, but U.S. residents aren't required by etiquette rules to make this gesture (however, U.S. citizens may bow or curtsy if they wish).

➤ Don't turn your back on royalty when leaving the room; back up three paces, and then turn.

➤ No matter how familiar they seem (after all, you've seen their faces plastered all over *People* magazine!), don't call a member of the royal family by his or her first name.

Royal Has-Beens

Some countries (in fact, most countries) used to have kings and queens that somehow got lost along the way. A former royal is still given a title out of respect, even if the person's own government doesn't recognize that title. Therefore, a Russian princess is still called "Princess," even though her own country annihilated the Russian royal family years ago.

Global Guide

The wives of ambassadors are always given the title "Madame" (unless they come from English-speaking countries).

You Are Excellent!

European heads of state, ambassadors, cabinet officers and other high-ranking members of the clergy can be referred to as "His (or Her) Excellency" and addressed as "Your Excellency." If you were writing a letter, you would address it:

His Excellency, the Ambassador of the Republic of Ireland

If you wanted to include his wife, it would read:

His Excellency, the Ambassador of Chile and Madame La Paz

The Least You Need to Know

➤ Never be first to touch or speak to a member of the Royal Family.

➤ Often, the title for correspondence is different than the way you address a foreign official in person.

➤ European heads of state, ambassadors, cabinet officers, and other high-ranking members of the clergy can be referred to as "His (or Her) Excellency" and addressed as "Your Excellency."

➤ A former royal from a country that has abolished the throne is still given a royal title.

Chapter 3

KONICHIWA

Hosting International Visitors

In This Chapter

➤ Learn the most appropriate gifts that won't offend

➤ Discover how eye contact, body language and gestures all carry different meanings

➤ Find out how to avoid cultural food taboos

➤ Remember that in some cultures, leaving food on the plate is the right thing to do

➤ Work on flexibility when it comes to other cultures' views on punctuality

Knowing whether to bow or shake hands isn't important only when you're taking a trip abroad—it's also important to know how to treat visitors from other countries who come to the United States.

One of the easiest ways to make your guest feel welcome is to learn a few words or phrases in your guest's native language. Americans have gotten the reputation for being chauvinistic, believing that everyone in the world should speak English. Learning some words in a stranger's language is a charming way to show you're willing to go out of your way to make someone else feel comfortable.

Bagels and Beer

Serving and sharing food is a terrific way to break the ice and get to know others from foreign countries—as long as you don't violate religious or cultural taboos while you're doing it.

Isolated as the U.S. is from most other countries, many Americans grow up feeling as if everyone in the world thinks and feels the way they do. Many believe that their own attitudes are simply "the way things are," rather than the way things are *in the United States*. Thus, Americans tend not to understand the power of culturally related food taboos (so what's so bad about eating a lobster?).

To help understand the strength of these taboos, imagine how you would feel if an Asian served you a meal of dog, considered to be a delicacy in some Asian countries. Most Americans have an immediate, visceral reaction to the idea of eating what we consider to be man's best friend—which is exactly how others feel about their own food taboos. In fact, it was an understanding of the intense cultural taboo against eating canines that prompted Korean restaurants to take "dog" off the menu during the 1988 Olympics, so as not to offend their Western visitors.

Faux Pas

You may know about some common food taboos for other cultures, but are you aware that one group of the earliest Americans—the Navajo nation—doesn't eat fish?

Some international food taboos are well known—most Americans know that Muslims and Jews don't eat pork—but they may not realize that Muslims also don't eat shellfish or drink alcohol, either. Be sure you fully understand your guests' food taboos before preparing or serving food that may not be acceptable to them.

If you're hosting international visitors, keep these food taboos in mind:

➤ **Alcohol:** Don't serve to Muslims, Hindus, Mormons, and some Protestant sects.

➤ **Pineapple:** Don't serve to some Puerto Ricans in combination with other food.

➤ **Beef:** Don't serve to Hindus.

➤ **Pork:** Don't serve to Muslims and Jews.

➤ **Fish:** If it's got scales or fins, don't serve to Muslims or Jews.

➤ **Meat:** Seventh Day Adventists don't eat meat.

Holy Day Taboos

What you eat isn't the only food taboo—when you eat it can also create problems. What may be perfectly okay to eat on one day may be taboo on a holy day—in much the way that Roman Catholics couldn't eat any meat on Fridays (until 1966). Today, Catholics can eat as many steaks as they can swallow on Fridays, but they still can't eat meat on Good Friday or Ash Wednesday.

Observant Jews can't eat leavened bread (or use any leavening agent) during the eight days of the festival of Passover. (Look for special unleavened food called "kosher for Passover" To serve during this festival.) Moreover, observant Jews may not mix dairy with meat (which means get rid of the cheeseburgers).

Thanks, but No Thanks

In many parts of Asia, it's customary to refuse food three times before accepting, so as not to appear greedy. Americans, however, are far more straight-forward, offering food once and then, not wishing to seem pushy, not offering any more. You can avoid this situation by simply serving food and beverages without bothering to ask your guests— or you can go ahead and offer three times, if you can bring yourself to do it.

Faux Pas

While many Asian cultures slurp their food to show appreciation, the Chinese and Thais consider slurping to be bad manners.

Slurping and Burping

Many Asian cultures look upon eating noises with enormous favor—so don't be surprised if you hear your otherwise-model guests belching, slurping, and smacking their lips over their meal. It doesn't mean they're hopeless cretins in the politeness department—they're simply following their own cultural customs. In Japan and Hong Kong, slurping is a sign that you've done a great job in the kitchen. (And yet, while slurping and smacking lips is considered perfectly okay in Japan, leaving your mouth open while you do it is not. That's why the Japanese cover their mouths when they laugh.)

The Clean Plate Club

You probably grew up knowing if you didn't clean your plate there wouldn't be any dessert. In some cultures, however, cleaning the plate is a hint that means you want more food, whereas leaving some food behind means you've had enough.

Some cultures—including the Jordanians, Filipinos, and Egyptians—leave a small bit of food on the plate to show that they're not greedy pigs and that you've done a good job of filling them up.

In Chinese tradition, you don't want to take the last bit of food from the serving plate—that shows that you're still hungry. On the other hand, some cultures (such as the Cambodians) that clean their plate do so to indicate that they want more food.

If you're dining with visitors from other parts of the world and you're not sure how they view cleaning the plate, quietly observe what everybody else is doing, and follow suit. If you're really in doubt—ask.

Gifts That Keep on Giving

Gift-giving seems like a simple thing and one that can hardly go wrong—you want to give a gift to a person from another culture. However, depending on where the recipient comes from, you may run into hidden obstacles having to do with the color, the number or amount of gifts, or even the gift itself.

Colors of the Rainbow

If you think that color doesn't matter in America, ask your grandmother what would she think if you decided to buy a black wedding dress? What would your mother say if you appeared at the funeral of your father dressed in a bright orange miniskirt with purple polka dots? Both of those choices would be interpreted—at least by older, more conservative Americans—as being in shockingly poor taste. As you can see, colors can carry very strong connotations.

Some of the biggest taboos in giving gifts to those of other cultures occur when you give a gift of an inappropriate or wrong color (often, of colors associated with death or mourning). These include:

Global Guide

Find out whether it is socially acceptable to give a gift to foreign friends or colleagues with your company logo emblazoned on it. In some cultures, it's considered boastful.

➤ **White:** While we in the U.S. think of white as the "wedding" color, in many Asian cultures, it's the color of funerals; in China, do not give white gifts, use white wrapping paper, or wear white ties.

➤ **Blue:** This is the color of funerals in some countries.

➤ **Black:** Again, this is the color of sadness and funerals in some places.

➤ **Purple:** This color symbolizes bad luck it Italy.

➤ **Yellow:** This is a "bad" color in many countries.

Stop and Smell the Flowers

It may be hard to imagine that a beautiful bloom could offend anybody, but in many cultures there are taboos on certain flowers because of the association with death, or because they are inappropriate in another way. These include:

➤ **Chrysanthemums:** Many countries consider these blooms to be "funeral flowers."

➤ **Red roses:** In many cultures, red roses are the color of love and intimate relationships, and therefore are not appropriate for gift giving.

➤ **White lilies:** These are considered a "funeral flower" in many countries, including the United Kingdom.

Faux Pas

In some countries, an even numbers of flowers is considered to be bad luck. Also, 13 of any type of flower can mean bad luck.

➤ **White asters:** This is another funeral flower (especially in Switzerland).

➤ **Yellow flowers:** In many cultures (including Iranians, Mexicans and Peruvians), the color yellow has a negative connotation.

➤ **Dahlias:** These flowers are associated with death in Spain.

➤ **Carnations:** In Scandinavia, these are associated with death.

Other Objects

When you're giving gifts, try to avoid giving the following objects to people from certain cultures:

➤ **Cheese:** Many Asians are lactose intolerant.

➤ **Knives, brooches or handkerchiefs:** In many Asian countries and some European ones (such as Italy), these items are linked to sadness or severing relationships.

➤ **Straw sandals:** In many Asian countries, these are bad luck.

➤ **Green hat:** In China, getting a green hat means that you're a cuckold.

➤ **Handkerchiefs:** These are associated with sadness and mourning in many countries, including China.

➤ **Storks and cranes:** These birds are associated with death in China.

Faux Pas

Bringing wine to the hostess is an accepted American tradition, but in some cultures, it's considered an insult—as if you didn't trust the host to pick out a good enough wine.

Wine and Liquor

While many countries consider wine and liquor to be a gift of excellent taste, people of some countries famous for fine vineyards are not impressed with these gifts. If you know that a particular country has extraordinary wine harvests, avoid this type of gift.

Wrap It Up

While you can't judge a book by its cover, the paper and ribbons that you wrap a present in may have some negative connotations in some cultures, especially the Chinese and Japanese. Avoid paper in shades of white, black, or blue (because of the connotations with death)—good colors to choose are red (it's lucky!), pink, or yellow.

Not Too Expensive

Since many cultures believe their gift to you should equal your gift to them, giving an expensive present may not be in the best taste. Furthermore, some Asian cultures have strong feelings against people who try to impress others by being ostentatious. Humility and modesty are the hallmarks in most Asian countries.

Unfortunately, Americans have gotten a bad reputation in many places for being boors and braggarts, eager to show off and display wealth. Giving a Rolex watch to an Asian colleague would therefore not earn you any points, but would rather bolster a sour opinion of Western humility.

The Envelope, Please

Traditionally, Chinese children are given a red envelope filled with cash at the start of the Chinese New Year. It's a charming custom, and if you decide to present a Chinese child you know with a red envelope, make sure you:

➤ Include crisp new bills.

➤ Give an even number of bills.

Be On Time

In many parts of the world (especially Latin and Middle Eastern cultures), punctuality is not something to worry about very much, so natives from these countries may not understand the import we in the U.S. place on arriving on time. On the other hand, Asian, many European, and Scandinavian cultures prize punctuality.

When dealing with newcomers to the U.S., try to be sensitive about the cultural attitudes toward punctuality in their country of origin; their lateness may be normal for their homeland and not a reflection of their own attitude toward you or toward being responsible.

Up Close and Personal

If you've ever walked down the street with a non-American of the same sex and had that person impulsively take hold of your hand, you know first-hand of the cultural jolt that can be caused by the clash of different cultural attitudes toward touching. Many other countries believe that Americans' innate discomfort at close personal contact between people of the same sex is a sign of a cold and distant nature. In fact, it's simple acculturation that makes us recoil in surprise when someone punctures our privacy bubble.

Global Guide

We in America keep a comfortable "bubble" of space between conversation partners, but many Latin Americans and Middle Easterners stand much closer.

In many parts of the world, however, it's not at all uncommon for two men or two women to stroll down the street hand in hand, or casually drape an arm over a shoulder. If this should happen to you, it's far better to grit your teeth and endure this familiarity as the gesture of warmth and friendship that it is instead of jerking away and hurting someone else's feelings.

In a similar way, it's not at all unusual for people in Latin American, Asian, and Middle Eastern cultures to share sleeping arrangements with family members out of simple affection (or a shortage of sleeping quarters). Most middle-class Americans are accustomed to a private bed in a private room for every member of the family, no matter how small.

As American children become close friends and spend time with youngsters from other cultures, they may be exposed to different attitudes toward sharing a bed. Grandmothers may sleep with granddaughters—and her American friend. Your children may likely accept these different arrangements far more easily than you can.

Cover Up!

Almost every country has some rules about what is and what isn't proper attire. Many countries are more conservative than the U.S. when it comes to what may be revealed, although a few countries are more lax.

Asian and Muslim countries in particular have strict rules about not revealing the body (especially for women), no matter how hot and sticky the weather gets. This can be a problem especially for children, who may be teased by U.S. children when a Muslim girl refuses to remove a scarf or an Asian boy won't take off a shirt during a tennis match.

Try to be sensitive to the clothing taboos, which are often rooted in religious beliefs, especially when visiting the home of foreign guests.

Taking off shoes when entering the house is a very common rule in Asian homes; disregarding this rule is deeply disrespectful. The shoe-removal tradition is common among the Japanese, Chinese, Koreans, Filipinos, Thais, Iranians, and Indian Buddhists. (Even some Americans, with newly installed light colored rugs, take off their shoes when entering their homes.)

If you see a row of shoes neatly lined up outside your host's door, take the hint and deposit your shoes there as well. This small sign of respect will mean a lot to your foreign friends.

Global Guide

Some Middle Eastern and Asian cultures believe it's impolite to show the soles of the feet to anyone; crossing your legs may thus be considered to be disrespectful.

Line Up!

If you've grown up in the United States, you know the intense peer pressure that is brought to bear when somebody tries to butt in line. Typically, the transgressor is sent—in disgrace—to the back of the line to wait his or her turn in abject misery. "No cuts!" his friends shriek. Nothing is as outraged as a young American whose feeling of fairness has been thus injured.

This American passion for orderly line-waiting—the dictum of "first come, first served"—is not, in fact, universal, no matter how natural it may feel to us. Indeed, the deeply held belief of neatly lining up to be served is rooted in the American reverence for democracy, fairness, and efficiency.

However, in many other countries (especially Soviet and Eastern European countries, where standing in line is a universal pastime), the concept of neat and orderly lining up is quite foreign. In many other countries, the person who pushes and shoves his way to the front of the line gets the reward; anybody who meekly waits his turn risks not getting any bread or sausage that day.

Many immigrants don't really understand the American passion for linestanding, and when they push or shove in line—an action that would be perfectly acceptable back home—their actions may appear to be extremely boorish. Politely letting them know the cultural rules in this country can be a friendly gesture (because if you don't, some other fellow in line won't hesitate to send them to the back of the line in disgrace).

Talk Is Cheap

When you're communicating with foreign visitors or immigrants, realize that not everyone is as bold and straightforward as an American: "When I say no, I mean no!"

In many Asian cultures, saying "no" can be extremely difficult, if not impossible. It all gets down to saving face. Saying "no" involves a loss of face and creates extreme discomfort: You're disappointing someone else and making them feel badly. You lose face; they lose face; everybody is unhappy. Instead, when a Japanese person needs to say "no," they may try to avoid the entire confrontation, or use indirect communication to get around the problem.

Tip of the Hat

If you detect a foreign friend shaking the head "no" when saying "yes," it's not a sign of confusion—it's just that in some cultures, the "no" head shake we use is their way of physically indicating "yes."

Great Job!

The opposite of saying "no" is saying "yes," and you'd be surprised at how many cultures also have problems with accepting compliments for a job well done.

Whether it's giving stars, a bonus, or getting your picture taken as "Employee of the Month," giving praise is an accepted way of rewarding good work and encouraging future performance in the United States. It's all part of the American emphasis on competition—which is not always valued so highly in other cultures (especially among Asians).

Many Asians feel uncomfortable at being praised, and will often react with great discomfort if you should heap accolades on their head. "Oh, it wasn't really a good report," they will respond after turning in a Pulitzer-winning performance. They may even believe that if you're praising them now, you are indirectly saying that they weren't doing a good enough job before. Looking at praise this way, it actually becomes a form of retroactive criticism.

Being praised also means that you're being singled out from your associates, which can lead to negative reactions from peers.

The flip side of praise is criticism—which is something else that American bosses tend to dole out in generous proportions. However, directly criticizing an Asian person can result in a significant loss of face for both of you.

If you're getting ready to praise or criticize a person from another culture, think hard about the best way to do this without causing loss of face or undue embarrassment.

Faux Pas

Telling an American woman that she's gained weight is considered to be an insult, but in the Middle East, getting a bit porky is considered a sign of success. Accept comments about weight gain in the spirit in which they're intended.

Eyes Up!

Anyone who's ever barked, "Look at me when I'm speaking to you!" to a recalcitrant teenager knows the importance of direct eye contact—at least to an American. To look away is usually interpreted in the U.S. as a sign of disrespect, anger, or downright sneakiness. Americans tend to look away when speaking, moving their eyes back to fasten on the other person's face when listening.

This is not the case among many immigrants from Asian, Latin American, and Caribbean cultures, who avoid eye contact as a sign of respect. Subtle cultural habits may be so ingrained that we don't recognize them until someone violates our traditions—and if you try to speak to someone who keeps staring at his toes, it can be truly disconcerting.

Be aware of the differences in eye contact and don't be too quick to make snap cultural conclusions.

Let a Smile Be Your Umbrella

In the United States, a smile connotes an open, happy, and friendly demeanor, but in many other countries, a smile may cover embarrassment, happiness, confusion—or even downright anger. Many Japanese don't smile for official photographs, since they believe that smiling at these times could be interpreted as a lack of respect.

Cultural Roundup

The more you know about another culture, the more you will be able to understand and work through cultural differences in behavior, gestures, language, and body movements. To an amazing degree, different cultures have evolved a wide variety of different cues in which everyone in that culture participates.

When we cross the boundaries of our own culture, we run the risks—and reap the benefits—of learning new ways of seeing, thinking, and behaving.

In fact, only by reaching out to those in other cultures can we bridge the surface differences and uncover the underlying humanity that unites us all.

The Least You Need to Know

➤ Be aware of different cultural implications of colors, numbers, and types of gifts.

➤ Table manners in different cultures may be opposite U.S. expectations.

➤ Cultural and religious clothing taboos may be much more conservative than U.S. habits.

➤ Rules of eye contact are often very different in other cultures.

➤ "Lining up" in an orderly fashion is not a world-wide custom.

Part 2
North America and South America

When it comes to travel in the Americas, you may feel completely at ease—after all, they're our neighbors. What could be difficult about traveling to Canada, for example, where most of us speak the same language and—well, it's pretty hard to tell the Canadians from the Americans just by looking. But there are differences—alternative ways of looking at life that may be critically important if you ignore them.

Read on to find out more about Canada, Mexico, and Latin America—how they're different, how they're the same—and what sorts of things you'll need to know to avoid inadvertently offending our neighbors.

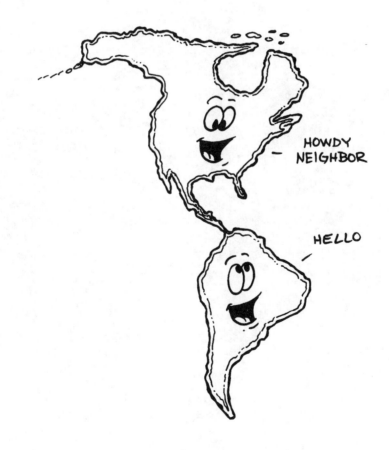

Canada

> ## In This Chapter
>
> ➤ Remember that culturally speaking, most of Canada is closer to Britain than the U.S.
>
> ➤ Understand that the cultural identity of Canada is separate from that of the U.S.
>
> ➤ Perceive the difference between French- and English-speaking Canada
>
> ➤ Learn what behavior Canadians expect and respond to best
>
> ➤ Discover the importance of punctuality

Canada may look and sound a great deal like the United States, but there's still a lot to know about the differences in cultural etiquette between the two, especially in the French-speaking province of Quebec.

If you don't remember anything else about Canada, keep these two things utmost in your mind when it comes to Canadian etiquette:

First, a separate Canadian cultural identity is of enormous importance here. Any indication that you consider Canada "a giant suburb of the United States" is deeply insulting to Canadians.

Second, never forget that many French Canadians consider themselves French first and Canadian second, and they get mighty touchy about their independence. Tread lightly when venturing into this tricky area—it's a political hot "pome de terre."

Tip of the Hat

Canada's valiant triumph over the unprovoked U.S. attack in the War of 1812 is taught to every Canadian school child. The U.S. was the first and only invader that British-controlled Canada ever faced, and to this day, the risk of U.S. economic or cultural annihilation haunts Canadians.

It's a fact: Most Canadians know far more about the United States than we know about Canada. They'll be able to tell you the U.S. states and capitals, the name of the president and other top U.S. officials, and so on.

Don't agree? Ask 10 Yanks to name the current Canadian Prime Minister, the capital of Manitoba, or the two houses of the Canadian parliament.

Read on for a quick rundown of some Canadian basics to help you navigate Canadian cultural waters.

Second Largest Country in the World

Canada has a highly developed, stable democracy, and while most Americans do know that Canada is that big chunk of a country on our northern border, most don't realize just how huge the place is—it's the second largest country in the world, stretching for 3.8 million square miles from one ocean to the other. Huge parts of Canada are still unsettled.

Look for tourist facilities everywhere—except in the northern and wilderness areas, where they are less developed and can be vast distances apart. In those areas, you'll need a plane to get around.

And the Prime Minister Is...

Canada has a parliamentary democracy, although its provinces have more power than do the individual states of the United States. The Canadian head of state is the British monarch (who is represented by the Governor General). However, the head of government is the Prime Minister. The Canadian parliament has two houses, the Senate, and the House of Commons.

Canada is similar in many ways to its southern cousin, as both are former British colonies—but the two countries actually evolved quite differently despite similar beginnings. Originally populated by Inuits (Eskimos), Canada's first foreign colony was established by the French, who called this new outpost "New France" (now Quebec) in 1534.

Not to be outdone, the British set up shop in Newfoundland 50 years later. For the next two centuries, the two countries eyed each other from their separate parts of Canada. This is the source of the bilingual tensions that exist to this day.

Eventually, the English managed to push out the French, who officially abandoned their unprofitable New France in 1760—but not all the French settlers left. While Canada became entirely a British possession, the French and English factions living in Canada were far from united.

While the two groups of settlers didn't get along, Canadians in general were treated quite differently by their British rulers, who had learned a thing or two about the dangers of ham-fisted control from their unruly Colonists to the south.

In an attempt to stave off more battles for independence in Canada like those they were struggling with in the U.S., the British allowed Canadians far more autonomy. As a result, Canadians were more than happy to accept a benevolent British rule. Eventually the far-flung separate colonies of Canada were united under British rule July 1, 1867—the date that Canada celebrates as its birthday.

It was not until 1931, however, that the British finally gave up control over Canada—peacefully—with the Statute of Westminster, which granted the Dominion of Canada complete independence from the U.K. Canada's last colony (Newfoundland) joined the Canadian confederation in 1949.

French vs. English

Long before Canada became a Dominion, the squabbling between the English and French had begun—and it has never been resolved. While French-speaking citizens became Anglicized throughout other parts of Canada, the residents of Quebec clung to their French heritage.

Today, they insist on their right to exist as a distinct society within Canada, and to maintain the language and the traditions of their mother country—that is, France.

Being considered a *distinct society* within Canada means far more than being allowed to list "soup" on your menu as "potage." Demands by French-speaking Canadians have ranged from basic changes in the Canadian constitution to separation as a separate, tiny little country. Quebec's independence party (le Parti Québécois) continues to demand sovereignty.

They aren't the only ones. Native Americans are also interested in *distinct society* status, and demand the return of vast tracts of their former land they lost to the invading Europeans. Meanwhile, the provinces in western Canada resent rule from Ottawa. (In fact, they feel they've got more things in common with the western United States than the *suits* in their own capital.)

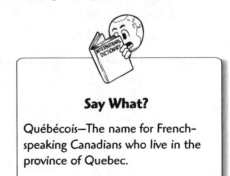

Say What?

Québécois—The name for French-speaking Canadians who live in the province of Quebec.

Despite these internecine squabbles, the Canadian government has never approved the designation of a distinct society to any of these groups, knowing that if the Québécois are awarded distinct society status, then many other segments of the population would also insist on the same designation.

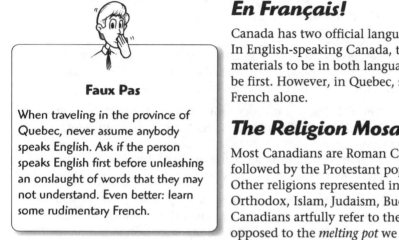

Faux Pas

When traveling in the province of Quebec, never assume anybody speaks English. Ask if the person speaks English first before unleashing an onslaught of words that they may not understand. Even better: learn some rudimentary French.

En Français!

Canada has two official languages—French and English. In English-speaking Canada, the law requires all written materials to be in both languages, although English may be first. However, in Quebec, signs are usually written in French alone.

The Religion Mosaic

Most Canadians are Roman Catholic (46 percent), followed by the Protestant population (41 percent). Other religions represented in Canada include Eastern Orthodox, Islam, Judaism, Buddhism, and Hinduism. Canadians artfully refer to their diversity as a *mosaic* (as opposed to the *melting pot* we think of here in the U.S.).

Religion in English-speaking Canada doesn't seem to exert a very strong influence on many citizens. However, it's a different story in French-speaking Quebec, where the Catholic Church holds much more influence in everyday life than it does even in France. Many French-speaking Canadians were educated in Catholic schools.

Let's Celebrate

Canadians do like their holidays, and they've amassed quite a list of celebrations. Many of these holidays are the same in the United States (except that Thanksgiving comes a month earlier, and New Year's is extended). Note also that Quebec, typically, has reserved some holidays of its own.

Be aware that when some holidays fall on a weekend, many businesses may close the Friday before or the Monday after the holiday as well:

Jan. 1-2: New Year's Holidays.

Jan. 3: New Year's (Quebec only).

Feb. 20: Family Day (Alberta only).

May 20: Victoria Day.

June 26: St. Jean Baptiste Day (Quebec only).

July 1: Canada Day.

Aug. 7: Civic Holiday (most provinces).

Sept. 4: Labor Day.

Oct. 14: Thanksgiving Day.

Nov. 11: Remembrance Day.

Dec. 26: Boxing Day.

Quelle Heure a-t-il?

When you're north of the border, expect to be on time for your appointments. In fact, most English-speaking Canadians have similar attitudes toward punctuality as do U.S. citizens. It's a *good* thing.

On the other hand, you may find that when you wander into French-speaking Canada, everybody takes a more relaxed view of the time clock (after all, they are more French than British!). It may not seem fair, but you'll still be expected to be on time here.

Global Guide

While French-speaking Canadians may stroll in to appointments late, you—as a foreign visitor—will still be expected to be on time.

Open for Business

As in the United States, expect the 9 A.M. to 5 P.M. standard business hours, Monday through Friday. If you've got an appointment, try to schedule it during the morning hours, which is the preferred Canadian time for meetings.

Most shops are open from 10 A.M. to 6 P.M. Monday through Saturday, but you may find more and more stores staying open until 9 P.M. these days. For many years, just as in many parts of the United States, Canadians had to confine their shopping to six days of the week because shop doors were legally closed on Sundays.

More recently, however, some provinces have made changes to the Lord's Day Act, leaving the option of Sunday hours under local jurisdiction.

If you've got banking to do, try to get there between 10 A.M. to 3 P.M. Monday through Thursday, and from 10 A.M. to 6 P.M. on Friday. (Some banks, as in the U.S., schedule longer hours and Saturday openings.) Fortunately, with ATM machines, these opening hours are less important than they once were.

If It's 2 p.m., It Must Be Quebec ...

Canada is a big country that takes up quite a few time zones: six in all. Fortunately for Americans, four of them are simply continuations of our own, so if you know what time it is in the United States, you can simply extend the boundary lines northward and get a rough idea. That's assuming that you know your Canadian geography, of course.

Most of Canada also operates on Daylight Savings Time, as does the United States, from the end of April through late October.

47

Global Guide

Newfoundland Island insists on its own time zone 30 minutes ahead of Atlantic Standard Time. Keep in mind that it's only the island that gets this special time; Labrador (the mainland part of Newfoundland Province) is on Atlantic Standard time.

To make sure you don't get zoned out with the time differences, here's a quick breakdown:

➤ **Atlantic Standard Time:** All Maritime Provinces (except for Newfoundland Island); Atlantic Standard is one hour *ahead* of Eastern Standard Time.

➤ **Eastern Standard Time:** Most of Quebec and Ontario.

➤ **Central Standard Time:** Western Ontario, Manitoba, and eastern Saskatchewan (including Regina).

➤ **Mountain Standard Time:** Western Saskatchewan, Alberta, and eastern British Columbia.

➤ **Pacific Standard Time:** Most of British Columbia.

Cultural Ins and Outs

It's very hard for many Europeans to tell the difference between English-speaking citizens of Canada and the United States, as the manners of both are very similar. As in the United States, your Canadian hosts will expect direct eye contact, an open and friendly attitude, and a firm handshake.

Despite these similarities, keep in mind that many Canadians are still culturally closer to their British cousins than to those of us in the United States—more reserved, formal, and polite than their neighbors to the south.

This means you need to be careful to rein in the more outrageous, boisterous parts of your personality, or you'll risk being thought of as overbearing and obnoxious. Think *Ugly American* here, and don't overdo it.

"Hi There!"

Sometimes it seems to outsiders that everyone in the United States is on a first-name basis. While many Canadians are quick to shift to first names, it's always best to follow the lead of your host before resorting to a first-name greeting.

Just as in the U.S., Canadians order their names beginning with the first name, the middle name, and then the surname. When first meeting and greeting, use a person's title and last name until told to do otherwise, or unless you notice that everyone is on a first-name basis.

When talking on the phone, French Canadians may use your first name and then revert to last names in person.

Everyone shakes hands on meeting in Canada, but be prepared to shake hands more often in French-speaking Canada—they'll also shake during introductions and when saying goodbye.

Friends in French Canada may well embrace and kiss the cheek—but you won't see a French-Canadian end a hug with a pat or two on the back, as you would in the United States.

Body Talk

When you think Canadian, you can often transpose *British*—so, not surprisingly, body language is usually more reserved among English-speaking Canadians. Keep your distance—about two feet—when talking to an English-speaking Canadian.

Still, while Canadians are very similar to those in the U.K., they are more relaxed than their British counterparts—back slapping is accepted (although it's not practiced among French Canadians). You'll notice Canadians also tend to be more informal when they sit than Brits would be; you'll find them propping an ankle on the opposite knee, or tilting back chairs and propping up feet. In the office, however, you'll need a less casual attitude.

Your French-speaking hosts, on the other hand, may be more outgoing—more in the manner of their Gallic ancestors. French Canadians may stand closer to each other than those in the United States are used to. And if you're squeamish about being touched, bite your lip, because French Canadians are more likely to touch you as they talk. They also may be more likely to hold the hand of a person of the same sex.

If your host takes your hand, don't jerk away in horror—it's considered a simple gesture of friendship.

Tip of the Hat

You can't tell a Canadian by the maple-leaf jacket. Canada is as much of an ethnic stew as any big city in the United States. The background of your hosts may include British, French, Inuit, German, Indian, Native American, Hong Kong Chinese, and so on. As a result, their behavior may be quite different from other Canadians.

Gestures

Close to the vest is a good rule of thumb when it comes to gestures. There's no need to gesticulate wildly in Canada; keep it conservative and calm and you'll do well. Follow these guidelines to avoid offense:

➤ Avoid pointing at another person; if you want to point at something else, however, use your index finger.

➤ Don't make the "V for Victory" sign with the palm facing in (it's an insult); instead, face the palm out.

➤ Both the "ok" sign (circle of the thumb and index finger) and the "thumbs up" (a fist with the thumbs upward) are accepted signs of approval.

Canadian Clothes

As in the U.K., clothing should be classic and understated; if you prefer obvious trendy outfits, you won't necessarily be perceived as *ahead of your time*.

If you're traveling in more rural areas, break out the jeans—the dress code will generally be less formal. (Still, if you're there on business and you're in doubt, it's better to err on the sign of conservatism.)

Remember that Canada is far north, and its winters can be downright freezing. Dress accordingly.

Sealed with a Kiss

When you're negotiating with Canadians, always remember that many tend to view people from the United States with amused tolerance, because they believe that folks in the U.S. have an inherent belief in their own superiority.

Global Guide

In Quebec, French is the only legal language of business. All signs must be posted in French. Outside Quebec, all communications must be in both French and English.

Remember this, and beware of overemphasizing the benefits of your company, product, or service. Try not to promote yourself too much.

Negotiating with your Canadian counterparts is otherwise rather similar to negotiating with someone in the U.S.—except at a slower tempo.

Don't forget about the dual language requirements in this country; if you are negotiating with French Canadians, all of your materials must be in French and English. If you really want to score points here, it's probably a good idea to have a bilingual representative from the U.S. do the negotiating.

Bring On the Cadeaux!

If you bring a gift, don't try to overwhelm your hosts with your incredible generosity and outrageous taste. A small, understated gift is acceptable, offered either when you arrive or when you leave. It's a nice touch to bring something from your own country.

It's acceptable in the Canadian business world to exchange gifts at Christmas. Choose one of these to make a good impression:

➤ office-related gift

➤ wine

➤ liquor

A business gift should be handed over when the deal is struck. Typically, the gift is unwrapped in your presence, and shown to the whole room—so don't give your Canadian colleague that outlandish pair of undershorts with the pictures of Bill Clinton, unless you wouldn't be embarrassed to have the whole gang see.

Instead of a tangible gift, it's quite popular and well accepted to take your host out for a meal or entertainment in lieu of a wrapped package. Then you don't need to worry about whether that Clinton underwear would go over well.

Global Guide

A hostess gift is a nice touch when visiting a Canadian home; as in the U.S., wine or liquor, flowers, or chocolates are all good choices.

Potage to Nuts

When it comes to dining out in Canada, you'll be in safe waters if you stick to the manners your mama taught you. Generally, what's considered acceptable in the United States is acceptable in Canada. Read on for the particulars.

While lunch is the most popular time to conduct business north of the border, dinner ranks a close second. While breakfast business meetings are beginning to crop up in Canada, they are still not that common.

Check, Please!

If you need to call the waiter, quietly wave your hand. If you want the check, make that busy little "writing" gesture on an imaginary piece of paper.

In French-speaking Canada, a simple backward tilt of the head or very discreet wave is enough to send the garçon scurrying over.

What's for Dinner?

Dinner is usually considered to be a social occasion, so if your hosts invite you out to eat, don't begin negotiations for that new maple syrup factory during the canapés. If business is going to be discussed, your hosts will bring it up at the end of the meal—but wait for them to broach the subject first.

Faux Pas

If you're invited to a French-Canadian's home, don't go barging into the kitchen as you would in the U.S. Certain areas are considered *private*—including the kitchen—and you should enter only when invited.

If you are invited out for a business dinner, expect to be taken to a restaurant or a nightclub; it would be unusual for a business associate you've just met to invite you to dine at their home.

However, as in the United States, things are more informal out west. Don't be surprised if you're invited over for an American *barbecue*.

The Least You Need to Know

➤ French-speaking Canadians and English-speaking Canadians have different cultural expectations and attitudes; friction between the two factions exists today.

➤ Canadians, as a rule, resent being considered as a sort of *U.S. annex* and insist on their own cultural individuality.

➤ Canadians will expect direct eye contact, an open and friendly attitude, and a firm handshake, but tend to be a bit more conservative and formal than their southern business colleagues.

➤ Don't start speaking English automatically in Quebec—if you try to learn some French, it will be appreciated.

➤ A small, understated business gift is best.

➤ If you are negotiating with French Canadians, all you materials must be in both French and English.

Chapter 5

Mexico

In This Chapter

➤ Master the ins and outs of "saving face" here

➤ Get the details on what you should not call a Mexican citizen

➤ Learn how to play the punctuality game

➤ Find out when to kiss and when to shake hands

➤ Discover the importance of family

The United States of Mexico and of America are so geographically close and yet so culturally far apart. It's more than a language that separates the U.S.A. from Mexico, and this chapter explores the differences and the similarities between these two neighbors.

Just as Canadians are sensitive about their own independence and differences from the United States, Mexicans likewise are proud of their own independence and unique qualities. They don't like to think they are somehow a lesser appendage to the larger and wealthier neighbor to their north.

It's All North American

Even though Mexico technically is also part of the North American continent, polite Mexicans will call a U.S. citizen a "norteamericano," meaning a "North American." They'll call Canadians "canadienses" to tell them apart from the norteamericanos.

Mexico is one of the Central American countries, which makes it technically part of North America. Bordering the U.S. to the north and Guatemala and Belize to the south, it is more than three times the size of Texas, with coasts on the Pacific Ocean and the Gulf of Mexico.

The country has a rapidly developing economy, and luxury accommodations in major cities are widely available, although tourist facilities in more remote areas may be limited. Driving to these remote places may be even more of a challenge.

Faux Pas

When in Mexico, don't refer to a U.S. citizen as an "American"—Mexicans are Americans, too. (In fact, the official name of Mexico translates into the "United States of Mexico.")

El Presidente

Mexico has a federal republic led by a president who serves for six years. (After that, he or she can't be re-elected). The current ruling party (the Partido Revolucionario Institucional) has been holding the Mexican reins for many years.

The original Mexicans were the Mayan and Aztec Indians, two extremely advanced pre-Colombian societies. Gifted as they were in astronomy, architecture, and crafts, they were still destroyed by the conquering Spanish in the 1500s. Ruled by colonial Spain since 1521, Mexico did not achieve independence until 1810.

Speaking the Lingo

The official language of Mexico is Spanish, but most educated people and business executives in the country also speak English. In addition to these two languages, there are also more than 100 Indian languages spoken in Mexico as well.

If you will be attempting to speak Spanish and you're not fluent, remember that the Spanish language has two forms of the pronoun "you"—the informal "tú" (pronounced "too") and the formal "usted" (pronounced "oo-sted"). When speaking to someone you don't know well, it's usually best to use "usted"—wait for the other fellow to switch to the familiar form before you do.

If you don't speak Spanish, buy a dictionary and try to learn a few phrases so you can establish that you don't speak the language and that you'll need someone to help you translate. Most businesses in urban areas have at least one bilingual employee, but don't go into a store expecting all their employees to speak your language.

Global Guide

If you're struggling to be understood, remain calm and polite. Usually you can get your point across despite not speaking the language.

Even if you're pretty sure everyone there speaks English, don't just start babbling in your native tongue at the top of your voice. If you must speak English, at least ask if anyone there speaks English first. Remember—you're in a foreign country, even if it is just over the border from the U.S.—and it's not their duty to speak your language.

If nobody there speaks English, remember that speaking in a louder voice isn't going to help anyone understand you any better. Try hand gestures. If you're taking a taxi, carry a map so you can point out where you're going in case the driver doesn't understand you.

Keeping the Faith

There is no "official" Mexican religion, but for all intents and purposes, it's Roman Catholic as almost 90 percent of Mexicans belong to this faith. More recently, more and more Protestant sects are cropping up (primarily Evangelical), but they are still very much in the minority.

Life Is a Holiday

There are 11 national holidays in Mexico, but some of the days fluctuate—so check to make sure before finalizing your travel and business plans. As in the United States, if a holiday falls on a Saturday or Sunday, businesses may close down the Friday before or the Monday after. Likewise, it's a good idea to avoid planning on traveling to Mexico for business during the Christmas and Easter holidays. Other major holidays include:

Jan. 1: New Year's Day.

Feb. 5: Constitution Day.

March 21: Benito Juarez' birthday.

Late March: Spring Equinox (Temple of Kukulkan at Chichén Itzá, special alignment with the sun).

May 1: Labor Day.

May 5: Victory at Puebla/Cinco de Mayo.

Sept. 16: Independence Day.

Oct. 12: Columbus Day (Dia de la Raza).

Nov. 20: 1910 Revolution Anniversary.

Dec. 12: The Day of the Virgin of Guadalupe.

Dec. 31: New Year's Eve.

Tip of the Hat

Images of the Virgin of Guadalupe are everywhere, symbol of a miracle that occurred to a poor Aztec, Juan Diego, in 1513. Diego believed the Virgin Mary appeared to him three times, telling him to build a church in Tepeyac, which is now a popular basilica. Today, the Virgin of Guadalupe is a symbol of Mexican nationality and the unity between the Aztec and Spanish cultures.

On Time, Sometimes

Mexicans admire punctuality although they often don't seem to be able to achieve it themselves. As a foreigner, you'll be expected to be right on time—but be sure to pack a bunch of work in your briefcase to occupy yourself until your Mexican colleagues show up.

On the other hand, the punctuality rules are thrown out the window when it comes to private parties. For these gatherings, everyone—even U.S. visitors—are expected to be at least 30 minutes late. If you're in Mexico City, make that an hour.

Before you leave the U.S., make your appointments with Mexican colleagues by mail or fax from two to four weeks early. Try to make contact with the most senior members of the firm that you can.

Open and Closed for Business

Business hours begin at 9 A.M. and end at 6 P.M. (well, more or less—there's that punctuality thing again). Don't forget about that two-hour siesta in between, from 1 P.M. to 3 P.M., when many places close down. You'll find banks are open from 9 A.M. to 1:30 P.M. Monday through Friday (Saturday hours don't exist here).

Government offices, on the other hand, open up earlier than any others—at 8 A.M.—but close down by 2:30 P.M., Monday through Friday.

There is only one time zone in Mexico, and it's one hour behind Eastern Standard Time. If it's 2 P.M. in New York, then it's 1 P.M. in Mexico.

Socially Speaking

The elite in Mexico (and Mexico has the largest upper class of all Latin American cultures) enjoy a wonderful life in a beautiful country with a rich cultural heritage. But the sad fact is that many other Mexicans toil at the other end of the continuum, enduring great hardships, working long hours, and earning very low wages.

Global Guide

Many Mexicans will place the importance of their family ahead of anything else, including their job or career.

To Mexicans, individual worth is not the only way of measuring a person's success, however—social status is of great importance. Social status is measured by the groups to whom you belong, namely your friends and your family. These social relationships can provide both strength and pressure on behavior.

The family is revered in Mexico, and hiring—and not firing—family members is a venerated Mexican practice.

A person's dignity means a great deal in Mexico, no mater what his social status. For this reason, never deliberately embarrass anyone and don't publicly criticize your hosts (even if it's deserved). The best way to get excellent service in Mexico is to show respect, courtesy, and manners to everyone you deal with.

In dealing with strangers, whether a taxi driver, a store owner, or a hotel desk clerk, it is always best to be polite and courteous. Remember that you are a guest in their country.

¡Hasta la Vista!

After the pleasantries and handshakes, you can expect someone to ask you what you've seen so far in Mexico, or what you think of their country. Mexicans have enormous pride in their cultural heritage and like to find out how much you know about your southern neighbors.

You don't have to be an expert on Aztec artifacts to succeed here. Showing a simple respect for the country's history and culture is a good start. If you haven't had time to tour sights such as Chichén Itzá, at least read up on some and explain that you're looking forward to checking out the sights.

Personal friendship counts for a great deal in Mexico, so you'll be wise to spend lots of time getting to know your colleagues here. In any business transaction, Mexicans are looking for long-term relationships with individuals they can respect.

The well-known company you represent will mean less than your own relationship with your Mexican colleagues, so don't forget them the minute your plane leaves the taxiway. Once you get home, pick up the phone. Call, or send a note. Stay in touch.

¿El Capitán?

If you've got a title, trot it out in Mexico—and be sure to use everyone else's title when you address them. If you're going to use a title, remember that in Mexico you should use the person's title by itself—call Dr. Susan Jones "Doctor," and not "Dr. Jones."

If the person you're talking to doesn't have a professional title, then use Señor (Mr.), Señora (Mrs.), or Señorita (Miss). Don't be the first to call anyone by his or her first name.

Names can get confusing in Latin America, and this is certainly true in Mexico, where people walk around with a whole string of names. Hispanics typically use two last names—one from dad (this one comes first) and one from mom. This means that you would call Señor Luis Juan Pedro Lopez Morales, "Señor Lopez."

When a woman marries, she usually tacks on her husband's last name. Therefore, if Señorita Maria Ana Garcia Zedillo married Señor Luis Juan Pedro Lopez Morales, her name would be Señora Maria Ana Garcia Zedillo de Morales. You'd call her "Señora de Morales" (or informally, Señora Morales). Or, to avoid all that, just smile!

Charmed, I'm Sure!

Greetings are more formal in Mexico than in the United States. Traditionally, men shake hands upon meeting and women may shake hands with men—it's up to the woman, so wait and see if a woman extends her hand before shaking hers.

Mexican men—always extremely polite—may bow slightly while shaking a woman's hand.

If you're a woman, don't be surprised if another woman kisses you on the cheek while embracing, or pats you on the arm in lieu of a kiss. No shrieking and running for a hanky—this is acceptable behavior in Mexico.

For women, a handshake will do for first meetings of both men and women, but with friends and acquaintances, both men and women, both a handshake and a kiss on the cheek are in order. It may feel awkward at first, but remember that it seems perfectly natural to the Mexican people.

When you're entering a party, bow slightly to everyone as you come in and then work your way around the room, shaking hands with everyone. Be prepared to shake hands with everyone all over again when it's time to leave.

Up Close and Personal

Don't be surprised to find your nose within inches of your Mexican colleagues' face. People here maintain a much closer physical distance while talking. This may make you feel decidedly uncomfortable, but try to avoid flinching or backing up—your hosts may feel you're being unfriendly. If you back up, they may simply step closer again to close up the gap.

Don't be surprised to be touched by a Mexican while you're talking, rubbing shoulders, or making other contact. It's an insult to flinch or pull away, so grit your teeth and don't move.

If you're talking to a Mexican and you notice his eyes seem permanently riveted to the ground, don't worry. It's not that he's not paying attention—he's showing respect to a superior (boss) by looking away.

When you're interacting with Mexican colleagues, you may gaze into the eyes of another person intermittently—then look away. Avoid a direct, constant eye contact, which will be interpreted as aggressive. The person who is talking is the one who gets to maintain direct eye contact.

Here are some other body language errors to avoid:

➤ Don't put your hands in your pockets.

➤ Don't put your hands on your hips (it's interpreted as a challenge).

➤ Put your cash into a clerk's hand—don't put it onto the counter.

➤ Use your index finger when indicating height.

Señorita Power

The situation for Mexican women is changing fairly rapidly, especially in major cities. Many women report that ageism, not sexism, is a real problem—that it's not nearly so hard to find and keep a job if you're a woman as it is to find and keep a job once you reach the age of 35 or 40.

Many older workers are concerned about keeping their jobs, knowing that for every position an older worker holds, there are 10 or 20 younger workers clamoring for that same spot. In fact, almost three quarters of the population are younger than 29 (and half of those are under age 15). Essentially a primarily young country, many older workers (who are not protected by law) find themselves out of a job just when they may need the income the most.

While Mexico historically has been a male-dominated society, the Latin expectation that men should be gentlemen virtually guarantees that female executives are treated with respect and politeness.

In fact, women may find it easier than some of their male colleagues to get ahead; successful Mexican women tend to be enormously efficient, tough, and hard-working while still projecting an image of femininity.

Suit or Serape?

It's fine to appear in Mexico in stylish, well-tailored clothes, but dressing up for the sake of showing off is frowned upon in Mexico. Leave that ostentatious jewelry at home. Remember that many Mexicans are very poor, and the rest of the country doesn't believe in wasting money.

Choose a conservative dark suit and tie (men); women should opt for a nice dress, or skirt and blouse. While women have made great strides in Mexico, even the most professional Mexican women strive to appear feminine and stylish.

If you're going to spend some time relaxing and you're used to sunbathing topless in other countries, remember that it isn't okay to go topless on most Mexican beaches. Always wear a bathing suit; bikinis are fine for women.

Faux Pas

Foreign women shouldn't invite male Mexican colleagues to a business dinner unless other colleagues or spouses come along. Business lunches are okay, but have the bill added to your hotel tab or you'll have an argument on your hands.

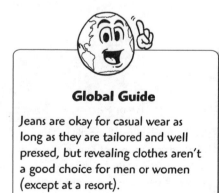

Global Guide

Jeans are okay for casual wear as long as they are tailored and well pressed, but revealing clothes aren't a good choice for men or women (except at a resort).

Tactful Time

Directness is valued in the United States, but think twice before spouting off to the Mexicans what you thought about the boss' last speech. Be courteous, be tactful, and above all, be polite. When in doubt, flatter and keep your criticism to yourself.

Artful Negotiation

Mexicans love a good bargaining session, but arguing is another matter entirely. The polite thing is to tell someone what he or she wants to hear, and that may not be necessarily the truth.

Don't be surprised at the leisurely pace—things get done, but they take more time. Expect delays (in fact, you should plan for delays) as the decisions which are made at the top must first be discussed at lower levels.

Remember when you negotiate that status counts for quite a lot in Mexico. Dress well, stay in a very good hotel, eat at excellent restaurants, and be sure to mention any university degrees you hold. Make sure that if you bring a negotiating team to Mexico, some higher-level management should be represented.

Don't forget that Mexicans hate to seem impolite or hurt anyone's feelings, so they'll find it hard to say "no." Instead, you may hear a "maybe" or even more vague, "it depends" or "we'll see." If you do manage to squeeze an agreement out of your hosts, make sure they sign an agreement right away before you find that "yes" really meant "no, but I can't bear to tell you that."

If you want to win at negotiating in Mexico, your colleagues there will want to hear how the deal will benefit the individual, his family, or his pride. Mexico is not the country where literal, linear thinking shines—go with your emotions. Don't stress logic or the bottom line—point out how compatible you are and how much you trust each other.

Compromise is good, but don't go too far or the ever-present machismo will appear and look down upon your own weakness.

Faux Pas

Don't give gifts made of silver. Silver is linked to the sort of tawdry trinkets snapped up by visiting gringos. Knives aren't a good choice either; it implies you're interested in severing a relationship.

To Give or Not To Give ...

If you're doing business in Mexico, custom doesn't require that you exchange gifts among executives. However, small items might be nice—on a first visit, perhaps something with your company's logo. On a follow-up visit, you can move on to something more substantial, such as a bottle of liquor or wine.

Secretaries, however, do expect to be remembered. Government secretaries expect a token gift for providing any type of service; secretaries in private businesses appreciate something more substantial, such as a scarf or perfume. If you're a married man, don't sign a gift to a secretary with your own name. You should tell the secretary that the gift is from your wife.

Por La Señorita ...

When going to a Mexican home for a meal, it's not necessary to bring a gift, but a gift does make a nice impression. Choose candy, flowers, or a local gift from your hometown.

If you decide to bring flowers, you should know that Mexican folklore has assigned certain meanings to certain types of blooms:

➤ **Red flowers:** They cast spells.

➤ **White flowers:** They lift spells.

➤ **Yellow flowers:** These represent death.

Entertainment Mexico Style

If you're doing business in Mexico, you'll also be doing a lot of socializing, so pack a few fancy duds and enjoy yourself. Don't expect to sit down in the middle of a party and talk business, however—socializing is strictly for having fun. Business will not be discussed.

Mi Casa es Su Casa

If you get invited into a Mexican home, you should be deeply honored. The Mexicans don't just drag home any Tom, Dick, or Harriet who crosses their path. If you've been invited home, you've been accepted as a friend of the family with all the honor and obligation that brings.

Quinceanera

If you're well thought of, you may be invited to attend a girl's 15th birthday party, which is called a "Quinceanera" in Mexico. It's sort of like a debutante's "coming-out" party in the United States. It's a fancy deal in Mexico and being invited is an honor.

Gazpacho to Nuts

Business lunches or dinner is common practice in Mexico. If you're eating as part of a group, the oldest person in the group usually pays the tab. It's good manners to argue about who pays the bill, however. If you lose, invite the other person out for another meal, explaining that you'll pay that time.

Minding Your Mexican Manners

Acceptable dining repartee includes your family, sights you've enjoyed in Mexico, and your job back home.

Faux Pas

No matter how strong your feelings, don't bring up the problem of illegal aliens, the Mexican-American war, or other sensitive historical topics at dinner.

Global Guide

Wine or a glass of tequila is a very common accompaniment to a meal (especially lunch) in Mexico. Drink up and enjoy! Remember that the altitude of Mexico City means that alcohol's effects may be intensified.

When dining out with a Mexican family, it is common for them to treat. Although you should offer to pay, it is not likely that they will concede and let you buy dinner. It's best to graciously accept their offer, but you should insist on paying for drinks and tip, or offer to take them out to dinner on a later date to return the favor.

Siesta or Lunch?

The biggest meal of the day is lunch, so don't be surprised if your business lunch lasts for more than two hours (from 2 P.M. to 4 P.M.) On the other hand, if you're visiting an area close to the border, you may find that the northern American tradition of a noontime lunch has been adopted. (In any case, it will still stretch on for at least two hours.)

Late-Night Dining

If you go out to dinner in Mexico, get plenty of sleep beforehand. Dinner hours here generally begins between 8:30 P.M. and 9:30 P.M. (and of course, you arrive about 30 minutes late to be polite).

Because of the value that Mexicans place on the family, there are many family-oriented restaurants throughout Mexico. Unlike some upscale restaurants in the United States and Europe that tend to frown on young children, many fancy restaurants in Mexico welcome families with children. If you'll be traveling with young children, don't hesitate to take them to a nice restaurant.

The Least You Need to Know

➤ Don't flash money, dress provocatively or criticize your hosts.

➤ Mexicans value the family above all else.

➤ Don't be surprised when the entire country shuts down for lunch.

➤ If you're doing business in Mexico, a small gift is a nice gesture.

➤ Avoid blunt directness in favor or polite courtesy.

➤ Don't be surprised at the leisurely pace of business.

Chapter 6

PLEASED TO MEET YOU.

Latin America

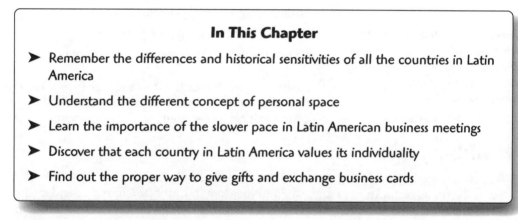

In This Chapter

➤ Remember the differences and historical sensitivities of all the countries in Latin America

➤ Understand the different concept of personal space

➤ Learn the importance of the slower pace in Latin American business meetings

➤ Discover that each country in Latin America values its individuality

➤ Find out the proper way to give gifts and exchange business cards

From Panama to Peru, Venezuela to Brazil, this chapter tells you what you need to know. Although each Latin American country maintains a unique personality, some customs remain the same.

As a traveler visiting any place south of the U.S. border, it helps to embark on your sojourn equipped with some knowledge of how things are done in this part of the world.

It's All America

Never refer to your home base as "America"—rather, say you're from the United States. South and Central Americans find North Americans a bit egocentric when referring to "back home" as America. After all, they all live in America, too.

And remember, the climate in Central and South America is mostly tropical, although it can be quite cold in the mountains.

Speaking the Lingo

The primary language spoken throughout Central and South America is Spanish, with the exception of Brazil, where Portuguese is the official tongue. (Brazilians take pride in their Portuguese heritage, so to call locals Spanish-Americans would be insulting.) Frequently, the spelling of Portuguese words is exactly the same as Spanish, but the pronunciation differs greatly. Before opening your mouth in this east coast country, learn to speak a few words and avoid committing a cultural offense.

Faux Pas

Remember that Brazilians resent being spoken to in Spanish. Be sure all your documentation—including business cards—is printed in both Portuguese and English.

Before you go, see if you can learn a few simple phrases in Spanish:

"¿Dónde está el baño?" (doan-day es-tah el bahn-do)—Where is the bathroom?

"Por favor," (pour-fa-vor)—Please.

"Gracias," (grah-see-us)—Thank you.

"De nada," (day-nah-da)—You are welcome.

"Hasta luego" (ah-stah loo-ay-go)—Goodbye.

Spanish is not that difficult a language (many Eastern European tongues are much harder to speak). Your efforts will be appreciated.

Holiday Time

Avoid scheduling appointments two or three days before a holiday. Most of the holidays in Latin America are related to the Roman Catholic Church calendar (the primary religion in almost all of Latin America), although local variations are common. Check before you go.

Never on Time

Try not to be exasperated by the Latin America attitude toward punctuality—this culture is not that interested. In general, South Americans are not picky about being punctual, but they will expect North Americans to be right on time.

In many areas of Latin America, in fact, the idea that a person should be ruled by a clock is thought to be a joke. It's fine if you want to roll in on time, but it's also okay if you're late. That's life ...

If timing is crucial, use a qualifying phrase, such as *"en punto"* (ahn-poontoe; on the dot).

Do You Have an Appointment?

You'll probably need an introduction to a Latin before you can make an appointment. This can come from somebody you both know, a trade organization, or a professional "go-between" (sometimes called an *"enchufado" [ahn-choo-fah-do]*). Family is of primary importance in Latin America, however, so an introduction by a businessperson's relative is often the best way.

While making appointments is a good idea, build in lots of flexibility and waiting time. Meetings can start and end late. Also, always keep a back-up meeting in the event a scheduled appointment is cancelled or postponed. Here are some specific appointment tips:

➤ Argentine executives put in a very long day, often lasting until 10 P.M.—it's not unusual to have evening appointments, perhaps as late as 8 P.M.

➤ In Chile, schedule appointments from 10 A.M. to noon and from 2:30 P.M. to 5 P.M. Following up a late morning appointment with lunch is also popular.

➤ Be a few minutes early to your appointment in Venezuela, and allow extra time to compensate for terrible traffic.

➤ Make appointments at least two weeks in advance in Brazil, and never make an impromptu visit. Schedule meetings from 10 A.M. to noon, and 3 P.M. to 5 P.M. If your business runs into lunch, be prepared to spend at least two hours.

Time is of the essence in São Paulo and tardiness is considered inconsiderate. In Rio de Janeiro, however, your host may not always be so punctual. If you called a meeting at 3 P.M., a Rio resident may interpret gathering time as "around 3" (like maybe 3:15 or so). Even if your agenda notes are wilting and the pastries are getting tough, whatever you do, don't indicate that you were concerned about the late arrival. Ironically, there's a double standard here—and it doesn't necessarily give *you* permission to wander in a few minutes late. During meetings in São Paulo, expect tight scheduling. In Rio, you may feel more like you've stepped into a social club—try not to hurry things along.

Tip of the Hat

Do all you can to stifle a yawn. Public yawning is not acceptable in most Latin American countries, especially in Argentina, Bolivia, and El Salvador. If you find one coming on, turn your head and cover your mouth.

In general, the business day starts and ends later in Latin American than it does in the United States. Lunch normally starts at 1 P.M. or 2 P.M. Plan meetings between 9 A.M. to noon, and from 3 P.M. to 6 P.M.

Getting Down to Business

In general, Latin Americans prefer to do business with folks they like, period. Conversely, most executives in the United States have a host of rules that govern whom they collaborate with. For example, they may be required to work with the lowest bidder on a particular project, or to prepare reports to justify hiring or promoting certain people.

In Latin America, the boss pretty much gets to do as he or she pleases, based on nothing more scientific than a gut reaction. If he likes you, you're in. If he doesn't—well, *hasta la vista* (goodbye)*!*

When you come to Latin America to do business, you're building a personal relationship, not just closing a deal. Latin Americans do business with you yourself, not your company logo. If you quit, they won't simply take up with the new guy where you left off—your replacement will have to start over from the beginning and build up a relationship all over again.

That's why it's imperative to establish a good first impression, because the development of the entire relationship begins there. After that first meeting, don't pass up an opportunity to get to know your contact better. If he suggests a business lunch or dinner, take him up on it. Any invitations to special parties or social organizations should be quickly accepted with pleasure. Don't assume the American way is the only way. Be open-minded.

It's important to understand that this Latin emphasis on getting to know you means that you shouldn't stride into a meeting, throw your briefcase on the table, and pull out your agenda. Socialize a bit. Bring up business after everyone has had time to loosen up a bit.

Tip of the Hat

In Latin America, "Yes" does not always mean, "I agree"; it may simply mean, "I hear you."

Remember that building relationships takes time, so don't expect to conquer Latin America on your first business trip. You might spend the entire first meeting nibbling pastry and focusing on social pleasantries. You may need to sit through many meetings before you reach the *"amigo"* stage.

Between appointments, check out the countryside—your colleagues will ask you your impressions of their country and they will want to know what you've seen. It's important to understand the uniqueness of each country and be aware of which countries are historical rivals. (For example, Argentines don't like being mistaken for Chileans, Brazilians resent being spoken to in Spanish, and so forth.)

If your business destination is Rio de Janeiro, you'll find a casual environment—what else would you expect in the land of Carnival and the samba? However, when scheduling meetings in São Paulo, you'll find business settings just the opposite—quite formal. Personal relationships are far more important than corporate ones in Argentina. Changing your representative may stop a negotiation process.

Compared to other parts of South America, Argentines are more serious and formal. Calling someone "not serious" is one of the worst accusations an Argentine can make.

Decision-making in Chile is centralized, residing mostly with the *presidente* (president). Be patient; several trips may be necessary to accomplish a transaction.

Never dominate the conversation or pressure your Latin American colleagues; they like to feel in control. Don't mention attorneys until negotiations are complete. Remember that Latin Americans value the person they do business with more than the firm name.

Global Guide

Sometimes Latin Americans find U.S. aggressive business attitudes offensive—don't expect to get right to the point. Avoid confrontations and hide any frustrations.

Hello, Goodbye

The standard greeting in most of Latin America is a nod and a hearty handshake. Greeting close friends may include a kiss, as well as the full embrace (the *abrazo [ah-brah-zo]*)—which entails a hug, handshakes, and (for men) several thumps on the shoulder. Brazilian greetings can be effusive, from extended handshakes at the first encounter to embraces once a friendship has been established.

Latin American women often kiss each other on alternating cheeks: twice if they are married, three times if single. The third kiss is for "good luck" in finding a spouse. Alternatively, they may greet each other with light opposite cheek touching. Hollywood folks know this as the "air kiss."

In addition, Latin American women often pat each other on the right forearm or shoulder.

At parties, greet each person individually. Don't ask a person his job; wait for the information to be volunteered.

What's Your Title?

Titles are important in Latin America, and many Latin Americans are status-conscious. During introductions, they'll announce their full names; you should do the same.

Most Hispanics have one surname from their father, which is listed first, and a second from their mother. Only the father's surname is commonly used when addressing someone verbally.

Use the title and surname, which comes first on the business card: Señor Juan Rodriguez Valdez would be Señor Rodriguez. Don't address anyone by first name unless invited to do so.

Always use a title with your host's first name—in Portuguese, this is Señor, Señora, or Señorita (Mr., Mrs., or Miss). The surname is not generally used. Soon after this formality, the title is usually dropped by the request of your host. In that manner, once you've become friendly with Señora Maria, you would be expected to simply call her Maria.

Offer Your Card

Shaking hands, introducing and exchanging business cards begins a meeting Latin-style. Unlike the situation in many Asian countries, you don't need to go through a formal presentation when you exchange business cards in Latin America. As the Nike folks say: Just do it. Offer your card—but don't be disappointed if you don't receive a card in return.

Bring plenty of your own cards along, and remember to treat others' cards with respect. It's a good idea to keep a client's card in front of you during a meeting—don't immediately pop it into your pocket (especially a pocket in the seat of your pants).

Group Hug!

Hugs are big in Latin America. This is a very friendly sector of the world where physical contact—be it a kiss on the cheek or a pat on the back—are all part of the culture.

Most Latin Americans converse at a closer distance than you're used to—often with a hand on your lapel or shoulder. You may feel invaded, but that's just Latin style; try not to back away.

For the most part, Latin America is an incredibly friendly group of nations. You should be as warm as possible when dealing with someone from any of those countries; smile at every opportunity (but don't fake it). Return any hug that comes your way.

But while hugging is in, staring at folks is out. During conversation, remember that direct, intense eye contact is considered challenging and aggressive. Look away while others are talking, and don't assume someone is untrustworthy or embarrassed if they don't look you in the eye. It's considered impolite to do so.

Gestures That Work

In at least six Latin American countries—Argentina, Colombia, Guatemala, Peru, Bolivia, and Mexico—the way to call someone to join you is to thrust your arm in front of you and keep your palm facing down. Then curl your fingers toward you back and forth a couple of times. Any local will know that you are interested in grabbing his or her attention and should head your way.

If your Brazilian host is displaying a scratching motion with the fingers together and palms down, walk over to your business contact. In Brazil this hand motion means, "come over here." If you are indicating approval on a business matter in Brazil, never give the okay sign of a ring formed by the thumb and index finger. This is an obscene gesture here. Instead, close the fist and shoot the thumb up.

Chivalry Lives

Be courteous. Chivalry is not dead in Latin America. When a woman enters a room, all the men present usually stand as a form of recognition. When a door needs to be entered, a Latin man is happy to oblige by opening it to let the woman pass through. Even if you are male and from the United States, it is best to be on your best behavior and use your manners at all times.

Global Guide

Carefully manicured nails are very important throughout Latin America for business women (and if you wear open-toed shoes, don't forget your feet—get a pedicure).

While women are beginning to make strides toward equality in Latin America, the success of those initial steps vary from one country to the next. In general, Latin America remains an area in which machismo still exists. However, innate politeness often conceals some of the more obvious inequalities.

Stylish but Conservative

Bringing along comfortable yet easy going clothes for business down Rio way, and packing conservative dark suits or dresses will provide the right look for corporate São Paulo. The Argentines have adopted British traditions toward clothing, usually wearing formal, conservative outfits, so you should, too. Businesswomen in Argentina should be sure to wear stylish shoes. Brazil is at the other extreme, stylish but casual. Here, style is the most important factor in Brazilian dress.

Brazilian execs are expected to turn out in well-cut, fashionable clothing (although ties aren't required). But remember that Brazil is very large, and the degree of casualness varies. For example, Rio de Janeiro is more casual than São Paulo, which itself is more casual than Brasilia.

The Art of Conversation

Generally speaking, Latin Americans enjoy a fun-loving, family oriented culture. During work forays here, inquire about your hosts' social activities and children.

It's normal for South American conversations to be highly animated, with many interruptions, many statements of "no," and lots of hugging and touching.

Small Package, Big Heart

Be generous. Gifts are happily accepted in most Latin American countries, even in the form of a small memento commemorating your company or your country. It can be a good way to establish business relationships.

Don't try giving perfume to a female colleague in Latin America, however, as this is far too personal a gift—and besides, how to you know what scent she prefers? Instead, use common sense and make the most appropriate gesture by picking a present the best you can and you should be greeted with a big smile and possibly a hug.

While many gifts are appropriate, here are a few you should stay away from:

➤ **Knives or scissors:** Blades represent severing relationships, just as they do in the Asian countries.

➤ **Carved elephants:** Some Latin American countries have all sorts of superstitions about elephants—especially that you should own only three: one bought, one found and one given. All these elephants should have trunks curving upwards to ensure that the luck doesn't "run out of the trunk."

➤ **Handkerchiefs:** These gifts are linked to sorrow and mourning.

➤ **Yellow flowers:** These blooms are associated with death because Mexicans use them in their Day of the Dead ceremonies (yellow roses also have negative connotations).

The paper that the gift comes in is also important; steer clear of black or purple paper, as these are the colors that symbolize Holy Week processions.

If you've spent some time shopping for the perfect gift, don't destroy all your hard work by throwing it into a paper bag and handing it over. Take the time to wrap the gift perfectly, address a card with a timely message, and then present the item graciously and at just the right moment. If you do all this successfully, you'll convince your Latin American colleagues that you're really worth having on their team.

Tip of the Hat

For ideas of the best culturally appropriate gifts, visit the GetCustoms Web site at www.getcustoms.com.

Zuppa to Nuts

In general, meals are eaten much later than they are in the United States—it's not uncommon for them to go on until midnight—with great enjoyment and lingering over the meal. Good conversation and fine food is considered an art in Latin America; choose an excellent restaurant and don't discuss business during the meal.

Though many restaurants and hotels now accept credit cards, acceptance is not as widespread as in the U.S.; travelers checks are accepted at major hotels and may be exchanged for local currency at authorized exchange facilities (*"casas de cambio"*).

Everybody arrives late for meals here in Latin America, and even foreigners are allowed to wander in about 15 minutes late (you can be 30 minutes late to a party).

In the evening, social dining often involves alcoholic beverages in South America. Many local drinks are potent—be aware. In Brazil, for example, if your host invites you to join him or her in a glass of *caipurinha* (*cay-pure-een-a*), beware. This refreshing citrus cooler may remind you of lemonade, and you probably will want to gulp it down. But don't. Your head will end up spinning.

Global Guide

During the business day you will most likely be offered *cafezinho* (*cah-fay seen-ho*), a very strong Brazilian coffee. Accept it graciously as not to offend your host. If coffee is not your thing, sip slowly. If you're a connoisseur, rejoice.

The Least You Need to Know

➤ Don't refer to your homeland as "America"—it's the U.S.

➤ Remember that Brazil does not consider itself part of Latin America (Brazilians are Portuguese speaking).

➤ It's normal for Latin Americans to be animated and excitable, often interrupting others trying to speak.

➤ Punctuality is not a Latin American attitude, but you'll be expected to be on time.

➤ Shaking hands, presenting business cards, and introductions begin meetings in Latin America.

Part 3
Eastern and Western Europe

The English are reserved. The Germans are neat. The Swiss are punctual. The French are haughty. It's easy to categorize (and sometimes dismiss) entire populations with throwaway labels, to pigeonhole and stereotype by mass characteristics. And yet when you travel to these countries, you may meet a bubbly English person (look at Sarah, Duchess of York!), a sloppy German, a procrastinating Swiss, and a warm, open Frenchman. What this book does is to provide a guideline to certain cultural attributes to help you know what to expect, and what will be expected of you.

If you don't understand the importance of punctuality in many European countries, you could make the mistake of arriving late for a business meeting. If you don't realize that saunas are an important part of Finnish socializing, you might not be sure how to react when presented with the opportunity. We'll give you lots of tips and suggestions for how to handle yourself throughout Europe, so that you're never surprised and never at a loss. Read on!

Chapter 7

Belgium

In This Chapter

➤ Learn the difference between the French-speaking Walloons and the Flemish-speaking Flemings

➤ Understand the value of tradition, manners, privacy and family in Belgium

➤ Discover the importance of the country's three languages: French, Flemish, and German

➤ Figure out the importance of serious, important business attitudes

➤ Learn the basics of etiquette in Belgium: conservative!

It may sound like France and look like Switzerland, but Belgium has its own unique charm and its own culture. It's a tiny country (just about the size of the state of Maryland) and because there's not much room for its 10 million citizens, it's plenty crowded—the second most densely populated country in Europe.

What's important to remember about this country is that there is not just one "Belgian" way of interacting with the world. Rather, the ethnic backgrounds—either French, Flemish, or German—influences everybody's cultural values. Understanding these cultural differences is of utmost importance when doing business in Belgium.

German Belgians are more likely to follow a strict behavior code, dealing in abstract ideas of right and wrong. For the French and Flemish, interpersonal relationships are of much greater importance.

This is not to say that Belgium is just one big happy international melting pot of a family. There is bias between the three primary ethnic groups in Belgium. While most

Belgians speak at least two and usually all three of their country's primary languages, that doesn't mean they are necessarily so broadminded about the others who share their small country.

French-speaking Belgians (they're called Walloons) think they are the aristocracy of the country; they tend to feel superior to the Flemish. In fact, it would be hard to find two more different European cultures than the Dutch and French.

Neither of them have much to say for the Belgian Germans.

Say What?

Walloons and Flemings: Walloons are French-speaking Belgians who live in the south and east; Flemings speak a dialect of Dutch called "Flemish" who live in the north and west.

Chocolates and Beer

When they hear the world "Belgium," most Americans think of chocolates and beer—but might have trouble actually locating the country on a map, or listing the principal folks in charge. It may help to learn a bit about the background of Belgium if you want to understand the people of today.

You'll find Belgium sandwiched between the English channel on the west and Germany on the east, and between the Netherlands on the north and France on the south.

While its coastline only contains 40 miles of white sandy beaches stretching from the French to the Dutch border, elegant resorts offer cozy hotels and good dining. The Ardennes, in the south of Belgium, are a hunting and fishing paradise, a country of mysterious forests and haunting legends.

Belgium enjoys a temperate, maritime climate—characterized as rather unpredictable, but seldom very hot or extremely cold.

Who's In Charge of the Netherlands?

Belgium has a highly developed and stable democracy with a modern economy, and tourist facilities are widely available. Unfortunately, Belgium's past hasn't been any bed of tulips. The country has been traded back and forth from country to country and duchy to duchy so often it's no wonder the populace speaks three different languages. Such transitions been going on ever since Julius Caesar first whacked his way through the countryside in 50 B.C.

Often yoked together with the Netherlands by one country after another, Belgium and the Netherlands were handed to Spain in 1516—and christened Spanish Netherlands.

But the Protestant Dutch in the Netherlands, who didn't much like being ruled by the Catholic Spanish king, revolted and formed the Dutch Republic. Catholic Belgium didn't follow suit; eventually, Belgium was handed over to the control of Austria, and then France.

Belgium was then handed back to the Netherlands in 1815 by the Congress of Vienna when the map of Europe was redrawn, but the Belgians—who didn't care to be ruled by the Dutch—broke away in 1830, with the help of Britain and France, to become the independent Kingdom of Belgium.

Today, Belgium has a constitutional monarchy, with a two-house parliament (a House of Representatives and a Senate). The king is the chief of state while the prime minister (as in the U.K.) holds the real power. However, over time, power has gradually changed hands from a central authority to regional control: Flanders in the north (Flemish-speaking), Wallonia in the south (French speaking), and Brussels (the capital regions divided into 19 bilingual communes).

As in the U.S., power over day-to-day life (such as health and education) remains in the hands of local government at the community and regional level.

French, German, Flemish ...

As a result of this ancient pattern of changing loyalties, modern Belgium maintains three official languages and a very diverse ethnic background. The Belgian Constitution recognizes this triumvirate: French, German, and Flemish (a variance of Dutch).

The capital of Belgium is Brussels, which is officially bilingual (although there are far more French-speaking Walloons than Flemish-speaking Belgians here). If you travel north, be prepared to hear Flemish, while you'll confront French in the south. Venture east and you'll run into German.

Global Guide

While most Belgian professionals and business executives speak English, if you're going to be presenting materials to a colleague in Belgium, you should translate the material into his or her language (either German, Flemish, or French).

Roman Catholic

You may get a headache trying to figure out the language situation in Belgium, but the religion is straightforward—almost everybody is Roman Catholic. They tend to have a very strong faith, and have a deeply felt respect for humanitarian causes.

However, there are four officially recognized religions in Belgium: Catholicism, Protestantism, Judaism, and Islam. Their official representatives are paid by the Belgian state.

Time for a Break

Belgian holidays and all cultural festivals are determined by the Catholic church calendar. When a holiday fall on a weekend, businesses may also close down on the Friday before or the Monday after the holiday.

As do most Europeans, most Belgians take a one-month vacation every year:

> **Jan. 1:** New Year's Day.
>
> **May 1:** Labor Day.
>
> **July 21:** National Independence Day.
>
> **Nov. 11:** Armistice (Veteran's) Day.
>
> **Dec. 31:** New Year's Eve.

Don't Be Late

Appointments are serious business in Belgian businesses. If you desire an appointment, write for one at least a week in advance, and then wait for the company to set the time.

If you're told to show up at 11:30 A.M., don't worry about whether or not to cram a couple of extra croissants in your briefcase; you can assume that you will be conducting business over lunch.

Don't be surprised if your hosts don't mention a word about those import/export agreements during your first appointment, however; most Belgians want to get to know you a bit before they decide whether or not they want to do business with you. Relax, have a sip of that good Belgian beer, and relax. You'll find out sooner or later whether or not you have a deal.

9 to 5?

You'll find most businesses open bright and early, by 8:30 A.M., and close by 5:30 P.M. during the week. (Some places stay open until 9 P.M. on Fridays.) Stores, on the other hand, are usually open from 9 A.M. to 6 P.M. Monday through Saturday.

Take this Job ...

In Belgium, workers appear to have garnered a pretty good deal—one of the shortest work weeks in the world (35.8 hours) and most Belgians take a one-month vacation every year.

If It's 2 P.M., It Must Be Brussels ...

The entire country lies within one time zone, one hour ahead of Greenwich Mean Time (GMT)—meaning it's six hours ahead of U.S. Eastern Standard Time. So if it's noon in New York, it's 6 P.M. in Belgium.

Think Conservative

When it comes to etiquette in Belgium, there are just two words: Think conservative. As a rule, Belgians tend to be restrained, traditional, and conservative, with a quiet demeanor. However, you do need to keep in mind the part of the country in which you're working or traveling.

While the Flemish tend to be great planners—these folks think like engineers—the Walloons are more impulsive and improvisational. This is another reason why management styles of the two groups don't always work well together.

Belgians appreciate dealing with folks who are discreet, which means you shouldn't brag about being the top salesman in your district or pass out photos of your daughter at her debutante cotillion. Downplay wealth; don't flash credit cards and francs, no matter how many of them you carry.

Likewise, mutual trust is of utmost importance. If you promise to deliver something by a certain date, don't figure that a week or two here or there will be okay—it won't. If a Belgian colleague calls you with a request, respond promptly and politely.

Privacy, Please

Belgians are a private people who respect others—so no barging into an office if the door is closed—even if a secretary has told you that you may go on in.

May I Present My Card?

Business cards are commonly exchanged in Belgium. It's a nice touch if you have some bilingual cards printed; one side may be in English, and the other should be in the language of whichever area you do the most business (generally, French, Flemish, or German).

When you present a card, don't just fling the thing across a table. Elegance of presentation never hurt anyone, and it will take you much farther in Belgium. Present the card with the language of your host facing him or her.

How D'You Do?

It's not surprising that in a country as conservative and traditional as Belgium, handshakes are *de rigeur*.

If there's one thing a Belgian likes to do, it's shake hands. Belgians zip around a room shaking hands with everyone in the room when they come in and when they leave.

Faux Pas

One of the quickest ways to alienate a Belgian is to confuse the cultural and language divisions of the country. Spend extra time on the plane getting it straight before you get there.

Global Guide

Remember, too, that doors are closed not just in the office, but also in private homes.

Don't expect a kiss among business acquaintances, but it's accepted in Belgium that among friends—men and women—you touch cheeks and kiss the air three times, alternating cheeks.

What's In a Name?

When it comes to calling people by name, go ahead and follow the European custom: It's not appropriate to call anyone but close friends by their first name.

This doesn't mean that name-calling is simple in Belgium. You'll need to know which language to use when addressing someone else—and in multilingual Belgium, this can get to be a real headache. Remember that there are three languages in Belgium (French, German, and Flemish) and that it won't be appreciated if you use the wrong language with the wrong person.

Faux Pas

Never use the French titles "Monsieur," "Madame," or "Mademoiselle" with a Flemish speaker. Use the English titles instead.

Here's the title you should use, depending on the language of your host:

➤ **German or Flemish speakers:** Use the English terms "Mr.," "Mrs.," "Miss," or "Ms."

➤ **French speaker:** Use "Monsieur" (Mr.), "Madame" (Mrs.) or "Mademoiselle" (Miss).

Nix on Gestures

It's best to avoid gesturing at all rather than risk being dismissed as a stereotypically effervescent, gesticulating American. In fact, the more restrained, mild-mannered, and just plain buttoned-up you can be in Belgium, the better off you'll be.

If in doubt, imagine you're the Queen of England. If she wouldn't make the gesture, you shouldn't, either.

Try to avoid all of the following:

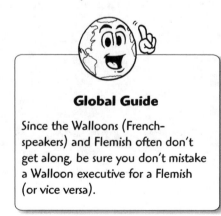

Global Guide

Since the Walloons (French-speakers) and Flemish often don't get along, be sure you don't mistake a Walloon executive for a Flemish (or vice versa).

➤ **Snapping your fingers.** You're not Elvis Presley, and in Belgium, this act is considered vulgar.

➤ **Pointing with your index finger.** It's rude.

➤ **Talking with your hands in your pockets.** Rude again.

You've Come a Long Way, Mlle.

Like their female counterparts in many parts of the world, Belgian women have come a long way—but they haven't gotten *all* the way. Unfortunately, Belgian women are not yet earning equal pay and equal respect for equal work.

Still, it's always safe to treat women business colleagues politely in traditional and conservative Belgium, such as standing when a woman enters a room, or opening a door for a woman.

Dress Up

Like life in general in Belgium, dress is always in conservative good taste. You should avoid:

➤ **Slip-on shoes** (like loafers).

➤ **Unpolished shoes.**

➤ **Sloppy clothes on Sunday** (Belgians dress up even if they are only gong to wander down to the deli for a croque monsieur).

Don't Get Personal

When it comes to conversation starters, you may bring up the current weather or the state of the world's economy, but don't ask your host about that upcoming divorce. In fact, you should steer clear of all personal subjects—and that includes the all-time favorite American opener: "What do *you* do?"

Fair and Proud

Negotiations with Belgians are straightforward, as Belgians are particularly fair-minded and open to facts and theories. Proud of a fine intellectual heritage, the Belgians believe in compromise and common sense.

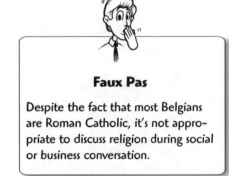

Faux Pas

Despite the fact that most Belgians are Roman Catholic, it's not appropriate to discuss religion during social or business conversation.

However, in any negotiation, the Belgian sense of humanitarianism and faith dictates that emotions play a strong part in the outcome. In general, how well you get along with your Belgian colleagues can have a real impact on what gets done and what is agreed to.

This doesn't mean that coming to a decision will be quick—it won't be. All points of view must be explored and many outside and tangential concerns are discussed.

To Give or Not To Give ...

Unlike life in the United States, you aren't expected to bestow gifts among your Belgian business contacts. If you happen to have a close business connection to someone in Belgium, you may give a gift—but bypass that ceramic mug or knit shirt emblazoned with your company's logo. In fact, you should not include your business card at all with the gift.

Should you be invited into the home of your Belgian host—congratulate yourself. It's quite a coup. And remember to bring along a *hostess gift*—either chocolates or flowers are appropriate. Be sure to present the gift before you sit down to a meal, not after you've polished off a five-course dinner.

If you decide to present flowers to your Belgian hostess when visiting the home, avoid:

➤ **Chrysanthemums** (they signify death).

➤ **Red roses** (appropriate only for lovers).

➤ **Thirteen of any flower** (unlucky).

Guess Who's Coming to Dinner?

While you're congratulating yourself on being invited into a Belgian home, remember that politeness still counts here. If you're invited to someone's home in the country for a social occasion and you've trekked through the mud to get there, leave your oxfords on the doormat. In rural Belgian homes, it's considered polite to leave dirty shoes outside.

If you're attending a party at a Belgian home and there is an attractive arrangement of hors d'oeuvres on the table, don't dive into the spinach pâé until your host gives the signal.

Pistou to Nuts

Dining out can be a real treat in Belgium, home of a marvelous array of cooking. In fact, the country boasts the highest density of Michelin star-rated restaurants in Europe.

Belgians are extremely proud of their country's cuisine, so be sure to compliment what you eat. It won't be hard, because odds are what you're eating will be exquisite: from chocolates and waffles to the national dish of Belgium (mussels), there's quite a lot that is worthy of praise.

Tip of the Hat

We call them "French," but the Belgians insist that French fries were a Belgian invention, not dreamed up by the French.

Whether you're dining in a restaurant or at home, remember what your mother taught you and try to finish everything on your plate. Belgians look with disfavor on wastefulness, which is what they consider a meal left unfinished. And in a country that prides itself on its cuisine, it's an added insult to leave that pate on your plate.

The food may have been delicious and you gorged yourself at table, but avoid using a toothpick in public afterwards. Belgians find the habit disgusting (and so do plenty of Americans, while we're at it).

Time to Eat

You can expect to eat dinner sometime between 7 p.m. and 8 p.m. in Belgium. When you sit down to eat, wait for your hosts to bring up business. If they don't—and they may not—you'll just have to wait to discuss your agenda.

To the Host!

Toasting is lots of fun in Belgium, a country that produces more than 400 different beers—all of them exquisite. (Keep in mind: The strongest beers are brewed by monks in the monasteries of Orval, Chimay, and Postel.)

But no matter how thirsty you are, and no matter how tempting that glorious Belgian beer may look in the glass, no drinking until the toast has been made.

If you're toasting among the Flemish, be prepared to hoist your glass twice: once during the verbal toast and then again, after exchanging glances. Only after the second glass-raising can you begin to drink.

The Least You Need to Know

➤ The French-speaking Walloons and the Flemish-speaking Flemings have very different management styles and historically do not get along well.

➤ Belgium is a traditional, conservative country; its people value manners, privacy and family.

➤ Belgium recognizes three languages: French, Flemish, and German.

➤ All Belgian holidays are determined by the Catholic Church calendars.

➤ Belgians appreciate discretion; don't brag.

➤ Shaking hands is the popular greeting; don't expect to kiss business acquaintances.

France

Chapter 8

In This Chapter

➤ Learn how to shake hands and when to kiss the cheek

➤ Discover what to do if you don't speak the language

➤ Master appropriate eye contact and body language

➤ Figure out the dress code in fashion-conscious France

➤ Find out the French attitude toward business behavior

If you've ever been intimidated by a tray-wielding *garçon*, read this chapter and discover the ins and outs of true French culture. Parisians in particular have a reputation for being notoriously rude and arrogant (even among the French themselves). Consequently, many travelers arrive with a chip on their shoulder the size of the Arc de Triomphe, just waiting for the slightest hint of injustice.

Be prepared to be pleasantly surprised—manners still matter in France! Before asking a question on the street, try beginning your query with a polite *"Bonjour Madame"* (*bahn-joor, mah-dahm*) or *"Excusez moi, Monsieur"* (*excusay-mwah, meh-syoor*). Your trip will be much more rewarding if you learn at least a few basic French phrases, and you will be less likely to meet with French arrogance.

Ou Est la France?

Contrary to reports, France is not an especially large country—it's actually just about the size of Texas, but with much better food. France was formerly a primarily rural country of small farms; one in three Frenchmen used to be a farmer; today farmers number one in sixteen.

Despite its small size, there's something for just about everyone in France. In fact, one of the most interesting things about the country is the incredible regional diversity: Former President Charles de Gaulle once asked, "How can you govern a people with 365 different cheeses?" (And the retort: "How can you live in a country without them?")

As most people already know, France is part of western Europe, bordering the English Channel on the west, sitting between Belgium and Spain. The Mediterranean Sea lies off the southern coast of France, between Italy and Spain. The largest West European nation, France generally enjoys cool winters and mild summers, but you'll note mild winters and hot summers along the Mediterranean. There is an occasional strong, cold, dry, north-to-northwesterly wind known as the *mistral*.

Who's In Charge of France?

Boasting one of the four West European trillion-dollar economies, France has a developed and stable democracy ruled by a president. The political system is based on a written constitution enacted by referendum in 1958. The president names a prime minister as head of the government, who then presides over the cabinet; there is a parliament of two houses (a national assembly and a senate). The political system here is a blend of both parliamentary and presidential methods, resulting in the president and the prime minister sometimes representing opposite parties.

Parlez-vous le Francais?

Of course, the official language of France is French—and it's something that the French take very, very seriously (as anyone with a rudimentary grasp of the language knows).

In fact, the French are so passionate about their language that they've appointed a committee to keep watch over its evolution. Because the French really believe that everyone should speak French (and in the early days of our own country, most of our diplomats and politicians did)—they don't have much tolerance for Americans who can't. The more you try to speak their language, the more respect and support you'll find among the French.

Global Guide

Even if you remember your high school French, remember that if you sally forth into the countryside, you may run into one of the seven dialects still found in France; Provencal, Breton, Alsatian, Corsican, Catalan, Basque, or Flemish.

In most parts of France, timid French is better than eloquent English, so practice a bit before you go and at least make a few attempts. Apologize first, especially if you can't muster a word or two, and you'll probably be forgiven your lapse. Fortunately, many French executives do speak English as well.

If you can speak a bit of French, remember that the French use the formal "vous" (you) rather than the intimate "tu" for everyone other than close friends or family members of the same age or younger. Even today, you'll find French teenagers using the formal "vous" form to their elders.

Faithfully Yours

While France has no official religion and all faiths are practiced here, most of the people (almost 90 percent) are Roman Catholic—but very few of the people carry this belief past the cathedral steps. Only about 16 percent of the people actually attend church. This leaves about 2 percent of the population Protestant and 1 percent Jewish; with the influx of folks from the Mediterranean areas, the Muslim population has risen to about 1 percent, and another 6 percent of the French are atheists or unaffiliated.

Tip of the Hat

Anticlerical laws enacted during the French Revolution are still on the books, so it's no surprise that religion doesn't play a very large part in the lives of many French citizens.

Let's Go On Holiday

When it comes to holidays, summer is the favorite time in France; just about everyone in the urban areas takes off for vacation beginning with Bastille Day (July 14) and continuing through August. Most French people get four or five weeks of vacation, and this is when they take it—so if you're hoping to get lots of business accomplished, don't choose this time to arrive.

Unless you're working in the tourist industry, you don't want to be in France during the mass migration.

On the other hand, some people like the calmer aspect of Paris in August—it's certainly easier to drive during this month! (But remember that resorts, camping areas, and beaches will be packed because this is where all those French folks are heading!)

Things get back to normal in September, when French children go back to school. October is really delightful—the weather is still warm and pleasant. Paris, however, may be so crowded in October with business conventions and special events that you may not be able to uncover a hotel room or get a restaurant reservation.

Holidays include:

Jan. 1: New Year's Day.

Jan. 6: Epiphany.

February before Lent (varies): Carnival.

(varies): Good Friday.

(varies): Easter (Paques).

May 1: Labor Day.

May 8: Veteran's Day (WWII).

July 14: Bastille Day (French National Day).

Aug. 15: The Assumption.

Nov. 1: All Saints Day.

Nov. 11: Armistice Day.

Dec. 25: Christmas Day.

Quelle Heure a-t-il?

While you are expected to be on time, your French colleague may be late. Don't expect an apology. In fact, time is not something taken very seriously in France, although the person in the lower position is expected to be on time. This means that on the French pecking order, a secretary must be on time, but the boss is free to stroll in at any time.

On the other hand, most people try to arrive on time for lunch, since they all have to trek back to the office afterward (although it may be two hours afterward, since that's the normal lunch "hour").

Remember that in France, *le dejeuner* (*leh day-jeu-nay*) is still taken seriously. You'll find shops close down between noon and 3 P.M., allowing everyone (well, everyone except waiters!) to chow down. You'll be able to find restaurants, post offices, banks and supermarkets open, but that's about all. Shops may not open again until 4 P.M., but then they will stay open until about 7 P.M. or 8 P.M.

Global Guide

All of France lies in one time zone, which is six hours ahead of Eastern Standard Time. If it's noon in New York, it's 6 P.M. in Paris.

Dinner is another matter, since you'll have the whole night to waste. Most people don't expect to be on time for this meal; 30 minutes behind schedule is about normal.

Wiggling Away

If you're trying to schedule a business meeting, don't be surprised if you find your French colleagues hard to pin down. It seems sometimes as if the French hate to make any sort of commitment they can't wriggle out of, and will put off scheduling meetings until the very last minute. They are also not averse to rescheduling like mad.

Open Up!

Other than that pesky lunchtime closing, expect to find most businesses open from 8 A.M. until 7 P.M. or 8 P.M. The post office is open from 8 A.M. to 7 P.M. Monday through Friday, and until noon on Saturday. You can usually get into a bank from 9 A.M. until 4:30 P.M. Monday through Friday, and the Stock Exchange (Bourse) from 11:30 A.M. to 2:30 P.M.

Never on Sunday

Don't be surprised to wake up on Sunday and find the town deserted. You're not trapped in the Twilight Zone—it's just Sunday, when almost everyone spends the whole day getting ready for Sunday dinner. Almost no one works on Sunday (except the clergy and folks selling food).

Those shops that do stay open on Sunday (usually the butcher and pastry shop) usually close on Monday, but they take turns—there will always be at least one purveyor of croissants and sausages open each day to serve you.

Formality—*Oui!*

Contrary to the popular U.S. opinion of the French, France is really a country of great dignity and formality in many aspects of daily life. French society today—despite the wholesale rolling of heads during the Revolution—remains rigidly divided into different classes who compete financially, politically, and economically.

Yet, despite this, there is also a curious laissez-faire attitude among the French when it comes to following the rules. They certainly *have* these rules of lining up in an orderly fashion and taking turns, but you'll find lots of French people who resist. The result is that when someone smokes where he isn't supposed to, or parks in a no parking zone, the others will assume he had a good reason and they'll look the other way.

Faux Pas

The quickest way to make a French colleague uncomfortable is to talk about money—especially your own. Don't brag about how much you have, or ask the price of something your host has.

Privacy

The French are a private bunch. You'll notice they quietly go around closing doors behind them when they enter a room. Always knock at a closed door, and wait for an *entrer* before going in.

While they feel perfectly free to walk around in the nude or confide amazingly intimate private comments on their sex lives, mention money and they'll clamp their jaws shut tighter than a pit bull on a pork chop.

Money is simply not discussed in France—it's almost as if they are embarrassed to admit people go around and make money at all. Inheriting money, or being able to earn lots of it, won't win you any popularity contests here. This also means that asking someone you don't know what they do for a living is considered too personal. When it comes to their career and their income, it's not something to be shared.

What's In a Name?

Remember that the French can be formal. Don't use first names until you're given the green light. Address senior people (and strangers) by their titles. Therefore, use "Monsieur" or "Madame" with the appropriate title ("Monsieur le professeur," not "Monsieur Hervais"). Once they get to know you better, your French acquaintances will invite you to call them by their first names.

Maybe it's all that regimentation in school, but when introducing themselves, the French sometimes say their last names first; Etienne Payen might introduce himself as "Payen, Etienne."

Don't be outraged if you're referred to as "Madame" even if you're single. "Madame" usually is used for any woman over 18 years, married or not. (One exception: If you're in a restaurant, call the waitress "mademoiselle" regardless of her age.)

Shake Your Groove Thing

Handshaking and cheek-kissing are obligatory. In fact, in France it's an art that is learned in the cradle. If you want to fit in, you should always shake hands upon meeting as well as leaving. French employees have to go around shaking everyone's hand in the office, both in the morning and when they leave at night. The smallest office ritual can still mean working your way through several hundred handshakes a day—so brief is better!

Probably because they must spend so much time at it, the French don't put a lot of oomph into their handshakes, which aren't generally as firm as in the U.S. In fact, the handshake really barely qualifies as a "shake" at all—primarily because you have to go through the ritual so many times during a day.

Remember that as you briefly touch the hands, you give an even quicker visual acknowledgment.

A Kiss Is Just a Kiss ...

If you're not shaking hands with someone, you're probably "kissing" them. The "double kiss" (touching cheeks and kissing the air) is used between friends in social settings, but you don't need to try it with your casual business associates. It's not expected in business (certainly not between two men).

Say What?

Les Bises (*lay beez*) is the French word for the "double kiss" used between friends in social situations.

Most Americans are a bit uncomfortable the first time they realize they're expected to do the double kiss. To perform this maneuver, start with right cheek touching.

If you're uncomfortable with actually touching the cheek, then it's okay to kiss the air instead of actually establishing lip-to-skin contact. Lots of French folks kiss the air, too.

You should expect "les bises" between

➤ Men and women.

➤ Two women.

➤ Adults and children.

➤ Men who are members of the same family.

While the two-cheek kiss is typical, greater affection may lead to a three-kiss embrace (alternating cheeks each time). This is more common in Paris, where you might even find a four-kiss extravaganza between two really close female friends.

The Eyes Have It

French eye contact is frequent and intense—so much so that North Americans may be intimidated by that relentless gaze. Don't interpret it as rude, however; it's just the French way.

Because the French use eye contact to recognize another person's identity, you should usually avoid eye contact when strolling down the street (especially if you're a woman). If you're a woman and you notice a male stranger making eye contact, remember that if you smile or return the look boldly, it's considered an invitation.

On the other hand, if you refuse to make eye contact in business, or during dining or social situations, it will be interpreted as a putdown.

Let a Smile Be Your Parapluie

No matter how funny you may find things in France, wipe that smile off your face! Nonstop smiling for no apparent reason is not considered good business in France—and it's not going to make you wildly popular on the social circuit, either.

The reason you should try not to keep a smile plastered on your face for long periods of time is that in France, a constant smiler is believed to be either condescending or stupid. Remember, this is the country that invented existentialism—which is about the least funny sort of personal philosophy you could come up with. If you're inclined to sport a silly grin, think "Jean-Paul Sartre." That ought to sober you up!

Global Guide

Remember that everyday relations between men and women may tend to be far more flirtatious than you are used to in the U.S. and not confrontational.

Doing the Wave ...

One thing you'll find right away in France is that a lot of talking gets done—but not out loud. While they're verbalizing, the French also chatter away with a rich, expressive range of hand gestures.

Here are a few you'll be sure to run into:

> ➤ To indicate that everything is okay, make the "thumbs up" gesture.

> ➤ The sign for OK common in the U.S. (the circle of the thumb and forefinger) means "zero" in France.

> ➤ Kiss the tips of your fingers to indicate something is delicious.

> ➤ Thumbs down means "bad."

> ➤ If you've had it "up to here," wipe your hand across your forehead.

> ➤ Shaking the fingers of one hand in front of the chest means great surprise (either good or bad)—usually to the tune of a Gallic "ooo-la-la!"

> ➤ Using the back of the fingers to stroke the right cheek means "It's a bore."

> ➤ If you slap your open palm over your closed fist, it's considered vulgar.

> ➤ Snapping your fingers is a no-no—it's considered rude.

> ➤ Another no-no—touching your finger below your eye. It means *"mon oeil"* (*mohn oy*) in French, which indicates you think the other fellow is lying.

Men and Women

French law protects women in many ways, but as in most countries, this doesn't guarantee equality. The May 1968 student uprising (such uprisings happen a lot in France) led to a great many changes in French society, including the situation for women, which then greatly improved. Still, the women's rights movement has a long way to go.

Women's lib came very late to this country. Women only earned the right to open their own mail in 1923, and have been protected legally from sexual harassment only since 1992.

In the work place, a woman may still have a way to go before finding total equality. It's still traditional in France to find the male as the head of the family—and this tenet also holds true in the business world as well. While many French people say they believe in equal rights for women, in practice it's not always a reality.

Still, in France a woman keeps her maiden name all her life, voting and paying taxes under this name (although socially she takes her husband's name). It's also true that men and women here tend to celebrate gender differences, and they make an important distinction between what is sexy behavior—and what is just plain sexist.

Wear the Best

Not surprisingly, the country that gave birth to Givenchy and Chanel is not known for tawdry fashion. Sometimes it seems as if just about everyone in France, from the meekest secretary to the most senior executive, strives to buy the best, most classic styles they can afford. And since most French people tend to be on the thin side with ramrod posture, their elegant clothes look even better. Even if someone isn't particularly physically attractive, the inherent pride and grace with which the French tend to conduct themselves makes them seem more attractive.

In the Business World

Business clothing tends to be elegantly cut and formal, and perhaps because of this trend, French business executives are formal as well. They aren't likely to fling that expensive jacket carelessly on the sofa; in fact, most don't even loosen their ties in the office.

Likewise, French women dress astonishingly well, with an innate sense of style. If you want to fit in, opt for a simple, chic tailored look. Don't go clomping in to your business meeting in earth shoes or floppy sandals, and ditch the wrinkled clothes and chartreuse nails. Think elegance and classic style, and buy the best shoes you can afford if you want to blend in with French businesswomen.

Tip of the Hat

When young French boys jog off to military service, they are customarily clad in a serviceable blue shirt. For this reason, it's a good idea to avoid wearing a blue shirt to a business meeting, since this will scream *"un bleu"* (greenhorn) to the French.

This doesn't mean that the French never wear casual clothes; indeed, especially among young French people, blue jeans and other weekend wear are popular—but somehow, the French always manage to look pulled together, even when they are casually clothed.

And Then There's the Beach

If you happen to end up on a French beach, especially on the Riviera, don't be surprised if most of the women are topless. (You can also expect partial or total nudity on French TV, even during prime time.) If you're not comfortable in your birthday suit, don't worry about it. The French will be far too well bred to laugh.

Talk Is Cheap

The French value eloquence, but that doesn't mean entertaining your business colleagues with a blow-by-blow review of your 10K marathon race. You'll be labeled a bore.

The art of conversation has been elevated to an Olympic sport in this country, but you need to observe the rules before you leap in. Don't be surprised if you're not automatically granted the floor the minute you open your mouth.

In fact, when you do converse with the French, be prepared to be interrupted—often! In France, you can't expect to pontificate for five minutes and then turn the floor over to the next fellow, who then talks for another five minutes, and so on. Instead, there is a lively give-and-take, frequently escalating to raised and passionate voices.

What's refreshing is that no matter how odd or just plain nuts your opinion may be, if you can articulate it well, you'll find an appreciative audience in France. It's also worthwhile to note that you don't need to follow doggedly down every conversational alley; the French don't expect you to refute every opinion—just fling it out there in the open and watch what happens.

No matter how witty your repartee, remember to let those pearls of wisdom roll off your tongue in a quiet voice. Americans have a nasty reputation in France for being, well, loudmouths. Keep your voice down to avoid sounding like an obnoxious Yankee executive who makes up in volume what is lacking in substance. Loud banter is considered brash, while speaking in low tones is considered far more elegant.

Visiting *Chez Nous*

If you've been dying to visit a French home, don't hold your breath. Expatriate Americans often live in France for years without seeing the inside of a Frenchman's home— it's just considered too private.

If you do get invited home, observe these rules:

➤ Don't arrive earlier than the stated time.

➤ This isn't the time to wear sweat pants. Dress as if you were going to a nice restaurant.

Global Guide

If you decide you'd like to pop in and see one of your new friends, however, make a date ahead of time. Spontaneity may be valued around your neighborhood, but in France, you should never "drop in" unannounced.

➤ The later the invited hour to dine, the better you should dress.

➤ When you arrive, you'll be offered an aperitif. Do NOT ask for wine—that will be served with the meal.

➤ Stand to receive the drink, and stand to greet other guests.

➤ Do not expect a "house tour" when you arrive. It's considered a breach of their privacy. Don't follow your hostess into the kitchen to help.

➤ Don't help yourself at the bar unless invited to do so.

Hostess Gifts

If you are invited to the home of your French hosts, you should feel honored—the French don't often invite those they don't know very well home to share their croissants. If you are invited to dine *en famille* (*ohn fa-meal*), you may bring flowers or candy.

It's probably not a good idea to tote along a bottle of wine. Many French people are serious wine connoisseurs and have probably spent a good deal of time selecting the perfect wine for the upcoming meal. Bringing your own bottle of wine implies that you know more about wine than does your host—which you don't want to do unless you're a California vintner.

The next day, write a thank-you note or call to let your hosts know how much you appreciated the hospitality.

Bouillabaisse to Nuts

When in France, you don't eat, you dine—and if you're there on business, you can rest assured that doing business means sharing meals. Enjoy! Compliment the meal when you've enjoyed it, and your appreciation will definitely add points!

Garçon, Beware!

To an amazing degree, Americans tend to be intimidated by French waiters, who are at best perceived as rude and anti-American. In fact, if you make an attempt to communicate—even with rudimentary French—you'll be pleasantly surprised.

When your waiter gives you a menu, smile and say *"Bonjour."* When it's time to give your order, smile and make eye contact. Ask for a description of the dishes, which should probably prompt an in-depth discussion and recommendation. If you don't speak French, practice ahead of time or use hand motions.

Minding Your Ps and Qs

If you are invited out to talk business over a meal, remember that food is an event in France. Before bringing out your briefcase, praise the food. (It won't be hard!) If you're a little nervous about how the French waiters will treat you, remember to make brief eye contact during the meal. You'll get a much friendlier response.

Here are a few things to keep in mind when dining out with others:

➤ Whoever does the inviting does the paying.

➤ When choosing a restaurant, pick a French one. Don't worry about the French not wanting to eat in restaurants featuring their own food; it's preferable to ethnic eateries.

➤ You'll need to make reservations in most restaurants (except cafes and smaller informal eateries).

Faux Pas

Don't ask for a doggy bag if you can't eat everything; it's considered an insult.

➤ If you have drunk only half a bottle of wine at your hotel, they'll usually keep it for you and let you drink it at the next meal.

➤ You can use your bread to soak up those delicious sauces—but only if your host does it first.

➤ Break your bread from the main loaf (don't cut it).

➤ When the cheese board reaches you, cut off a share of the cheese (along with the rind); watch how others cut if you're not sure.

➤ Peel and slice the fruit with a knife before gulping it down.

There's a Dog at My Table!

No matter how much you think you like dogs, you may be jolted to find one lying at your feet under a cafe table in France. Unlike the U.S., where strict public health laws prohibit dogs and cats from restaurants, you'll find pets cozily snoozing at restaurants all over France.

Should you happen to look up from *your Boeuf à la Bordelaise* long enough to notice, it's perfectly okay to feed that sad-eyed French poodle from the table. If you've brought your own dog along on your trip, feel free to drag him along to dinner with you. No one else will mind.

Breaking Your Fast

Unless you're dining at a large hotel that caters to many Americans, expect to enjoy a typical French breakfast—with no eggs in sight. Instead, you can expect to find delicious French bread or rolls, butter and preserves, and hot chocolate or cafe au lait. Go ahead and dunk your bread in your beverage—everyone else is.

But don't expect to see Parisians there. They seldom eat breakfast in restaurants. Patisseries and boulangeries (bakeries) sell croissants and other breads and pastries, or you can buy coffee and a croissant in a cafe. Brunch, however, is catching on in some U.S.-style restaurants.

Take Me to Le Cafe!

Nowhere will you have quite the same dining experience as in a Parisian cafe, where you can slouch the afternoon away reading a paper and drinking *un cafe*. If this is what you're after, you may choose an "express" (little cups of espresso); when you pour in a pile of hot milk, it's "cafe creme" (water it down and serve it in a large cup and—voila! it's cafe Americain").

Not a coffee buff? Then try a "citron presse" (*see-trohn press*; fresh-squeezed lemon juice with water and sugar added to taste). You don't need to worry about lingering without buying much; your waiter will never clear your place, flick the lights, or otherwise try to shove you out the door.

You can also get a simple hot lunch at a cafe, but things get busy around noontime; if it's a relaxed nosh you want, go around 2 P.M. If you're by yourself, you may want to sit at the bar (*le zinc; leu zeenk*), but if you pick up your drink and move on to a table, the price of whatever you bought will rise.

Dinner Is Served

Dinners in France can be a formal affair. Don't be surprised if you're facing a seven-course meal at a restaurant. The order of courses at a formal French meal would be as follows: soup, fish, sorbet, meat/fowl, salad, dessert, and coffee. Most people eat dinner very late in France (it's not uncommon for families to eat at 10 P.M., and also accept telephone calls until midnight!).

Try to finish everything on your plate—and remember that asking for seconds is considered a compliment to the chef. (Of course, if you're in the middle of a six-course meal, it's not a good idea to pipe up with "More, please!" It may interrupt the flow of the performance.)

Raise a Glass

You'll find the French don't drink hard liquor before meals—they believe it deadens the taste buds. And since all that great French food to follow will be worth the wait, go along with their plan.

Tip of the Hat

From the time a child is big enough to hang onto a wine glass, he drinks wine with the family (however, a child must be 14 to be served in a restaurant).

Wine is drunk at every meal in France except breakfast, and alcoholism is a serious problem in France. However, odds are you won't find a Frenchman staggering through the Bois de Bologne. And any sign of public intoxication isn't acceptable in France, and you'll do well to remember that.

Wine is served with the first course, and there will be a brief toast ("Salut!") from the host. Once you've started the meal, feel free to propose a toast.

The Least You Need to Know

➤ The French shake hands constantly, always on "hello" and "goodbye."

➤ Double-kissing the cheeks (or air) is acceptable for acquaintances and friends.

➤ Attempting to speak just a little French is better than not trying at all.

➤ The French are a private, conservative people but are not inherently rude to Americans without provocation.

➤ Don't use first names until you're told to do so.

➤ France remains rigidly divided into social classes.

Chapter 9

Germany and Austria

In This Chapter

➤ Discover the intricacies of German names and titles

➤ Learn what to expect when negotiating with German firms

➤ Find out the importance of punctuality

➤ Learn about bias in Germany

➤ Understand the importance of planning, orderliness, and control

You can't learn the truth about these two countries by watching old war movies; reality is far more complex, especially in Germany and Austria. In general, you'll find that Germans place enormous emphasis on social factors that are almost as important in this country as religious values.

Germans believe that every citizen has a responsibility to be orderly and controlled. It's a country deeply interested in thrift, cleanliness, orderliness—in short, Germans believe that life is serious business. When you think of Germany, think of a well-oiled machine: organized, methodical, well-planned. Germans may not make lots of jokes, but they get the job done. Austrians, while still valuing many of the responsibilities Germans find so important, find the time to be far more relaxed and gregarious.

Stuff You Should Have Learned in School

Germany and Austria both have stable democracies with modern economies; Tourist facilities throughout Austria and Germany are highly developed (except for some areas in eastern Germany).

Tip of the Hat

One interesting aspect of German culture is the country's almost religious zeal for environmental protection, leading to the establishment of the most rigorous packaging and recycling laws in the world. The land—especially the forests—are worshipped.

Where It's At

Austria and Germany are situated in southern Central Europe; their neighbors include Switzerland, the Czech Republic, Liechtenstein, Hungary, Italy, Slovenia, and Slovakia.

These two countries, situated at the heart of a continent, have always been a junction for communication links between the trade and cultural centers of Europe.

Under the current German Constitution (called the "Basic Law"), the federal Republic of Germany has a parliamentary democracy with two houses in its legislature. Executive power is wielded by a Prime Minister (called Chancellor). The president, who is elected to a five-year term, has lots of ceremonial duties but little real power.

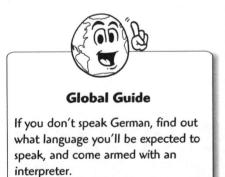

Global Guide

If you don't speak German, find out what language you'll be expected to speak, and come armed with an interpreter.

Austria has a democratic republic, with legislative power in the hands of the people. The constitution is guided by the rule of law and based on the republican, democratic, and federal principles as well as on the strict division of legislative and executive powers and of the judiciary and administration.

The constitutional guarantee of basic rights in Austria looks back on a tradition more than a century old, and the constitution is supplemented by the provisions of the European Convention for the Protection of Human Rights and Fundamental Freedoms. The head of the Austrian state is the president.

Sprechen zie Deutsche?

German is the official language in both Austria and Germany. In Germany, 99 percent of the people speak German, but there are also several dialects (such as Bavarian), which may be quite different from traditional German.

You'll find that English is widely spoken in both Germany and Austria, although some German business people may prefer to converse in German.

Half and Half

In Germany, half the population is Catholic (mostly found in the south) and the other half Protestant (mostly Lutheran, found primarily in the north). A few small pockets of Jews and Muslims can also be found.

Much more of Austria is Roman Catholic, where 78 percent of the population is Catholic, with 5 percent Protestant. About 4.5 percent belong to other groups, and the remaining 9 percent do not claim any specific faith (3.5 percent provided no information). According to Austrian law, every child over the age of 14 can freely choose a religion (for children up to the age of 14, parents get to decide what church their kids attend).

Holidays in Germany and Austria

There are a fair number of holidays in Germany and Austria—but also a large number of regional holidays. The national holidays celebrated in most areas include:

Jan. 1: New Year's Day.

Jan. 6: Epiphany (only in Bavaria and Baden-Wuerttemberg).

Spring: Good Friday.

Spring: Easter Monday.

May 1: Labor Day (May Day).

Varies: Ascension Day.

Varies: Whitmonday.

June 6: Corpus Christi (only in parts of Germany).

Varies: German Unity Day.

Oct. 31: Reformation Day (only in parts of Germany).

Nov. 1: All Saints Day (only in parts of Germany).

Dec. 25/26: Christmas.

Germans and Austrians, like many Europeans, enjoy a nice, long vacation. Almost everyone takes an entire month, usually during July, August, or December. If you've come to Germany prepared to work, don't expect to get much done during festivals such as Oktoberfest or the three-day Carnival before Lent.

Be There!

If there's ever a place where you always need to be on time, it's Germany, whether you're attending a business or social function. Being on time is also a good idea in Austria.

The quickest way to alienate a German executive is to stroll in late to a meeting or appointment. Even a minute or two past your appointed hour is insulting (especially if you're in a lesser position).

Open and Close

Business hours in Austria and Germany run from 8 A.M. or 9 A.M. through 4 P.M. or 5 P.M. Monday through Friday.

Shops are open from 8 A.M. to 6:30 P.M. Monday through Friday, with a one- or two-hour schnitzel break at lunch. On Saturday, expect shops to close up for the day by early afternoon. (In Germany, many shops stay open late one Saturday a month.) Banks usually close between 3 P.M. or 4 P.M. through the week, and don't open at all on the weekends.

Appointment, Please!

Be sure to make your appointments well in advance—at least one or two weeks' notice for an appointment made by telephone or e-mail, or at least a month for an appointment made by mail. (Airmail letters may take at least a week to be delivered.) If time is of the essence, a brief meeting can be arranged with only a few days' notice.

Global Guide

When it comes to appointments, favored times are between 11 A.M. and 1 P.M., or between 3 P.M. and 5 P.M. Avoid scheduling appointments late on Fridays (some offices close by 3 P.M. Friday).

In the days of a divided Germany, East Germans did not schedule any appointments on Wednesdays. While this practice has been slowly changing since the country was reunified, you still may run into this mid-week holiday in parts of what had been East Germany.

If It's 2 P.M., It Must Be Berlin!

Germany and Austria are small countries; both countries fit into one time zone, six hours ahead of Eastern Standard Time. If it's noon in New York, it's 6 P.M. in Germany and Austria.

"Our Kind"

A wide range of subtle biases exist in Germany against Gypsies, refugees, foreign workers, and the East Germans, who may be perceived as a threat to the job situation. Class status means a great deal in Germany, whose citizens believe that the different roles and classes give structure to the society. While the law guarantees equal rights to everyone, in reality it's not so.

Austria, in general, is smaller, more homogenous, and less biased. The cultural status emphasis is less noticeable in Austria.

Auf Wiedersen!

You're expected to say hello and goodbye when you enter or leave a shop or restaurant in Austria or Germany. Always say *Guten Tag* (*goo-ten tahg*; good day) or *Guten Abend* (*goo-ten ah-ben*; good evening) when meeting someone or entering a shop, and

Auf Wiedersehen (*ow-vee-der-zshane*; goodbye) when leaving. Most Austrians and Germans shake hands in the beginning and ending of meetings—firmly but briefly. (Customs may differ in certain parts of Germany, but the general rule is to shake both times.)

Failing to make a slight bow when shaking hands in Germany is a mistake—especially when shaking hands with a superior. All that's needed is a slight nod of the head—but don't forget it.

If introductions are going on at the same time in the room, take turns in shaking. It's rude to reach over someone else's handshake. It's also rude to keep one hand in your pocket while shaking.

As warm and outgoing as Austrians are, Germans may seem cold and distant on first meeting, whether business or as friends. However, once that initial ice is broken, Germans can be as gregarious as their Austrian neighbors.

Remember that Germans are nothing if not formal, so try to have a third party introduce you in both business and social situations. Sometimes this just isn't possible, so if no third party is in the vicinity, go ahead and introduce yourself.

Who Goes First?

In Germany, age comes before youth, but not before rank. If there are a group of business people entering a room, the oldest person gets to go in first. If you're introducing folks, you should introduce the younger person to the older one (assuming that the older one has a higher rank).

Thus, if you've got a younger CEO in the room with an older, lower-ranking exec, the CEO—albeit a young whippersnapper—takes precedence over the older, lower-ranking drone.

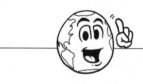

Global Guide

It may be a republic, but there are still lots of old Royals floating around in Germany and Austria. Socially speaking, a member of the nobility—no matter how young—takes presence over a doddering commoner.

Lots of Titles

When in Germany, always remember to use every conceivable title you can think of. (It's especially true when you're writing a letter.) Use "Mr." or "Mrs." followed by the last name; in German, this is "Herr" for Mr., and "Frau" for Mrs. or Ms.

"Fraulein" (Miss) is not used in Germany any more for any woman under age 18. You should address a business woman as "Frau" whether she's married or not.

So what do you do if you're addressing a German overachiever with a bunch of titles longer than a string of sausages? Use them all. Keep the Mr./Herr or Mrs./Frau, but instead of using the last name, use the other titles. So, Dr. Susan Smith would be "Frau Doktor," and a college professor with a Ph.D. would be called "Herr Professor Doktor."

Keep in mind that just about every German professional you see will use a title, including pastors, politicians, lawyers, and engineers.

You may get to a first-name basis if you are very close friends, but don't hold your breath at reaching this milestone with German colleagues. You may never get to be on a first-name basis with executives at work.

Your Card, Sir ...

Because most Germans and Austrians speak English, you don't need to use business cards with German translations on one side. However, because education and a solid reputation are important, it's a good idea to include the following on your business cards:

> ➤ Include the founding date of your company (if it's been around for a long time).

> ➤ If you're got any sort of advanced degree (beyond undergraduate level), add it after your name.

Bring lots of business cards with you, as many of your colleagues may want to exchange cards.

Stiff and Straight

Personal space is inviolate in Germany—so stand about six inches farther back in Germany. This holds true not just for your own body, but also for the placement of your office furniture. If you sit down to chat with a German executive and you find yourself facing him or her across a wide expanse of rug, don't hitch your chair closer. This could be viewed as insulting by many German executives.

You can extrapolate this sense of personal space to German cars as well. Don't even think of touching someone else's car in this country. The last thing you'd want to do is set a bag of groceries on top of someone else's hood. In fact, never put anything on top of anybody else's car in Germany.

Faux Pas

If you must get someone's attention farther afield, don't flap, wave, or beckon wildly. Make yourself known by raising your hand (palm out) with your index finger extended.

You may cross your knee over the other, but don't prop your ankle over your knee, leaving your other knee to flop untidily. And while you're at it, never prop your feet up on anything except a footstool.

German Gestures

Don't expect to walk down the street and find German men walking hand in hand. Public displays of affection between any two people are unusual in Germany.

If you want to flag down a colleague across the street, don't leap up into the air, hollering and waiving frantically. Germans don't like public displays of any kind, and will wait until they are very close to you before trying to get your attention. If you're holding a conversation in Germany, don't stuff your hands in your pockets.

Gender in Germany

In Germany, women still have a tough row to hoe—life isn't yet equal there between the sexes in status, careers, or pay. If several people approach a doorway, and they are all about the same in status and age—the men walk in first.

When walking down the street, the man walks closest to the curb; on a corridor, he will walk on the woman's left. If you're a triumvirate, the sole man walks in the middle of the two women; the sole woman walks in the middle of the two men. If two women are walking on the street, the younger one walks on the curb side (or the left).

When you are introduced to a German or Austrian woman, wait to see if she extends her hand before shaking it. In formal social situations, however, older Germans may bend and kiss the hand of a woman when they greet. Don't try this on your own, however; it's not expected of foreign-born men, and even among Germans, it's fairly rare.

Most of the time, men will still stand when a woman enters the room, and will remain standing as long as she does. (It's not necessary for a woman to rise, however, when a man enters.)

Lederhosen, Nien!

Austrians are pretty casual when it comes to the clothes department, unless you're going to an exclusive restaurant. If you're going out on the town, to the theater, or the opera, however, you'll be expected to dress up.

When in Germany, think conservative for men and women alike: white shirt or blouse, dark suit, and restrained tie. (If all you've got are gray flannels and blue blazers, don't worry. In Germany, this is also considered formal.)

And when we say formal, we mean formal—even in the sweltering heat, most German executives won't think of stripping off coat or tie. You should follow suit.

When it's time for dress-down day, jeans are acceptable casual wear—but make sure they are clean and don't have rips. If it's summer, most German men flop around in sandals.

Can We *Sprechen?*

When you're talking, whether in German or English, be careful to speak in complete sentences. In German, the end of the sentence (often the final word) is very important and Germans are in the habit of listening for the end of the sentence.

IF you want to chew gum, fine—but don't do so while you're trying to hold a conversation.

Take a Letter ...

When you're writing a business letter, remember that correctness and formality are very important in Germany. You may write business letters in English, but make it grammatically correct and free from slang. You should address a business letter to the company ("Dear Ladies and Gentlemen ... ") and not to a particular executive.

Global Guide

While you don't need to translate business cards, it's essential to provide German translations of all written material, instruction manuals, and promotional information.

If you get a business letter with two signatures, this means you'll need to wait for both signees to make a decision—and they will both have to agree before this decision is made.

It's No Joke

While Germans can enjoy a joke as much as the next fellow, you don't want to try this in the business world. Business is not funny to most German executives, so don't feel that you need to pepper your presentations and speeches with little jokes. You won't be taken seriously, and in this country, that's the kiss of death.

Negotiation Auf Deutsche

When negotiating in Germany, remember that age is respected here, so older, sober U.S. executives may get more respect than a brash, young well-scrubbed yuppie, no matter how brilliant.

Whoever comes over to represent your company, however, should be prepared to back up any claims with facts and studies—and plenty of them. Germans don't much care for wild generalizations and slick talk. Be prepared to trot out as many examples and case studies as you can dig up.

Cold, hard facts impress the German business community, not how glamorous or fun a product or service may be. Be prepared to fork over lots of information in excruciating detail. Present your ideas clearly, succinctly, and with a minimum of bravado.

If you've got bad news to impart, don't begin by trying to soften the blow with compliments, as you would in the United States. German executives don't expect flattery—they assume things are running well if they don't hear complaints. If you've got a problem, come out with it bluntly.

Many U.S. business people make the mistake of thinking that since German products are so similar to those of the U.S., their companies must be, too. Actually, the decision-making process in Germany is much more laborious and painstaking than in the U.S.; once you've worked your way through the official German chain of command, a sort of *backstairs* group of advisors must also give their approval.

Don't expect snap decisions when dealing with German companies. Plodding, thorough, and detailed-based, Germans value planning and methodical attention to detail. This isn't the time to push and shove your own opinion.

It Is Better to Give ...

German executives don't expect lavish gifts; choose something of quality and value, such as imported liquor or a quality pen. Remember that Germans don't like to get personal when they do business, so don't opt for a personal gift such as clothing or perfume. Mouthwash and soap are definite *neins!*

However, you may find that many German executives are very interested in unusual aspects of American culture. If you know your colleague loves cowboy novels or Amish quilting, this could make a nice business gift.

Tip of the Hat

In Northern Germany, heather is often planted on graves because it's so hardy. It makes a nice cemetery planting, but it's not a good idea to include heather in a bouquet you intend to present to your hostess.

If you're invited to someone's home, a gift of unwrapped flowers is a must (not too showy). Choose an uneven number of stems (as long as they don't add up to 13!), but avoid red flowers (they're for lovers) or calla lilies (they're for funerals).

Avoid bringing a local wine for a hostess gift (it may be interpreted as a slight on your host's wine cellar)—but you can feel confident in toting along a wine from your home, or even a fine imported wine (as long as it's not German). Because German beer is so outstanding, it's not likely you could find a foreign beer that would pique their interest.

Off to the Biergarten!

If you're attending opening night of a play, a concert, or the opera, you should go very formal—dark tuxedo for men, or long evening gowns for women. Otherwise, business clothes are acceptable for formal social events.

You'll have to check your coat in German theaters, so bring a sweater if it's cold.

Remember that punctuality in Germany is prized; if you're late to a performing event, better bring a novel because the doors will be closed until intermission.

It's also a good idea to remember that German audiences are among the most respectful and attentive in the world. Don't wiggle in your seat, crack your knuckles, cough, or even sneeze—you'll be "shushed."

Souppe to Nuts

Every German and Austrian city has its share of fancy gourmet restaurants, but at the other end of the spectrum are the *wuerstl* (sausage) stands that dot the streets and squares where you can select from several local variations that put the American hot dog to shame.

You may enjoy exchanging business banter over bagels, but breakfast meetings in Germany are *verboten* (*fer-bo-ten*)! It's just something that's not common. Instead, expect to meet for a business lunch.

Before taking the first bite of a meal, say *Guten Appetit* (*goo-ten ah-pe-tet*). Remember that no matter what you're served, Germans don't often eat with their fingers—they hate the mess. Always use utensils. When you're finished, line up your utensils neatly on the plate.

Business Lunching

Expect to talk business before lunch or after lunch, but never during lunch. When it comes to the check, whoever invites, pays.

Dinner Is Served

Remember that punctuality is required even on social occasions. Drinks will usually be served before the meal, but don't expect lots of luscious little canapes and hors d'oeuvres. The meal will begin soon after you arrive.

Raising a Glass

Before taking the first sip of a drink, remember to wish others in your party *Prost* (*pro-st*; cheers)!

> **The Least You Need to Know**
>
> ➤ Be polite, restrained, punctual, and organized.
> ➤ Use all the titles that a person has earned.
> ➤ Don't try to be funny in a business situation.
> ➤ Remember that age and education are respected.
> ➤ Present lots of data to back up your claims when doing business in Germany.
> ➤ Thrift, cleanliness, and orderliness are prized here.

Chapter 10

Italy

In This Chapter

➤ Learn the ins and outs of Italian holidays

➤ Discover the correct way to address an Italian

➤ Understand the importance of family in Italy

➤ Learn what business items you can and can't bring into the country

➤ Discover the lunch–break schedule in Italy

You may think Italy is just a fun-loving romp through lots of pasta and pizza, but there are cultural dos and don'ts here, too. Italy has a developed democracy with a modern economy. It's also a highly regional land, with quite different geography and spirit in different areas. Most Italians identify most strongly with their particular area, whether that's north or south, Sicily, Sardinia, and so on.

Italians have been excelling in business for hundreds of years, so they've had plenty of time to learn the art of subtle negotiation and terrible red tape. The draft bill of exchange was invented by the Florentines; double-entry bookkeeping was thought up by the Sienese; the Medici bank developed the modern idea of a holding company. In fact, the whole idea of banking and insurance was introduced to the English by the Lombards, the "Pope's merchants."

The Boot

Italy, a boot-shaped peninsula about the size of California, lies in southern Europe, extending into the central Mediterranean Sea (that is slightly larger than the state of Arizona). Its strategic location dominates the central Mediterranean, as well as southern sea and air approaches to Western Europe.

Since the 1400s, popes have been inviting people of all religions to come to Rome, a city influenced by ancient Roman, Judeo, and Christian traditions. Today, the city authorities have already started sandblasting monuments, buying new city buses, expanding the subway system, rerouting traffic, and landscaping parks in preparation for an estimated 15 million tourists who will visit the Eternal City in the year 2000, a Papal Jubilee year.

Tip of the Hat

The insurance policies of Lloyds of London reveals its Italian origins in the wording of its *"polizza"* (a promise).

Its climate is predominantly Mediterranean, with cool weather in the far north and hot and dry weather in the south. Fully 70 percent of the country is mountainous, with 1600 kilometers of coastline.

Who's Running the Government?

The Chief of State is the president; the head of government is the Prime Minister (referred to in Italy as the president of the Council of Ministers). A Council of Ministers is nominated by the prime minister and approved by the president.

This is very old civilization in a fairly new nation, which until 1860 was simply a collection of squabbling states that couldn't get along. Since World War II, the Italian economy has changed from one based on agriculture into a ranking industrial economy, with approximately the same total and per capita output as France and the United Kingdom. The economy is still divided into a developed industrial north, dominated by private companies, and a less developed agricultural south, with large public enterprises and more than 20 percent unemployment.

In the second half of 1992, Rome was shocked to learn it might not qualify to participate in EU (European Union) plans for economic and monetary union later in the decade. As a result, Italy finally began to address its huge fiscal imbalance. The government adopted fairly stringent budgets, abandoned its inflationary wage system, and cut back its generous social welfare programs.

Parlo Lei Italiano?

Obviously, Italian is the national language of Italy, but there are many dialects of Italian; some dialects are so different from others that communication between the two may be difficult.

As if the dialects weren't problematic enough, not everyone in Italy speaks Italian. In fact, parts of the Trentino-Alto Adige region are predominantly German-speaking, and there is a small French-speaking minority in Valle d'Aosta region. Also, you'll find a Slovene-speaking minority in the Trieste-Gorizia area.

However, you'll find that most business people do speak English. If you speak another Romance language (French or Spanish), you'll be surprised at how much Italian you can puzzle out. A few years of Latin will also help, because the Italian spoken today is really the evolution of ancient Latin. After the Roman Empire fell, spoken Latin began to deteriorate into regional dialects. Because Tuscany was the dominant region of the Middle Ages and the Renaissance, it's language was eventually adopted as the national language. It still is today, and it's Tuscan that is taught in school.

Tip of the Hat

The great writers Dante, Petrarch, and Boccaccio were all Tuscans, and wrote in this language during the 14th century.

No Official Religion?

It should come as no surprise that most Italians are Roman Catholic, although the Republic of Italy has no actual official religion. While the Catholic church still exerts influence here, it couldn't prevent the legalization of abortion and divorce during the 1970s. (While 98 percent of Italians are Catholics, as many as 60 percent don't practice their beliefs.)

Nevertheless, the Italian culture is thoroughly Catholic, and the church is the heart of both social structure and local power.

Italian Holidays

Italy has fewer holidays than most other European countries—but they make up for that with their regional holidays celebrating patron saints. Almost every city shuts down during the feast day of its patron saint, which is considered (in that city) as a legal holiday.

Jan. 1: New Year's Day.

Spring: Easter Monday.

April 25: Anniversary of the Liberation.

May 1: Labor Day.

June 24: St. John (in Genoa and Florence).

June 29: Sts. Peter and Paul (in Rome).

July 15: St. Rosalia (in Palermo).

Varies: Ferragosto and Assumption.

Nov. 1: All Saints Day.

Dec. 7: St. Ambrogio (Milan).

Dec. 26: St. Stephen's Day.

Dec. 31: New Year's Eve.

Various Italian regions may have their own feast days and holidays during which businesses are closed. As in other parts of Europe, you'll find that many people take vacations during July and August, and also over the Christmas/New Years' holidays. It may be wise to plan a trip (especially for business) during other times.

Global Guide

You'll need to make business appointments long before leaving for your trip to Italy. And when you do, aim for between 10 A.M. and 11 A.M., or after 3 P.M.

On Time, Pronto! ...

While many people assume that Italians have a *laissez-faire* attitude when it comes to punctuality, this habit is respected here. Americans in particular are expected to be prompt. Therefore: Be on time, especially in the industrial north. If you're five minutes late, the Tower of Pisa won't collapse, but any later than that requires an apologetic phone call.

Don't be upset, though, if you arrive at a meeting and your contact does not. It's best to reconfirm a couple of times, if at all possible. And learn to be patient.

Business Hours

You'll find most businesses and stores open from 8 A.M. or 9 A.M. to noon. After a longish lunch break, everything opens up again from about 3 P.M. through 6 or 7 P.M. The government, however, doesn't take that long of a lunch break, so you'll find an open door there from 8 A.M. through 2 P.M. Banks are open Monday through Friday only, from 8:30 A.M. through 1:30 P.M.; they open again from 3 P.M. to 4 P.M. Many businesses may be open on Saturday.

All of Italy lies in one time zone, which falls six hours ahead of the Eastern Standard Time. Therefore, if it's noon in New York city, it's 6 P.M. in Italy.

What to Expect

Italians are a warm, friendly, outgoing people and it can be a real pleasure to visit for work or pleasure. Don't be surprised, however, at an underlying formality and conservativism. Business executives will most likely be more old-fashioned and status-conscious than you would have predicted. This is not likely a place where you will see the executives going out to lunch with the fellows from the mailroom.

At home, the family is still important in Italy. However, recent economic changes have altered the historical importance Italians felt toward their close-knit clans. In the past, family formed the social glue that held the country together, frequently joining several generations in one house. More recently, Italians are having fewer babies and most women must work to make ends meet. Just as in the United States, economic changes have forced many Italians to move away from their hometowns in search of work, which has further fragmented the family. You would not often find an extended family living all together in modern Italy.

Up Close and Personal

Americans have a stereotypical idea that Italians are very touchy-feely people. In fact, there's a lot of touching going on, but it's only done by Italian men toward other men. Italian women, on the other hand, very rarely touch other women.

On the other hand, they do like to be up close and personal—Italians feel comfortable standing closer together than the normal U.S. range of two feet.

Faux Pas

Don't back away from an advancing Italian, who will probably stand closer to you than you feel comfortable with. It's an insult to do so.

Gestures—Yes!

Italians love to converse, but—as the Latins—they also tend to use their hands a great deal while chattering away. A gesture you may notice: to indicate derision, stroke the fingertips under the chin and then thrust them forward.

Here are some other gestures you may encounter in Italy:

➤ **Crossed fingers in front of the mouth:** I swear!

➤ **Pushing a finger into the cheek:** Good or delicious.

➤ **Kissing the tips of all fingers:** Excellent!

➤ **Pointing directly at someone:** Bad luck to you!

Ciao, Baby!

When first greeting someone in Italy, take off your hat, bow slightly, and (if it's a formal situation) you may kiss a woman's hand. Otherwise, shake hands with everyone when arriving and leaving.

If no one leaps forward to introduce you, it's okay to introduce yourself. The most respect automatically goes to the oldest (or most senior) person in the room. Women may "kiss" good friends on either cheek (more like pressing the sides of each face together).

Italians are enthusiastic greeters; when you shake hands, don't be surprised if the other fellow grabs your arm with the other hand. Backslapping and embraces between close friends and male relatives are expected.

And Your Name Is ...

In Italy, titles are used in all forms of address. Professors and doctors are considered Big Cheesees here, so use their titles ("Dottore" for a man, "Dottoressa" for a woman). You can use a title with a last name (or without, if you've forgotten it). Therefore, Doctor Lolobrigita could be "Dottoressa Lolobrigita" or "Signora Dottoressa."

Titles you may find handy include:

➤ **Padrone** or **commendatore**   the boss

➤ **Ingegnere**—technical or engineering boss

➤ **Ragionniere**—financial boss

➤ **Avocato**—lawyer

➤ **Architetto**—architect

➤ **Geometra**—surveyor

➤ **Signor** (Mr.) or **Signora** (Mrs.)—general terms that are acceptable

And no matter who you're talking to, don't use their first names unless you're invited to do so. Executives and their employees don't usually address each other by first names.

Your Card ...

Business cards are used in Italy, and many Italians have three—a social card, and two business cards: one filled with all details (including degrees and titles), and a second without titles and degrees.

The social card, which lists only a name (no titles), address and phone number, is used as a visiting card for social occasions. The business card with titles includes all relevant business information, including education degrees, titles, and contact information. If you're handed this card, you should address the person using the appropriate title as indicated on the card.

The second business card omits the titles (some folks simply cross them out). If you're given this card, it means you've moved on to a more informal relationship and you can now omit the titles when addressing the person.

Cards are a popular source of introduction in Italy. However, don't present your card at the beginning of a meeting; instead, hand out your business card when you're about to leave.

The Art of Conversation

Conversation is an art in Italy, but that doesn't mean that everyone is willing to sit by and listen to you pontificate. Don't be surprised if you're in a meeting or a group and everyone is talking at once. Meetings don't have to be conducted this way, however. If you are looking for an orderly meeting, you'll need to set down the rules at the very beginning.

Good choices for conversation are food, wine, art, sports, film, and Italian culture. Don't criticize the country, no matter how maddening you find it, even if your host is ripping it to shreds.

Topics to avoid include:

➤ World War II
➤ Politics
➤ Religion
➤ Off-color jokes

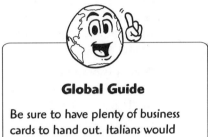

Global Guide

Be sure to have plenty of business cards to hand out. Italians would consider it impolite to have to ask you how to spell your name.

Faux Pas

This may be Italy, but flirting and flattering in the office are frowned upon. Save that for after-hours fraternizing.

No Pinching, Please

Things are not always easy for women in Italy, where a woman alone still invites unwanted attention. If you're eating in a restaurant by yourself in the north, you may be left alone as long as you don't smile at other diners. Bring some work along, or a good book, and bury your nose in it.

In the south, however, it may be more difficult to convince men that you aren't interested in company. In this part of Italy, it's still unusual for women to dine alone. Again, bring work along and make it clear you don't want to be disturbed.

Still, it's not hopeless for women in Italy, where women are making slow, gradual progress toward equality. The Italian legislature recognizes the equality of men and women in all areas, although (as in many other countries) the culture remains a male-oriented one.

Armani a Armani

In Italy, as in France, there's one thing that natives understand: fashion! Dress your best in this fashion-forward European country. The whole world looks to Italy for their power wardrobes. For business, you should wear good clothes of quiet elegance, fashionable and conservative. You'll be judged by the quality of your fashions, so don't buy cheap! Women may wear slacks in Italy, but avoid shorts, especially if you intend to enter a church.

Women should not wear sleeveless shirts or shorts to a church, nor should they enter a church without a head covering. The rules for clothing are posted on the outside of the building.

If you're going to a business lunch, men usually wear a coat and tie to lunch (a dark suit to dinner); women should wear a business suit or dark dress.

The World's Worst Red Tape

When it comes to dealing with bureaucracy, Italy wrote the book! In fact, Italy has been writing this book for the past 2,000 years, which is one reason why things are so maddeningly slow and infuriatingly tangled up in red tape. Laws enacted during the height of the Roman Empire are still on the books (they keep adding new ones, but they don't strike out the old ones). This is one reason why Italy is known as the "Land of 250,000 Laws."

The Art of Negotiation

If you're negotiating for business, remember that the more important the contract, the slower the negotiation. If you approach the Italians with a frenzied sense of urgency, your position will be much weaker. In the past, government corruption was a major problem in doing business in Italy, but laws enacted in the early 1990s were aimed at cleaning up the political abuses.

Also keep in mind that what passes for an organizational structure in the United States isn't necessarily used in Italy. In the middle of negotiations, you may be suddenly introduced to someone completely new who has been brought in because of his or her experience and seniority. Try to be flexible. Rather than the traditional top-to-bottom corporate structure that Americans are used to, Italians prefer a horizontal level of authority—sort of the "all on one team" philosophy. It's important to have a company contact who can understand the allegiances between executives, which are forged with personal concerns.

Global Guide

When it comes to doing business in Italy, who you know counts for a great deal. In fact, you may not want to come to Italy at all for business reasons unless you have at least some previous connection (however slight) with a representative who can make introductions for you.

Getting Down to Business

Before leaving the U.S., write for an appointment—don't expect to just pick up the phone once you get to Italy. (Write for the appointment in Italy if you want a prompt reply; if you are not literate in Italian, hire someone who is.) Once you've mailed off your letter, follow up with a phone call or fax.

Before actually sitting down to discuss what you came for, plan for a little chat session to get to know each other first. Italians don't like doing business with strangers. They'll ask you about your town and your family.

Presents, Si!

Be prepared to exchange business gifts if you're dealing with senior management. Think small and well-made (especially crafts from your home town). Liquor is also a good choice here. However, lose the mugs and baseball caps with your company's logo plastered all over them—that's not considered to be in good taste.

If you'd like to reward a secretary who's been very helpful, flowers are a nice touch. You could also choose some small item such as a good pen or a silver key chain.

If you are invited to an Italian home, you should bring a small hostess gift of flowers, pastry, or nicely wrapped chocolates. Try to avoid the following:

➤ **Chrysanthemums:** They are funeral flowers.

➤ **Even numbers of flowers:** (Bad luck)

➤ **Knives, brooches or handkerchiefs:** Linked to sadness.

➤ **Jug wine:** Make sure wine gifts are of excellent quality; Italians know their wines!

➤ **Any gift of a purple color:** It's bad luck.

Guess Who's Coming To Dinner?

Consider yourself honored if you've been invited home to dinner with an Italian family, as friends are usually entertained in a restaurant. You'll want to arrive on time, and remember bring a small hostess gift (see the previous section). Expect to be served an aperitif and a few appetizers. Leave your drink behind when you go into the dining room for the meal.

Don't look for a signal from you hostess indicating that the evening is over—or you'll be waiting all night! It's up to you to decide when to leave. Send a note the next day thanking your hosts (you can send flowers if you had a really good time).

Entertainment, Italian Style

When you're in Italy, you can expect really world-class entertainment, from the Festival dei due mondi at Spoleto, to the opera season in some really spectacular settings. But what to wear?

You'll be safe if your dress matches the formality of the occasion, and the number of lire you've plunked down for your ticket. Thus, for opening night at La Scala in Milan, you'll wear black tie (or long gown); a circus would call for much more casual attire!

Zuppa to Nuts

Italian hospitality is legendary, and for good reason! If you're in Italy for business, you may well be invited out to a restaurant. Even if you're still suffering from jet lag and just want to sleep, don't turn down an invitation. No matter how good your reason, your hosts may well be offended.

If you want to save some money in this sometimes pricey country, try eating alone at a restaurant counter. Customers who opt to stand for their meals pay dramatically less expensive prices for the same meals they'd be enjoying at a table in the same cafe. It's not unusual to see an Italian eating breakfast or lunch standing up.

Faux Pas

When dining in Italy, don't put your hands in your lap, and don't eat anything with your fingers except grapes or cherries. (Cheese should be eaten with a knife.)

At the same time, don't be surprised or offended if your Italian contact wants to join you for a meal at a cafe counter. Often, power-talks take place in this casual setting, so don't view this kind of an invitation as a waste of time.

Expect to find several varieties of pizza, none of which will be exactly what you're accustomed to eating outside of Italy. You'll encounter thick, sauceless varieties served at room temperature (straight from walk-up display cases) as well as super-thin, piping-hot pies straight from wood-burning ovens and covered with a variety of toppings and presented in sit-down restaurants. The thin ones are usually served to one person, and are eaten with a knife and a fork.

The Most Important Meal of the Day

Just as in France, breakfast in Italy is simple—rolls, jam, butter, and coffee or chocolate. (That's where we got the "continental breakfast" idea, you see ...) If you try breakfast at a cafe, remember to first pay for a ticket at the cash desk, and then hand it to the person behind the counter when you place your order. Breakfast is served from 6:30 A.M. to 10 A.M. in coffee bars.

Once you get your coffee, you're supposed to drink it standing up. If you feel you really must sit down, tables are available—but you have to pay to sit there.

In general, however, Italians eat just twice a day—at lunch, and again at dinner. They may dine at a *trattoria*: a simple, down-to-earth place offering "homestyle" food; a restaurant will be more expensive and formal. A *Tavola Calda* is a self-service diner offering quick snacks.

Luncheon Is Served

Restaurants are usually open from noon to 3 P.M. for lunch, which is the main meal of the day. When you sit down to the table in Italy, don't panic if you see a pile of plates at your place. The one on top is for serving antipasto (a selection of cold cuts); the deep dish beneath that is intended for soup or pasta; the biggest plate under that is reserved for the main course.

The menu for lunch is about the same as for dinner, although selections may be a bit heavier at lunch, which is the main meal of the day. Lunch is served around 1 P.M., beginning with an antipasto (a selection of cold cuts), and followed by a pasta or rice dish.

Next comes *il secondo* (the main course), which is usually a choice of meat, poultry or fish, accompanied by vegetables and followed by salad. Cheese is served next, then dessert or fruit (or sometimes both). Should you have room for dessert, remember to eat it with your teaspoon. That's the Italian way. Lastly, espresso is served.

Dinner a la Roma

Dinner is a lighter meal than lunch, although you may see many of the same courses that you were offered at lunch. You'll see all the courses listed separately on the menu, so don't expect to order an entree and expect that it will arrive accompanied with the "vegetable of the day" and a salad: It won't. If you want vegetables and a salad, you have to order them specifically. (Of course, some restaurants do offer a special tourist menu, but it's usually rather dull and unexciting.)

Restaurants are usually open for dinner between 7 P.M. and 11 P.M. You probably won't find any restaurants open after 11 P.M.

If you're going out for a business dinner, don't expect to see half the company sit down at the table. Typically, only a small group of the most important executives will attend. If you're hosting dinner, don't assume you can figure out who should be invited and who shouldn't—check with your Italian client for hints.

If you were invited out to eat, the bill's not your responsibility. However, if it's clear that it would be appropriate for you to split the bill, that's certainly acceptable in Italy. Say: *"Facciamo alla romana"* (*fah-see-ah-moe ah-la-ro-mahn-oh*; "Let's go 'Dutch'") and then split the bill down the middle. Haggling over individual items by sitting there with a calculator mumbling, "Now, who had the *pasta alla parmegiano*?" (*pahsta ah-la pahr-may-gee-ahno*) is considered rude.

Raise a Glass

Italy is certainly wine country, but that doesn't mean you have to be a sot. Wine is for sipping, according to the Italians. They view public drunkenness with a very prejudiced eye; it's offensive to them.

Most Italians don't really get enthusiastic about cocktails, although they may opt for an aperitif (vermouth or white wine, perhaps). Instead, they usually cut right to the wine, which they drink before, during, and after the meal.

The Least You Need to Know

➤ Every region in Italy has its own feast day holidays when stores and businesses will close.

➤ Always use a title when addressing someone in Italy, and don't use first names.

➤ Family and privacy is extremely important in Italy; don't be hurt if you aren't invited home to dinner.

➤ Don't underestimate your business colleagues; Italians are some of the best business experts in the world.

➤ When greeting an Italian, take off your hat and bow, and then shake hands.

➤ Titles are used in all forms of address.

Chapter 11

Portugal

> ### In This Chapter
>
> ➤ Learn about the intricacies of the Portuguese language
>
> ➤ Discover the melancholy nature of the Portuguese attitudes
>
> ➤ Explore the importance of personal relationships in business situations
>
> ➤ Find out how the Portuguese feel about religion and family
>
> ➤ Understand the key to dressing appropriately

It's small, it's beautiful, and Americans know far too little about Spain's tiny neighbor to the west. Portuguese culture today contains remnants of its history as both conqueror and conquered while maintaining one of the best economic performances and lowest unemployment rates in Europe. While many Americans know almost nothing about Portugal, there are many attractions waiting to be discovered: medieval hilltop towns with cobbled streets and storybook castles, coastal villages of neat whitewashed cottages and lush foliage, sun-drenched beach resorts, and outstanding wine cellars and vineyards.

Here or There?

Slightly smaller than Indiana, Portugal lies in southwestern Europe, between the North Atlantic Ocean on the west and Spain on the east. Geographically, Portugal is a long, narrow country characterized by mountains and an extensive seacoast marked by beaches, marshes, cliffs, and many excellent harbors.

Jutting out into the Atlantic Ocean, the country enjoys a maritime temperate climate that is cool and rainy in the north and warmer and drier in the south. The southern coasts have a near-Mediterranean climate, while some rain can be expected along the northern coasts and in the northern valleys.

The best time is visit is from May through June or the end of September through October, when the weather isn't too hot (although it can be a bit cool for lying on the beaches). Days will be warm with very little rain, and nights definitely require a sweater. In the summer, it can be hot on the beaches, and the winters are wet, often foggy and windy and really quite uncomfortable on the coast. If you're traveling in winter, plan to spend most of your time inland.

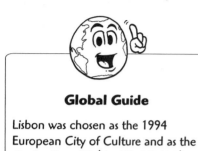

Global Guide

Lisbon was chosen as the 1994 European City of Culture and as the site for Expo 98 (the World's Fair).

Formerly Lusitania

Portugal has a moderately developed and stable democracy with tourist facilities widely available. The chief of state is the president; the prime minister is head of government. A Council of Ministers is appointed by the president on the recommendation of the prime minister.

Hundreds of years ago, vulnerable Portugal (known then as Lusitania) spent all its time putting up with its share of invaders from the sea——the Phoenicians, Romans, Moors, and Celts. Taking a page from their military notebook, Portugal finally went on the offensive from 1400 to 1600 and began to develop its own territories throughout South America, Africa, India and Asia. That 200-year era of Colonialism is known as Portugal's Golden Age. Indeed, Portugal was so attached to its ideas of colonial acquisition that it hung onto the last of its colonies until 1975.

Its glory days long past, Portugal has nevertheless been able to maintain a strong economy even without a flotilla of colonies to back it up. The Socialist government's primary economic goal is to place Portugal in the initial group of countries adopting the single European currency. Lisbon, its capital, is also is working to modernize and increase competitiveness.

Speaking Portuguese

Portuguese is spoken throughout the country, although French is often used in business, and some English is spoken in tourist areas. While it's true that Portuguese and Spanish are related and similar, they aren't the same language at all. If you'd like to try a bit of the local lingo, bring a Portuguese phrasebook, but don't hold your breath. Portuguese is notoriously difficult to speak.

If you speak Spanish (or another Romance language), you may be able to figure out the meanings of a lot of written Portuguese. But Portuguese, while the seventh most common spoken language in the world, is full of odd pronunciation rules that can add up to a real mouthful. Unlike the French, however, if you give it a try—no matter how dreadfully you bungle it—the Portuguese will find your efforts charming and will be delighted at your attempts.

While many of your business associates may indeed speak English, it's a nice touch to hire an interpreter for business meetings. And while most Portuguese associates understand English, it will be appreciated if you have documents translated into their native tongue.

Faux Pas

Don't assume that the Portuguese speak Spanish, and don't try to communicate with the Portuguese in Spanish—it's considered insulting. The Portuguese have their own language and are proud of it.

Religion

While there is no *official* religion in Portugal, most of the people are Roman Catholic (97 percent); a few are Protestant (1 percent), and the rest are primarily Jewish or Muslim. Freedom of religion is guaranteed in the Portuguese constitution.

The church and the family provide a strong sense of social structure and stability to the country. While individuals are responsible for their own decisions, the impact of the family and the employer has strong influence. This is why your connections are much more important than your abilities when looking for a job in Portugal.

How important is the Catholic church? When you get to Portugal, look around. You may notice the color black is everywhere, but especially in the clothing of the women. That's because the Portuguese have elevated mourning to a high art here. Women enshroud themselves in black from 7 to 10 years after the death of a parent, and for two or three years after the death of an in-law. After the death of a husband—well, many widows never emerge from their widow's weeds, but drown themselves in black for the rest of their lives. (Oddly enough, nobody goes into mourning for the death of a child.)

How to Have Fun

Despite their tendency to dwell on pessimism (the glass is always half empty in Portugal), the people do know how to put on a holiday. It's said that there is a different market day or festival every day of the year in Portugal. Religious festivals (called *romarias*) are held throughout the year. Market days, whether in big cities or small towns, are an irresistible attraction.

Jan. 1: New Year's Day.

Feb. 11: Mardi Gras.

Say What?

Ponte (*pont*): Literally, this is the Portuguese word for "bridge," but it's used to refer to a "long weekend." If a national holiday falls on a Tuesday or Thursday, many businesses will call for a "ponte" and also close on the Monday or Friday in between.

123

Spring: Good Friday.

April 25: Liberty Day.

May 1: Labor Day.

June 13: St. Anthony's Day.

August 15: Assumption.

Oct. 5: Republic Day.

Nov. 1: All Saints' Day.

Dec. 1: Independence Day.

Dec. 8: Feast of the Immaculate Conception.

Dec. 24: Christmas Eve.

Dec. 25: Christmas Day.

You Be on Time, I'll Be Late ...

Portuguese business people usually arrive within 15 to 30 minutes of when a scheduled meeting is to begin, but they expect that you'll be on time. If you're going to be late, call with an explanation.

Work Week

The Portuguese work week runs from 9 A.M. through 5 P.M. Monday through Friday, but there's a nice break in the middle—a two-hour lunch from noon to 2 P.M. Businesses are open from 9 A.M. through 1 P.M. Monday through Friday, and again from 3 P.M. to 7 P.M.

Banks are generally open weekdays from 8:30 A.M. to 3 P.M., although money exchanges at airports and train stations are usually open all day (24 hours at the airport).

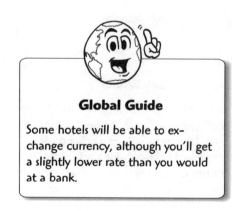

Global Guide

Some hotels will be able to exchange currency, although you'll get a slightly lower rate than you would at a bank.

Most museums open at 10 A.M., close for lunch between 12:30 P.M. and 2 P.M., and close for good at 5 P.M. (a few big ones stay open at midday—check beforehand). Museums are closed on Monday and holidays; palaces close on Tuesday and holidays.

One of the most inconvenient things about shopping in Portugal is the midday closing of most shops for about two hours. Store hours are weekdays from 9 A.M. to 1 P.M. and from 3 P.M. to 7 P.M. Saturday hours are from 9 A.M. to 1 P.M. (In December, Saturday hours are the same as weekdays.) Shops are closed on Sunday, although some *hipermercados* (supermarkets) and shopping centers are open seven days a week, 10 A.M. through midnight.

Portugal is six hours ahead of Eastern Standard Time, so when it's noon in New York City, it's 6 P.M. in Portugal. Clocks are turned ahead an hour on the last Sunday in March, and back an hour on the last Sunday in September.

A Handshake Will Do

When greeting Portuguese associates, extend a firm handshake to everyone present, looking each person in the eye as you greet them. Shake hands again when leaving.

On social occasions, don't be surprised if men grab other men with a brief embrace. Women do the "air kiss" or kiss on both cheeks when greeting each other.

And Your Title Is ...

Given names come first in Portugal followed by family names, the same as in the U.S. But just because you happen to know someone's first name in Portugal, this doesn't mean you should use it; using first names is reserved for very close friends.

Don't be surprised if that well-respected teacher or engineer is introduced as *Doctor*, despite the fact that you know he never attended medical school. The title is given out of respect.

Card Me!

Business cards are important in Portugal. Before you leave the U.S., have your business cards printed with English on one side and Portuguese on the other. When you get to Portugal, offer your card with the Portuguese side facing the recipient.

Tip of the Hat

When you're given a card, don't be surprised if it arrives with one corner turned down, which may be a holdover from the early days when the landed gentry used a calling card with a turned-down corner in lieu of immediate payment.

Stiffly and Straight

When it comes to body language and gestures, the Portuguese are fairly stiff. As a general rule, avoid pointing with your finger. To get someone's attention, keep your palm down and wave with your fingers or your whole hand, like you're patting someone on the head.

Equality: Yes or No?

Women shouldn't go to Portugal expecting to find equality—it's an extremely macho society. This means that when you walk down the street, you'll likely hear hissing or clucks of approval, although you'll still encounter less sexual harassment that you would in many Latin countries.

On the other hand, the facts that almost everyone in Portugal is ethnic Portuguese and speaks the same language lends a sense of equality. This doesn't mean that there is economic equality in this country, however: Portugal is a land of economic extremes, with a tiny upper class, a moderate middle class, and a huge lower class.

Dress Up

It may seem like a laid-back, romantic country, but when dressing in Portugal, think conservative and formal. The Portuguese, like the Spanish, tend to dress up more than Americans or the British. In fact, Portuguese men even wear a suit and tie when going to the movies. And no matter how sweltering it gets, don't take off your jacket until your hosts do. Women don't usually wear suits; instead, choose a quiet-colored dress.

Faux Pas

For the most part, there's no dress code, but don't wear shorts in churches, or bathing suits on the street or in restaurants and shops.

Remember that the climate here can be harsh. Summer can be brutally hot, spring and fall are mild to chilly; and winter is cold and rainy. If you're going sightseeing, dress in casual, comfortable clothing. If you're going out to a restaurant or nightclub in the city, however, you'll need dressier outfits.

If you like to travel incognito without being recognized as an American, it's possible—but you'll have to ditch your Reboks. If you want to blend in, wear leather shoes, not sneakers. Jeans, on the other hand, let you blend into the crowd no matter where you go or who you are.

Can We Talk?

While the Portuguese are friendly and like to talk, privacy is important here. Don't pry into personal matters——let them set the boundaries for small talk. Good choices for discussion are your own personal hobbies, positive comments on Portuguese culture, and the family.

Other cultural don'ts:

➤ Don't discuss politics or government.

➤ Don't use American slang.

Negotiating Portuguese-Style

The Portuguese are a warm, gentle people with a haunting melancholy that pervades their personality, music, and art. Their state of mind is called *saudade* (*so-dad*), a difficult-to-translate concept that refers to poignant longing for something just out of reach. This passive yearning is best expressed in the music called *fado* (*fah-do*), which involves soul-baring, gut-wrenching angst. (Think Romeo and Juliet with a guitar.) In fact, so vulnerable are the Portuguese to this music, that during the 1974 revolution, it was illegal to broadcast fado on the radio because the government feared it encouraged fatalism and listlessness and got in the way of social progress.

Dignified and proud, the Portuguese are extremely tolerant—almost indulgent—with foreigners. As a general rule, business relations in Portugal are casual and often based on trusting, personal relationships. The Portuguese like to do business with people they feel they know, so if you spend the time to make good contacts here, you'll be much farther ahead. If you want to boost your negotiation strength, emphasize how committed you'll be to your Portuguese clients. Make frequent visits to drive this point home.

This doesn't mean that lots of personal contact will grease the wheels and get decisions moving on a rapid pace. Things take time in Portugal, and you'll need to develop patience if you want to succeed here. Change is not something that is looked upon with much favor here.

First of all, during that first meeting, let your Portuguese colleagues start the negotiation ball rolling. Refreshments or small talk may precede getting down to business. Always accept coffee, a soda, or an alcoholic beverage when offered by your Portuguese colleagues, even if you're not thirsty.

Once the meeting does begin, don't be surprised if it degenerates into an arena for competition and personal gain. That Portuguese colleague who seems so eager to consider outside input in private can turn into an aggressive Donald Trump at the boardroom table.

Hold the Gifts

Business gifts are exchanged in Portugal, but never on the first meeting. When you do decide the time is right to come up with a gift, steer a middle course: Don't buy a present that's too expensive, but don't choose the cheap route, either.

If you're buying a gift to give to a business associate, don't be tacky about it, and don't be so obvious that you give a gift with your company logo plastered all over it. Likewise, when you present the gift, include a handwritten card, not your business card.

Slow and Soulful

Music is all-important in Portugal. Saudade, the soulful undercurrent that defines Portugal's traditional fado music, is a mèlange of nostalgic longing and pride in the past. Fado's popularity in contemporary Portugal isn't surprising in a land that was once a wealthy world power known for its bold navigators only to end up as a largely ignored international backwater, the European equivalent of a hick town.

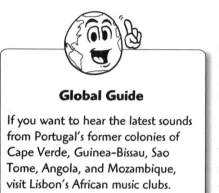

Global Guide

If you want to hear the latest sounds from Portugal's former colonies of Cape Verde, Guinea-Bissau, Sao Tome, Angola, and Mozambique, visit Lisbon's African music clubs.

If you're looking for something a bit more energetic than a musical interlude, try a bullfight. But don't expect Portuguese bullfights to be bloodbaths like those seen in Spain. In Portugal, the bull is wrestled to the ground, and the inevitably injured beast is slaughtered after the crowds have left.

Home for Dinner

When invited to your Portuguese counterparts' home for dinner, you can bring a small gift, which will be opened right away. Flowers for the hostess and wine for the host are good choices.

If you do bring flowers to your Portuguese hostess, don't skimp; be sure to present a nice, big, impressive bouquet (a cheap handful of wilting blooms is insulting). You'll also want to avoid:

➤ **Thirteen flowers of any kind.** (Bad luck)

➤ **Chrysanthemums.** (Associated with death)

➤ **Roses.** (Too intimate)

You aren't required to bring a hostess gift, however. If you prefer, you may simply repay the dinner invitation by inviting your hosts to a meal in turn.

Sopas to Nuts

For the best food in Portugal, pass up that high brow French fare in favor of peasant Portuguese dishes found at nice *tasca*s (taverns) or a *restaurante tipico*. If you go where the locals go, choose the *prato do dia* (plate of the day) and you won't be disappointed.

Faux Pas

If you don't want to offend while in Portugal, don't walk down the street while you're eating, and don't leave your hands in your lap during mealtimes; both are considered rude.

While you often need a magnifying glass to find your food on your plate in some European countries, you'll likely have the opposite problem in Portugal—enormous portions that soon have your waist billowing over your belt. Feel free to request a *half portion* option—most menus list the rate, which usually costs two-thirds of the full price.

Women who figure they'd like to grab a meal on their own in a restaurant better pack a fat briefcase and make it really obvious you're on a working meal—otherwise, you'll likely be bothered (or at least approached) by men who can't bear to see a woman eating alone. (Or, as is likely in this macho culture, that a woman eating alone is advertising her wish to be approached.)

Breakfast

Don't expect to find big plates of bacon and eggs on your breakfast table—Portugal is part of Europe, after all, the home of the *continental breakfast*. In Portugal, breakfast usually consists of a cup of coffee and a roll, followed by another cup of coffee mid-morning. If you're lucky, you'll get some butter for your bread.

Lunch Is King

Breakfast might be spartan, but lunch is quite another story: It's the big meal of the day in Portugal. If you're here on business, expect to conduct business during this meal. Most Portuguese sit down for lunch around 12:30 P.M. to 1 P.M., and eat for about two hours. Many Portuguese enjoy eating at a special eatery called a *casas de cha* (*casa da sha*; tea house).

Almost all restaurants offer an *ementa turistica* (*ay-men-tah toor-ees-te-kah*; tourist menu), a set-price meal at lunchtime. Don't forget to finish your meal with a glass of port.

Once lunch is over, expect a mid-afternoon cup of tea or coffee to fortify you until dinner.

Dinner Is Served

Dinner is usually served around 8 P.M., and is typically a simple but heavy meal. Most restaurants serve fresh, reasonable Portuguese cuisine, characterized by grilled sardines, steaks and cutlets, fresh seafood, and salads. Local specialties include a thick bread-and-shellfish stew, or thick and spicy meat stews (especially in the north). If you want something a little different, try a restaurant that specializes in colonial Portuguese food (principally Brazilian).

If you like meat and seafood, you'll be happy with Portuguese cuisine; if you're a vegetarian, you may have a harder time. Outside the big cities, it may be almost impossible to find plentiful fresh vegetables and vegetarian meals.

When invited to dinner by business colleagues, don't plan on discussing business unless the host brings up the subject first. Dinners are generally family style, with the host serving himself first and passing dishes around the table. Don't eat until everyone has been served and the host begins.

Drink a Glass

Drinking is a popular pastime in Portugal (they have those great port wines, after all!) but the Portuguese rarely get drunk, despite the rock-bottom wine prices.

You may crave a Coke with your hamburger and fries, but when dining in Portugal, expect to be served wine to drink with your meals. The Portuguese are very proud of their vineyards and their ports. If you read up a bit on the subject before you go, you'll earn points in Portugal.

Global Guide

If you're invited to dine by your Portuguese host, you'll be expected to return the favor. Just don't mention anything about owing the other person a meal.

Traditional, sprawling *cervejarias* (beer halls/restaurants) are everywhere. But be careful when ordering vintage ports in restaurants—you could end up with a staggering tab! Be sure you know what you're getting, and how much it's going to cost.

Local wines are considered a sort of health tonic—they're called *vinho da casa* (vin-ho da cah sa; house wine) they of good quality. Others prefer the brandy-like *aguardente* (ah-gwar-dahn-tay), which is distilled from wine, or the fiery *bagaceira* (bahg-a-chaira), distilled from the dregs of pressed grapes. Portugal also brews some fine beers and also has a wide range of its own bottled waters. If you prefer fresh fruit juice—well, good luck: It's almost impossible to find.

Tipping

Service is included in cafè, restaurant, and hotel bills, but waiters and other service people are poorly paid; you can be sure your contribution will be appreciated. However, if you received bad service, never feel obligated (or intimidated) to leave a tip.

An acceptable tip is 10 to 15 percent of the total bill, although if you just have a sandwich or *petiscos* (pay-tees-cohs; appetizers) at a bar, leave less.

The Least You Need to Know

➤ The Portuguese are formal and gentle people, and resistant to change.

➤ Never start speaking Spanish to a Portuguese and expect him or her to be able to understand.

➤ Personal relationships are vital to business success.

➤ Church and family are an important part of Portuguese life.

➤ Don't expect to find gender or social equality in Portugal.

➤ Think conservative and formal when dressing.

Spain

In This Chapter

➤ Discover the ins and outs of the Spanish language and titles

➤ Understand the proper way to tip in Spain

➤ Learn how to combine business with dining

If this is your first visit to Spain, you may wonder when anything gets done.

The Spanish seem to spend most of their time eating, drinking, and enjoying life: Their long lunches are legendary, they spend their evenings hopping from *tapas* bar to tapas bar, and eventually they get around to eating dinner.

This breezy approach to life doesn't mean the Spanish are lazy louts with nothing better to do with their time—they just love life with passion and drama, from El Greco to flamenco dancing to the thrill of the bullfight.

Where It's At

Catalonia and the Basque region in the north were granted autonomy in 1980, but political violence continues as some Basques still seek total independence from Spain. Spain continues its tussle over the return of Gibralter, which has been under British control since 1704.

The months of April through June as well as September and October are the best times to visit. It can be a bit cool in October in the higher elevations and the Basque area. Sweaters will be needed for evenings. July and August are generally very hot; winter, though generally mild, can be rainy, foggy, and windy. Winter, even on the Costa del Sol, is on the cool side—much too cool to sunbathe and swim.

Spain has a highly developed and stable constitutional monarchy with a modern economy. Its current constitution dates back only to 1978, and the country is ruled by the king as chief of state, the prime minister as head of government, and a bicameral parliament.

Spanish, Por Favor

Spain's official language is Spanish (the Castillian dialect is used by most Spaniards); Spanish is also the standard business language. English and French are the most common foreign languages spoken in Madrid, especially among young people. Most cabdrivers don't speak English, although it's understood at major hotels, restaurants, and at business meetings. The Basques, the Galicians, and the Catalans all speak their own languages, which may have quite different pronunciations and spellings.

Tip of the Hat

The native language of the Basques (Euskera) is not related to Spanish at all. In fact, it is linguistically unrelated to any known language.

Don't automatically expect English to be the predominant language in a Spanish business meeting. Try to find out ahead of time. If Spanish reigns, try to arrange an interpreter through your hotel concierge. Even if you do hire a bilingual expert, put your two cents into the conversation in the native tongue whenever you can. Your foreign colleague will admire your effort—even if the only words you utter are *buenos diás* (good day). And even though you struggled through those four years of Spanish in school, don't be shocked when you hear how fast people speak. If you try to join in, don't forget to lisp your z's. (For example, Ibiza is pronounced "ee-BEETH-ah.")

Even if you think most people you'll be meeting do understand English, have all of your materials printed in Spanish, along with a Spanish side to your business cards.

Romance languages typically differentiate between the formal "you" (*usted*) and the intimate "you" (*tu*, which is used only for family, close friends, and young people). However, in Spain, these pronoun forms are used differently than in the rest of Latin America. You'll find that Spaniards:

➤ Use the formal "usted" (singular) or "ustedes" (plural) to speak to servants as a way of conferring dignity to the servant as a person.

➤ Are more likely to use the informal "tú" pronoun in the office—sometimes even the employees use the "tú" pronoun to their bosses.

Religion

While there is no "official" religion in Spain, 97 percent of the people are Roman Catholic and the country observes many rituals and holidays associated with the Catholic religion.

Historically, this religion has wielded great power in Spain; its opposition to birth control and divorce are the reasons why large families were common in Spain. These days, the church has less of a direct impact on day-to-day Spanish life. However, the more educated a person is, the more likely he or she is to be a practicing Catholic.

Cultural Roundup

You'll find that Spain is still rigidly divided along class, occupational and professional lines. The middle class is expanding, and the rural poor are less evident. The extended family, once the norm throughout the country, is being replaced by the nuclear family. And while the idea of personal responsibility is strong, the best interests of family or the group are always kept in mind.

Global Guide

When it comes to keeping a job, your family and friend relationships are more important than how well you do your work.

Life Is a Holiday

In addition to the following national holidays, other parts of Spain celebrate regional holidays as well. Most Spaniards get 30 days paid vacation and take them in July or August. In addition, there are the following holidays:

Jan. 1: New Year's Day.

May 1: Labor Day.

May 16: San Isidro (Madrid).

Sept. 24: Our Lady of Mercy (Barcelona).

Oct. 12: National Day and Hispanic Day.

Nov. 9: Our Lady of Almudena (Madrid).

Dec. 6: Constitution Day.

Dec. 26: St. Stephen's Day (Barcelona).

Laid-Back Spain

It may be the climate or the long hours of sun in Spain, but natives tend to get up later in the morning and stay out later at night than the rest of Europe. Meetings may not begin promptly, either, so try to be patient. Taking a *siesta* in the afternoons helps in getting adjusted to the Spanish schedule.

Spain is six hours ahead of Eastern Standard Time, so if it's noon in New York City, it's 6 P.M. in Spain. Daylight Saving Time is observed from late March to late October.

Typically, people work 40 hours a week in Spain, but specific business hours will vary. Most shops are open Monday through Friday from 9:30 A.M. to 1:30 P.M. or 2 P.M., and then again from 5 P.M. to 8:30 P.M.; however, more and more stores are beginning to stay open during traditional siesta hours. (Saturday hours usually run from 9:30 A.M. to 1:30 P.M. or 2 P.M.) Large department stores are open Monday through Saturday from 9:30 A.M. to 9 P.M. A few department stores, large supermarkets, and shopping centers are open on designated Sundays, the dates of which are usually announced in the newspapers in the days before. Those hours are from noon to 8 P.M. In tourist areas, however, a business may keep summer hours, staying open until 10 P.M. or 11 P.M. seven days a week.

Banking hours vary according to the bank and the season. During the summer (June 1 through September 30) banks close up tight on Saturdays.

If you get a hankering for a box of Chicklets at 2 A.M., you'll be glad to know that "VIP"s (a convenience store/cafeteria chain) remain open until 3 A.M.

Many businesses in Madrid close down for part or all of August because of summer vacation. It's wise to phone ahead to most places during this time.

Daily Business Life

Knowing a few details in advance on how business is conducted in Spain will eliminate a lot of visitor frustration: All kinds of interruptions are commonplace during meetings. If that happens to you, don't be insulted, but give your host the floor, wait until he or she is finished, and then graciously resume.

Faux Pas

If your host corrects you, don't fly off the handle and stomp out of the room. Spaniards find confrontation as a progressive negotiating tool.

Similarly, you'll also find the "me first" (*yo primero*) attitude to be common in Spain, which means that orderly queues are almost unheard of. If you're in charge of sales for multiple customers, be sure to provide some type of crowd control (such as "taking a number").

When you're in meetings, don't be surprised if it's hard to pry facts out of your Spanish colleagues. Information is considered to be a valuable commodity here.

Shake, Shake, Shake

Once underway, usual greetings involve firm handshakes and direct eye contact. Shaking hands is a very important custom in Spain: People shake hands when they meet and when they part. Spanish men often pat the back in addition, or even give a hug.

Women practice that "air kiss" and may lightly embrace. Professional Spanish women also may greet a close colleague (including men) this way.

Let's Play Cards

Business cards are generally handed out at the close of meetings, and are thankfully accepted if printed in both Spanish and English. If you do have both languages on your card, present the card with the Spanish side up facing the other person.

¡Titles, Sí!

First names are only for young people or close friends. Wait for your Spanish colleagues to call you by your first name before you begin. This also applies to the intimate form of the word "you" (*tu*) as opposed to the formal "you" (*usted*). (See "Lingo" for more details.)

When you want to address a colleague, use the titles of Señor (Mr.), Señora (Mrs.), or Señorita (Miss) preceding the last name: "Senor Valdez," for example. If you are introduced to an older person or someone in an elevated position (high-level execs, for instance) use the title "Don" (for a man) or "Dona" (for a woman), followed by the first name. You'd say, "Don Pedro," or "Dona Maria."

As in most Spanish-speaking countries, most Spaniards have two last names, one from their father (listed first) and one from their mother. Only the father's surname is used when addressing someone aloud: Señor Pedro Juan Nunez de Martinez would be called "Señor Nunez" in person.

When a woman gets married, she usually tacks her husband's surname on to the end of the string. Before marriage, she would be Señorita Maria Francesca Mira de Acevedo; after marriage, she would be Señora Maria Francesca Mira Acevedo de Blasco. After marriage, you would call her Señora de Blasco (or informally, Señora Blasco).

Global Guide

As a rule, you would use only one surname when speaking directly to someone, but you'd use both surnames when writing.

Can We Talk?

When you're dealing with the Spanish, aim for a warm personal style. Strive to maintain dignity and diplomacy, and don't be surprised if the Spanish seem a bit restrained at first. It takes a while for a personal relationship to begin in this country.

If you're searching for a good topic of conversation, choose politics, sports, and travel. Just don't get into religion, and don't criticize bullfighting. If you can't find anything good to say about this sport, keep your trap shut.

Don't be surprised if you find your Spanish colleagues leaning over and offering you all sorts of personal advice. They'll do it freely among themselves and foreigners—they don't mean to offend. They're trying to be helpful.

Faux Pas

Don't make the "A-OK" sign with a circle of the first finger and thumb. It's considered rude.

Spaniards are well-known for a strong sense of personal honor and pride—but oddly enough, business expertise may not necessarily be honored in Spain. You'll find that Spaniards may take more pride in personal characteristics than in their business skills—so watch what you compliment!

Spanish Eyes

Don't be surprised if you find your Spanish counterpart smashed right up against your face during a conversation. Whatever you do, don't jump back. Instead, rise to this friendly occasion and stay put.

You may find hands flapping in different ways in Spain as many gestures are used in daily conversation; their meanings, however, may differ depending on what part of Spain you're in.

If you want to beckon someone, turn your palm down and wave your fingers or your whole hand. If you want to make a point and drive it home, snap your hand downward.

Señorita Freedoms

With the end of the puritan Franco era, Spanish women have begun to demand equal freedoms, and women are now found more prominently in education, politics, and the work force. According to Spanish law, women and men are completely equal.

However, Spain is the country that just about invented the idea of "machismo," which is still the norm in this country—you'll need to be careful not to insult a man's honor. Especially watch out for jokes in poor taste, which can easily trigger an angry response or a botched business deal.

Women visiting Spain on business may have a difficult time playing the host and picking up the tab. As a whole, Spanish men feel it's their duty to treat women to a meal. If you're a woman and you don't go along with this, you can win by making arrangements in advance with the maìtre d' to pay—if it's really important to you.

Women may be the object of more unwanted attention here than in northern Europe, particularly if they're traveling alone or visiting Andalusia or the southern Mediterranean coast. If you're bothered, the best response is no response at all—any attention given is likely to be misinterpreted.

Neat and Formal

People dress casually but conservatively for sightseeing, especially in the summer when short sleeves are common, even for natives of Madrid. However, don't wear shorts in churches; wear them only on beaches and at beach resorts.

For business, a neat, formal appearance will earn you a good impression in this southern European destination. In fact, the dress in Spain is still more formal than in most other European countries. Designer labels won't go unnoticed, either. When you arrive in Spain, have your clothes pressed (or better yet, have an iron sent to your room for any last-minute wrinkle removals). Crisp and tailored is the look you're aiming for.

Suits are acceptable for both men and women. In general, men should be conservative and women may be stylish. Men usually wear dark colors during the winter and lighter shades during the summer. Plaid or checked suits or jackets are a tad unusual. Avoid them. When dining, top restaurants will require men to wear coats and ties.

Meet the Family

Don't expect to be invited home to meet your Spanish colleague's family, as this honor is usually reserved for intimate friends. In fact, if you do get an invitation, you may decline at first—accept only if pressed. (Typically, these first invitations may be given only out of politeness. If the invitation is extended a second time, they really mean it and you may then accept.)

If you do visit a Spanish home, it's customary to bring along a small gift, such as pastry, chocolate or flowers. If you do take flowers, avoid these:

➤ Dahlias (associated with death).

➤ Chrysanthemums (associated with death).

➤ Thirteen of any type of flower (bad luck).

Giving a Gift

Business gifts are sometimes given, but not at a first meeting. If you're given a gift, you should usually open it right away.

If you're doing the giving, choose a corporate gift carefully. Buy name brands and high quality, wrapped elegantly. Stay away from items plastered with your company logo (unless it's a nice, tasteful pen). Good choices include

➤ Local crafts.

➤ Shirts or caps with sports logos (for kids).

➤ Shirts or caps with university logos (for kids).

➤ Illustrated books from your home.

Sopa to Nuts

Eating will almost surely be part of the establishment of your business partnerships. In fact, it may seem as if you can't get rid of your Spanish friends, as they join you for breakfast, lunch, afternoon snack, and dinner.

Most cafeterias and restaurants are classified by the Spanish government, which issues a "fork" rating displayed on the restaurant's front door. Five forks signify the highest quality (rather like the stars of the Michelin Guide). This rating partly reflects the food quality, but also includes the decor, number of dishes on the menu, prices, languages used on the menu, and languages spoken by the head waiter.

Global Guide

For most Spaniards, the dinner hour begins sometime around 10:30 P.M. However, you can start digging in as early as 9:30 P.M. without attracting notice.

If you've found a "four- or five-forker" you'd like to try, you can figure that breakfast usually begins from 7 A.M. to 10 A.M., lunch from 1:30 P.M. to 4 P.M.; and dinner from 9 P.M. to midnight. However, in summer these hours are often expanded and many places offer continuous service. Many serve food into the small hours of the night.

If you want to take a Spanish client out for a meal, choose an excellent restaurant. Many Spaniards are gourmands. Making reservations for lunch and dinner in most restaurants is a good idea, especially on weekends.

While we in the U.S. may be fully aware of what the Surgeon General has to say about smoking, that news hasn't really hit home in Spain. Don't complain about cigarette smoke in bars; you'll either be laughed at or thrown out—and forget about looking for that "No Smoking" sections in restaurants. There is no such thing in Spain.

Breakfast

Breakfast in Spain is a real thrill for chocoholics—typically, you'll be eating *churros con chocolate* (*chew-ros cahn sho-co-laht*; deep-fried squiggles of dough served hot and sprinkled with sugar). The best way to eat them is to dunk them into a cup of rich, hot chocolate. All bars and cafés serve coffee, tea, and rolls. You may want to try the Spanish *tortilla* (potato and onion omelette) found all over Spain.

A business breakfast should be scheduled late (no earlier than 8:30 A.M.)—remember, those Spaniards are getting up late and staying up late.

Lunch Is Served

Don't attempt to schedule a meeting between the hours of 1:30 P.M. and 4:30 P.M. Traditionally, this is the lunch break when Spaniards chow down on a large midday meal, and then go crawl in the sack to rest up for the evening. Today, many of these southern Europeans are working longer hours and may not follow these relaxed practices. If your business contact is of this latter persuasion, a luncheon may be acceptable. Otherwise, to be on the safe side, plan dinner meetings and let your host decide whether or not to arrange a business lunch.

If you do decide on a business lunch, it is okay to talk over business, but if that's where you're heading, get set for a siege—a Spanish business lunch may last up to three hours. In general, you'll start out with informal conversation during the first course, and usually you won't start discussing business until the main course comes or dessert is served. If your host doesn't bring up business, wait until coffee is served before you bring it up.

Tapas Time

Roughly similar to the British idea of "high tea," many Spaniards trot out for a drink and a plate of hors d'oeuvres called "tapas." (After all, they'll probably still be going strong until the wee hours, so they need to tide themselves over!) Don't expect to plop comfortably down for a few hours of tapas-eating, however; Spaniards typically cruise from bar to bar, grabbing a potato omelette in one place, octopus in the next. Typically, sherry is a nice accompaniment to the tapas.

Say What?

Tapas (hors d'oeuvres) are usually served at bars called *tabernas, bars, mesones,* or *cafes*.

Dinner Is Served

Business dinners are appropriate only when a friendship exists between colleagues. In any case, never schedule a business diner before 9 P.M. (you have to give those tapas time to digest)!

Taste the Bubbly

Spaniards do enjoy a taste of the bubbly; bars are usually open all day and close late at night, well past midnight. In summer, they may stay open until past 3 A.M. or 4 A.M. In big cities such as Madrid and Barcelona, bars and discos often stay open until dawn (even in winter).

Mind Your Manners

In Spain, if you place your knife and fork side by side on the plate, you've signaled you're finished. Cross the utensils on opposite sides of the plate and you're asking for seconds. Keep your hands on top of the table, and feel free to let your compliments flow (to the host and to the waiters).

Global Guide

Remember that tips are not obligatory—any reasonable amount is appreciated. You won't get thrown out if you don't tip.

If you've been invited out by others, you should return the honor at a later date—but don't say anything about "repaying their hospitality."

Tips on Tips

You'll find that most establishments in Spain include a surcharge for service—but you'll still see most folks leaving a tip anyway, which can vary from 5 percent to 7 percent of the total bill. Tipping is especially common in bars and restaurants, but now also often includes hotel porters, theater ushers, and taxi drivers. Round up the bill in restaurants. Taxi drivers expect a tip of 10 percent of the fare.

The Least You Need to Know

➤ Meetings will probably start late and take forever.

➤ Spaniards get up late, and eat and drink long into the night.

➤ Dress more formally in Spain than you would for most European countries.

➤ In general, expect to be treated with respect, integrity, and conservatism.

➤ Choose a warm, personal style but maintain your dignity.

➤ Give a firm handshake and direct eye contact.

Chapter 13

Switzerland

In This Chapter

➤ Learn about the importance of punctuality, neatness, and hard work

➤ Discover the three primary cultures of Switzerland and how they differ

➤ Find out what to talk about so you don't offend

➤ Understand the cultural beliefs of decency, fairness, patriotism, and the importance of family

➤ Learn the ways the Swiss greet and depart

With dizzying speed, the language changes from Italian to German to French and back again depending on where you are in this small country; don't lose sight of your etiquette while you struggle to keep track.

Switzerland looks so much like a post card that it can be almost unbelievable: spectacular Alpine scenery, cozy half-timbered chalets, sparkling ski runs, geranium-stuffed flower boxes, neat cities beside still lakes, elegant grand hotels, and punctual trains. There are few places as clean, safe, and orderly as Switzerland. But to first-time visitors, the Swiss passion for order and cleanliness can be a bit unnerving.

Where It's At

Slightly less than twice the size of New Jersey, its terrain is mostly mountains (with the Alps in the south and the Jura in the northwest), with a central plateau of rolling hills, plains, and large lakes. This landlocked country is at the crossroads of northern and southern Europe. Together with southeastern France and northern Italy, Switzerland contains the highest mountains in Europe.

Still, despite the fact that Switzerland may be sitting right up there in the Alps, it's not always as cold as you may think. In fact, spring, summer, and autumn are all quite comfortable. (Of course, summer brings its own plague—hordes of tourists, but that's another story.) Typically, temperatures vary with altitude, but in general, the winters are cold, cloudy, rainy, and snowy while summers are cool to warm, with cloudy, humid weather and occasional showers.

Global Guide

The best time to visit Switzerland may be in May, unless skiing is part of your itinerary (many resort hotels close down for the month).

The Big Emmenthaler

The president of the Swiss Confederation is both the chief of state and head of government, and is in charge of guiding the 28 sovereign cantons (states). Historically neutral, Switzerland has kept to herself and didn't take part in either World War. In fact, the country hasn't taken up arms since Napoleon came galloping over its borders in 1815.

Instead, Switzerland was one of the world's earliest democracies, formed in 1291 when three cantons joined together to protect their borders. Today, the cantons have far more individual power than the states of the United States have when it comes to governing themselves; in Switzerland, the cantons have broad, autonomous powers.

Home to four different cultures within the boundaries of one tiny country, Switzerland somehow makes it all work. It's one of the most politically stable countries in Europe. The country's strength lies in its wealth, its generally conservative nature and, perhaps most importantly, the citizens' common belief in a policy of armed neutrality. (Nevertheless, that position of neutrality, as well as the country's saintly image, have been damaged with revelations about Swiss bankers' possible dealings with the Nazis during World War II.)

In any case, its prosperous and stable modern economy is a bit perplexing because the country has no raw materials, no natural resources, and little fertile land. What it has is an efficient army of Swiss workers with a tradition of responsibility and an incredibly strong work ethic.

Even sturdy Switzerland—as much of the world—has been experiencing some recent economic difficulties, however. Weak domestic consumer demand is partly at fault, together with stagnating disposable income and a reluctance to reduce saving rates in the face of a shaky employment outlook. Still, experts expect the economy to continue to improve into the new millennium.

Four Languages Here

Switzerland encompasses four cultures: French (Geneva and the surrounding western area), Italian (Lugano and the surrounding southern area), Swiss-German (Zurich and the surrounding eastern area) and Romansh (St. Moritz and the surrounding southeastern region). In general, the French and Italian areas are more lively and cosmo-politan, while the German area is more conservative and sedate. The Romansh area is the least known and developed, but the Swiss take pains to retain this minority language and culture.

With all these cultures, it's not surprising that Switzerland has four official languages as well: Swiss-German (Schwyzerdutsch), French, Italian, and Romansch. The language you hear depends on which of the 26 Swiss states you're in. Still, you can make generalities: Most Swiss (74 percent) are Swiss-German and speak that language (mostly in central and northeastern Switzerland). French is spoken by about 20 percent of the people (mostly in the west), followed by Italian in the south (4 percent). A peasant dialect of Romansch is spoken by a few (less than 1 percent) in the southeast.

Almost all Swiss speak at least two of these languages, and many are also fluent in English.

If you don't speak any of these four languages (and many Americans don't), you need not hire translators for business, as most transcontinental business in Switzerland will be conducted in English anyway.

Faux Pas

Don't give a tip to your interpreter. Instead, come up with a personalized gift.

Still, it's a nice gesture to find out in advance what language your host speaks so you can learn a few words. This show of good will as you begin negotiations will get you off to a good start.

Religion

In this country where its citizens speak four different languages and come from four different cultures, their cohesion as a Swiss culture come from their shared beliefs in decency, fairness, patriotism, and the importance of family. Believing that their ideals are important, they exert considerable peer pressure to make sure everyone conforms to the Swiss behavior patterns—which is surely the best way.

Despite their strong moral stance, the Swiss believe that a person's individual religious beliefs are very private. This may have something to do with the fact that in the 15th century, the Protestant Reformation was born right in the midst of their country, and the resulting years of bitter warfare between Catholics and Protestants devastated Switzerland.

Even today, the lingering cultural memory of that long-ago enmity prompts the Swiss to keep silent on the subject of other people's religious beliefs. They won't poke their nose into your practices, and they expect you to keep yours out of theirs.

Their four cultures today share a wide variety of religious beliefs, but most Swiss (46 percent) are Roman Catholic; Protestants make up another 40 percent, and most of the world's religions make up the rest.

Take a Holiday

Most people take their vacations in July and August, so if you are scheduling a business trip you may want to avoid late summer—no one will be in the office. The following are the holidays:

Jan. 1: New Year's Day.

Jan. 2: Baerzelistag Day (in some cantons).

Spring: Easter holidays.

Varies: Whit Monday.

May 1: Labor Day (in some cantons).

May: Corpus Christi (in Roman Catholic cantons).

June 5: Ascension (or Pentecostal Monday).

June 18: Fete-Dieu (in some cantons).

Aug. 1: Swiss National Day.

Aug. 15: Assumption Day (in some cantons).

Nov. 1: Toussaint (in some cantons).

Dec. 6: St. Nicholas' Day (in some cantons).

Dec. 25: Christmas Day.

Dec. 26: St. Stephen's Day/Boxing Day.

On Time—No Excuses!

When it comes to punctuality, Switzerland pretty much wrote the book. Play by the rules when you come here: You're expected to be punctual, and punctual you must be. This goes not just for personal punctuality—everything is expected to be on time here, including public transportation, the newspaper, and any other sort of deadline.

If being late is unavoidable when meeting with a Swiss contact, don't scurry into your meeting offering profuse apologies. Instead, call beforehand and notify your host of your predicament. This should take the edge off of your late arrival where an air of understanding will most likely prevail.

We're Open!

Stores are open from Monday through Friday from 9 A.M. to 6:30 P.M. Many close for lunch, although large department stores remain open. Late-night shopping is on Thursday, when stores are open to 9 P.M.; Saturday hours are from 8 A.M. to 4 P.M., with no closing for lunch. All stores are closed on Sunday. At the Hauptbahnhof (main railway station), a grocery store operates Monday through Friday from 7 A.M. to 8 P.M. (open later on Thursday to 9 P.M.) and is open Saturday and Sunday from 8 A.M. to 8 P.M.

Tip of the Hat

Switzerland has season-related hours; in the hotter months, you'll find stores open from 9 A.M. to 6:30 P.M. Many small businesses (such as bakers and butchers) open even earlier—by 7:30 A.M.

In the colder months (the end of winter and beginning of spring), shops usually close earlier, but it depends in part on the weather and the number of tourists.

It should be no surprise that banks, in this finance-friendly country, open early and stay open late (at least, for banks)—from 8:30 A.M. until 4:30 P.M. Monday through Friday.

Switzerland is six hours ahead of Eastern Standard Time, which means that if it's noon in New York City, it's 6 P.M. in Switzerland.

Greetings

In a country so intent on universal politeness, it is easily understood that the ritual of comings and goings is likewise conservative and formal. Greet the Swiss with a firm handshake and a hardy hello, and be sure to maintain eye contact.

As you're shaking hands, address your Swiss contact by title, followed by his or her last name. At the meeting's end, again offer a handshake. (Even children are expected to come up with this formal greeting.)

In some parts of Switzerland (especially among the French), if you've met before, you can expect a gentle brushing cheek to cheek three times (also known as the "air kiss") instead of a handshake. However, if you've just been introduced, you'll likely be offered a handshake instead (especially if you're an American) and not an air kiss. In German areas, women may embrace upon meeting, but men don't. Embracing is more common among the French and Italian Swiss.

Global Guide

If you want to meet someone, wait to be introduced by a third person, and always rise for the occasion.

By now, it should come as no surprise that in Switzerland, everyone is either addressed as "Mr.," "Mrs.," or "Miss." Don't use first names with anybody (except children).

Swiss Miss

As a general rule, the Swiss passion for tolerance means that most people get a fair shake here when it comes to equality. However, it's also true that there are still some role differences between men and women, and you can still find sexual discrimination toward women. Equal rights for men are guaranteed by law.

Card Sharps

Before you leave home, be sure you've got plenty of business cards, since you'll need at least two for every appointment. (You present one to the secretary who files it away, and then you present the second to the person you really came to see.)

At the start of any meeting during a visit to Switzerland, offer your business card as you receive one from each person in attendance.

Give and Take

Be well-prepared before meeting with a Swiss counterpart. Chances are you will be highly scrutinized, and to be well received, you will have had to do your homework—and then some.

When you sit down to negotiations, be prepared with small entertaining small talk if you're dealing with Swiss-French or -Italians—but expect to get right down to business if you've got Swiss-Germans sitting across the table.

If you want to know how the Swiss conduct business, think of the precision of a Swiss watch—and you'll instantly understand what makes this country tick. In Switzerland, research is thorough, presentations are exact, and punctuality is paramount. If you can adopt the same work ethics as your colleagues in Switzerland, then you should be able to build solid business relationships.

On the other hand, there's a downside to all this precision and exactitude: In a country where everything runs like clockwork, they don't have much practice in dealing with breakdowns. This means that when a problem occurs, the Swiss aren't always so good at improvising and being flexible. They just don't have much practice at it.

Faux Pas

You may be itching to share that latest Clinton joke, but your Swiss colleagues won't be amused. To them, business is serious and they won't appreciate your humor on the job. (This is especially true amongst the Swiss-Germans.)

Age Before Beauty

As in many Asian countries, the Swiss respect age and seniority. It's not a good idea to send a young gen-X'er to do your negotiating—send one of the more senior executives to represent your company.

If your company was established so long ago it bought ad space in Poor Richard's Almanac, that will impress the Swiss—put the date of establishment right there on your stationery and business cards. The longer your business has been in operation, the better, as far as the Swiss are concerned.

Molasses in January

The speed of negotiations in Switzerland can be agonizingly slow, no matter how much of a whiz you are at high-pressure tactics. The Swiss take a long time to form personal relationships, and they take an even longer time to make business decisions.

Sit Up Straight

You may be at your most creative lolling in your chair with your feet on your desk blotter, but this lax attitude won't go over well in Switzerland. Avoid bad posture when both sitting and standing, and keep your body language formal.

You'll do fine in Switzerland if you remember that the country values modesty and restraint. This means:

➤ Don't chew gum.

➤ Don't litter.

➤ Don't talk with your hands in your pockets.

➤ Don't sit with one ankle propped on your knee.

➤ Don't slap anybody's back.

On the street, Swiss-German men tip their hats when passing people they know on the street; everywhere in Switzerland, it's common to address each stranger in passing with a "hello" or a nod and a smile. When you pop into a Swiss shop, expect a polite "hello" and "goodbye"—and offer one as well.

If you're caught doing something wrong (let's say you've suddenly got an urge to spit on the street), don't be surprised if a resident (especially a Swiss-German) takes you to task in public for your transgression.

Safe Talk

Don't talk about World War II. Switzerland was neutral, but most Swiss endured their own share of tragedies with friends or families in other countries who had to fight.

Faux Pas

Don't pick flowers that seem to be growing wild (many were hand planted by armies of gardeners) and don't pick fruit you find behind fences.

Faux Pas

Even if it seems called for, try not to swear in public. The Swiss tend to adhere to a fairly strict moral code and they don't appreciate profanity.

If you're looking for a safe topic of conversation, try discussing travel, politics, work, good things about Switzerland, and sports. Topics to avoid discussing in Switzerland:

➤ The draft.

➤ The military.

➤ Dieting (especially when sitting at the table gorging on raclette, a type of Swiss cheese fondue).

➤ Personal questions or observations.

Think Elegant

The Swiss are naturally elegant, albeit conservative, dressers. Avoid flamboyant colors and go for a classic look—you'll blend in. (A classic expensive look is even better.) Remember that Switzerland has the highest standard of living in Europe; they can afford to look terrific.

Global Guide

Maintain a clean, neat appearance at all times.

This doesn't mean that you should go for the ostentatious look, however. Just because you own a tiara doesn't mean you need to wear it to the bank.

Go for simple, expensively elegant—but not overblown or flamboyant.

First-class restaurants, hotel dining rooms, and important social occasions may warrant jackets and ties. Black tie is usually specified when required.

Take a sweater year round (a light raincoat and folding umbrella might come in handy, too).

Gifting

Gift-giving habits are different in different parts of Switzerland. In general, the Swiss appreciate quality and craftsmanship, as long as it doesn't appear that you're trying to bribe them. Typically, a small, tasteful remembrance is valued more highly than a huge, gaudy, or ostentatious present. Good choices would include a craft or art from your hometown or state. When you give a gift, it's usually opened in front of you right away.

That's Entertainment

Try to attend one of the *hornusen* (horn-oozen; a game in which a disc is swatted about) if you're visiting in the summer. If you're touring in the spring, you may find it interesting to attend the open-air parliament in the canton of Glarus, even if you don't speak the language.

Most major towns and resorts have nightclubs or discotheques with music and dancing, sometimes serving food. There are also cinemas and theatres, and some bars and restaurants have local folk entertainment. However, if you're a night owl, don't expect nightlife to continue here until the small hours: Switzerland is primarily an outdoors destination.

In a Swiss Home ...

Take along a small present of a plant, flowers, or chocolates when invited to dinner. Alternatively, you could give unwrapped flowers to the hostess when invited for a meal. Flowers to avoid include

➤ Red roses (too personal).

➤ Chrysanthemums (funeral flowers).

➤ White asters (funeral flowers).

Don't arrive late, and be careful not to overstay your welcome. If you're offered a glass of wine, wait until your host has made a toast before drinking. The traditional drinking toast is *"Prosit!"* (*Prost*).

Raclette to Nuts

Sometimes it may seem as if Switzerland's primary raison d'etre is to eat out; there are so many restaurants here. Indeed, eating in a restaurant is a very popular way to conduct business. Business lunches and dinners are very popular (but don't hold your breath for a business breakfast; it's not done in Switzerland).

The great specialty is fondue, the delicious concoction of Gruyère and Emmenthal cheese, melted and mixed with white wine, flour, Kirsch, and a little garlic. Regional specialties include *viande seche* (*vee-ahnd sesch*; dried beef or pork) from Valais and the Grisons; *papet vaudoir* (*pah-pet voh-dwahr*) is a delicious leek and potato dish. Geneva's great speciality is *pieds de porc* (*pee-ay deh pork*; pigs feet). Pork sausages or salami come prepared in a variety of local recipes.

Try *rosti* (*roasty*; shredded fried potatoes) and *fondue Bourguignonne* (*fahn-do boar-gie-nee-un*; cubed meat with various sauces). *Leckerli* (*leck-er-lee*) are Basel specialities (spiced honey cakes topped with icing sugar); in Bern, they are decorated with a white sugar bear. Although there are many self-service snack bars, table service is normal.

Lunch and Dinner

Business lunches are popular, but if you're hoping for a quiet fondue in some little chalet, forget it. Many business people do their business lunches in the company cafeteria. It may not be very elegant, but it gets the job done.

If you're taking a Swiss client out to dinner to discuss business, aim for a very fine, elegant restaurant.

When dining in Switzerland, the rule of thumb is that if you can stab your fork through it, it needs just a fork to cut. Many Swiss consider cutting food with a knife to be an insult to the cook—as if it were an indication that the dish is not tender or that it has been badly prepared.

Odds are that your host will probably notice if you start sawing away with your knife. To the Swiss, using your knife this way is rather vulgar. (You are allowed to use a knife with steak and other meats.) Salad, however, does not come under the "a knife is okay to use" heading.

Tip of the Hat

It's customary and polite to keep your hands on the dining table in Switzerland.

Expect a 15 percent tip to be included on most hotel, café, restaurant, and bar bills (it's the law). Tip extra only for extraordinary service.

Down the Hatch!

A great variety of Swiss wines and lagers are available throughout the country. There are also spirits made from fruit, the most popular being Kirsch, Marc, and Williams. So drink up and enjoy!

Toasting is popular in Switzerland—and, surprise surprise, there's a formal, preordained way to do it. Your host will propose the toast—when he does, lock eyes and respond with an all-purpose comment such as, "To our health." (Practice saying this in your host's language.) Next, touch glasses with everyone at the table within clinking distance. Only then do you get to drink.

The Least You Need to Know

➤ The Swiss value punctuality, fairness, and hard work.

➤ Be formal and conservative in actions and dress and you'll do fine in Switzerland.

➤ Although Switzerland was neutral during the wars, war is a sensitive topic that the Swiss prefer not to discuss.

➤ Allow time for the Swiss to make business decisions.

➤ The Swiss respect age and seniority.

➤ If you do something incorrect, don't be surprised if a Swiss national takes you to task in public.

Chapter 14

United Kingdom

In This Chapter

➤ Understanding the U.K. way of life: private and traditional

➤ Remembering regional differences

➤ Learning when to toast and when to sit silent

➤ Knowing when to curtsy

➤ Figuring out the aristocracy

Most Americans feel at home in the U.K., but there are still many ways to embarrass yourself if you don't pay attention and do your homework before you leave.

In general, you're safest if you dress conservatively, speak slowly and quietly, rein in your more flamboyant gestures, listen politely, and don't poke fun at U.K. politics and their Royals. Stay away from probing, personal, or demanding questions and curtail any temptation to boast, brag, or talk excessively about yourself.

Stuff You Should Have Learned In School

By this time in your life, most of us should have learned the basics about the United Kingdom, such as its government, geography, and religion. If you've forgotten all that (or you never learned it in the first place)—read on!

Remember that the *United Kingdom* consists of four distinct regions: England, Scotland, Northern Ireland, and Wales. Each of the four parts of the U.K. has a separate history, culture, religion, and ancestral language. "Britain" or "Great Britain" refers to the island that contains England, Scotland, and Wales.

Faux Pas

The quickest way to offend the Scots, Welsh, and Irish is to lump them together with their English neighbors.

Northern Ireland is across the Irish Sea, on the northern part of the island of Eire. The Republic of Ireland (that's the bigger, southern chunk of the Irish island) is a separate country and not part of the U.K. at all.

You'll be surprised how easy it is to make a foreign *faux pas* if you don't know the United Kingdom from Great Britain. While you may notice that your English hosts call everyone from the U.K. "Brits," don't you make this mistake—the Welsh and Scots will take offense. Even worse: calling a native of Northern Ireland (which is part of the United Kingdom) a "Brit." It's considered both incorrect and insulting.

Is the Queen in Charge?

Despite what the Labour Party may wish, the country is still officially governed by a constitutional monarchy, which means that the monarch is chief of state, while the prime minister is head of the government. The Queen has lots of social clout, but the pound sterling stops at the door of the Prime Minister. The real power is wielded via the cabinet, selected from Parliament by the prime minister.

The Parliament includes the House of Commons and the House of Lords, with the real power resting with the elected members of the Commons. The House of Lords is an hereditary post only. The prime minister is the leader of the majority party in the House of Commons.

The country is guided by an unwritten constitution, and includes some enacted laws and other "common laws." Unlike the United States, the English judicial system can't rule on the constitutionality of laws.

Real English

We all know that English is the first language of the U.K.—although it sounds so much better when they speak it! Be aware that Welsh and Gaelic are also spoken in the United Kingdom, especially in the rural parts of the country. Keep in mind, however, that while we all speak English (of course, those in the U.K. think we speak "American"), there are some words in the U.K. that have very different meanings.

For example, if you table a discussion in the U.S., you don't want to talk about it—but "tabling" something in the U.K. means to bring it up (to "put it on the table").

Likewise, if you're on the first floor in the United States, you're on the second floor in the U.K., and if you want to buy some kerosene in England, you'll have to ask for "paraffin." The list goes on and on …

Religion

When we think of religion in the U.K., Americans tend to think of the Anglican Church (also known as the "Church of England" or the Episcopal church). There's also a Church of Scotland (the Presbyterian church). Wales and Northern Ireland have no established state "church."

Most people in the UK are Christian: 21 percent Catholic, 20 percent Anglican, and 14 percent Presbyterian. The remainder of the Christians make up a variety of smaller denominations. Of non-Christians, most in the U.K. are Muslims (11 percent), followed by Sikhs (4 percent) and Hindus (2 percent).

Religion is considered to be a very private subject here, so keep that in mind when you're casting about for cocktail party patter. Don't ask.

Vacations

Americans share two national holidays with our cousins in the U.K.—New Year's Day and Christmas. There are lots of other holidays you'll need to be aware of, however. Americans seem far more eager for an excuse for a three-day weekend, because in the U.K., there are only seven national holidays. Besides the two mentioned above, be prepared to celebrate:

> **May 6:** May Day.
>
> **May 27:** Spring Holiday.
>
> **June 11:** The Queen's Birthday.
>
> **Aug. 26:** Summer Bank Holiday.
>
> **Dec. 26:** Boxing Day.

Global Guide

This list of national U.K. holidays is a good place to start, but check with your local hosts for details on regional special holidays (especially during July, August, and September).

Right on Schedule

Life in the U.K. tootles along fairly much like things on this side of the Atlantic: The work week stretches from 9 A.M. to 5 P.M. Monday through Friday, with the exception of government offices. There, workers close up shop for a pork pie break from 1 P.M. to 2 P.M., but they compensate (well, a little bit) by keeping their doors open until 5:30 P.M. Most executives are out the door every day by 5:30 P.M.

Pub hours usually run from 11 A.M. through 11 P.M., but don't be surprised if pubs out in the country close down between 3 P.M. to 5:30 P.M. for a nap break.

If you want to make points in the U.K., you'll show up on time for all your appointments and social events. Punctuality is a virtue here. To make sure you don't make a mistake, keep in mind that the U.K. observes Greenwich Mean Time—five hours head of our Eastern Standard Time. If it's 10 A.M. in New York, it's 3 P.M. in London.

Be warned, however: Especially if you're in one of the big cities, traffic can be a royal pain. Be sure to allow plenty of time to reach your appointments so that you aren't late.

It's not a good idea to show up the day you want to have a business meeting and try to make the appointment. Instead, schedule the meeting a few days earlier and then remember to confirm your appointment once you arrive in the country.

The Daily Grind

Life in the U.K. is bound by rules and laws. This gives an enormous sense of stability to the country and her people, but it can be frustrating sometimes to visitors. When it comes to daily life or business life, think "private and traditional."

As part of this, deadlines and results are extremely important. Missing a deadline here is not something taken lightly, so try not to let things slide. At the same time, you won't get a split-second decision, so don't waste time trying. Decisions are to be made with all due deliberation.

The term "stiff upper lip" wasn't invented for the fun of it; the U.K. is often a formal, restrained, and understated place where physical touching in public is not encouraged.

Ta, Ta!

If you want to meet a businessperson in the U.K., it's best to arrange an introduction via a third party. However, once that initial contact has been made, you can't keep going back to the original introducer and ask him or her to intervene again on your behalf. If you didn't cut the mustard the first time, you're out of luck.

Don't know anybody in the business? Then you should write directly to the company, not to a specific person in the company you've never met. Once you arrive in person, you can expect the secretary to introduce you to the executive. If that doesn't happen, introduce yourself.

A firm handshake is standard in the U.K. business world. When you're signing a business deal, a light, firm handshake is fine—no need to go overboard. Remember that "stiff upper lip" the Brits are famous for. Restrain yourself. On the other hand, if you're gathering on a social occasion, a handshake may not be appropriate. If in doubt, pay attention to what everyone else is doing, and follow along.

When you're introduced to someone, you should ask "How do you do?" (It's rhetorical—no need to go into your latest prostate operation!) Avoid saying something too casual such as, "Nice to meet you."

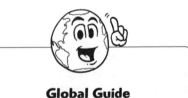

Global Guide

Remember that people who live in the United Kingdom, despite the fact that they are a part of the European Union, do not consider themselves European.

Look, Don't Touch

Look, but don't touch—at least in public. This prohibition doesn't just mean you need to avoid wild embraces and loud smacking kisses—even a backslap or throwing your arm around your host may be considered excessive. "Up close and personal" doesn't cut it in the U.K. If you're having a conversation—business or social—be sure to keep your distance.

Gestures

There are lots of dos and don'ts when it comes to gestures in the U.K., which isn't surprising considering the restraint with which you are expected to handle yourself. No matter how much you feel like your hosts are "just like you," don't assume that a gesture that is okay in the United States will not offend anyone in the U.K. Follow these guidelines:

➤ Don't talk with your hands in your pockets.

➤ Don't point with your fingers. If you must indicate something, use your head—literally.

➤ Want to give the "V for Victory" sign? Go ahead—but be sure to make the gesture with your palm facing outward. The gesture is considered obscene in the U.K. if you give the sign with the palm in.

➤ Don't gesture wildly at all. The fewer hand gestures you use, the better.

Global Guide

If you tap your nose, you're indicating to your hosts that you're about to reveal a confidence or secret. If that's not what you intend, keep your hands away from your face.

To Bow or Not to Bow ...

No matter what you may read in the tabloids about the Royal Family, it's not okay to insult the Queen or any of her brood in front of your U.K. hosts. Natives may enjoy a joke at her expense, but—while there may be plenty of opportunity—don't join in. You should always show respect to the Royals, including standing for "God Save the Queen."

This does not mean that you need to carry this respect as far as bowing or curtsying to members of the Royal Family if you're an American citizen, however. It's a nice touch if you want to fall in line and blend in with your hosts, but as an American, you are not required to perform this act of obeisance.

On the other hand, whether you come from Kansas or the Cotswolds, there are some little niceties you will be expected to observe. To wit: You do not touch or speak to a member of the Royal Family first. (President Carter got in trouble for this when he impulsively bussed the Queen Mother. She was, it was later reported, appalled.) And if you're wondering what to call a member of the Royal Family, check out Chapter Two.

Global Guide

If you want to break the ice, don't ask, "What do you do?" This is considered too personal of a question. Don't even venture a "What part of the country do you come from?"

Gender Gap

When compared to the world outside the U.K., women have a great deal of equality in pay and power. On the other hand, remember that those in the U.K. still respect the traditions of men holding open doors for women, rising when women enter the room, and giving up their seats to a woman on crowded public transportation.

When it comes to day-to-day etiquette, remember that women in the U.K. do not necessarily shake hands. If you're not sure whether or not to shake a woman's hand in the U.K., wait to see if she extends a hand to shake. If she does, fine. If she doesn't, don't lean out and grab her hand. Keep your distance.

Saville Row

The way you dress when you travel to another country, especially if you're traveling on business, is very important. The U.K. business world is not the place for those Hawaiian shirts or that dress made entirely out of beer tabs. While London may have been the home of Mary Quant and white lipstick, in the business world, conservative dress for men and women is still very important.

Faux Pas

If you must have pockets, keep them empty. Don't stick a bunch of pens and protractors in there, and nix the pocket protector while you're at it, even if you are an engineer.

This means:

➤ No loafers.

➤ No shirts with pockets.

➤ Wear top quality clothes.

Do keep in mind the unpredictable weather in the U.K., however; it's often cold and wet, which is why tweed is so popular here. Tweed skirts, suit jackets, and coats are warm and extremely water-repellant.

Say What?

Public schools: In Britain, these schools are what we in the U.S. would call a "private school" (and vice versa).

If you don't want to get all tied up in an embarrassing social situation, avoid striped ties when traveling to England. Graduates of certain British public schools sometimes wear very distinctive striped ties, known as "old school ties." These should be worn only by people who actually attended these schools. You'll risk looking as if you're trying to mimic the British regimental or school ties, which aren't worn by anyone in the U.K. unless he or she actually served in that regiment or attended that school. The easiest way to avoid this is not to wear stripes (or buy your ties in the U.K.).

Talk Is Cheap

When talking with folks in the U.K., you may notice that they seem to do a lot of apologizing. This is especially fascinating to Americans because it usually occurs after minor transgressions, or for things over which they have no control. This doesn't mean that citizens of the U.K. are wimps or that they are especially insecure; they're just polite. Americans may find it takes some getting used to.

Most people you'll meet in the U.K. tend to be unemotional in public, although it's also true that a uniquely British sense of humor—often self-deprecating—is quite common. Most people in the U.K. love a good joke and will poke fun at almost anything.

Sealed with a Kiss

When it comes to negotiations in the U.K., it's "just the facts, ma'am." The only truth, as far as someone from the U.K. is concerned, is an objective fact. *Feelings* don't enter into the discussion. Because facts can be so ... well, factual ... convincing U.K. natives to change their minds is not going to be an easy row to hoe. Once they make up their mind, they're not easily moved from their position. Laws and rules count here, so keep that in mind when negotiating.

If you're prone to wild generalizations and blustering postures, rein yourself in. Those in the U.K. invented the art of understatement. This also means that if you're facing a dangerous or very serious situation, don't expect your U.K. counterparts to point it out—traditionally, they'll underplay the situation. Anyone who doubts that should listen to someone from the U.K. refer to the continual often-savage strife between Northern Ireland and England as "The Troubles."

Keep these suggestions in mind when you need to negotiate with someone from the U.K.:

➤ Avoid a "hard sell."

➤ As an American, you may be stereotyped as "condescending." Watch your behavior and avoid anything that could be misconstrued as arrogance.

➤ Executives in the U.K. are known for their directness. If they don't like your suggestion, they'll tell you so.

➤ Don't rush your hosts for a decision.

Most simple business agreements are settled by a firm handshake. Don't worry that your host will try to wiggle out of a verbal "ok" down the road; in the U.K., verbal agreements are binding. The agreement is often followed by a written confirmation, but only major agreements require legal procedures.

In the U.S., there may be an attorney behind every bush, but in the U.K. you need to be discreet when suggesting the advisability of contacting an attorney. (If you do decide to look for a lawyer, remember they are called "solicitors" here.)

Faux Pas

While flowers make a nice hostess gift, presenting your hostess with white lilies as a gift is considered bad form, as white lilies signify death.

Global Guide

If you smoke, always offer cigarettes to others first before lighting up.

To Give or Not To Give ...

Beware of Americans bringing gifts: If you're in the UK on business, it's better to offer to treat your hosts to dinner and a show. On the other hand, if you're invited to visit someone's home, it's okay to bring a "hostess gift." You could choose chocolates, liquor or champagne, or flowers. The next day, it's good form to write a brief, handwritten thank-you note. Have it delivered by messenger instead of by mail for extra points.

Let Me Entertain You ...

One of the favorite ways of entertaining in the U.K. is to take visitors to see a play. Keep in mind that when you go, you'll be charged for your program. Make sure you have change ready for the usher. If you're a guest, don't wait for your hosts to end the evening. It's up to you get that ball rolling and head for the door.

If you go to a pub, either as a guest or a host, remember that the British as a rule love their beer and lager. Expect to stand your share of the rounds.

Oxtail Soup to Nuts

Dining out in the U.K. is nothing if not complicated. While we in the United States think nothing of suggesting a meal to someone we may know only slightly, it's not good form in the U.K. to invite a business associate to dine unless you know the person fairly well.

When you do decide to entertain your U.K. friends, keep in mind that social order is still very important here. While Americans are far less inclined to restrict the guest list according to social status, it's a good idea when in the U.K. to limit your guest list to people of the same background and professional level.

Table Manners

When it comes to manners in the U.K., remember to mind yours because they are extremely important here. Try to remember everything your mother ever said, and watch what your neighbors are doing so you don't make mistakes.

Always keep your hands above the table (as long as you don't lean your elbows there!). No matter how delicious the meal looks on your neighbor's table, resist the impulse to shout, "Hey! What's that guy in the tweed jacket got in his soup bowl?" It's considered impolite to ask about someone else's food. It's also not a good idea to reach across the table and stab a bit of your partner's dinner with your fork so you can taste it. If you simply must sample the bubble and squeak, order your own.

Mealtime

Don't be surprised if your host suggests a business breakfast. They're common in the U.K.. Remember that if the breakfast is scheduled in a hotel, it's likely to be quite a large meal.

Be prepared for luncheon anywhere from noon to 2 P.M. If it's going to be a business lunch, prepare to head to the local pub for a light repast. On the other hand, if you're noshing with the company's top brass, odds are you'll be dining in an exclusive restaurant or executive dining room.

Faux Pas

When you go out with your U.K. friends after hours, bringing up work is considered a no-no (unless your friends mention it first). You'll be considered a bore.

Tea for Two

When you think of eating in the U.K., chances are you think of tea—that wonderful excuse for chowing down on a few high-calorie sweet cakes and tea between lunch and dinner. When your business associates mention tea, however, they probably refer to "afternoon tea." "High tea" is a term that once referred to a working-man's supper, and is usually far more substantial than afternoon tea.

If your hosts suggest a business break for afternoon tea, you can expect a small meal including freshly-brewed tea, fancy little sandwiches, scones, pound cake, fruit tarts, and cookies (called "biscuits"). If you're having afternoon tea at a restaurant or hotel, you'll usually have a choice between an à la carte selection of pastries and sandwiches, or a "full" tea, which comes with a number of these goodies on your plate.

Tea is serious business in the U.K., and it won't arrive at your table packed in little flow-through bags floating in tepid water. Instead, your host will pour your tea from a community pot (filled with piping hot water and loose tea leaves) through a strainer which rests on your cup to collect the loose leaves. (The strainer then goes into a small bowl.) You'll have a choice of milk (never cream), lemon, or sugar. If the tea is too strong, you can dilute it with hot water available from a smaller hot-water pitcher.

The accompaniments for scones and biscuits (butter, jam, and clotted cream) are served in dishes for the entire table; place a bit of each on your plate and return the spoon or knife so others can help themselves.

If you are offered scones, don't slather jelly all over the scone and stuff the thing in your mouth at once. Think restraint! Cut one in half and then spread each bite with butter, jam, and/or clotted cream before popping them in your mouth. Tea

Say What?

"Clotted cream": A type of thickened cream (also known as Devonshire cream) that looks much like whipped cream (except it's not sweetened) that you eat with scones.

sandwiches may be tiny, but don't pop the entire thing in your mouth at once, either (no matter how hungry you are). These small finger sandwiches are eaten one tiny bite at a time.

Dinner Is Served!

Expect to eat dinner anywhere from 7 P.M. to 11 P.M. Don't be disappointed if you aren't invited to the home of your hosts for a business meal; it's not because your hosts find you unappealing. Most business entertaining is conducted away from home.

When dining out in a U.K. restaurant, remember that you don't need to whistle, or stand up and scream "Garçon!" to call a waiter. Simply raise your hand and a server will appear.

Now, what's on the menu? Remember that while many Americans seem to dote on talking about diets and the current health food risks, your U.K. hosts may well not be at all interested in that Mayo Clinic report on the dietary risks of beef. On the other hand, it's not considered bad form to be a vegetarian. (Remember, those in the U.K. are nuts about animals!) Your vegetarian peccadilloes will be respected here.

Toasts

Toasting one's companions is a veddy British thing to do. While you're lifting your glass, however, keep in mind that it's not a good idea to offer a toast in the U.K. to those who are older or more senior than you.

If you want to blend in among your Irish hosts (especially if they have the Gaelic), try this Irish Gaelic toast: *"Slainte"* (*Slahn-sha*; "to your health").

Global Guide

Because of the National Health Insurance rules, it's a good idea to make sure you have health insurance that will cover you while you visit the U.K.

Tip of the Hat

The word *toast* was coined in England, and refers to the tradition of dipping a piece of scorched bread into a mug of beer or wine to improve the taste of the beverage.

The Least You Need to Know

➤ The United Kingdom consists of England, Scotland, Northern Ireland, and Wales, each with its own history, culture, religion, and ancestral language.

➤ Treat the Royal Family with respect, but you aren't required to bow or curtsy on meeting them if you're a U.S. citizen.

➤ If in doubt, act with restraint, dress conservatively, and don't boast or talk loudly.

➤ Facts more than feelings are important in British business.

➤ Don't point or talk with your hands in your pockets.

➤ If you want to meet a business person, arrange a meeting through a third party.

Chapter 15

Greece

In This Chapter

➤ Learn about the two forms of the Greek language

➤ Understand the Greek concept of punctuality

➤ Discover the proper way to dress for business

➤ Uncover the Greek attitude toward those of different social classes

➤ Find out the best times to visit

This friendly country is hospitable to visitors, but it still pays to mind your Alphas and Omegas. You may have lots of romantic illusions about Greece (especially Athens) and its historic treasures—but don't be surprised if you encounter pollution, traffic jams, and noise.

Things are looking up, however. Athens, for example, is spending $2.8 billion (U.S.) to extend and improve the subway system, a project designed to reduce traffic and pollution.

One of the reasons for all this sprucing up is that tourism is the big money-earner in Greece, which is among the poorest European Union (EU) countries as far as per capita income. Economic struggles are the result of a huge public sector, substantial budget and balance-of-payments deficits, and a 10 percent unemployment rate.

Still, economic growth is slowly strengthening, and the government's strict fiscal and monetary policies are responsible for the decline in inflation and the budget deficit. Despite widespread howling from labor unions and farmers, the government is taking further steps to beef up tax collection and cut expenses to prepare Greece for participation in the EU's single currency unit by 2001.

Tip of the Hat

More than 5 million tourists—a number equal to half the country's population—flock to Greece each year to explore the ruins of this ancient civilization.

With the impressive expansion of Greek hotel and tourist facilities in recent years, modern and comfortable accommodations can be found in most areas you're likely to visit. Growing tourist travel makes advance hotel reservations advisable, however, particularly during late spring and summer.

The Land of the Greek Gods

The landscape of Greece is surprisingly varied, ranging from the cool, wetter, mountainous regions of the northwest and the coastal hills of the Peloponnese to the plains of Macedonia and the sun-drenched, rocky islands that lie off the coast in three different seas.

Slightly smaller than Alabama, Greece lies at the southern extremity of the Balkan peninsula in southeastern Europe. It is bordered by the Aegean Sea, the Ionian Sea, and the Mediterranean Sea, between Albania and Turkey. Roughly four-fifths of Greece is mountainous, with most of the land at 1500 meters above sea level. Epiros and Macedonia, in northern Greece, still have extensive forests, but the rest of the country has been seriously denuded by goat grazing, tree felling, and forest fires.

The peninsula of mainland Greece is surrounded by about 1400 islands, of which 169 are inhabited. The islands are divided into six groups:

➤ Cyclades.

➤ Dodecanese.

➤ The islands of the Northeastern Aegean.

➤ Sporades.

➤ Saronic Gulf islands.

➤ Crete and Evia (the two largest islands). These don't belong to any group.

Greece has mild wet winters and hot dry summers. Winter temperatures can be severe in the mountains, and even Athens can get viciously cold. Maximum temperatures on the islands hover around 30 degrees Celsius in summer, but the heat is often tempered by the northerly wind.

The best times to visit are from mid-May to mid-June and from mid-September to the latter part of October (when the temperatures are mild). Between Easter and mid-June, the weather is pleasantly warm in most places, but not too hot. During this time of year, beaches and ancient sites are relatively uncrowded, public transport operates on close to full schedules, and rooms are cheaper and easier to find than in the mid-June to end of August high season. Conditions are once more ideal from the end of August until the end of November as the tourist season winds down.

While the winter months are generally fine for visiting, it's usually too cold to swim or lie on the beach, and most of the fun tourist stuff goes into hibernation from the end of November to the beginning of April.

Unless you really like to bake, stay away from Greece during the latter part of June to the first part of September—it's hot and crowded with tourists.

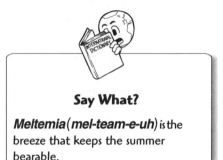

Say What?

Meltemia (*mel-team-e-uh*) is the breeze that keeps the summer bearable.

Who's Running the Parthenon?

Greece has an ancient democracy, but its ancient democracy in Athens was fairly short lived. It was followed by a long series of dictatorships.

Although its recorded history goes back thousands of years, modern-day Greece was shaped largely in the past several centuries. Today, Greece is the sum total of both these long-ago political beginnings, tugged between the history of democracy and a heritage of regional violence and strife.

The long history of domination by other cultures has made Greeks profoundly nationalistic. The Ottoman Empire took control of Greece in the fifteenth century and governed until 1821 when the War of Independence began. A monarchy, installed in 1832 under Prince Otto of Bavaria, was abolished and reinstated twice during the twentieth century. During the 1960s, the king had planned a series of liberalizing moves. Before these could be enacted, a military coup occurred in 1967. The military junta gave Greece some stability at the expense of human rights, but by 1973, student and military opposition forced reforms. However, by late 1973, Greek military police staged their own coup, leading to the establishment of the Greek Republic in 1974, when the nation finally returned to democracy, a concept that was born there two and a half millennia earlier.

Today, Greece has a parliamentary republic. The chief of state is a president; the head of government is a prime minister. The cabinet is appointed by the president on the recommendation of the prime minister.

Say What?

The population of Greece is almost entirely Greek, except for a few Turks, Albanians, and Macedonians. Greek is the official language, and it's spoken by 96 percent of the people. While it's used for all business and official purposes, language isn't a major barrier to foreign business visitors, as most local officials and business people speak English or French.

Greek is written in its own ancient alphabet, which was first developed around 1000 B.C. There are currently two forms of the language—Demotic is the popular form, used in government documents and the media only since 1976. In the past, only the pure form of the language (Katharevoussa) was used. You can still find Katharevoussa in technical publications.

Tip of the Hat

If you want to have the best chance of finding your way around, learn the Greek alphabet. It's not hard; college students pledging fraternities and sororities do it all the time.

Religion

Most of the people are Greek Orthodox (98 percent), and the state supports the church. Greek Orthodox principles are learned in schools. However, a few Greeks are Muslim (1.3 percent), and assorted religions make up the rest (0.7 percent) (Protestants, Jews, Greek and Roman Catholics). Regardless of denomination, freedom of religion is guaranteed.

Holiday Time

Most of the holidays you'll run into in Greece are religious, linked to the Greek Orthodox church.

> **Jan. 1:** New Year's Day.
>
> **Jan. 6:** Epiphany.
>
> **March 25:** Independence Day.
>
> **(spring):** Good Friday.
>
> **(spring):** Holy Saturday.
>
> **(spring):** Easter/Easter Monday.

(varies): Kathara Deftera (49 days prior to Greek Easter Sunday).

(varies): Whit Monday (50 days after Greek Easter Sunday).

May 1: Labor Day/May Day.

Aug. 15: Assumption.

Oct. 28: National Holiday (OXI Day).

Dec. 24: Christmas Eve.

Dec. 25: Christmas.

Dec. 26: Boxing Day.

Dec. 31: New Year's Eve.

There are also several regional holidays celebrated:

Feb. 20: Liberation of Ioannina (observed in Ioannina only).

March 7: Dodecanese Accession Day (observed in Dodecanese Islands only).

Oct. 4: Liberation of Xanthi (observed in Xanthi only).

Oct. 26: St. Demetrios Day (observed in Thessaloniki only).

Nov. 30: St. Andreas Day (observed in Patras only).

What Time Is It?

Greeks aren't known for their punctuality, so don't expect your business contact to show up on time; if you automatically assume there will be a delay of at least half an hour (sometimes even longer), you'll be a lot happier and less stressed.

On the other hand, you should be on time; while some Greeks aren't always prompt, others are. If you do show up on time, you're covered. Bring along some extra paperwork and you won't feel as if you're wasting time.

You don't necessarily need to set up an appointment ahead of time, but it's a polite thing to do if you can. You don't need to set up a limited time for the appointment; keep it open-ended.

Open for Business

The business work week in Greece during the summer (from May to October) runs from Monday through Friday between 8 A.M. and 1:30 P.M. and then from 4 P.M. to 7 P.M. During the winter (October to May), workers get to spend a bit longer lingering over lunch, working from 8 A.M. to 1 P.M. and from 4:30 P.M. to 7:30 P.M. Stores, on the other hand, are generally open from 8 A.M. to 2:30 P.M., when they close for good for the day.

Greece is seven hours ahead of Eastern Standard Time, so if it's noon in New York City, it's 7 P.M. in Greece.

Greece is no longer dirt cheap. Allow at least US $30 per day if you've left your college-student fondness for living in hostels far behind. You will still need to do a fair bit of self-catering on this budget, though. If you really want a comfortable holiday with great rooms and restaurants all the way, you'll need closer to US$45 a day.

Global Guide

Keep in mind that banks will exchange currency in either cash or travelers' checks, but the commission is lower for cash. All post offices have exchange facilities and they're often quicker and charge a lesser commission than banks.

Credit cards are only accepted in larger, more expensive establishments, but most banks have ATMs where you can access your debit account through Maestro and Cirrus networks; you'll also find a number of 24-hour banknote exchange machines.

If you live to bargain, you'll be disappointed to find that haggling isn't as widespread in Greece as it is further east. Prices in most shops are clearly marked and non-negotiable, but your haggling skills can be useful at markets. It's always worth bargaining over the price of hotel rooms, especially if you are intending to stay a few days.

Service with a Smile

You come to Greece for business, for the experience, or the scenery, but not for the great service. Don't expect Greek people to be service-oriented—taxi drivers may shut the door in your face if your destination isn't far enough or if it's not on their way.

Greetings

When meeting someone for the first time, don't automatically assume you should get in a good brisk handshake. While this may happen, don't be surprised to find yourself hugged and even kissed during that first meeting—and at every meeting after that, as well. During that first introduction, do what your Greek colleagues are doing. And try not to flinch.

Age is respected in Greece, so older people are always addressed using titles. First and last names are given in the same order as in the U.S.

Grin and Bear It

If you've just complimented your colleague on a brilliant presentation, don't be surprised if he puffs air at you though his lips. He's not blowing you a kiss—it's the Greek way of warding off the "evil eye" in the wake of a compliment.

At the same time, don't be taken in by a smile, either. A smile isn't just a smile in Greece—locals grin when they're happy or cheerful, but they may also grin when angry or upset.

If you want to nix the CEO's newest idea, don't shake your head "no"—move your head in an upward direction, almost as if you were nodding "yes." On the other hand, if you do want to say "yes," tilt your head to either side.

While you're at it, don't point a finger at anyone while you're in Greece, either. In this culture, pointing means that you're angry or that you're delivering a threat. Obviously, this isn't a good idea when trying to negotiate a deal on unfamiliar turf.

You'll want to avoid these signals:

➤ Don't make the "OK" sign (circle with thumb and finger)—it's obscene.

➤ Don't signal the number "5" by holding up five fingers (it's the Greek symbol for the evil eye).

➤ Don't stick out your thumb at a motorist in Greece, even if you're hitchhiking—the gesture is an obscene insult in Greece.

Pecking Order

As in most countries, there's a class pecking order. There is some bias against certain classes, ethnic groups, and religions, but basically the Greeks do have an inherent trust in others. You'll find big contrasts between the "haves" and the "have-nots" in Greece. Machismo is very strong, and women's equality has a way to go in this conservative country.

Tip of the Hat

The Greek sense of stability is enhanced by a definite social role, strong extended family, and many solid friendships.

Suit Yourself

Greek dress tends to be middle of the road—you won't see patched jeans nor expensive suits, although locals tend to dress up for nightclubs and *bouzoukia*.

In the summer, you'll need lightweight, casual clothing and good walking shoes, with a light sweater or jacket for cool evenings. There's no need for rain gear in summer, but don't forget sunglasses and a sun hat. Be prepared for cooler weather and some rain in spring and fall, and in winter, add a warm coat.

Greece is not the place to trot out that wild orange tie or a shiny see-through blouse. Opt for conservative clothing for business; women should wear suits or dresses in colors that aren't too loud. Casual attire is acceptable everywhere except in the most expensive restaurants in large cities, but you should dress conservatively when visiting churches or monasteries.

Some stricter monasteries and churches will not admit improperly dressed men or women (men wearing shorts and women in pants), although oftentimes long skirts or some sort of draping garb will be provided at the entrance. Revealing too much skin may lead to unwelcome harassment.

Faux Pas

Don't dress to shock if you plan to enter a church. No matter how hot, women are expected to cover their arms, so take along a shawl, sweater, or shirt with long sleeves.

It's Greek to Me

Get ready for some lively conversation during your working venture to Greece. In general, sharing information has been raised to an art form in this European country where few topics are taboo—except, perhaps, for politics. It's best to stay away from conversations regarding Turkey, especially if you plan to say something nice about that country. Emotions have run high over Greece's eastern neighbor ever since Helen was spirited away to Troy. Also, try to listen politely (or gracefully change the subject) if the conversation turns to Macedonia or Albania.

As you chat, keep your eye on your Greek companion's hands as well as his eyes because there will be a lot going on with the hand gestures.

Basic Business 101

Greek business people are astute bargainers. Success in business dealings depends on a combination of patience and quick judgment. Greeks are warm and cordial in their personal relationships. A wealth of good restaurants and places of entertainment makes it easy for a business visitor to reciprocate the courtesies shown.

No matter what happens during negotiations or a business meeting, never to blame a Greek counterpart—even if it's obvious who messed up. Like the Asian concept of "losing face," blaming someone in Greece causes instant shame. They don't get over it easily. The response may range from embarrassment to outright hostility—which isn't going to help your cause.

Beware of Greeks ...

Despite that old axiom, "Beware of Greeks bearing gifts," the Greeks are very generous—so if you ooh and ahh over your colleague's necktie, he just might whip it off and hand it to you.

Business associates don't usually give a gift the first time they meet; when it is time to exchange presents, aim for a moderately priced item. Don't choose a gift that's too cheap or too lavish, and don't opt for something with your company logo all over the front.

If you're invited to the home of a Greek colleague, don't show up empty-handed. Bring something small for the children, and don't neglect your hostess, either; bring along some flowers, a bottle of wine, a box of cookies, or a cake to show your appreciation.

Let Me Entertain You

In Athens, you can find anything from nightclubs with disco, rock, jazz, and blues, Latin, retro, pop, and Greek music to piano bars, tea bars, and gay bars. Bouzouki clubs are where the natives go when they want to really enjoy themselves. (Bouzoukis are guitar-like instruments that are said to bring on *kefi*, or exceptionally good humor.) Generally, entertainment is provided by Greek pop or folk singers.

You may think that you have two left feet, but put your reservations about dancing aside when in Greece. You'll likely be asked to dance while at a social event. Try not to decline; join in and have fun!

The trick for travelers in Greece is to find the balance between environment and history, crowds and quiet. With a bit of planning, you can sniff out beautiful settings to ease your soul while centuries of art and history invigorate your mind.

If you're invited to dine in a Greek home, most likely you will be urged to have seconds and even thirds—don't refuse! It's considered a compliment to the cook if you chow down repeatedly.

Faux Pas

Don't smash plates, buy flowers to throw on stage, or offer a drink of champagne to the singer unless you feel like spending a lot of money—after an evening doing those things, you might receive a bill for more than 485,000 drachmas (as opposed to a more normal 24,000 to 48,500 dr. for more conservative diners).

Easter Soup to Nuts

Eating out in Greece is a national pastime and a leisurely pleasure. Whether dining at a local *taverna* (as traditional to Greeks as the pub is to the English) or an elegant restaurant, Greeks take their time over food.

Remember, too, that food is important here. Don't refuse offers of food or drink from business associates—it's considered an insult. Greeks love to do business over coffee and *ouzo* (the national liquor). Enjoy!

If you go into a Greek restaurant expecting to find food that you've eaten in Greek restaurants at home—think again! The native cuisine is uncomplicated, relying on simple seasonings and fresh meat and vegetables.

In fact, things are so informal that patrons may troop into the restaurant kitchen to peer into the pans if they can't decide what to order. Once

Global Guide

In Greece, the older diners are always served first out of respect.

you've ordered, don't be surprised if everyone shares the food with everyone else at the table.

Breaking Your Fast

You may live for eggs and bacon, but keep in mind that Greece is not the land of hearty American-style breakfasts. If your hotel has a dining room that serves eggs, toast, marmalade, and coffee, go for it—you won't find much better outside. If you choose to travel on the Greek breakfast circuit, you'll choose a coffee and a cheese-pie (tiropita) or spinach pie (spanikopita) from a small shop or bakery.

Lunch Is on the Table

Your stomach might be growling around noon, but in Greece, lunch won't arrive until late afternoon, generally around 2 P.M. When it does come, don't look for a Big Mac. It's common for Greeks to make a lunch simply of *mezedes* (*may-zee-deze*; hors d'oeuvres). Typical appetizer dishes include fried meatballs, squash balls, octopus, shrimp, squid, cheese, olives, stuffed vine leaves, *tzatziki* (*szaht-zeé-key*; garlicky yogurt and cucumbers), eggplant dip, small sausages, and giant beans.

Say What?

An **ouzeri** (**ooze-aír-ee**) is a restaurant serving ouzo (**ooze-oh**), an anise-flavored liqueur, and appetizers. A **mezedopolio** (**meh-zeh-doh-polio**) is a restaurant serving locally produced wine or beer and appetizers (both of these types of restaurants are open only during the day).

Dinner Is Served

Dinner is likewise served late—10 P.M. or 11 P.M. To stave off hunger in between, you'll find locals enjoy snacking on *souvlaki* (garlic-marinated lamb kabobs or tiropitas bought from a street vendor. Greek tavernas serve such specialties as *moussaka* (lamb and eggplant with béchamel sauce), kebabs, *pastitsio* (lamb or goat meat with macaroni and tomatoes), *stifado* (braised beef with onions), and *paithakia* (*pahs-téet-see-oh*; grilled lamb or goat chops).

Tipping

In restaurants, tipping can get confusing. It's customary to leave some extra change on your plate for the waiter and some additional extra change on the table for the busboy. (This assumes that the service charge has already been included. If it hasn't, you'll want to tip 15 percent.)

Generally, menus in restaurants will show prices with the tip included on one side and without the tip on the other. If you're unsure about what's been added on your bill, ask. Don't tip cabdrivers; just round up the fare to the nearest 50 or 100 drachma.

The Least You Need to Know

➤ Dress conservatively for business in Greece.

➤ Friendships and relationships are important here.

➤ Greeks are very generous, and may give you an object that you've openly admired.

➤ The best times to visit are mid-May to mid-June and mid-September to the end of October.

➤ Learn the Greek alphabet and you'll have an easier time getting around.

➤ Don't expect punctuality in Greece.

Chapter 16

Scandinavia

In This Chapter

➤ Learn the differences between the five countries of Scandinavia

➤ Discover the unique languages of Norway, Denmark, Iceland, Sweden, and Finland

➤ Find out what negotiation approach works best in Scandinavia

➤ Understand the importance of punctuality here

➤ Find out the business card rules

The Scandinavian countries of Denmark, Sweden, Norway, and Iceland share a common Norse heritage, including culture, customs, and history. Linked as they are by geography, there are still variations between each country—not to mention a fair dose of sibling rivalry. While these countries aren't as foreign to Americans as other destinations tend to be, there are still plenty of cultural differences you'll need to understand. It may seem as if everyone speaks English here and just loves Americans, but if you don't wish to offend, you'll need to read up on Scandinavian culture.

Be sure to allow for the fact that each country in this part of Europe has a distinct personality and should be recognized as a separate entity from its neighbors. Praise the place you're visiting and don't compare it with other Scandinavian countries; negotiations will go a lot smoother.

Scandinavians tend to be prosperous, orderly and neat, and appreciate balance, understatement, and good design. Like its people, the area's sights are impressive without being imposing.

Stuff You Need to Know

The Scandinavian countries have highly developed, stable democracies (although Sweden, Denmark, and Norway are monarchies) with modern economies. Finland is the least like the other Scandinavian countries; its people are not Nordic and its language is totally unrelated to the other Scandinavian tongues. In the past, Denmark and Norway were both ruled by a single monarchy for several hundred years until Sweden took control. After breaking with Sweden in 1905, Norway became independent. Finland, too, was part of Sweden for 600 years, and then became a Russian Grand Duchy for another hundred years until the Bolshevik Revolution. Denmark ruled Iceland until its independence in 1944. Today, Scandinavia has two republics (Iceland and Finland) and three moderate monarchies (Sweden, Denmark, and Norway).

Sweden's well-educated population has a system of government that allows for private enterprise (Saab, the automobile company, and Ikea, the chair company, are local companies), while also providing a cradle-to-grave social welfare system. However, in recent years, the country has had to reconsider its commitment to those social programs as its economy has slowed. Stockholm, the country's capital, is a progressive city, although there are pockets that have a village feel (if you can ignore all those trendy Ikea chairs).

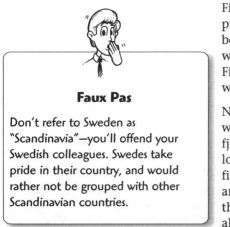

Faux Pas

Don't refer to Sweden as "Scandinavia"—you'll offend your Swedish colleagues. Swedes take pride in their country, and would rather not be grouped with other Scandinavian countries.

Finland, the seventh largest country in Europe, nestles precariously between Sweden and Russia; it also shares a border with Norway's arctic north and Sweden's northwest. Recovering from recent economic setbacks, Finland is one of the least polluted countries in the world.

Norway is one of the loveliest countries in the world, with a dramatic mix of mountains, sea, forests, and fjords. The "Land of the Midnight Sun" has delightfully long summer days, pleasantly low-key cities, unspoiled fishing villages, and rich historic sites with Viking ships and medieval churches. Its standard of living is among the highest in the world, in part because the country is almost self-sufficient in its energy needs.

Denmark borders the Baltic Sea and the North Sea on a peninsula north of Germany. Its climate is temperate, often humid and overcast, with mild, windy winters and cool summers. Denmark is the only Nordic/Baltic member of both the European Union and NATO. Despite Scandinavia's reputation as the Land of the Midnight Sun, don't expect to see the sun blazing 24 hours a day in Denmark during the winter; on the longest day, it'll be dark by 10:30 P.M. in Copenhagen.

Although considered part of Scandinavia, Iceland is really closer to Greenland, with startling scenery that gave birth to the nickname "Land of Ice and Fire." This island, steeped in myth and folklore, is Europe's second-largest, yet it has fewer residents than Luxembourg.

Tip of the Hat

Denmark has two other dependencies: Greenland, a self-governing dependency, and The Faroes, an island group in the North Atlantic Ocean that is a self-governing overseas administrative division of Denmark.

Best Time to Visit

Because so much of Scandinavia is north of the Arctic Circle, it's not surprising that the best time to visit is in the late spring through early fall—before the mercury plummets and even the ocean freezes. While you'll most likely need to bundle up in a sweater for evenings even in summer, it beats the winter, which in Scandinavia is long, dreary, cold, and uncomfortable for most touring activities. Even in summer, don't forget an umbrella and a raincoat for the frequent drizzle.

In addition to the mild temperatures, you'll be so far north that you can enjoy incredibly long days; the "midnight sun" lasts from about mid-May to the end of July in the far north. (Even southern Norway has daylight from 4 A.M. to 11 P.M. in midsummer.) Everything has its price, of course, and the downside to this perpetual sunlight is the winter darkness, when the sun does not rise in the north from the end of November to the end of January.

Who's Who

Finland and Iceland have republics, with presidents and prime ministers; Denmark, Norway, and Sweden have low-key constitutional monarchies with prime ministers appointed by the crown.

Banking Business

Scandinavia's banking system is first rate, and it's easy to change money or cash traveler's checks wherever you go—but banking fees are hefty here. ATMs are found everywhere and are an easy way to get a cash advance with a credit card.

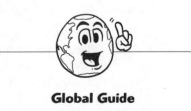

Global Guide

In Scandinavia, some banks charge a fee per check; you'll save money by bringing travelers' checks in higher denominations.

Everybody Speaks English

Fortunately for anyone who has tried to get a handle on those impossible Scandinavian language vowels, English is required in schools throughout Scandinavia—which means that most of the people in Scandinavia will probably be able to understand you. In fact, most Scandinavians are eager to try out their English.

Swedish is a Germanic language and is spoken throughout Sweden and in parts of Finland. Swedes, Danes, and Norwegians can make themselves mutually understood since their languages are similar.

Global Guide

If you're visiting Scandinavia on business, it's a nice touch to learn at least a word or two in your host's language. (Difficult, but nice!)

Finland is officially a bilingual country—six percent of the people speak *Finlandssvenska,* or "Finland's Swedish," (very similar to the language spoken in Sweden, but with many Finnish words). There are small Lapp-and Russian-speaking minorities in Finland as well.

The Danish language belongs to the northern branch of the Germanic language group, and bears a strong resemblance to other Scandinavian tongues. The official language in Denmark is Danish, but English is widely spoken and understood, especially in stores, hotels, and business meetings. Other languages you'll hear include Danish, Faroese, Greenlandic (an Eskimo dialect), and German (spoken by a small minority).

The language of Norway is of Germanic origin, but there are many dialects. Until about 1850, the official language was *Riksmal*—a written tongue heavily influenced by Danish back in the days when the two nations were united. "Country Language" (called *Landsmal*) was created after 1850 as a sort of mixture of various country dialects. Eventually, the Norwegians reached a compromise in which both languages were given equal status; this was called *Bokmal* ("book language") for the written Riksmal, and *Nynorsk* ("New Norwegian") for spoken language. In fact, there isn't much difference between Bokmal and Nynorsk; Bokmal is the language that's usually taught in schools. In addition, most newspapers and TV stations use Bokmal, as do almost all business publications. Norwegians are true linguists, who are required to learn English in school—but also frequently speak French and German in addition.

Modern-day Icelanders speak a language that's basically the same as Old Norse of the long-ago Vikings—it hasn't changed because the Icelanders refuse to allow foreign terms to describe modern technology. Therefore, the word for computer is *tolva* (which means "number prophetess"). It's an extremely difficult language for foreigners to learn, with complicated grammar and complex pronunciations, but because English is taught in the schools, most Icelanders will be able to understand you.

What They Believe

The overwhelming majority of people in Scandinavia are Lutherans, with a variety of other denominations and religions making up the balance.

Painfully Punctual

The Scandinavians are painfully punctual for appointments and take verbal agreements and commitments seriously. Business is normally conducted during regular office hours and over lunch; call ahead if you are likely to be delayed.

In Scandinavia, it's a good idea to ask the front desk for two consecutive wake-up calls in order to make sure you're not late for early morning appointments. With extra-long winter nights and short summer evenings, you can't always rely on dawn beginning at a respectable hour of 5 A.M. or 6 A.M. This is important because throughout Scandinavia, business begins promptly at the pre-arranged time. If you have a meeting scheduled at 7 A.M., be there at 7 A.M. Late arrival on your part can put your contacts in a less receptive mood. Call if you're going to be late. Only in mellow Iceland can you get away with being late for an appointment.

Make appointments at least two weeks in advance in Scandinavia, but don't try to make business appointments in Denmark on the weekend. Saturdays and Sundays are reserved for time with the family.

Open for Business

Most businesses are open from Monday through Friday from about 8 A.M. to 5 P.M. Most banks are open Monday through Friday from 9 A.M. to 4 P.M. (banks in some countries offer late hours at least night). Shopping hours are generally Monday through Friday from 9:30 A.M. until 5:30 P.M., and on Saturdays from 9 A.M. to noon or 2 P.M. Various kiosks and small convenience stores are open later to sell sale tobacco, newspapers, and candy. Within the last year, Danish 7-Elevens (open 24 hours a day) can be found in all parts of Copenhagen. Bakeries, florists, and delis will often stay open late.

Norway, Denmark, and Sweden are six hours ahead of Eastern Standard Time, so if it's noon in New York City, it's 6 P.M. there. Finland is an hour later; it's seven hours ahead of Eastern Standard Time. Iceland is four hours ahead.

On Holiday

Most Scandinavians get four or five weeks of vacation each year, so take this into account when you're planning a business trip. And keep in mind the following holidays:

Jan. 1: New Year's Day.

Jan. 6: Epiphany and the 13th day of Christmas (Sweden).

Spring: Good Friday, Easter, Easter Monday.

April 16: National holiday (Birthday of the Danish Queen).

Faux Pas

In Scandinavia, scheduling business meetings during July and August is inconsiderate; many firms close down during these two months.

May 1: Labor Day (Sweden).

May 3: General Prayer Day (Denmark).

June 5: Constitution Day (Denmark).

June 17: Independence (Iceland).

late June: Midsummer Eve.

early Aug.: Verslunarmannahelgi (Iceland).

early Sept.: Rettadgur (sheep celebration, Iceland).

Nov. 1: All Saints' Day.

Dec. 25: Christmas.

Dec. 26: Boxing Day.

Dec. 31: New Year's Eve.

Global Guide

No matter how relaxed you think your Scandinavian colleagues are, never forget your manners. Being polite is an important foray into positive business negotiations.

Formal or Informal? It Depends!

Iceland is probably the most relaxed of the Scandinavian countries, where you can comfortably call a colleague by his or her first name upon meeting. If you want to get to know someone, you won't be considered rude if you just drop by his or her office unannounced. This is an easygoing country with its own particular practice of etiquette.

Denmark is more formal than Iceland, but still relaxed; you can introduce yourself to executives you don't know, and even go by first names. In all of Scandinavia, Sweden is the most formal; if your business takes you here, keep the casual attitude out of the business setting.

Hello, Goodbye

In Scandinavia, everyone involved in business meetings shakes hands at both the opening and close of negotiations. Get extra points by adding a greeting in the appropriate language (for example, in Swedish you'd accompany handshakes with a verbal greeting such as, *"God dag"* (pronounced goo dag), or *"God morgon"* (pronounced goo MORN-ahn); both mean, "Good day."

Be prepared to offer your heartiest handshake in Norway, not only to new contacts but even to those you've met many times before. This gesture is as important as saying hello, which, by the way, is translated in Norwegian as *"Morn"*—not be confused with "Good Morning" since you'll be greeted this way from day until night.

The all-purpose greeting (both hello and goodbye) in Danish sounds, conveniently enough, exactly like "Hi" in English. It's written *"heij."*

Titles

Learn to pronounce the last name of your Scandinavian contact before arriving, as you will be using it a lot. Proper name-calling reigns here, so using Mr., Mrs., Miss, or Dr. (preceding the last name) is appreciated—"Hey, Sven!" will most likely raise an eyebrow. As soon as a genuine attempt at constant formality is recognized, your host may insist on being called by his or her first name. That's when you know you're making headway.

You'll have an interesting time of it in Iceland, where only about 10 percent of the residents have last names. Instead, everybody uses a "patronym"—the first name of the father, followed by *"son"* or *"dottir"* to denote (of course) "son" or "daughter." The daughter of Jon would be "Jondottir;" the son's name would be "Jonson." It's such a small country that just about everyone is related.

Business Cards

In general, business cards are an important business tool in Scandinavia.

If your company has a long history, have your company's establishment date printed on your business cards. Most Scandinavians respect age and tradition. Present your card either at the beginning or somewhere in the middle of a meeting.

Body of Evidence

In winter months, Scandinavians spend a lot of time being chivalrous with their hats and coats. A gentleman frequently removes his hat when speaking to, or passing, a woman in the street. At the same time, hats and coats are always removed when entering a place of business. Upon leaving, wait until you're out the door before putting on your coat. (Otherwise, your colleagues will think you're anxious to leave.)

Sweden is considered the most formal of all the countries of Scandinavia. Don't overdo it when gesticulating—Swedes find these actions offensive. Finns don't appreciate folded arms (it seems too arrogant).

Many gestures we take for granted in the U.S. are not polite in Scandinavia; some are downright obscene. Avoid:

➤ The North American gesture for "OK" (circle formed by thumb and forefinger) is an insult in Denmark.

Faux Pas

In the Scandinavian workplace, avoid all physical contact, except between relatives and close friends. Don't pat your contact on the back or even touch his or her arm with affection.

Global Guide

Norwegians don't always rise when another person enters the room. Don't be offended by this.

➤ Talking with your hands in your pockets.

➤ Patting the back or backslapping; it's too much physical contact.

We're All Equal

Known throughout the world for their tolerance and social forward thinking, it's not surprising that in general, Scandinavians treat women with equality. Indeed, one of the reasons why so many women are able to work outside the home is the presence of quality subsidized day care for children throughout Scandinavia. It's not unusual for Scandinavian women to pick up the check (especially if she has an expense account).

You'll find lots of Swedish women in middle management; the Swedish equivalent of a glass ceiling is evident in that very few women work in top leadership positions in business. Politically, you will find Swedish women in parliament and local councils.

Icelandic women not only bring home the bacon and fry it up in the pan, they could butcher the pig and design the pan as well. Icelandic women held down the fort for years while their seafaring men were plundering and conquering elsewhere, and this tradition hasn't faded. When you think of Icelandic women, think of the mythological Valkyrie—the handmaidens of Odin—and you'll get the right idea here. Iceland is the site of the first-ever democratically elected woman president, and the first-ever Woman's Party. Women are well-represented everywhere in society; 7 out of 10 Iceland women have jobs.

In any other country of Europe, the situation for Finnish women would be exemplary, but Scandinavia has high standards for gender equality, and Finland has a way to go for true equality. Women do have very good working conditions and generous maternity leave and child care allowances. About 38 percent of the parliament jobs go to women, as do a few top industrial positions. While career opportunities are improving, Finnish women still don't earn the same as Finnish men.

Danes try to downplay social differences of all kinds; this is made easier by their homogeneous population. Danish women and men share household and child care responsibilities. For every 100 Danish men with a job, there are about 76 working Danish women—one of the highest ratios in Europe.

Conservative Dresser

You'll always be on the safe side in Scandinavia if you grab your clothes from the "conservative" section of the closet. Business suits for men and women are the norm for office wear. Chances are you'll be asked to participate in a black-tie affair during a business venture in Scandinavia, so take along a tuxedo (women should bring an evening gown). Danes lean toward subdued color choices and casual dress rather than the high fashion. A coat and tie may be required in many restaurants after 6 P.M. Casually speaking, Danes are fairly conservative—except when they get to the beach, when topless bathing suits are quite common.

Tip of the Hat

You'll find the weather in Scandinavia often unpredictable, so layer your clothing and keep an umbrella and raincoat handy.

The Art of Conversation

While it's easy to lump Europe's Scandinavian countries together, each nation possesses a distinct personality and should be recognized as a separate entity from neighboring nations.

The Swedish love to socialize, but keep your voice tone quiet and well modulated while you're doing it. Swedes are a relatively quiet people.

Taboo subjects of discussion include politics and religion. Instead, talk to your Swedish acquaintances about their beautiful countryside and cities, or ask how they spent their last vacation. While the Swede's have a reputation for coolness toward strangers, once you break the ice, there's a genuine friendliness. Swedes may brood a bit during the winter (who wouldn't?) but they come alive in summer.

In Norway, modesty is the best policy; Norwegians don't flaunt their success, wealth, or material possessions. Don't ask, "How are you?" without expecting to listen to an elaborate response. Norwegians are very proud of their history, culture, and landscape. To endear yourself, make time to comment on the beautiful countryside or the rich culture. Your compliments will be highly appreciated. Play up Norway's independence; you'll be sure to win points with your patriotic Norwegian contacts. However, don't compare Norway to America or imply that America is better in any way. Boasting only serves as a way to alienate.

The Finns love a good joke, although they're famously reluctant to make small talk. They also love to talk politics (they have a host of government parties, so there's lots to talk about). At a loss for what to talk about? Try sports (cross-country skiing and downhill skiing are popular), travel, hobbies, or politics.

When you're conversing with a Dane, steer clear of any sort of personal remarks; these could offend. Even a simple, "Wow, that's a beautiful ski sweater" could be taken as too personal. Note that the Danish sense of humor is very dry and reserved. On the other hand, Danes are also very frank—sometimes brutally so, but they never mean to insult.

Getting Down to Business

When it comes to negotiations, one of the biggest lessons is not to offend. Keep in mind when visiting here that most Scandinavians are intensely patriotic—so never, ever criticize their country. Expect a reserved exterior with an underlying delightfully dry sense of humor. Still, as similar as the countries of Scandinavia are, there are still cultural differences that can be important if you're trying to finalize negotiations.

Sweden

Never wing it. Swedes carefully plan out their meeting agendas and expect the same from business counterparts. Following prompt arrival, expect a short time of casual small talk, then down to the business at hand.

In presentations, be very precise and concrete; don't launch into parables and hard-to-understand examples. And forget that "opening joke" your pals back at Toastmasters were so fond of; humor is not usually part of Swedish negotiations. Unlike the Danes, Swedes tend to be serious to the point of stuffiness in business. Do not show emotion during negotiations. Remember that Swedes value consensus and prefer to avoid confrontation, so don't start pounding the table in a huff when you don't get your way.

Norway

Yes, like all Scandinavians, there's that famous Norwegian reserve—but in fact, you'll find Norwegians to be enormously friendly if you make the first move. They may not run up to you and grab your hand, but they're always open and warm when approached.

Norwegians consider some Americans to be too smooth-talking and polished. Try hard for sincerity, and negotiations should go smoothly. Even if you're anxious to get your point across, always speak in a soft voice. The louder you talk, the less likely your ideas will be heard.

Denmark

Danes like to burrow in and aim for a warm, intimate mood—it's how Danes approach their personal lives, from designing their homes to their fondness for small cafés and pubs. Danes are relaxed, casual, and very tolerant of different life styles. In fact, in 1989 Denmark became the first European country to legalize same-sex marriages and offer gay partnerships the same rights as heterosexual couples.

Say What?

The Danish word **hygge** for "cozy and snug" is used to indicate a special Danish get-together at home with friends.

Finland

No need to worry about small talk with a Finn; just get down to business and they'll be happy. You'll find the Finns unemotional and direct during negotiations, and prone to long silences. Don't let this unnerve you.

Iceland

It seems that Scandinavians may be self-possessed (but never dour) and almost always easy going—and the Icelanders are just as quiet but also easy to get along with. Break the ice with Icelanders and you'll find a wonderful, dry sense of humor and an active interest in world affairs beyond their tiny island.

When dealing with an Icelander, you'll be on a first-name basis almost immediately—even with the top executives of the firm— as there are very few class barriers here. (There is also only a small group with last names, which is probably the other reason why everyone is so casual!)

Global Guide

Gifts aren't required when doing business in Scandinavia, but a craft or illustrated book from your hometown in the U.S. is a nice touch. Business gifts shouldn't be too costly or too cheap.

Home in Scandinavia

If you're invited to a colleague's house, it's a nice touch to bring along some pastry, chocolates, or wine for your hostess. If you're invited home for dinner, send flowers to the hostess the morning of the dinner (but avoid carnations and only-white flowers, which are reserved for funerals).

Danes can stretch a meal out forever—in a Danish home, you'll spend up to five hours at the table, but don't get up from the table before your host does. When you're finished eating, place your knife and fork side by side on the plate with the fork's tines pointed up (pointed down means you want more food).

Take off your shoes before you enter the home of an Icelander (they'll probably be full of snow and ice most of the year anyway!).

Sauna Rules

Don't be surprised during your Finland trip if you're invited to a colleague's home for dinner—and a sauna. Saunas are a national pastime many locals enjoy every day—guests or no guests. In fact, the casual setting inside a little wooden room creates an apt environment for the perfect cultural schmooze session.

If your host is male and you're a woman, don't worry. Saunas are usually segregated affairs, and women get to go in first. While Finns usually enjoy their saunas nude, they won't mind if you prefer to wear a towel or bathing suit. Aprés sauna, expect to be given a small meal of sausage, bread, and salty fish (the fish replaces the salt you lost back there sweating in the sauna).

Suppe to Nuts

You're in for a dietary treat in Scandinavia, which features a host of delicious seafood and plenty of spicy, tasty national dishes. Business is commonly discussed over lunch or dinner.

Tip of the Hat

A common sight on most Norwegian breakfast tables is sweet brown goat cheese (called **geitost**[**guyt-ohst**]) and pickled herring.

Teatime

In Denmark, a break for coffee somewhere between 2 P.M. and 4 P.M. is common. If you've got a sweet tooth, you'll be in pastry heaven in Denmark, the country that invented "the danish" (except they call it *wienerbrod* [*veener-bdrd*] here). In fact, there's a bakery on almost every Danish street corner. Coffee is strong here, all the better to marry with the danish pastries. You can sample this combo in a *konditori* (*kahn-de-tory*), a bakery, or confectioner's (tearoom) all over the city.

Dinner Is Served

When you think Danish, think smorrebrod (literally 'buttered bread'), an open-faced sandwich that ranges from very basic fare to elaborately sculpted creations. Danish food relies heavily on fish, meat, and potatoes. Typical dishes:

➤ *flъskesteg (flisk-a-sty):*—roast pork with cracklings.

➤ *gravad laks (grah-vahd lahks):*—cured or salted salmon marinated in dill and served with a sweet mustard sauce.

➤ *hvid labskovs (vid labskoff):*—a stew made of square cuts of beef boiled with potatoes, bay leaves, and pepper.

➤ *hakkebøf med løg (hakboof mit loy):*—hamburger in onions.

➤ *biksemad:*—meat-and-potato hash with an egg on top.

If you're visiting Copenhagen, try a typical Danish "cold table" lunch—hot and cold fish dishes served with ice-cold schnapps followed by smorrebrod with beer, and finished with a wide variety of cheeses and fruit.

If you're at dinner with Danish colleagues, don't eat and run. That's considered rude, as polite conversation afterwards is the right way to digest the evening meal.

Finnish food has elements of both Swedish and Russian cuisines, but with lots of variations and specialties. The potato is a staple, and it comes with various fish or meat sauces. If you're hankering for a traditional meal, it will probably include game (try snow grouse, reindeer stew, salmon, or raw pickled salmon).

In Sweden, business lunches and dinners are quite popular; choose a formal restaurant if you're scheduling a business meal. Popular dishes include fish, which is typically served poached or fried in lard. Pickled herring is especially popular, and the potato is basically indispensable.

Norwegian dishes include *laks* (*lahks*; grilled or smoked salmon), *reker* (boiled shrimp), and *torsk* (cod). Popular at Christmas time is *lutefisk* (*loot-a-fisk*; dried cod made near-gelatinous by smoking in lye)—definitely an acquired taste.

Skoal!

In general, it seems that Scandinavians love to drink and they love to toast—but don't jump up and offer a toast before your host has a chance. In fact, don't even touch your glass before your host offers the toast.

The typical Scandinavian toast goes like this: your host lifts a glass and announces *"skoal"* (this is Swedish, but the toasts in other Scandinavian tongues are very similar). In turn, other party members raise their glasses, make direct eye contact, and grin before downing a healthy swig. This silent gesture collectively indicates the same sentiment to the entire table. This eye contact is an important part of the process—first the eye contact, then the toast, then the clink of glasses amid more eye contact, and then the tossing back of the liquor. (Extra points are awarded if you don't blink or choke).

Strong beer, wines, and spirits are usually sold by state monopoly, and this, plus import restrictions, makes prices usually quite high. This is one reason why many Scandinavians take their partying so seriously. Denmark's Carlsberg and Tuborg breweries both produce excellent beers, but the most popular spirit in Denmark is *aquavit*. It's easy to find beer, wine, and spirits in most restaurants, cafés, and grocery stores. However, in Norway, alcohol may be hard to find in some rural communities where virtual prohibition is common.

Global Guide

In Copenhagen, sales of alcohol are forbidden after 8 P.M.

Tipping Policy

In Scandinavia, tipping is generally not necessary because service charges are usually included in almost all restaurants and hotels in all five countries. For exceptional service in a restaurant, you may want to round up the bill.

The Least You Need to Know

➤ Scandinavians are reserved, polite, and kind, with a dry sense of humor once they get to know you.

➤ In general, Scandinavian countries are clean, safe, and well run.

➤ Punctuality is important in Scandinavia; don't be late, and call if you are running behind.

➤ English is widely spoken in Scandinavia, so it's not hard to make yourself understood.

➤ Scandinavia's banking system is first rate; it's easy to change money here.

Chapter 17

Eastern Bloc: Czech Republic, Poland, and Hungary

HOW DO YOU DO?

In This Chapter

➤ Learn about the Czech, Magyar, and Polish languages

➤ Understand the conservative approach of the Eastern bloc

➤ Find out what subjects to avoid discussing

➤ Discover the importance of handshakes here

➤ Find out what the gender equality situation is

Many Americans still can't figure out the difference between the Eastern bloc countries and all those new little countries that have been carved up out of the former USSR—much less puzzle out the cultural ramifications of the new borders and alliances.

Tourist facilities, particularly those found in the capitals, are quickly approaching the level of those found in most European countries. Outside of the urban centers, however, your chances of finding good places to stay are not so hot. Indeed, some goods and services taken for granted in other European countries may not yet be available. It's an up-and-coming geography, but it's still the Eastern bloc.

Who's on First?

The Czech Republic, Poland, and Hungary are all rapidly-developing European nation undergoing profound economic and social change. They are considered to be three of the most successful countries of the Eastern Bloc. All three have democratic republics with a president and prime minister:

Tip of the Hat

Fairly small countries, the Czech Republic, Poland, and Hungary are all landlocked areas in Central Europe. Temperate in climate, the three countries enjoy cool summers and slog through cold, cloudy, and humid winters.

➤ Poland is a moderately developed European nation working to build a new political system and a market economy.

➤ Hungary has a stable democracy completing the transition to a market economy—Budapest now ranks as the fourth most popular tourist destination in Europe.

➤ Political and financial crises in 1997 shattered the Czech Republic's image as one of the most stable and prosperous of post-Communist states, but it's slowly making a comeback.

Not surprising for a part of the world with constantly shifting boundaries, Czech citizens come from many surrounding areas: Almost 95 percent are Czech, followed by Slovak (3 percent), Polish (0.6 percent), German (0.5 percent), Gypsy (0.3 percent), and Hungarian (0.2 percent). Hungary has a significant minority population including German, Slovak, Romanian, and Gypsy. Poland, however, is very homogenous; 98 percent of the population are Poles.

Say What?

Some helpful Hungarian words to know before you arrive:

➤ **halo:** (hay-lo; accent on the "o") can be used for both hello and goodbye.

➤ **orvendek:** (uhr-ven-deck) means "Pleased to meet you."

Learn the Language

Czech, a consonant-rich Slavic language, is among the world's most complicated. It contains sounds that are difficult for English speakers to produce. However, a growing number of businesspeople, politicians, and shopkeepers (at least in Prague) speak English (particularly in the city's center). Many older folks also speak German.

Closely related to Czech, Polish is the official language of Poland. It is a part of the Slavic branch of the Indo-European language family (along with English).

Polish may be easier for Americans to read because it's not written with the Russian Cyrillic alphabet but rather with the modified Latin alphabet. It's considered to be the most difficult Indo-European language for English speakers to learn.

Magyar (Hungarian) is also extremely difficult for Americans to master. Unrelated to most European languages, it is most closely allied with Finnish and Estonian. Most Hungarians speak Magyar.

Religion

True to its Communist roots, the majority of Czech citizens are atheist (39.8 percent), closely followed by Roman Catholic (39.2 percent). In Poland, however (the native land of the current Roman Catholic Pope), most are Roman Catholic, with about 1.5 percent Orthodox. In Hungary, about 68 percent are Roman Catholic and 28 percent are Protestants.

Holidays: Only a Few

There aren't a lot of holidays to celebrate in the Eastern Bloc, but many Christian holidays are still celebrated. On national holidays, you'll find schools, and most banks and stores, are closed:

Jan. 1: New Year's Day.

April-May: Easter/Easter Monday (varies).

May 1: Labor Day (Czech).

May 3: National Constitution Day (Poland).

May 8: National Liberation Day (Czech).

July 5: Sts. Cyril & Methodius.

July 6: Jan Hus Day (Czech).

Oct. 28: Founding of the Republic (Czech Republic).

Nov. 11: National Independence Day (Poland).

Dec. 24-25: Christmas holidays.

Dec. 26: Saint Stephen's Day/Boxing Day.

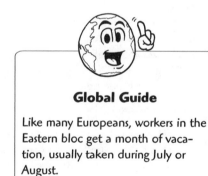

Global Guide

Like many Europeans, workers in the Eastern bloc get a month of vacation, usually taken during July or August.

Be on Time

Punctuality is prized here, where the workaday world often starts very early in the morning. Appointments are usually scheduled between 9 A.M. and noon or in early afternoon.

Most city businesses stay open all day, without a noontime break; typical business hours are 8:30 A.M. to 5 P.M. Monday through Friday. Most shops (and sometimes businesses) are open Saturday morning until noon or 1 P.M., but department stores and tourist-oriented shops in the center of bigger cities often remain open all day Saturday; some are open Sunday as well.

All three countries are six hours ahead of Eastern Standard time. If it's noon in New York City, it's 6 P.M. in Prague, Budapest, or Krakow.

It's a good idea to request appointments in writing (a week or two in advance)—but you may write your business letters in English. Don't make an appointment for Saturday.

Handshakes All Around

When you arrive and when you leave, handshakes are the way to go in the Eastern bloc. If you're dealing with an old-fashioned Magyar, expect a courtly bow to a woman. At the very least, a Hungarian man will wait for a woman to extend her hand before he shakes it. A traditional Polish man may kiss a woman's hand in greeting. (As an American, however, you won't be expected to do this.)

When you're greeting a close friend, a man will first shake hands, and then embrace and touch cheeks (left, then right). Women do the same, but they go right for the cheeks—they don't shake hands first.

Global Guide

Reverse the order of names in Hungary, so that the last name comes first and the first name comes last. Hungarian composer Bela Bartok, therefore, would be called Bartok Bela. (Your name will be listed in the usual American order, however.)

Card-o-Mania

Bring lots of business cards, and hand them out to everyone you meet. Have one side of the card printed in the language of your host country.

Titles

Folks are very formal in the Eastern bloc; use titles (Mister, Miss, Doctor) in all discussions. Your colleagues will let you know when it's okay to shift to a first-name basis.

The title of "Dr." can be obtained with far less education than required for the same degree in the United States. Often economists, teachers, and lawyers hold this prestigious title. Therefore, when this title is spelled out on a business card, you may not be sure what it means, but be sure to address a Hungarian as "Dr." anyway and follow it with the person's last name.

Body Language

Don't misinterpret that serious mien in the Eastern bloc as misery or depression. Many Slavs appear dour simply because smiling in public is not part of their cultural milieu.

There are a number of gestures to avoid:

➤ Don't chew gum in public.

➤ Don't litter.

➤ Don't be loud in public.

Slow and Steady

Historically, decision-making is slow here. Those in the Eastern bloc will be very gracious in conversations, but don't hold your breath for final decisions or actions to be taken quickly. Retain a long-term view in all business dealings. This is especially true if you have to negotiate with any government group.

On the other hand, some of the newer or younger business people in the Eastern bloc are eager to get new ventures underway, and may be more open to trying to untie monumental red tape.

It's a good idea to have a local representative from the country with whom you're negotiating to help move things along smoothly. Good secretarial skills are as scarce as hen's teeth in Hungary. One suggestion is to arrange support in advance with your hotel. If you anticipate needing a great deal of intricate clerical support, it might be wise to bring someone along to avoid the hassle.

It's a Man's World

The business arena in the countries of the Eastern Bloc is still a man's preserve, and you'll be hard put to find many women in the upper echelons of management. You may not like this situation, but becoming a one-person women's lib advocacy group won't help your relationship with your hosts. Attitudes take time to change. You'll find many men don't appreciate assertive women. For example, if a woman needs directions in Poland, she should approach a policeman; asking a Polish man may be interpreted as flirting.

In Hungary, you'll find less emphasis on the power of the male head of the household, especially since many more women are working outside the home.

Suit Up

Standard business dress for men is a dark suit, white shirt, and tasteful tie, although you might be able to get away without a jacket (and in some situations, not even the tie is necessary).

If you're going formal to a restaurant or theater, standard business suits are fine. Opera goers may want to choose either a dark suit or a tux (women should wear formal gowns).

For women, skirts and blouses are perhaps the most common outfit, although more and more women are wearing dress slacks.

When it comes to casual wear, shorts and tee shirts are fine for summer, and you can wear jeans, slacks, or skirts with sweaters in winter.

Tip of the Hat

It's always a good idea to carry an umbrella, and sturdy walking shoes are a must on the city's cobblestones and uneven pavements.

Keep It Pleasant

Folks in the Eastern bloc love to talk—feel free to chat about food, wine, sports, and sightseeing. In Hungary, horses are always a popular topic.

In major cities, you may find the air quality not so great, or the condition of historic buildings deplorable. Keep your mouth shut. Those in the Eastern bloc take great pride in their country and would rather discuss attributes like the fine architecture, beautiful parks, and museums.

As you move around in the country, remember that Hungarians tend to be literal. If you tell a Hungarian contact, "I'll see you later," you can be sure a person from this society of literal communication will respond with, "When and where?" If you blurt out, "Next time you're in Boise, give me a call," a Hungarian may respond by pulling out a datebook and scheduling a time.

Topics to avoid:

➤ In Hungary, don't mention your background if you're Slovak, Polish, Gypsy, or Romanian (neighborly relations with these groups haven't always been top notch).

➤ In Poland, don't bring up your background if you're Russian, German, Austrian, or Hungarian.

➤ Don't bring up anti-semitism or the Holocaust in Poland (most of the Nazi concentration camps were in Poland, not Germany).

➤ Politics in general.

To Give or Not To Give ...

You don't have to bring gifts when visiting an Eastern bloc company, but if you're going to give a gift, don't just bring one for the CEO. Tote along a whole bag of small presents and hand them out liberally.

It's very unlikely that you'll be invited to anybody's home in the Eastern bloc—there's just no room. But if you are, bring a gift of flowers, chocolate, or Western liquor.

My House or Yours?

Times are still hard in the Eastern bloc, and most folks don't have lots of personal space at home. In fact, apartments are usually extremely cramped, so don't expect anyone from these countries to invite you home for a cuppa. Instead, you'll be invited out to a restaurant, cafè or bar. The person who extends the invitation also foots the bill.

Hungarians in particular are known for their love of entertainment, and you'll have a hard time paying the bill here—your hosts will always want to treat.

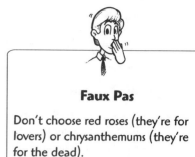

Faux Pas

Don't choose red roses (they're for lovers) or chrysanthemums (they're for the dead).

Goulash to Nuts

A cafè society has emerged once more in Prague, creating numerous places to sit and chat over a creamy cappuccino or a cool drink around the city. In addition to a simple breakfast and evening meal, Czechs enjoy a snack (*svacina*) at about 10 A.M.

You may love to discuss business over a double latte and a pile of bagels, but those in the Eastern bloc haven't yet warmed up to the idea of a breakfast business meeting.

Luncheon

The main meal of the day is eaten at noon, and usually consists of meat and dumplings, potatoes or rice, and soup. The national Czech dish is roast pork, sauerkraut, and dumplings. Another specialty is goulash, often served with dumplings.

Business lunches are often held quite late in Poland, around 4 p.m. or 5 p.m., so grab a snack to fortify yourself until it's time to sit down to discuss business! In Hungary, however, you'll probably not get much accomplished over lunch—food is to enjoy, not to discuss over. Get your Hungarian business done during non-eating meetings back at the office.

Dinner Is Served

Because so many of the good restaurants are quite small, they tend to fill up quickly. It's a good idea to reserve several days ahead. There aren't usually any dress requirements, although you might want to dress more formally for very expensive places.

Expect dinner to last into late evening in Hungary, with entertainment following the last course. When you go out to eat in Hungary, even if it's with your business associates, don't bring up work—eating and entertaining are not appropriate for discussing business.

Be prepared to encounter ultra-rich and incredibly spicy foods (especially in Hungary). If you struggle with a sensitive digestive tract, stick to milder dishes such as chicken paprika (it's considered mild in Hungary!). When you order a salad, you'll probably get cabbage.

195

Global Guide

In less expensive restaurants, it's not considered rude for a stranger to join you at your table if there are empty seats.

Global Guide

For extra points, let your host know you would like to sample a local wine—of which Hungarians are very proud.

Have a Brew

Tea is the most common beverage. However, Czech beer is famous worldwide. The best-known brands are Pilsner (Plzenske) and Budweiser (Budvar), but you won't go wrong with Radegast, Staropramen, os Velkopopovicky Kozel. Everyone's favorite aperitif is Becherovka (*bay-cher-oh-va*), a Czech-invented liqueur; this potent herbal beverage is said to have medicinal qualities. Plum brandy (*slivovice; sliv-a-vitch*) is popular.

In Poland, however, vodka is the drink of choice—beer is just a chaser. Don't drink too fast, however—your glass will be topped up as soon as it's empty, and you'll quicky be lying under the table instead of doing business over it if you get into a drinking contest with a Pole.

Tip Your Hat ...

In finer restaurants, it's a good idea to give about a 10 percent tip. Tip the waiter by stating the total amount you wish him or her to keep (meal price plus tip) as you hand over the money. In a taxi, if you feel the driver has quoted you an honest price at the end of your journey, round up. In hotels, tip the bellboy.

The Least You Need to Know

➤ Business people in the Eastern bloc are conservative and more formal than those in the United States.

➤ Don't expect to be invited home to your host's apartment; overcrowding makes this unlikely.

➤ Expect business decisions to take a long, tortuous time unless you're dealing with a very young and energetic entrepreneur.

➤ It's a man's world here; very few women are in upper management.

➤ Decision-making goes slowly here.

➤ Standard business dress is conservative and tasteful.

Chapter 18

Russia and the Commonwealth of Independent States

In This Chapter

➤ Learn the ins and outs of money within CIS

➤ Find out the attitude toward punctuality

➤ Discover the tricks to successful negotiating

➤ Decipher the keys to Russian names

➤ Learn what to do in a Russian home

➤ Understand the different kinds of gifts that are acceptable

The Commonwealth of Independent States (CIS) includes Armenia, Azerbaijan, Belarus, Georgia, Kazakhstan, Kyrgyzstan, Moldova, Russia, Tajikistan, Turkmenistan, Ukraine, and Uzbekistan. The CIS is currently undergoing fundamental political and economic changes, which can be confusing for travelers throughout the CIS. Many geographic names throughout the region have been changed with the breakup of the former U.S.S.R. Try to buy a map before your trip, but keep in mind that some place names may need to be updated. If your map and the street signs don't match up, you're not necessarily lost; the street may just have been renamed.

Geography and Economy

In the former Kazakh capital Alma Ata, an economic community agreement was reached in October 1991 between the former Soviet republics under the guidance of the Commonwealth of Independent States (CIS). This agreement allows for coordinated policies in energy, transport, finance and banking systems, customs and tariffs, and foreign economic relations. A large proportion of Russia's trade is conducted within the CIS, although there is a growing insistence for payment in hard currency rather than by the barter deals of previous times.

Despite the disintegration of its empire, Russia is still huge—its borders stretch from Estonia, Latvia, Belarus, Ukraine, and Turkey to the west and then pass Kazakhstan, Mongolia, and China to end up at the Pacific Ocean. The landscape is predominantly flat except for the low-rising Urals and the more substantial mountain ranges of the far east. Siberia occupies Russia's Far East, and is characterized by tundra, steppes, and vast expanses of nothingness.

This vast country, with a wealth of natural resources and a well-educated population, continues to experience serious problems as it evolves from the old centrally planned economy to a modern market. Many of the problems of Mother Russia are also seen in the variety of smaller Commonwealth Independent States. Although Russia has made progress since 1991 and avoided collapse, the Russian economy is still troubled by a weak infrastructure, such as poor roads, transport networks and telecommunications, together with poor distribution of goods and consequent shortages and waste.

A persistent, ugly civil war drags on in Chechnya while Russia's domestic problems become more entrenched. Throughout the CIS (but especially in Russia), the problems of corruption among officials, business people, financiers, police, and the Mafia have spread into every corner and level of society. Its people struggle with soaring drug abuse levels and a murder rate twice as high as in the U.S.

Since the beginning of the economic reforms in 1990, the total output of the Russian economy has been cut in half. However, if the economy manages to stabilize, there are reasons for long-term optimism as Russia is blessed with plenty of natural resources. Indeed, Moscow itself has been transformed more radically in the last five years than in the past 100. Shops once barely filled with merchandise have been turned into expensive restaurants, designer boutiques, and the Russian equivalent of a 7-11 convenience store. Moscow has completed its metamorphosis from a backward, uninspiring wallflower into one of the most vibrant courtesans in Europe. Free market reform has not been kind to Russia, however. Production and investment are in diabolical decline because of uncertainty induced by the rapid changes and suspicions born of corruption. More than 40 million Russians struggle below the poverty line.

Global Guide

When planning a trip to the CIS, there may be areas of instability throughout the region; it may not be safe or wise to travel through these troubled areas. For updated information on a specific country, consult that country's current Consular Information Sheet (available from the U.S. State Department).

Keep in mind that while you can find good tourist facilities in Moscow, St. Petersburg, and some other large cities, such amenities don't exist in the rest of the CIS. Many items and services you'd take for granted in other countries aren't yet available. Travel to some parts of the CIS is downright dangerous.

July and August are the warmest months and the main holiday season in Russia. They're also the wettest (expect rain one out of every three days). Moscow and St. Petersburg share similar summer temperatures, but by the end of November, Moscow is iced over, with snow remaining until early April; the average January temperature is around –12° Celsius. St. Petersburg is so far north that the sun doesn't set in summer, and winter usually offers only five hours of dim light a day. Vladivostok, on Russia's Pacific coast, enjoys slightly milder weather than elsewhere in the Russian Far East, but its winter temperature hovers around –13° Celsius—a paradise compared to Oymyakon in the northeast, the coldest inhabited place on earth. Its winter temperatures drops to –65° Celsius.

If you want to avoid the crowds and the rain, visit Russia between May and June or September to October. Although the winters are bitterly cold, but you'll find that the theaters are open, the vodka is flowing, most buildings are warm, and the snow is beautiful. Spring, on the other hand, is slushy, muddy, and generally unpleasant.

The Native Tongue

Russian is the official language of Russia, used for state business; it's also the native tongue of over half the population. Central Asian populations speak Turkic. But while Russian is the official language of Russia, but it's not a popular choice in ethnically non-Russian areas of the Russian Federation and the CIS. In general, the languages of the CIS (especially Russian) aren't easy languages to learn—but if you try, you'll earn big points. English, French, or German are spoken by some people.

Spend plenty of time with your interpreter to make sure the two of you understand each other; if your translator misinterprets your discussions, you could end up importing beets when what you really wanted was caviar.

However (at least in Russia), most residents learn English in school. Odds are that if you're talking to anyone under the age of 40, he or she will at least maintain a working knowledge of English.

Tip of the Hat

Even before discussions get underway, have your interpreter explain that you're sorry you can't speak in Russian. As the interpreter translates, maintain continuous eye contact with your Russian colleagues.

Religion

Despite the years of Communism, the Russian Orthodox Church nevertheless survived and is of growing importance today in Russia. Other religions include Muslim and Buddhist. Many of Russia's Jews have emigrated because of entrenched anti-Semitism.

Holidays!

This list is just a guide—obviously, holidays will differ slightly form one CIS country to the next, and from one locality to the other. The following is a list of holidays:

Jan. 1-2: New Year.

Jan. 7: Orthodox Christmas.

March 8: International Women's Day.

May 1: Labor Day.

May 2: Spring Day.

May 9: Victory Day (1945).

June 12: Independence Day (Russia).

Nov. 7: Anniversary of the Great October Socialist Revolution, 1917.

Global Guide

Remember that the Russian Orthodox Church uses the Julian calendar (not the Gregorian one you thought everyone in the world—including the U.S.—follows!). Currently, the Julian calendar runs about 13 days behind the Gregorian calendar.

Faux Pas

Don't get up and leave a meeting if it runs late. Once things do get underway, it's not uncommon for business meetings to run two or three hours over the limit. Plan for this.

Just Try to Be on Time!

There's almost no place on earth where it's as difficult to be punctual as Russia and the CIS, where getting anywhere seems to take forever—and you never know what sort of problem will crop up along the way. Being late will most likely not upset your Russian colleagues, but aim for promptness nonetheless.

In the old Communist days, you could be as late as you wanted and nobody cared—you were guaranteed a job no matter how slothful you were. Old habits die hard, so don't expect folks to be on time. Indeed, Russians spent so much of their life waiting in lines—for bread, for vodka, and for meat—that they had little time left over for anything else. Who could be on time when you had to spend all your life in line? In Russia, patience is the virtue.

When it comes to Russian time zones, you need a laptop to keep track of them all. The Russian federation crosses 11 time zones—and when you throw in Daylight Savings Time (during the end of March and October), it's a wonder anyone knows what time it really is.

Moscow and St. Petersburg are in the farthest western zone, which is eight hours ahead of Eastern Standard Time. Therefore, when it's noon in New York City, it's 8 P.M. in Moscow.

Open Late, Leave Early

Technically, business hours are from 9 A.M. to 5 P.M. Monday through Friday, but most people arrive late and leave early. Banks are usually open from 9 A.M. to 5 P.M. Monday through Friday, although some banks are now open a bit on Saturdays. Large stores are open from 9 A.M. to 8 P.M. or 9 P.M. Monday through Saturday; most shops close for an hour at lunch. Groceries are open on Sundays.

Appointment, Please

Nowhere does that legendary Russian patience come in more handy than when you're trying to pin someone down to set up an appointment. Be patient and don't give up. Eventually you'll be written down in the appointment calendar. Once you do wrangle an appointment, don't cancel. You may never get another chance!

Grip and Greet

When being greeted by a Russian for the first time, chances are you'll get a hearty handshake and a brisk repeat of your name instead of a "How do you do?" sort of greeting. You should respond the same way—with a handshake and by repeating the other person's name. Once things progress in the friendship department, you can expect a lot of hugging and cheek-kissing.

Remember to shake hands firmly when greeting and saying goodbye. Russians shake hands often, and don't be surprised if you get heartily kissed on both cheeks (this applies to men as well as women).

Take a Card ...

In a country where the telephone company expected 9 million Muscovites to make do with 250,000 copies of its Moscow telephone book, you can appreciate the value of business cards inscribed with phone numbers and addresses. When you print yours, try to have one side of them printed in Russian.

Titles

If you've ever tried to slog through a Russian novel, you know just how complicated Russian names can be. While they're listed in the same order as in the west, the middle name is patronymic (that is, it's a name derived from the first name of the person's father). If you've just met Mikhail Nikolaievich Baryshnikov, remember that his first name is Mikhail, his last name is Baryshnikov, and his middle name means "son of Nikolai." Mikhail's friends would likely call him by a nickname, such as "Misha" or "Mishka"—or they might call him his first name and patronymic (Mikhail Nikolaievich). If Mikhail had a wife, she would add an "a" to her last name—she would be called Anastasia Baryshnikova.

Don't use first names unless you've been asked to do so. Use a professional title if the person has one; otherwise, the standard "Mr." or "Mrs." works well together with the last name.

Faux Pas

Don't talk or laugh too loudly in public. And don't whistle, either (Slavic superstition says it will make you lose money!).

Talk Tips

Don't be surprised if you hear Russians ripping their own country apart (they have a lot of fodder). No matter how agonizingly irritating your experiences might be in this still-evolving land, you shouldn't jump in and start tearing the country down, too. While Russians are nothing if not critical of their own country, they're conversely very proud and will resent it if outsiders take the same liberties. Never forget the long history of Russian cultural and artistic achievements in your zeal to point out all the flaws you see today.

Space Bubbles

Don't be surprised if you find Russians standing in your face when they talk to you. The Russian personal space bubble is much smaller than is yours in the United States. Expect lots of physical contact, and don't back down.

There are a number of gestures you should try to avoid while traveling in Russia, some of which will be interpreted as obscene or considered bad luck:

➤ Don't shake hands while standing in a doorway over a threshold (it will start an argument).

➤ Don't whistle indoors, or after a performance (it means you didn't like it).

➤ Don't gesture with your thumb between your first two fingers (it's obscene).

➤ Don't light a cigarette from a candle (it brings bad luck).

➤ The American "OK" sign with the thumb and forefinger touching in a circle is obscene.

➤ Don't shake your fist; it's vulgar.

➤ Men should avoid sitting with an ankle on a knee.

➤ Don't show the soles of your feet (it's rude).

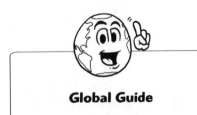

Global Guide

Women should wear a hat or scarf if visiting an orthodox church.

Less Equal Than Others

While Russia and the CIS have granted legal equality between men and women, in reality, conditions are far less equal. Sexual harassment is not at all unusual in business and in government, and women should be prepared for sexist and patronizing behavior from male colleagues.

Western women should also expect conversation that would be inappropriate in the west, such as comments about appearance. Attempted flattery is very much part of Russian culture.

Sartorial Swingers

Each region has its own characteristic mode of dress, some quite unlike Western styles, so don't be surprised at what you see. Most Russians expect a lot in the sartorial department from Western business people—so dress conservatively, but dress well. Although modest Western-style clothing is appropriate in the CIS, women should take pains to dress conservatively in areas outside the capitals—if you wear pants, short skirts, or sleeveless blouses, you face a risk of harassment.

Don't wear your coat or boots when you go into a public building (especially a theater); leave your coat in the cloakroom.

Cold War Blues

The Cold War may be history, but there can still be distinct tension between Russians and Americans. Even as you try to build bridges, never forget that many Russians and others in the CIS still don't entirely trust outsiders. Some see Americans as too direct and too concerned about money.

Be extremely careful to treat your Russian colleagues as equals. Don't even think of flaunting that new Rolex you got for your birthday; it won't help you build strong business relationships. Russians wrote the book on financial modesty, so act accordingly.

Instead, work hard to build a good relationship with your Russian colleagues. Slavic business associations are often based on a personal, individual relationship. Be sincere in your business dealings, and you'll build trusting bonds that should pay off in the long haul. Russians respect age and experience, so it's a good idea to send senior businessmen or -women to negotiate here.

If you remember Nikita Kruschev banging that shoe on the table—or recall seeing the entire Russian delegation stalking out of the United Nations in a huff—you'll have a key to the negotiating strategy that works in Russia. It's called "hardball." Russians are the cultural opposite of the Japanese: They don't hold their emotions in when they negotiate. They expect tantrums and walkouts and pessimism.

Don't cave in and you'll do fine—the most persistent and tenacious business person will come out ahead in negotiations with the Russians. Since the Russians are naturally as tenacious as a pit bull with a pork loin, they're hard to beat in the boardroom.

Global Guide

It's customary at business meetings to offer tea, coffee, and snacks.

What with all this walking out and issuing ultimatums and pounding the table, business negotiations in Russia tend to take time—you may need to return for several visits before you can take care of all the red tape and details. Don't give up just because you couldn't make a fast deal on a quick visit.

On the other hand, don't get cocky until you have a signed agreement in your hands. Once you do, don't figure you can go back to the bargaining table later on and fine tune the contract. What you've signed is what you're stuck with.

Say What?

If you want to get something done in Russia, you've got to use *blat* (*blaht*; influence or connections): You give me some of your caviar and I'll give you some toast points.

To Gift or Not to Gift

A gift wears many faces in Russia; one sort of gift is what you hand out to your business contacts. Another sort is what you give to a Russian friend to help out—things that he or she can't get in Russia, such as blue jeans or peanut butter. The third is, quite frankly, a bribe (you can think of it as a "bargaining chip" if that makes it more palatable).

Remember that while you can give a small "gift" to cut through red tape and then deduct it as a business expensive, gifts given to obtain business are not legally deductible in the U.S. and can be prosecutable under the Foreign Corrupt Practices Act.

Visiting the Locals

It's an honor to be invited into a Russia home, especially because it may well present a problem for your host, who—according to Russian custom—must offer you a lavish meal that he or she probably can't afford.

Despite this, when you visit the home of a Russian associate, don't turn down any offers of either food or drink. To decline is considered extremely rude. After all, if you've stood in line for two hours to get a couple of croissants and a piece of beef, how would you feel if the guest of honor turned it down?

Russians often tend to serve massive amounts of food to show they enjoy an abundance of good fortune, so leave a few bits of food on your plate at the end of a meal. This shows you're honoring your host.

Always bring wine or flowers (an even number of blooms) if you're invited to a Russian home. When you arrive, take off your shoes before entering the home.

If you don't get any invites yourself, visits to homes and cities can be organized by Intourist. You'll find that, although the people vary from region to region and from city to city, they are welcoming and hospitable.

Entertainment Russian-Style

Russia has probably produced more famous dancers, composers, and musicians than any other country in the world, and Moscow is the city for experiencing these performing arts. Go ahead and enjoy—tickets are incredibly cheap (less than a few U.S. dollars) for almost everything. Nearly always, performances begin at 7 P.M. Tickets are available in advance or from ticket booths right before the start of the performances. In the course of one month, 30 different productions may be presented by the Bolshoi Opera and Ballet Company.

While traditional cultural events are a real treat here, you can also sample the more decadent side of life in Moscow, now one of the wildest, most worldly cities in Europe. Choose from a wide spectrum of clubs, discos, and bars:

➤ Mafia-infested, super-expensive casino/strip joints

➤ Stylish yuppie bars

➤ Rave and techno clubs

You can dance in many of the Intourist restaurants and night bars, as well as in the main local restaurants. Moscow alone boasts 69 casinos, with plenty of discos and cabarets.

Your new Russian friends may invite you to a Russian *banya* (sauna), where you're expected to strip naked and sweat in a steam room while being beaten with birch twigs. (It's a favorite pastime for President Yeltsin, who loves to do this with visiting heads of state.) A compulsory part of the banya experience is heavy drinking: It's considered rude not to drain your glass when drinking a toast.

Faux Pas

Don't face the stage when you enter a row of seats in the theater; it's considered rude to squeeze past people with your back to them.

Borscht to Nuts

The kind of food visitors will eat from day-to-day depends on which city you visit and the time of year. Reservations are recommended for most restaurants; you can ask the hotel receptionist to make reservations for you (some restaurants won't have employees who speak any English). In Moscow, restaurants are usually open every day of the week, with very few exceptions. Restaurant dinner hours usually begin at 7 P.M. and run until 11 P.M.

If a restaurant is going to accept a credit card (most likely only in Moscow or a very large city), it will probably be American Express, VISA, or MasterCard.

If you find yourself in a tug of war over your coat with the restaurant's hat check girl, give in gracefully—it's considered uncivilized to wear outdoor clothes inside. (This usually means you should leave your boots at the door, too.)

Once you're seated, don't be surprised if the hostess seats strangers at your table. Many restaurants have only large tables where everyone sits together. And when you get the menu, always choose several things you'd like to have because a listing on the menu doesn't mean it's really in the kitchen. About one third to half of all items on any given menu aren't available. Smoking is acceptable unless stated otherwise.

Breakfast

If you have a hankering for bacon and eggs, stop for breakfast at your hotel; it's almost impossible to get breakfast anywhere else. But be prepared: Breakfast in the CIS is often similar to Scandinavia, with cold meats, boiled eggs, and bread served with Russian tea. *Kasha* (*kah-sha*; porridge) is a staple breakfast dish, made with milk and oats, buckwheat, or semolina.

Lunch and Dinner

Trying to find a good restaurant in Moscow used to be harder than finding a needle in the Kremlin—but not any more! Moscow now has a good selection of restaurants in all price ranges, though eating out is still relatively expensive by international standards.

In the big cities, ethnic cuisine seems to be disappearing under the influx of everything from sushi to pizza, but you can still find authentic Russian food, depending on the region:

➤ *borshch* (*bor-scht*)—beetroot soup served hot with sour cream.

➤ *akroshka* (*ah-kro-shka*)—a kvas soup served cold.

➤ *blini* (*blee-knee*)—small pancakes filled with caviar, fish, melted butter, or sour cream.

➤ *aladyi* (*ah-lahd-ee*)—crumpets with the same fillings as blini, plus jam.

➤ *pirozhky* (*peer-oh-shkey*)—fried rolls with different fillings, usually meat.

➤ *prostakvasha* (*pros-tahk-vah-sha*)—yogurt.

➤ *rossolnik* (*ross-ohl-nik*)—hot soup, usually made of pickled vegetables.

➤ *shchi* (*she*)—cabbage soup.

➤ *morozhenoye* (*mohr-ohzne-uh*)—ice cream.

➤ *ponchiki* (*pohn-she-key*)—hot, sugared doughnuts.

➤ *vareniki* (*vah-ren-nee-kee*)—dumplings containing fresh berries, cherries, or jam.

Global Guide

If no Russian food tempts your palate, you'll be glad to know that Moscow and St. Petersburg have Western–style supermarkets where you can stock up.

Whole roast suckling pig, roast goose stuffed with buckwheat, roast duck stuffed with apples, and *shashlik* (shish kebab) are served at parties and for special occasions. A vegetable variant of shashlik also exists.

Tips on Tipping

Very few places in Russia expect you to tip. If you're visiting a high-priced hotels or restaurant, a 5 percent to 15 percent gratuity is usually added to your bill. Give about $1 (U.S.) per bag to porters. You can't haggle at a shop, but in the markets, you'll be expected to bargain.

Vodka All Around

It's immediately apparent in Russia that most residents spend an awful lot of time drinking vodka. You can buy it everywhere: at street corners, shops, bars, and restaurants, in a dizzying array of styles. You'll find it served straight or flavored with pepper, berries, bison grass, apple leaves, lemon, or ginger and cloves. However they drink it, the average citizen drinks more than liter of vodka a week—usually in chilled shots tossed back with abandon.

If you don't fancy vodka, you have lots of other choices. *Krushon* (*kroo-shon*) is a highly recommended cold punch made with champagne, brandy, and summer fruit poured into a hollowed watermelon. (White wine and cucumber are used to make a drier variety.) *Nastoika* (*nas-tóy-ka*) is a fortified wine made of herbs, leaves, flowers, fruit, and roots of plants with medicinal properties. *Nalivka* (*nah-leev-ka*) is a sweet liqueur made with fruit or berries. Russian champagne is surprisingly good and reasonably priced. Imported wines from Georgia, Ukraine, and Moldova are excellent, as is Armenian Cognac. *Kvas* (*kvas*) is a fermented rye bread water that is only mildly alcoholic and refreshing in summer.

When you're seated at a restaurant, you'll probably see one bottle of water and one of vodka on the table. Note that there is usually no way to reseal the vodka—you're expected to drink it at one sitting. Because of the group seating at many places, you may find yourself sitting with a table of rowdy Russians. Expect them to invite you to drink with them. Even people from other tables may come over to toast international friendship.

It's next to impossible to refuse a drink in Russia. If you don't want to wake up with a jackhammer in your head, take small sips and stall! If you're really not in the mood, the only way you can get out of enforced drinking is to say you are an alcoholic.

Faux Pas

If you decide to have wine with your meal, remember to never pour a glass of wine backhanded (it's an insult to the person whose glass you're filling).

Don't Leave Home Without It

The countries of the Commonwealth of Independent States operate on the basis of cash-only economies, and each has their own currency system. This means that all those traveler's checks you busily filled out and all those credit cards stuffed in your wallet won't be much use to you. Before you leave home, check with your credit card and travelers check companies to learn if and where these cash substitutes can be used in Russia and the CIS.

You may not be able to get cash advances from your credit card or wire transfers even at major hotels. Don't expect to find lots of automated teller machines (ATMs) either. Major hotels or the American Express offices in Moscow or St. Petersburg may be able to suggest where you can cash travelers checks or get a cash advance on a credit card.

Faux Pas

Anyone caught dealing on the black market can expect a visit from the local militia. Don't get involved.

Realize that Russia and the countries of the CIS are struggling with profound political and economic change. Recent economic difficulties include many bank closures. If you bring over lots of U.S. dollars, you can usually exchange them for local currency only at official exchange offices or in banks. The Russian ruble is the only legal tender within that country, but while rubles aren't available outside Russia, there are thousands of exchange desks and kiosks dotted all over Moscow, many open 24 hours a day. While it's easy to change dollars into rubles, you can expect some difficulty changing rubles into dollars in Russia.

Tip of the Hat

Take along crisp, new dollar bills to exchange (and remember that pre-1993 bills are rarely accepted because of the possibility of forgeries). If the bills are too old or dirty, they may not be exchangeable.

The Least You Need to Know

➤ Take hard cash to the CIS; credit cards and travelers checks are hard to use.

➤ Be pugnacious and tenacious when negotiating with the Russians.

➤ Patience is a cultural necessity in the CIS.

➤ Dress conservatively and don't flash expensive possessions.

➤ Be honest and sincere with your CIS colleagues if you want to break down inherent distrust.

Part 4

Asia and the Pacific Rim

Part of the fun of international travel is encountering different cultures and different people—it broadens your mind and sweeps out all those cobwebs that have been festering as you sat through the 322nd episode of Melrose Place back home. Travel through Asia will do just that, because the culture is so different—the food, the people, the expectations, the attitudes—and may be very different from anything you're used to back home. And as Martha says, that's a GOOD thing.

But there are lots of things to learn before you go. Should you bow? If so, how? What sorts of gifts are taboo? How do you take off your shoes, and when should you keep them on? What should you expect when negotiating a contract?

If you're planning on traveling to this part of the world, you'll need to know all this, and more. Sit back and read on—we'll tell you how.

MADE IN...

Chapter 19

Hong Kong and Taiwan

In This Chapter

➤ Learn the ins and outs of business entertaining

➤ Discover the best ways to conduct business in Taiwan and Hong Kong

➤ Find out the importance of humility, relationships, and the group

➤ Understand the attitude toward public displays of affection

➤ Learn the ins and outs of Chinese names

Hong Kong and Taiwan are both related to China, each in its own way with modern industrialized lands clinging to the vestiges of an ancient culture. Taiwan is populated mostly with refugees from mainland China who fled the country after the Communist takeover, and who one day hope to return; Hong Kong was once independent and was returned to mainland China in 1997 as a special administrative region.

Taiwan has always been a popular refuge from mainland China, welcoming everyone from fortune hunters and farmers to persecuted minorities and exiled royalty. Part of eastern Asia, its islands border the East China Sea, the Philippine Sea, the South China Sea, and the Taiwan Strait. It has a subtropical climate with moderate temperatures in the north; the southern areas have slightly higher temperatures.

Hong Kong, six times the size of Washington, D.C., is part of eastern Asia, bordering the South China Sea and China. Cool and humid in winter, hot and rainy from spring through summer, and warm and sunny in fall, Hong Kong has a bustling free market economy highly dependent on international trade. Natural resources are limited, and food and raw materials must be imported. Even before Hong Kong reverted to Chinese administration in July 1997, it had extensive trade and investment ties with China.

Best Time to Go

The high tourist season in Hong Kong and Taiwan is October through late December, popular then because the weather is pleasant, with sunny days and comfortable, cool

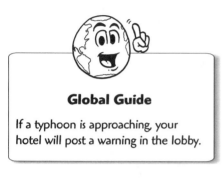

Global Guide

If a typhoon is approaching, your hotel will post a warning in the lobby.

nights. The months of June through September are the typhoon season, when the weather is hot and sticky, with lots of rain. All visitors to Hong Kong should know in advance that typhoons (called hurricanes in the Atlantic) must be treated with respect. Fortunately, Hong Kong is prepared for these blustery assaults.

Perched on an island 99 miles off the coast of China, Taiwan is subtropical, with mountains that can be chilly in summer and snowy in winter. Summer is hot and sticky all over the low parts of the island, with drenching rains in the mountains.

Who's on First?

Japan took Taiwan from China in 1895 and kept it until the end of World War II, when it was handed back to China. When Communist forces arrived on the mainland of China in 1949, Chinese president General Chiang Kaishek and his nationalist party (the Kuomintang)—together with one and a half million Chinese—fled to Taiwan to plan their reconquest of the mainland. They're still at it.

The leaders of both Communist mainland China and the Republic of China (Taiwan) claim to speak for all China, but the international community—almost to a country—sides with the mainland. In 1971, the Kuomintang lost its "Chinese" United Nations seat, and in 1979 the U.S. withdrew its recognition of Taiwan. Taiwanese politics is divided between those who want reunification with China (the Kuomintang bunch) and those who want Taiwanese independence. In 1995, relations between the two Chinas—never very warm—plunged to new lows as the two countries continued to jockey for position in the world's arena.

Today, Taiwan (the Republic of China) has a stable democracy and has a strong and well-developed economy; the president of Taiwan is the chief of state, and head of government is the Premier (President). Tourist facilities are widely available. Taiwan has a dynamic capitalist economy with gradually decreasing guidance of investment and foreign trade by government authorities and partial government ownership of some large banks and industrial firms. Spillover from the Asian financial crisis hit Taiwan in the fourth quarter of 1997, wreaking havoc on the stock and currency markets.

Hong Kong became a special administrative region of China on July 1, 1997. Under the terms of this agreement, China has promised that Hong Kong shall enjoy a high degree of autonomy in all matters except foreign and defense affairs.

What Language Is This?

In Taiwan, the official language is northern Chinese (Mandarin). Taiwanese is widely spoken, however, and English is taught as the primary foreign language in schools. Many people speak at least some English (especially younger people). In fact, many Chinese long for a chance to practice their English.

If you're having your written materials translated for use in Taiwan, be sure that they are written by a Taiwanese expert. You should not use the simplified Chinese characters used in the People's Republic of China (Communist China).

Hong Kong's population is 97 percent Chinese, most of whom speak Cantonese, not the Mandarin Chinese that is the official language of Taiwan. The official languages of Hong Kong are English and Chinese.

Written Chinese is understood by those who are literate in Chinese, but Cantonese is quite different from Mandarin—those who understand one won't be able to automatically understand the other. However, with the incorporation of Hong Kong into the People's Republic of China, the ability to speak Mandarin has become more important.

Religion

The primary religion of Taiwan is Buddhism, but other religions include Taoism, Christianity (Roman Catholic and Protestant), and Islam.

There is no official religion in Hong Kong; about one-half million Christians live in Hong Kong (half Protestant, half Catholic); there are also a few Hindus and Muslims.

Tip of the Hat

Many Chinese follow a religion in addition to the teachings of Confucius, or they may follow Taoism or Buddhism. These other ideologies influence many aspects of life in Taiwan and Hong Kong.

Let's Take a Holiday

Ancient festivals and customs are celebrated enthusiastically and traditional holidays are important.

Try to avoid traveling on major public holidays, especially Chinese New Year (usually early February), when shops and restaurants close and hotels are unusually expensive.

While October has pleasant weather, there are lots of holidays—November is a better choice. Late August or early September is Ghost Month, which means there will be no Chinese travelers on the road and temples will be at their most active.

You'll need a lunar calendar if you want to attend big events—most of them don't occur on the same date every year:

Say What?

Ghost Month is the period when ghosts from Hell walk the earth in Taiwan, and no one travels, swims, gets married, or moves. Instead, everyone visits Taoist temples.

First day of first lunar month: Chinese New Year.

15th day of first moon: The Lantern Festival.

19th day of second moon: Kuanyin's Birthday.

Early spring: Ching Ming Festival (Hong Kong).

Spring: Easter.

Spring: Tuen Ng Festival (Hong Kong).

Seventh lunar month: Ghost Month (Taiwan).

August (last Monday): Liberation Day.

Oct. 10: National Day (Taiwan).

Dec. 25: Christmas.

Early Birds Unite

No matter what, arrive early to a business meeting or dinner. This is considered a sign of respect and makes it look as if you care enough to save the host's precious time.

Faux Pas

Don't just drop by the office in Taiwan or Hong Kong and expect to pop in and see the boss—or anybody else, for that matter. An appointment is *de rigueur* for every business dealing.

Making somebody wait because you didn't get out of bed in time—or cancelling an appointment because you ate too many spring rolls the night before—will result in a severe loss of face. It's a big-time affront, so don't do it. Grit your teeth and get there on time.

In Taiwan and Hong Kong, punctuality is considered to be a virtue, so try hard to be on time. If you left your hotel in plenty of time and then got held up for an hour by snarled traffic, apologize anyway. Even if it's not your fault, you'll be expected to be sorry.

Both Taiwan and Hong Kong are 13 hours ahead of Eastern Standard Time, which means that if it's 7 A.M. in New York City, it's 8 P.M. over there.

Open Up

In Hong Kong, businesses are open from 9 A.M. to 5 P.M., Monday through Friday, with many companies open a half-day on Saturday. (Today, however, more and more firms are changing to a strict five-day week.)

Things start a bit earlier in Taiwan (8:30 A.M.) but then they crash to a halt for that two-hour customary luncheon nap before resuming from 2 P.M. to 5 P.M.; banks are also open on Saturday from 8:30 P.M. until noon.

Slow and Steady

Don't expect to sit down at your first business meeting and zip through that agenda before lunch time. In fact, business is never the first item discussed at a meeting. Typically, things start off with a short interval of polite general conversation, usually over tea. In a business setting, the highest-ranking executive will be the one who does most (if not all) of the talking. Your team should act the same way.

The Chinese see haste as a sign of suspicious behavior, so be patient in your business negotiations. No mater how agitated the boss is back home, remain calm and don't push. Decisions are a group activity here, and they can take months (or years!). Business dealings usually take time (and a few visits) before they can be worked out.

Name-dropping and self-promotion may boost you up the rungs of corporate America's ladder, but it won't get you far in China. The Chinese consider boasting to be a rude trait. Never exaggerate your abilities; humility is a virtue. Even if you did make the Fortune 1000 list, keep that fact to yourself. Chances are your accolades are already known, and you'll earn respect by being modest.

Don't direct all your information to the senior negotiator, whose presence may simply be ceremonial. The junior staff often gets the info to the group leader. Whoever you decide to target, present all your materials and your business ideas in a modest, patient way.

Global Guide

Many Chinese adhere to old beliefs, such as astrology and geomancy. Even senior executives may wait until a "lucky" day to make a decision.

Most top hotels in Hong Kong provide business centers for visiting business people, offering typing, duplication, translation, and other services.

Saving Face

It's important to understand the principle of "saving face," because your reputation and social standing is based on this complex concept. When you treat someone with respect, he gains face—if you berate that person, he loses face. Anybody who loses his temper in public loses face big time—and also causes a loss of face for the person he's angry with. It's the Eastern equivalent of a lose-lose situation.

Trust is everything here, but it's not necessarily something that's going to be easy to establish. In fact, as a Westerner, you'll probably be automatically distrusted until you prove yourself. Take several trips to establish a personal relationship. If you're going to do business in Taiwan and Hong Kong, expect to have to work for it. Chinese here are extremely competitive and they're going to want to know everything about your proposals. They also like to bargain, so be prepared to compromise.

Tip of the Hat

Causing someone to lose face—even if you didn't mean to—is a sure way to squash any deal you've come to finalize.

Moreover, your colleagues may seem extremely Westernized, with the same electronic gadgets and the zeal for capitalism as you're familiar with in the U.S.—but at heart they are Asian and very traditional. When you encounter delays, remember that the pace of business is much slower in the East, where patience is an art form.

Hello, Goodbye

In Taiwan and Hong Kong, handshaking is a common greeting, although when meeting someone for the first time a simple nod of the head is enough. If you want to earn points and show respect, bow slightly with hands at sides and feet together. Either English or Chinese traditions are appropriate, so it's okay to shake hands or bow. If you do bow, however—get it right. When bowing to a superior, you should bow more deeply and allow him to rise first.

Most Chinese women won't shake hands, so don't make a grab for her. Western women will have to make the first hand-shaking move; a Chinese man won't. When you're introduced to a person from Taiwan or Hong Kong, you may be asked if you've eaten; just say "Yes" even if you're starved. This question is similar to the Western, "How are you"—no one really wants to know how you are, and no one in the East really wants to find out if you've eaten.

Faux Pas

Don't call Foo Yung "Mr. Yung"— he's "Mr. Foo." In Taiwan and Hong Kong, as in many parts of Asia, the family name comes first and the given name comes last.

When you're mingling at a party and you spy someone you'd like to meet, don't just trot boldly up and introduce yourself over the *dim sum*. Ask a third person to be an intermediary.

Business Cards

Business cards are popular in Taiwan and Hong Kong, so bring along a lot of them. Put your name, company name, and title on one side, and duplicate the same info on the other side in Mandarin Chinese. Status and rank are important here.

When you first meet, present your bilingual business card to the others, with the Chinese translation side of your card facing the recipients. Holding the top corners with two fingers of both hands, offer your card to that person.

Accept others' cards the same way. Take a good look at it before putting it in your card case, but don't put it in your back pocket.

By Any Other Name

There are only about 400 different Chinese family names, but when they're translated into English, they may be spelled differently. For example, Huang, Wang, and Wong are all versions of the same Chinese clan name.

Official titles such as "General," "Committee Member," or "Bureau Chief" are used whenever possible, and are followed with the surname: "General Huang."

No Touching

If you want to hold hands in Hong Kong, make sure it's with somebody of the same sex—that won't raise eyebrows, but touching someone of the opposite sex will. Any other kind of physical contact won't be welcomed. In Taiwan, don't hold hands with (or touch) anybody at all.

While people in Hong Kong may not like to be touched while you talk, they'll stand much closer to you while holding a conversation than you may be used to back in the U.S. Try not to back up as they encroach upon your comfort zone.

A woman may get away with crossing her legs in Hong Kong and Taiwan, but men should keep those loafers planted solidly on the floor.

Try to avoid waving your hands when you speak; Chinese speakers don't talk with their hands in this way and they'll be distracted if you stand there and flap your fingers in their face while you talk. Here are some other gestures to avoid:

➤ Don't point with a finger at someone else.

➤ Don't crook your finger at someone else to beckon them over (instead, turn your hand palm down and wave the fingers toward the body).

➤ Don't wink.

Ancient Attitudes

No matter how modern Taiwan and Hong Kong may seem, these countries retain much of their ancient conservative attitudes. The equality of women is one of these entrenched norms. You won't find many women business executives in this part of the world; U.S. businesswomen, therefore, may have a tough row to hoe here.

Global Guide

You may point to your chest to refer to yourself, but a Taiwanese person will point to his or her nose to indicate selfhood.

Think Conservative

Dress is conservative in Hong Kong and Taiwan, with dark-colored, lightweight business suits for men and conservative skirts and blouses for women. Neatness counts in this part of the world—it may be hot and sticky, but you don't have to look like a slob. Modesty counts here, so ditch the revealing clothing. (Shorts for children are okay, however.)

Don't wear white or blue at any social function in Hong Kong; these colors are linked to mourning and death.

Talk Softly

Try to tone down that life-of-the-party attitude when you travel to Taiwan and Hong Kong. The reputation of Americans (loud and brassy) precedes you—so do all you can to break this stereotype by being reserved, quiet, and a study of self-control.

Global Guide

Smoking is widely acceptable and only prohibited where specified.

Being polite is one of the best things you can do when visiting Taiwan and Hong Kong. Try to be as humble and modest as your Western personality will allow. Don't just barge into someone else's office; wait to be invited. If your Taiwanese colleague praises your speech, politely demur. Feel free to compliment others, but deflect all compliments that flow your way.

Since the elderly are revered in this part of the world, go along—treat older people with respect. This means letting them go through a doorway first, not smoking in their presence, and so on.

Gifts All Around

Business gift giving is quite popular in Taiwan and Hong Kong—choose a small gift with your company logo (and make sure it wasn't manufactured in the country with whom you're doing business). If you don't want to give a business trinket, try one of these:

➤ fine pen or pencil set

➤ imported liquor

➤ food (but don't take food to a dinner party)

When you present your gift, don't be surprised if your colleague declines it three times; that's a sign of good breeding and modesty among Chinese. If you hang in there for the third refusal, your gift will be accepted. (They've wanted to do this all along, but politeness required otherwise.)

Avoid giving the following gifts to anyone in Taiwan or Hong Kong:

➤ straw sandals (bad luck)

➤ knives or cutting implements (suggests ending relationships)

➤ clocks (bad luck)

➤ anything colored white, black, or blue (association with death)

➤ handkerchiefs (associated with death)

➤ flowers (in the past, they were associated with death; if you do bring flowers, make sure your bouquet contains an odd number of flowers)

If you are given a gift, it's normal to return the favor by giving a gift of about the same value.

Let Me Entertain You

When you travel to Taiwan for business, expect to be entertained—and entertained—and entertained. In fact, you'll be invited out every night to night spots and clubs, usually until the wee hours of the morning.

If you're looking for fun, Taiwan has plenty of nightlife, and Taipei in particular is lively at night. You can find Western-style entertainment at hotels, and in the many discos, clubs, restaurants, and cinemas in Taipei. Other entertainment includes the popular KTVs (a type of sing-along club modeled after Japanese karaoke bars), as well as circuses and mime theater.

If your brow is more high than low, there's excellent Chinese drama, opera, and art. Despite rapid industrialization and development, the way of life is very much Chinese, steeped in tradition and old values. Taiwanese culture is very similar to that of China: both love opera, replete with beautiful costumes, music, acting, and atmosphere.

Say What?

A money gift traditionally given in a red envelope to children and service people during the Chinese New Year is called *hong bao*. The money is usually given in even number of crisp new bills.

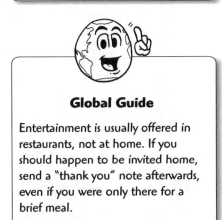

Global Guide

Entertainment is usually offered in restaurants, not at home. If you should happen to be invited home, send a "thank you" note afterwards, even if you were only there for a brief meal.

Changing Money

In Taiwan, travelers' checks and cash can be exchanged at international airports and large banks, but you might get stuck with uncashable checks in rural areas. Stick to U.S. dollars for cash and checks if you can (other currencies will cause you problems). Don't exchange your checks at the first place you find; commission costs can vary widely. There are no legal private money changers in Taiwan, but some jewelery shops will exchange cash. Major international credit cards can be used at big hotels and fancy restaurants; you also can get cash advances at your credit card's headquarters.

Soto to Nuts

People in Hong Kong and Taiwan love to eat, and they love to feed guests. Food here is similar to that in China, with a twist: subtropical flavors with seafood and the liberal use of sugar.

While many meals in Hong Kong and Taiwan are long (they may include 12 courses), it's not considered an insult to eat sparingly. However, a good appetite is always appreciated and it's good manners to taste every dish.

Lunch

A great choice for lunch are the *dim sum* restaurants that serve tasty Chinese hors d'oeuvres (come a bit early to avoid crowds). As the staff pushes trolleys past your table, they call out the names of dishes; point to what you want. Some items may seem less than enticing (congealed blood and giblets comes to mind...) but other *dim sum* tidbits such as spring rolls or steamed pork buns are delicious. Always check the cost of items labeled "market price"—the cost may skyrocket as a result of anything from heavy traffic to a devastating typhoon. Reservations are always a good idea, especially at lunchtime (between 1 P.M. and 2 P.M.) or on weekend nights.

Chopstick Tips

Before you leave home for your trip, get a bowl of rice and practice using chopsticks; you'll be expected to wield them like a pro. (Remember: If you drop them, it's bad luck!) The hardest thing you'll have to eat with chopsticks is rice; lucky for you, it usually arrives at the end of the meal. Because you'll be leaving part of your meal anyway (to show that you've eaten plenty and couldn't touch another bite), it won't matter if you don't scoop up all your rice. (Tip: It's okay to hold the bowl close to your mouth and shovel in the rice with your chopsticks.) Watch your neighbor and do what he does. In fact, that's good advice for all your meals—when you're eating during a business dinner or banquet, watch your hosts and do what they do. Don't eat or drink until they do, and never take the last bit of food from a serving plate. That would signify that you're still hungry. Finally, don't leave your chopsticks sticking straight up and down in your rice bowl, as this would suggest *insense sticks*, which are associated with death.

Dinner Is Served

Taiwan restaurants almost always have table service, although some hotels offer buffet/barbecue lunches. Most hotels have restaurants that offer both Western and Chinese cuisines, and some of the larger hotels offer several styles of Chinese cooking.

Although the Taiwanese use many ingredients that may turn a Westerner's stomach (bear organs, dog, or snake), you probably won't find them in most dinner menus. Favorite Taiwanese dishes include spring rolls with peanut butter, sweet-and-sour spare ribs, bean curd in red sauce, oyster omelets, and seafood. Special foods to keep an eye out for:

➤ moon cakes (made during the Moon Festival in autumn)

➤ spring rolls (sold in April)

➤ rice dumplings (made for the Dragon Boat Festival)

➤ red turtle cakes (for birthdays and temple worship)

Hong Kong is one of the great centers for international cuisine, where you can find many Indian, Vietnamese, Malaysian, and Thai restaurants. Of course, you can also get terrific authentic Chinese food from all the regions of China, including:

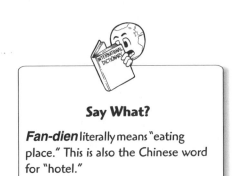

Say What?

Fan-dien literally means "eating place." This is also the Chinese word for "hotel."

➤ **Cantonese:** The Cantonese ideal is to bring out the natural taste of ingredients by cooking them quickly at very high temperatures, creating *wok chi*, a flash of energy that requires food to be served and eaten immediately. Cantonese food is parboiled, steamed, and quickly stir-fried without being greasy; specialties include dim sum (savory snacks, usually steamed and served in bamboo baskets).

➤ **Northern (Peking):** Everybody loves Peking duck—and nowhere is it better than in Hong Kong. For those of you who think that all Chinese cooking features rice, here's a new idea: Peking cuisine features northern noodles, not rice. Peking noodles, along with Mongolian barbecue and onion cakes, are big winners.

➤ **Shanghainese:** Expect good seafood with this style of cooking: Shanghai crabs, diced or shredded veggies stewed in soya or fried in sesame oil with pots of peppers and garlic (can be greasy).

➤ **Chiu Chow:** This style of preparation is hearty chow featuring thick shark's fin soup, whelk (tiny snails), bird's nest, and steamed lobsters served with tangerine jam.

➤ **Hakka:** Simple in style, baked chicken in salt is among the best dishes.

➤ **Szechwan:** Hot and spicy with plenty of chilies, this style features rice, bamboo, wheat, river fish, shellfish, chicken, and pork dishes with plenty of salt, anise, fennel seed, chili, and coriander.

Don't swoon when the bill arrives—you'll find you were charged for everything, including tea, rice, and even those side dishes you found on your table that you probably thought were freebie snacks.

Global Guide

Banquets are a large part of Hong Kong and Taiwan's Chinese culture. Celebrating a productive business meeting or a new alliance usually occurs over 8 to 12 courses of a well-prepared banquet.

221

Raise a Glass

Most Taiwan bars have counter service. There are no set licensing hours and alcohol is widely available. Taiwan beer houses, which sell draught beer and snacks, are also popular. In the northern district of Tienmu, there is a street of open-air beer houses.

In Hong Kong, cocktails aren't usually part of the Chinese experience, but beer and wine with dinner is another matter! Popular Chinese beers are the locally brewed San Miguel and Tsingtao (from China); other imported beers are widely available. Chinese wines and spirits include:

➤ **Zhian Jing** *(zhan jing)*: a rice wine served hot, like sake.

➤ **Liang hua pei** *(lang-wha-pay)*: potent plum brandy.

➤ **Kaolian** *(kao-le-ahn)*: whiskey.

Tea for Two

You also can sample both traditional and modern tea houses in Taiwan, open all day and in the evening. In the countryside around Mucha, you can visit all-night tea houses and sip locally produced teas. High-quality meals and snacks are also available. These tea houses are popular with local families, particularly on special occasions.

Tipping

In Taiwan, tipping is not an established custom, although it's more common now than it used to be. The only people who really expect you to cough up the cash are hotel bellhops and airport porters, who will expect about $1 (U.S.) per bag. Taipei hotels and restaurants add 10 percent service charge and 5 percent value-added tax (VAT) on your bill; extra tipping isn't expected. It's not customary to tip taxi drivers.

Today, tips are expected at most restaurants, even if a service charge is already to the bill. In more traditional Chinese restaurants, however, tips aren't expected.

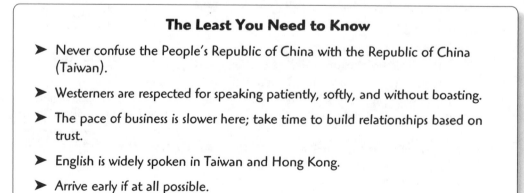

The Least You Need to Know

➤ Never confuse the People's Republic of China with the Republic of China (Taiwan).

➤ Westerners are respected for speaking patiently, softly, and without boasting.

➤ The pace of business is slower here; take time to build relationships based on trust.

➤ English is widely spoken in Taiwan and Hong Kong.

➤ Arrive early if at all possible.

Chapter 20

China

In This Chapter

➤ Learn about China's relationship with Taiwan and Hong Kong

➤ Discover the importance of business banquets

➤ Read about the intricacies of the Chinese language

➤ Find out the importance of humility, relationships, and the group

➤ Discover the power of Chinese officials

China is the most populous nation by far and the third-largest country in the world (it's bigger than all of Europe), with a coastline nearly 11,000 miles long. This great hulking land, long isolated from the rest of the world, remains steeped in mystery and very difficult for many Americans to decipher. Even as China courts new business and struggles to build a technological empire, in many ways, old customs, beliefs, and superstitions die hard. Even the most urbane Chinese business leader may consult a *feng shui* specialist about the most harmonious way to place a home, or burn joss sticks for good luck in an enterprise.

China is part of eastern Asia, bordering the East China Sea, Korea Bay, the Yellow Sea, and the South China Sea, between North Korea and Vietnam.

While many Americans refer to the People's Republic of China as "Mainland China," or "Communist China," when you're visiting on their turf, the only term you should use is the People's Republic of China (or the abbreviation, P.R.C.) At the same time, don't confuse the P.R.C. with the Republic of China (Taiwan), which the P.R.C. considers to be a sort of scofflaw district only temporarily beyond their jurisdiction.

China is a land of violent weather; there are frequent typhoons (about five per year along the southern and eastern coasts) as well as damaging floods, tsunamis, earthquakes, and droughts. Its climate is extremely diverse, ranging from tropical in the south to sub arctic in the north. China is a land of mostly mountains, with high plateaus and deserts in the west, and plains, deltas, and hills in the east. It has very hot summers in most parts of the country, with bitter winters in the north and comfortable winters in the south. Westerners may feel uncomfortable here because the heating is often too cold or too hot, but thick quilts and hot water bottles are provided everywhere. Spring rains can make southern cities humid.

Sandstorms can be a problem in the north (including Beijing) in spring and autumn. Tibet can be quite cold, even in the autumn and late spring. If you didn't bring warm enough clothing in the winter, you can easily find most practical cold-weather gear in most areas of China.

Tip of the Hat

It's a good idea to visit China from September to October, with April to May a close second. Heat and humidity make the summer less attractive, but on the other hand, there are fewer foreign tourists and prices can be a bit lower.

A One-Party State

The People's Republic of China has been a one-party state controlled by the Chinese Communist Party since its founding in 1949. Although this country boasts one of the world's largest and fastest growing economies, modern tourist facilities are still not widely available, except in major cities. The president is chief of state, and the premier is head of government. The cabinet is called the State Council, and it's appointed by the National People's Congress (NPC). No meaningful political opposition groups to Communism exist.

China was unified under the first of a series of dynasties beginning in 221 B.C., which finally ended with the Manchu dynasty in 1911. The dynasties were replaced by the Republic on February 12, 1912, followed by the People's Republic on October 1, 1949.

The legal system is a complex amalgam of custom and statute, which is largely based on criminal law. A rudimentary civil code has been in effect since 1987, and new legal codes have been in effect since 1980. Continuing efforts are being made to improve civil, administrative, criminal, and commercial law.

Beginning in late 1978, the Chinese leadership has been trying to shove the economy into the twentieth century, from a sluggish Soviet-style central system to a more market-oriented economy—all while maintaining rigid Communist Party control. Authorities improved the economy by:

➤ Ending collectives in favor of individually-owned farms.

➤ Giving more authority to local officials and plant managers.

➤ Allowing small-scale enterprises.

➤ Opening the economy to more foreign trade and investment.

As a result, agricultural output doubled in the 1980s, and industry posted major gains, especially in coastal areas near Hong Kong and opposite Taiwan, where foreign investment helped spur economic output.

This was not always successful, however, which forces Beijing to periodically backtrack and retighten central controls. By 1995–97, inflation dropped sharply, reflecting tighter monetary policies and stronger measures to control food prices. At the same time, the government struggled to collect taxes, reduce corruption, and boost the large shaky state-owned enterprises. The next few years may bear witness to increasing tensions between a highly centralized political system and an increasingly decentralized economic system.

Hong Kong's reversion on July 1, 1997, to Chinese administration is strengthening the already close ties between the two economies. At the same time, China considers Taiwan its twenty-third province.

Hong Kong

When Hong Kong reverted to Chinese sovereignty in 1997, many people feared that Hong Kong as everyone knew it would be gone forever. But there is the chance that assimilating Hong Kong may change China.

In recent years, China has begun to reform its own economy, setting up Shanghai to rival Hong Kong as a financial center.

The world is waiting to see what happens as young Hong Kong citizens push the limits of Beijing's tolerance of dissent. As in 1989, the central leadership tends to create an atmosphere that encourages dissenters to appear—and then makes examples of them.

Many Westerners confuse the Chinese acceptance of open markets with a recognition of civil rights or democracy. The two are very separate.

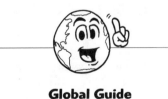

Global Guide

Many Chinese adhere to old beliefs, such as astrology. Even senior executives may wait until a "lucky" day to make a decision.

Travelin' Around

China is one of the most mysterious travel destinations in the world—and there are times when you may wonder why you went there at all. Restaurants tell you they're out of food but they serve Chinese patrons. Your trip off the beaten track will be cancelled without warning. Clerks in the shops get angry when you interrupt their personal conversations to ask a question.

The key to survival in China: No matter what has been promised by whom, Chinese officials always have the last word, and "capricious" is their middle name. Some decisions are based on politics; others are founded on an elaborate pecking order for preferential treatment. Group travel may be the best way to deal with these foibles, and could also be the only legal way you'll get to see certain parts of the country.

While improvements in China's tourism infrastructure have been noticeable, levels of competency and efficiency vary. Except in Hong Kong, the computerization of reservation systems is still only in the introductory phase.

Independent travel has become easier for agents to arrange, thanks in part to the introduction of competition among Chinese travel services. It's even possible to book some reservations directly with hotels in the larger Chinese cities. Travelers who want to make arrangements while on the road should be aware that they may encounter problems trying to arrange transportation and lodging locally.

Don't be surprised, however, if you draw a crowd; it's still unusual in many places to find Westerners.

Faux Pas

Be careful about booking Trans-Siberian Express tickets from Hong Kong—there are many black-market tickets. The Chinese won't confirm tickets bought outside the country more than two weeks ahead of departure, so if you buy one of these tickets, make sure it is "confirmed" and not just "open."

Chinese Spoken Here

The northern dialect of Mandarin (known as *Putonghua*, or Common Speech) is the official language in China, spoken by more than 70 percent of the people. (It's not the language spoken by most Chinese-Americans, however; they speak the southern dialect of Cantonese. Someone who understands Mandarin most likely won't be able to figure out Cantonese, and vice versa.)

Other major dialects include Shanghainese (*Wu*), Minbei (*Fuzhou*), Minnan (*Hokkien-Taiwanese*), Xiang, Gan, and Hakka. In fact, each of the 55 recognized minorities speak their own language.

However, while there are many dialects in China that are as different from each other as English is from French or Italian, all natives understand written Chinese characters.

Keep in mind that when the Communist Chinese took over in 1949, they made certain changes in their written and spoken languages. These changes were not enthusiastically adopted outside the country's boundaries, however; for example, Taiwan still uses the older form of written and spoken Chinese.

When you're having your written materials translated into Chinese, make sure they are written in "reformed" Chinese. And use only black and white in your materials (colors have great significance). One of the most challenging things to translate is your name; translating phonetically may result in an undesirable meaning, so be sure to get someone who speaks the language to advise you on this.

When discussing numbers, write them down, since it's easy to confuse numbers in China: for example, 50 (*wu shi*) can easily be misunderstood as 15 (*shi wu*). This confusion is similar to when an English speaker says, "16," and it may sound like, "60."

Tip of the Hat

Learn to count to 10 in Chinese. This will be helpful when shopping, as Western hand signals for numbers aren't the same in China. (For example, to a Chinese, the forefinger and thumb outstretched means "eight.")

While the Chinese don't expect you to speak their language like Mao Tse Tung, you'll earn the respect of your Chinese counterparts if you try to utter at least a few of the simplest phrases or words. Outside of the major hotels, you'll find few people who speak English, but your hosts will often bring an interpreter or a colleague who speaks English to a business meeting with English-speaking guests. However, many businesses don't have English speakers to answer the phone.

If you have trouble being understood (and you probably will), try calling your embassy for help. However, be advised that the U.S. Embassy in Beijing is notoriously hostile and unhelpful—even to its own citizens.

Religious Beliefs

Officially atheist, China is traditionally pragmatic and eclectic. Religions include Daoism (Taoism), Buddhism, Muslim, and Christian. The Chinese constitution does guarantee freedom of religion (with certain limits).

In addition to a formal religion, many Chinese also practice Confucianism, which is not technically a religion but rather a philosophy. Confucius believed that the family was the basic unit of society and that everyone had certain responsibilities in their dealings with everyone else in the family. Confucianism also grants specific rankings so that everyone knows who's doing what for whom (the son defers to the father, the younger brother defers to the older brother, and so on). Confucianism holds—and the Chinese believe—that the values of kindness, righteousness, intelligence, and faithfulness are profoundly important. These principles guide their everyday family and business life.

Local Holidays

China has many local holidays celebrated in different parts of the country as opposed to national holidays. Check with your local Chinese hosts to make sure your appointments won't conflict.

Jan. 1: New Year's Day.

Feb. 19-20: Spring festival.

May 1: Labor Day.

Oct. 1-2: National Day (celebrating the founding of the People's Republic of China in 1949).

Arrive Early

It's important to arrive early for business meetings or dinner. This is considered a sign of respect. Cancelling an appointment because you ate too much Beijing duck the night before is just rude. It's a big-time affront, so don't do it. Grit your teeth and get there on time.

Global Guide

During that time, the company may totally shut down so that employees can go home for lunch and a quick nap, so plan accordingly when scheduling business appointments or trying to phone somebody to make an appointment.

Doors Open Early

Although we may think Americans are workaholics, our work ethic pales by comparison to that of the Chinese. Until recently, the official work week in China was six longer-than-normal days (closed Sundays) with no break for lunch. Today, however, many businesses keep the more traditional 8 A.M. to 5 P.M. work schedule, with a lunch break from noon to 1:30 P.M. Banks stay open from 10 A.M. through 6 P.M., Monday through Friday. Shop hours are from 9 A.M. to 7 P.M. daily, although most stores in urban areas stay open until 10 P.M.

Timeliness

China may be huge, but it's all crammed into one time zone (including Beijing)—13 hours ahead of Eastern Standard Time. That means when it's 9 A.M. in New York City, it's 10 P.M. in China. (And by the way, China doesn't observe Daylight Saving Time.)

In formal China, you can't drop in without an appointment—it's mandatory for every business dealing in China.

Meet and Greet

When you're introduced, bow your head slightly (it's a sign of respect), but don't grab anyone's hand and start pumping. The Chinese don't like to be touched by strangers. In business, shaking hands is very common.

What's Your Title?

In China, as in many parts of Asia, the family name comes first and the given name comes last.

Because there are only about 400 different Chinese family names, you'd think it would be easy to spell them—but when they're translated into English, they may be spelled differently. For example, Huang, Wang and Wong are all versions of the same Chinese clan name.

Official titles such as "General," "Committee Member," or "Bureau Chief" are used whenever possible, and are followed with the surname: "General Huang."

Don't Be a Card

Exchanging business cards in China is like shaking hands in the U.S.—it's part of proper business etiquette. If you can, before venturing overseas have your business cards printed in both English and Chinese. If you didn't get around to this beforehand, ask your concierge or hotel business center manager if he or she can take care of having your cards reprinted in both languages (preferably using the local dialect). Again be careful about having your name literally translated, it may result in a offensive or unflattering meaning. Have a name selected that represents who you are as a person—something that conveys your good qualities.

You'll exchange business cards right away when you first meet. When you present your bilingual business card to a prospective client, make sure the Chinese translation side of your card is facing the recipient. Then, holding the upper corners of the card with the thumb and forefinger of both hands, offer your card to that person.

When someone gives you a business card, receive the card in the same way as you gave yours, and be sure to examine its contents before putting it carefully in your card case for future reference. (And by the way, don't park that card case in your back pocket, where you'll be sitting on it.) Simply stashing the card as soon as you receive it will

Faux Pas

Picking the wrong colors can be disastrous. Gold is the most prestigious color for your ink. Never write anyone's name with red ink. (Buddhists use red ink to print the names of the deceased.)

cause your contact to immediately lose face—not a good move if you're hoping to nurture a future business affiliation.

Getting Down to Business

Don't expect to sit down at your first business meeting and zip through that agenda before lunch time. In fact, business is never the first item discussed at a meeting. Typically, things start off with a short interval of polite general conversation, usually over tea.

In a business setting, the highest-ranking Chinese executive will be the one who does most (if not all) of the talking. Your team should act the same way.

The host may signal the end of a meeting by offering more tea. The correct response at this point is to demur, saying that you should be leaving quite soon.

Patience Is a Virtue

The Chinese see haste as a sign of suspicious behavior, so be patient in your business negotiations. No matter how agitated the boss is back home in Indiana, remain calm and don't push. Decisions are a group activity here, and they can take months (or years!). Business dealings usually take time (and a few visits) before they can be worked out.

No Boasting

Name-dropping and self-promotion may boost you up the rungs of corporate America's ladder, but it won't get you far in China. The Chinese consider boasting to be a rude trait. Never exaggerate your abilities. The Chinese believe humility is a virtue; they will investigate your claims.

Even if you did make the Fortune 1000 list, keep that fact to yourself. Chances are your accolades are already known, and you'll earn respect by being modest.

Teamwork

Emphasize company teamwork as opposed to individual business plans. The Chinese place a strong emphasis on the need to work together as if you are each part of a well-oiled machine. They tend to identify with the ideas of a firm as a whole, rather that those ideas of just one business associate.

If you want to do business in China, you'll spend time cultivating relationships. This is known as *guanxi* (gwon-shee)—the responsibilities you undertake by being connected to other people in a business sense.

In this way, a Chinese executive maintains certain obligations toward his employees, and they likewise have certain responsibilities toward him.

Saving Face

To function well in China it's important to understand the principle of "saving face." In China, your reputation and social standing is based on treating others with respect, and being treated this way yourself. Anybody who loses his temper in public loses face—and also causes a loss of face for the person he's angry with. It's a lose-lose situation.

For example, if you decline an invitation to a play because you've got a headache, you lose face simply because you are not available. To save face for both of you, you must apologize for not being able to accept the invitation, and then propose an alternative plan that would be acceptable to everyone.

Tip of the Hat

Causing someone to lose face—even if you didn't mean to—is a sure way to squash any deal you've come to China to finalize.

In some ways, this importance of "saving face" influences China to this day. The memory of humiliation by other countries in the nineteenth and twentieth centuries still rankles, which is one reason by China rebuffs foreign insistence on human rights. China sees these demands as unnecessary meddling in its own affairs.

If you're intent on doing business in China, never forget the Chinese opinion about foreign aggression in any form. It's likely that you'll tower over your Chinese colleagues, and size can be a form of intimidation. Since it's imperative that you develop trust among the Chinese business people, try to minimize your height difference by sitting instead of standing whenever you can. If you have to stand, search for ways to appear smaller (stand on a lower step, for example).

Hands Off!

When you're traveling in China, don't touch anybody! Business people don't hug, kiss, or touch in any way, except for shaking hands. You can get away with holding hands with someone of the same sex (if you're good friends), but any sort of public affection between the opposite sex (even if you're married) is not acceptable.

Speak Softly

The Chinese don't appreciate the "big" voice and expansive gestures of many Western-ers, so try to modulate your voice. Loudness is akin to rudeness here. You'll also want to take your time when you're ready to speak in China. Think about what you're going to say before you say it; a quick way to lose credibility with your Chinese counterpart is to make an inaccurate statement. So, get your facts straight or don't say a word. While you're at it, listen carefully when your Chinese hosts are speaking.

What is acceptable in the U.S. may offend the Chinese, and what is perfectly decent behavior in China may leave you gaping. For example, if you feel like spitting in public, go right ahead—it's perfectly acceptable. And if you've got a cold and you left your hanky behind, don't worry! The Chinese expect you to blow your nose onto the ground in public.

On the other hand, while you can spit and blow your nose in front of anybody, you should cover your mouth if you have to use a toothpick. In fact, you shouldn't be putting your hands into your mouth at all, whether you're nervously nibbling your finger nails or picking a bit of rice out of your teeth. Hands in the mouth are disgusting to the Chinese.

Here are some other gestures to avoid:

➤ Don't point with a finger at another person.

➤ Don't wiggle your finger at another person to call them over (turn your hand palm down and move your fingers toward your body).

➤ Don't be surprised (or offended) if Tibetans stick their tongues out at you. It's a friendly greeting.

Gender Gap

While women are said to be equal to men, Confucianism does not teach this; in fact, economic and social inequality for women continues in this country.

Suit Yourself

For business, men should wear conservative dark suits and ties (white shirts are okay, but not white ties or suits). Women can wear dresses or suits—but never all in white; it's the color of mourning. Women commonly wear boots in winter, even for business.

Women won't need high heels or a long, formal gown unless you're going to a formal reception given for a foreign diplomat.

Global Guide

Expect to have your clothes brushed as you wash your hands in the men's rooms of the fancier hotels. It's the custom.

Except in business settings, dress is casual in Beijing and it is becoming more liberal every year. It is perfectly acceptable for women to wear skirts without pantyhose and shorts in the summer; shorts and tee shirts aren't considered improper during the summer, but very few Chinese people (especially men) wear them. Also frowned upon are bright colors (especially red) when visiting Mao Tse Tung's mausoleum.

Open-toed sandals are considered unclean, so wear closed shoes whenever possible. Bathing suits in China are generally modest, although men generally wear the tighter, racing-style swimsuits that some Westerners avoid. Women, on the other hand, wear one-piece suits; bikinis are extremely rare, thongs are taboo, and topless or nude bathing is prohibited everywhere—even in foreign hotels.

Gifts Are Illegal, But ...

If you really want to follow the letter of the Chinese law, gift-giving is illegal here. But this is changing, and so you'll want to be prepared. It's acceptable for your company to present a gift to the entire Chinese company—make it clear that the gift is from your company to the entire Chinese organization. Give the gift to the company's leader (remember, always use both hands). If you're choosing this sort of company-wide gift, try one of these selections:

➤ historical gift from your state

➤ local crafts from the U.S.

➤ an illustrated book

If you want to give your Chinese hosts a gift, remember not to buy anything to expensive (it might embarrass the giftee). Good gifts for an individual might be a fine pen, stamps (the Chinese love to collect stamps), tee shirts with a U.S. sports team decal, solar-powered calculator, or excellent liquor. Food gifts are always a treat, but don't bring a gift of edible treats to a dinner party (it implies your host isn't going to feed you well enough). You can send candy or fruit afterwards.

Say What?

Hong bao is a money gift traditionally given in a red envelope to children and service people during the Chinese New Year. The money is usually given in even number of crisp new bills.

Present the gift to an individual in private—and only after all your business has been concluded. Remember that red is the color of luck in China, so that's a good color choice. If you do decide to give a gift, don't choose these:

➤ **Clocks:** The sound of the word in Chinese has an unpleasant connotation.

➤ **Green hat:** A green hat means you're a cuckold.

➤ **Cheese:** Many Chinese are lactose intolerant.

➤ **White tie:** White is the color of mourning.

➤ **Straw sandals:** These are associated with funerals.

➤ **Handkerchiefs:** These are associated with death.

➤ **Stork or crane:** These, too, are associated with death.

Even if you know what you're going to give before you leave the states, don't wrap the present before you get to China. They'll just unwrap it again in Customs. When you do wrap the gift, don't choose paper in shades of white, black, or blue (again, it's that mourning association). Good colors to pick are red (lucky color!), pink, or yellow (happy).

Let Me Entertain You

Try to visit the nightlife in Beijing, from the teahouses offering cabaret shows along with tea, to the dinner shows that serving Beijing duck along with pageantry inspired by the Qing or Ming dynasties.

If you want to go to the theater, buy your tickets directly from the various theaters. The concierge or front desk at many hotels can help you buy tickets to events. Tickets sold by folks outside events may or may not be tickets for the actual event taking place. Be careful when buying tickets this way—and avoid this if you can.

Tang to Nuts

Before you leave, get a bowl of rice and practice using chopsticks. (Don't drop them or you'll risk bad luck.) Remember to leave some food on your plate. Keep in mind that it's okay to hold a bowl close to your mouth as you eat. Watch your neighbor and do what she does. Don't eat or drink until your hosts do.

Usually reservations aren't required in most restaurants unless you have more than five people in your party, or it's a holiday.

Say What?

Kuaitzu is the Chinese word for "chopsticks" (it also means "hurry"— and that's what you'll have to do to keep up with the speed with which the Chinese manipulate them).

It will probably shock you when you first encounter this, but the Chinese who share your table may happily burp and slurp loudly as they spoon up that *Moo goo gai pan*. Don't worry—they're just showing they enjoy the meal.

For more tips on dining à la Chinoise, read on:

➤ Don't eat cheese in public; many Chinese consider dairy products disgusting.

➤ Don't try to order chop suey, chow mein, or fortune cookies. These dishes were invented in the U.S. and are unknown in China.

➤ Try White Rabbit candy or chocolate made by the Children's Food Factory—they're the best Chinese-made brands you'll find in Asia.

Tipping

Tipping is not expected in China, except for hotel porters who now expect a tip for carrying your bags to a hotel room or a waiting taxi. It's customary to let taxi drivers keep the change. However, don't tip at restaurants. It's not expected and may even be construed as an offense. Some restaurants may add a 15 percent service charge, which is enough to cover any gratuities.

Lunch Is On

Generally, lunch is served between 11 A.M. and 2 P.M.; restaurants close down between 2 P.M. and 5 P.M. or 6 P.M., and reopen for dinner between 6 P.M. and 10 P.M. A few places stay open continuously from 11 A.M. to 10 P.M.

Early Dinner

The Chinese aren't known for their late nights, and they don't have late business dinners, either. Expect to pick up your chopsticks by 6 P.M., and end no later than 9 P.M. Most restaurants open for dinner at 6 P.M. and stay open until 10 P.M. (most don't stay open later than that).

If your mouth can stand it, go for the fiery Szechwan cuisine; if you prefer the milder taste of Cantonese, sample dim sum at one of the many restaurants that serve several different types of Chinese cuisine. Try a restaurant specializing in Beijing duck, but go easy—the fatty duck meat often makes first-timers ill. And by the way, waiters in less expensive restaurants almost never speak English. (If they do, the price will be higher.) As a tip, when the fruit courseis served, that's the signal that the meal is over.

Banquets

Banquets are big in China. In fact, they're so big that you'll probably go to at least two on every business trip to China—one given by your hosts in your honor, and one given by you to honor your host. If you've been honored by such a banquet, this reciprocal banquet is really quite important for you to give.

Your host will probably give the first banquet; watch how he does things. He'll be in control of the whole shindig, and he may even pile different bits of food from serving dishes and put it on your plate, explaining what the various things are. No matter what happens, try everything—no matter how strange. Sometimes the Chinese like to test your mettle by serving items they know will be hard for a Westerner to swallow … do your best!

Correct seating is important at banquets. The host sits nearest the door (to direct the waiters). The guest of honor sits directly opposite him. Learn the protocol for seating arrangements, don't discuss business during the meal, and do prepare a toast.

You can expect the banquet to get underway between 6:30 P.M. and 7 P.M., and continue for about two hours. The guest of honor is the last to arrive and the first to leave.

You'll be expected to reciprocate, banquet for banquet. When you do, remember that face is important! Don't have your banquet be more lavish than the one your host threw for you, or he'll lose face. Make sure the dinner appears to cost the same (per person). Be sure to arrive at the site about a half-hour before your guests (who will troop in right on time).

Bars and Clubs

Karaoke bars are the center of nighttime activity for the Chinese. You will find them in every hotel as well as on every corner in the downtown and tourist areas of Beijing. (You can find them by some Chinese characters followed by the letters "OK" or "KTV.")

Be warned: Some karaoke bars charge outrageous prices and have been known to rough up customers who refused to pay a large bill. If you want to try a karaoke bar, go to one in a hotel. It will be more expensive, but at least you know what you're getting into.

Late-Night Dining

Some local restaurants are open 24 hours a day, but it takes a lot of walking or driving to find them. Your cab driver will certainly know, if you can communicate. Otherwise, go for a midnight bite at a Baskin-Robbins ice cream shop. It may not have the 33 flavors you'd find in the U.S., but there are plenty to choose from.

Say What?

Common toasts include: *"Gan bei!"* (*gan-bay*; Dry your glass!)–Mandarin; *"Yam sing!"* (*yam-sing*; Dry your glass!)–Cantonese; *"Yahm pai!"* (*yum-pie*)–Cantonese.

"Here's to You!"

Toasts are popular in China; typically, the Chinese offer toasts with *maotai* (*mao-tie*), a sorghum-based liquor.

When a toast is made, it's the practice to down the contents at one pop; you drink it out of tiny thimble-sized glasses. If you don't want to drink, turn your glass upside down. (To avoid offending, tell your hosts your doctor does not allow you to drink alcohol.) Ask the waiter for soda or bottled water, so that you can participate in the toast, which is expected. When the host rises and gives a toast or thanks the guests after dinner, don't sit down again. The toast is the Chinese equivalent of the singing fat lady—it's time to go.

The Least You Need to Know

➤ Never confuse the People's Republic of China with the Republic of China (Taiwan).

➤ If your host gives you a banquet, you must reciprocate with another banquet.

➤ Relationships are extremely important, and the group is always more important than the individual.

➤ Westerners are respected for speaking patiently, softly, and without boasting.

➤ Make sure your business materials are translated into "reformed Chinese."

➤ Chinese consider boasting and name dropping to be crude.

Chapter 21

Indonesia and Malaysia

In This Chapter

➤ Learn the similarities of Malaysia and Indonesia

➤ Discover the Muslim background that affects these cultures

➤ Find out the pace of business and what you can expect

➤ Understand the Indonesian and Malaysian calendars

➤ Discover the attitude toward punctuality

Malaysia and Indonesia have been welcoming visitors for hundreds of years. These two countries each combine major ethnic groups, which manage to combine unity and diversity while each maintains unique remnants of their own culture as they form separate nations.

Indonesia's population includes nearly 195 million Arabs, Chinese, Pakistanis, Indians, Europeans, and Eurasians in addition to the native Indonesians—it's the fourth most populous country in the world. This nation of villagers is an independent republic consisting of more than 13,500 islands spread over 3,000 miles, with a developing economy and plenty of services in major tourist areas.

While the original Malays (called *Bumiputera)* make up more then 60 percent of the population, they don't by any means control their own country. In Malaysia, business is dominated by ethnic Chinese, the government by original Malays, and the legal and educational community by Indians.

The Chinese began arriving in Malaysia during the fifteenth century, and Indian traders came more than 400 years ago. Many more Indians arrived after World War I. Historically, there has been resentment among the Malays bcause the Chinese have controlled the country's wealth; for this reason, the government has been handling the redistribution of wealth from the Chinese as an official government policy. This has done this in many different ways, such as controlling who can buy new stock options.

Who's In Charge?

Malaysia has a federal parliamentary democracy with a constitutional monarch. Its population of approximately 21 million is ethnically divided into Malay (58 percent), Chinese (26 percent), and Indian (7 percent).

Faux Pas

Beware of shortening the word "Indonesian" into "Indo"—in the past, Indo referred to the child of an Indonesian mother and a European father; Indonesians are sensitive to this term. Avoid this.

Things are a little more rocky over in Indonesia, where, after more than 30 years in office, the government of President Suharto came to an end in May 1998 amid widespread demonstrations, rioting, and looting throughout the country. Indonesia has entered a period of political and economic transition characterized by frequent demonstrations and occasional instances of significant civil unrest. What remains true is that Indonesia is a country of staggering contrasts, home to more than 400 ethnic groups and cultures ranging from Stone Age to modern technology, as well as a terrain that ranges from deserts to snowy mountain peaks.

Talk the Talk

Bahasa Malay is the official language of Malaysia, although English is widely spoken—especially around the water cooler. While Malaysia's three major ethnic groups all speak different languages, they all know English and will likely address you in your own tongue. In fact, because of the variety of dialects and languages in Malaysia, most people communicate in English, which is seen as a unifying force. (If they don't, it's not hard to find an interpreter.) However, business correspondence with government officials must be in Bahasa Malay.

The people of Indonesia speak about 600 languages or dialects among their 67,000 villages. However, the government has decided that Bahasa Indonesia is the official language; it's written in the Roman alphabet and evolved from the Malay trade language. All advertising copy, media communication, and official reports must be in Bahasa Indonesia, which is also taught in all schools.

Religion

Islam is the majority religion in both Indonesia and Malaysia. In Malaysia, most Malays and Indians are Muslim; however, about half the population is not Muslim. Buddhists make up about 17 percent, and the rest ascribe to a variety of beliefs.

Despite the fact that 87 percent of the Indonesian people practice Islam (making Indonesia the world's most populous Islamic nation), Islam is not the official religion in Indonesia. Stopping short of making Islam its official religion, Indonesia has declared itself officially "monotheistic." The government adopted an official belief (called *"Pancasila"*) that states that there is just one Supreme Being—this stance creates harmony with Christians, although it goes against the beliefs of resident minority Hindus.

All students and government workers in Indonesia are taught the five principles of Pancasila:

➤ There is one Supreme God.

➤ Humanity is just and civilized.

➤ Democracy is best.

➤ Indonesia should be unified.

➤ Obeying these rules will bring justice to everyone.

Holiday Time

While the primary religion in Indonesia and Malaysia is Islam, holidays are inclusive and represent the three major religions: Hinduism, Islam, and Christianity.

Indonesians and Malaysians typically use one of three calendars to keep track of the days: officially, everyone uses the Western (Gregorian) calendar. Islamic holidays are dated with the Arabic calendar (it loses about 11 days every year as compared to the Western calendar). Indonesians use the Java calendar, a method of marking days influenced by the Hindus.

Jan. 1-2: New Year.

Feb. 1: Kuala Lumpur City Day (Malaysia).

Varies: Chinese New Year (Malaysia).

Varies: Hari Raya Puasa (Malaysia).

Varies: Hari Raya Haji (Malaysia).

Varies: Idul Fitri.

March-April: Easter.

April-May: Ascension Day.

May 1: Labor Day (Malaysia).

Varies: Wesak Day (Buddhist holiday).

Varies: Awal Muharam.

Varies: Idul Adha (Haj New Year).

Varies: Moslem New Year.

June 1: Agong's Birthday (Malaysia).

Varies: Deepavali.

Aug. 17: Independence Day.

Varies: Mohammed's Birthday.

Dec. 25: Christmas.

Global Guide

When different calendars happen to coincide, that's considered a lucky day in Indonesia. For example, when the third day of a Western week falls on the third day of an Arabic week, that's a good day.

Jam karet (jaHM-carrot) is the Indonesia term meaning "rubber time" that refers to the Indonesia lack of concern about the ticking clock.

Relax, Be Happy

Time is relative in Malaysia and Indonesia, and nobody seems to be very concerned about getting anywhere in a big hurry. Oddly enough, however, while Malaysians aren't very worried about promptness, they do seem concerned with the future—long-term planning is a passion in this part of the world. Indeed, the government is busy looking far into the future, with plans so farsighted on their drawing board that they stretch well into the twenty-first century.

Take a Number...

If you're going to visit Malaysia, try to schedule appointments at least two weeks in advance. Malaysian executives are quite busy and travel frequently.

Once you've set up your appointments in Malaysia or Indonesia, you'll be expected to be prompt (everybody seems to know about the U.S. penchant for punctuality) but don't be surprised if your foreign hosts stroll in late. (The exception here is Chinese Malays, who—like most Chinese everywhere—are apt to be very prompt.)

Socially, however, no one expects you to be on time. Instead, plan to arrive about 15 minutes late.

Are You Open?

Although most Malaysians and Indonesians are Muslim, the two countries don't follow the traditional Muslim work week pattern (with Friday set aside as the Holy Day, and Thursday and Friday as the weekend days). In Indonesia, the work week runs for four full days, from Monday through Thursday, with two half days on Friday and Saturday.

Malaysian Muslims reached a different compromise; those who work in an area in which Friday is just another workday are granted a two-hour break on Friday to attend a mosque. Five of Malaysia's 13 states (all in the west) follow the Muslim work week:

➤ Kedah

➤ Kelantan

➤ Johor

➤ Perlis

➤ Terengganu

Otherwise, business hours in both countries are usually from 8 A.M. to 5 P.M. Monday through Friday (with some offices open for a half day on Saturday). Those following the Muslim work week may work a half-day on Thursday. The tradition lunch hour used to be a two-hour break in both countries, but modern employers are whittling this back to just an hour.

Most Malay and Indonesian government offices stay open from 8:30 A.M. to 4:45 P.M., with a half-day on Saturday (or Thursday in Muslim areas). Most Malay and Indonesian banks keep banker's hours of 9 A.M. to 3 P.M., with a few hours on Saturday morning.

Malaysia is 13 hours ahead of the U.S. Eastern Standard Time, but gigantic meandering Indonesia takes up three time zones all by itself:

➤ West Indonesia Standard Time: Java and Bali are 12 hours ahead of U.S. Eastern Standard Time.

➤ Central Indonesia Standard Time: Central Indonesia is 13 hours ahead of Eastern Standard Time.

➤ East Indonesia Standard Time: Eastern Indonesia (including Maluku and Irian Jaya) is 14 hours ahead of Eastern Standard Time.

Getting Down to Business

When you come to the islands of Malaysia and Indonesia, time takes on a different dimension—it slows down noticeably. Because of the slow pace of negotiations, it's unusual to complete a complicated deal in one trip to these areas. Little will happen at the first meeting, as Malaysians and Indonesians like to get to know you before getting on with business. In fact, business is never the first item discussed at a meeting. Typically, things start off with a short interval of polite general conversation, usually over tea.

Be patient in your business negotiations. Remain calm and don't push. Decisions can take months (or years!), because everyone has a say. Business dealings usually take time (and a few visits) before they can be worked out.

Tip of the Hat

In a business setting, the highest-ranking executive will be the one who does most (if not all) of the talking.

When doing business here, it's important to find out the ethnic background of your colleagues so you know what traditions you'll be dealing with. Each of the main ethnic groups (Chinese, Indian, Malay, and so on) has their own traditions; in general, most business people are Chinese in Malaysia and Indonesia.

No matter what the ethnic background, however, you'll do much better if you manage to hang onto your politeness, which is held in high esteem in this part of the world, although the precise standards of politeness may vary from one culture to the next.

For example, Americans like to cut to the chase and get quick "yes or no" answers to their questions—but it may be hard to get a straight answer in Malaysia and Indonesia. These are cultures influenced by Asia, in which the people find it difficult to say, "No." They also find it hard to disagree or argue with a superior, who must be treated with respect.

For this reason, don't be surprised if, as you're doing business in these countries, the only way you learn unpleasant news is from the employee grapevine. In Indonesia, this is referred to as "Keeping Father happy," and it's ingrained in even the youngest Indonesian child. If you're going to be successful here, you've got to set up a network to enable you to find out what people really think.

Limp and Long

The standard handshake in this part of the world is rather limp and lasts 10 or 12 seconds. (Most North American handshakes only last three or four seconds.) Often, both hands are used. A typical greeting is the rhetorical, "Where are you going?" Acceptable answers are, "For a walk," or, "Nowhere of importance".

Despite its Muslim underpinnings, Western women may shake a man's hand in Malaysia and Indonesia (he will usually wait for you to offer your hand, however, and a traditional Muslim will not want to shake your hand). If you don't want to shake hands, simply nodding your head will be fine. If you do decide to shake hands, don't do it too often; frenzied, frequent hand shaking will be misinterpreted as loose behavior.

Traditional Chinese Malaysians or Indonesians will bow as a greeting, but today most will shake hands instead. Westernized Indians will also shake hands with women, whereas more traditional Indian Hindus will not. The traditional Indian greeting in both Indonesia and Malaysia is a gesture made by placing the hands together as if praying. The traditional Malay greeting is a gesture made by touching the hands lightly and placing them over the heart.

In both countries, kissing between the sexes in public is taboo—so don't even try a quick peck on the cheek as a hello or goodbye.

Traditional Greetings

Americans ask how you're feeling without really wanting a blow-by-blow description of your throbbing migraine headache or your recent root canal. In the same way, Malaysians and Indonesians have a range of polite rhetorical greetings that they like to trot out on first meetings. The precise nature of the greetings differs depending on ethnic background. Chinese Malaysians may ask you, "Have you eaten?" You should say "yes" no matter what. A Malay will ask you, "Where are you going?" You should mumble something like, "Nowhere special." They don't really want to know your entire schedule.

Titles

The traditional Malay forms of Mr./Mrs./Miss are:

> *Encik:* Mr.
>
> *Puan:* Mrs. (married woman).
>
> *Cik:* Miss (unmarried woman).

Say What?

Selamat is the Indonesia word for "peace," which traditionally follows any greeting.

These are used in front of an individual's name; Mr. Ahmadi would be addressed as "Encik Ahmadi." You can use the title Puan ("Mrs.") for any adult female.

The traditional form of greeting in Indonesia should be the title and name. Traditional Indonesian titles are:

> *Ibu:* Used as Madam, Mrs., or Miss (mother).
>
> *Bapak:* Used as Mr. ("father"; this comes before any other title).

If you're giving a formal Indonesian introduction, here's the sequence (commit it to memory or write it on your wrist):

➤ Bapak/Ibu

➤ academic title

➤ noble title (as in "Lady")

➤ given name

➤ family name

➤ business/official title

This means that if John Doe were really talented, he'd be introduced as:

> Bapak Doctor Lord John Doe Chief Executive. (It's a mouthful, but at least everybody knows where John ranks in the status department.)

Traditionally, the lower classes will have just one name, and the middle classes tend to have two. The farther up the social scale you go, the more names and titles you run into. If you do have more than one name, you can shorten the other to an initial.

Play Your Cards Right

Since most Malaysian and Indonesian business people are Chinese, it may be a good idea to have your business cards printed in Chinese. Exchanging business cards here is part of proper business etiquette—more like a reverent ceremony.

You'll exchange business cards right away when you first meet. When you present your bilingual business card to a prospective client, make sure the Chinese translation side of your card is facing the recipient. Then, holding the upper corners of the card with the thumb and forefinger of both hands, offer your card to that person.

When someone gives you a business card, receive the card in the same way as you gave yours, and be sure to look at it before putting it carefully in your card case. (Don't put that card in your back pocket, where you'll sit on it.) If you stash the card as soon as you receive it, your contact will lose face.

Business cards are also important in Indonesia, which was once a colony of the Netherlands. It's not surprising, therefore, that they still use Dutch words for academic titles. Business cards may carry these abbreviations for degrees:

➤ *Dra:* A graduate in any field except engineering or law (feminine).

➤ *Drs:* The same as above, except masculine.

➤ *S H:* Anyone with a law degree.

➤ *Ir:* Anyone with an engineering degree.

Bite Your Lip

Never express anger in public: A person who loses his or her temper won't be trusted or respected. Traditionally, both the Indonesians and Malaysians were very soft spoken, although younger people are becoming more modern (and louder) as the countries become more sophisticated.

The word "No" is rude in both Malaysia and Indonesia, where "Yes" can mean "I agree," or "Maybe," or "I hope you can tell from my lack of enthusiasm that I really mean 'no.'"

Don't be surprised if your Indonesian colleague leans over in the middle of a meeting and asks you how much you earn or how many degrees you have. Status and rank is of vital importance here, and the Indonesians figure they can't really assess your worth unless they come right out and ask you. What seems intensely private to an American is fair game to an Indonesian. In fact, the native language of an Indonesian almost requires him or her to find out your status so he knows how to talk to you.

Silence is not a problem for Indonesians, who don't interpret silence as rejection or anger. In fact, you may find that Indonesians wait as long as 15 seconds after you've finished speaking before they respond. Too many times, this brief silence is interpreted as agreement, and the Westerner plunges on in the conversation before hearing the Indonesian's viewpoint.

Global Guide

Saying "no" isn't a problem if you happen to speak Bahasa Indonesia, as there are 12 ways to say "no" (there are even some ways to say, "I'm saying 'yes' but I'm meaning 'no'").

Taboos

Traditional Muslim taboos are alive and well in both countries. Among other things, you should not:

➤ Show the soles of the feet.

➤ Touch anything with the left hand (it's unclean).

➤ Touch anyone on the head (even a child).

➤ Point at anyone with your forefinger (it's an insult).

If you feel you really must point, then use your thumb, or make the pointing gesture with your chin. Look in the mirror and practice if you have to.

In Malaysia and Indonesia, don't touch anybody! Business people don't hug, kiss, or touch in any way. You can get away with holding hands with someone of the same sex (if you're good friends), but any sort of public affection between the opposite sex (even if you're married) is not acceptable.

Speak slowly. Think about what you're going to say before you say it, and listen carefully when your hosts speak.

Faux Pas

The Malaysians and Indonesians don't appreciate the loud voice and gestures of many Westerners, so try to soften your voice.

Separate and Unequal

You can find lots of royalty in Malaysia, and the gap between commoner and blueblood is great. Most states have sultans and elaborate forms of address to speak to such nobilities. While the country is not especially racist, there are plenty of stereotypes and a tendency to believe that one's own ethnic group is more important.

Since Malaysia is Islamic, women are considered (by Western standards) to be inferior to men, and the two sexes are not treated equally. Still, in Indonesia (although also Islamic) women are considered equal, and both sexes are expected to maintain the household and the family. Equal rights for women have always been important in the Indonesia community.

Suit Up

When it comes to clothing in Malaysia and Indonesia, remember that the majority Islamic and minority Hindu populations require modesty in dress—and they don't make exceptions for foreigners.

It's hot here, so you can be modest but still casual; standard office outfits for men includes dark trousers and light long-sleeved shirts with tie but no jacket (although lots of men get away with short-sleeved shirts). Businesswomen, however, aren't cut any "slack"—women must wear long-sleeved blouses (so that the arms are covered), with a skirt that should reach the knee (longer is better).

Shorts are okay for sports, but aren't worn in public and certainly not for business occasions.

Presenting a Present

Gift giving is a common practice in Indonesia and Malaysia—and it's always appreciated. If someone has invited you home in Indonesia, a small gift is welcome (flowers or food are nice). However, don't expect Malaysians or Indonesians to dive into your present in front of you.

Don't be surprised if your Indonesian contact gives you a lavish present to you if they're meeting you for the first time. It's something they feel they are honor-bound to do.

You may give a gift to someone with whom you've developed a friendship. Some good ideas are:

➤ Historical gift from your state.

➤ Local crafts from the U.S.

➤ An illustrated book.

➤ A fine pen.

➤ Tee shirts with a U.S. sports team decal.

Food gifts are always a treat, but don't give something that would violate a religious taboo.

When you give someone a gift, present it in private—and only after all your business has been concluded. Remember that red is the color of luck, so that's a good color choice. If you do decide to give a gift, don't choose these:

➤ Straw sandals: These have an association with funerals.

➤ Handkerchiefs: These are associated with death.

➤ Stork or crane: These are also associated with death.

On the Town

Take advantage of any invitations to social events, although invitations may not come immediately. If you send out written invitations in Indonesia, don't be surprised if you don't get a response—they're reluctant to commit themselves to an event in the future. (What if a car should run over his foot and he can't make it?)

Going "Dutch treat" isn't done in Indonesia or Malaysia; the person who does the inviting does the paying.

246

As you've read earlier, it's perfectly okay to be late in both countries to a social invitation—but just *how* late can be tricky. Because of the importance of status in both countries, many people try to time their lateness to coincide with the proper appearance of others with a similar status. Thus, you wouldn't want to stroll in after somebody who had more status than you do.

While "dropping in" on someone in many parts of the world is a definite no-no, in Indonesia it's welcomed. Just stop by *mampir* (unannounced)—they will be charmed. Residents do it all the time.

Global Guide

Some invitations will actually state a time for you to arrive and then direct you to arrive "15 minutes early"—this is your signal to avoid upstaging the more important guest.

Soto to Nuts

Food is vital when doing business in Malaysia and Indonesia. Spouses in Malaysia are usually invited to lunch, but not dinner. Utensils can either be the traditional spoon and fork, or the use of hands. Remember the traditional Muslim taboos against pork and alcohol; in addition, remember that Hindus do not eat beef.

If you're going to be dining in this part of the world, however, brace yourself for some of the more unusual items:

➤ **Dog** (especially black dog): This is considered quite tasty.

➤ **Beef brain curry**: West Sumatrans swear by this very hot, spicy curry.

➤ **Goat curry**: You've probably figured it out by now; if it's got the word *"Gulai"* in it, it means curry. This dish is made with goat.

➤ **Fried intestines**: This dish uses the lungs, liver, chicken giblets, and kidneys that you'll find throughout Indonesia.

➤ **Fried dried chicken's blood**: Here's an interesting food that's often given to children.

➤ **Elephant's intestines**: This dish used to be prepared from elephant intestines, but today, fried beef is substituted.

➤ **Leg of goat soup**: Here's a real winner, involving goat sinew mixed up with intestines, lungs, bladder, and chopped penis blended in coconut cream.

The Least You Need to Know

➤ Malaysians and Indonesians are primarily Muslim, with the same food taboos and many of the same beliefs of protecting women as found in the Middle East.

➤ Saying "no" and giving bad news to superiors is difficult for both cultures.

➤ Both Malaysia and Indonesia have "unity in diversity" with several primary ethnic groups making up each country.

➤ Royalty and social class are very important here.

➤ Don't express anger in public; you won't be trusted.

➤ Dress convervatively here, modest but casual.

Chapter 22

Singapore

In This Chapter

➤ Discover the various cultures of modern Singapore

➤ Learn the importance of following the rules and laws

➤ Find out the importance of food and dining in Singapore

➤ Understand the pace of business in Singapore

➤ Find out the importance of business cards

Industrialization has come rapidly to Singapore, bringing with it social change, high-rise buildings, and new technology. While Singapore may appear to look quite Westernized, especially with the younger, more modern Singaporeans, it's important not to forget the Asian ethnic culture that forms the background of the island and its people.

Singapore lies in southeastern Asia between Malaysia and Indonesia, slightly more than 3.5 times the size of Washington, D.C. Like most of Southeast Asia, Singapore is tropical—hot, humid, and rainy. There are no pronounced rainy or dry seasons—it just rains most of the time (thunderstorms occur on 40 percent of all days, and occur 67 percent of the time in April). Both an island and a country, it's best described as a city-state that combines Western development with Eastern tranquility—a modern country where you feel safe walking the streets and where you can work in an efficient Asian business center.

Many guide books claim that June through August is the best time to visit, but even then it rains often.

Who's In Charge?

Singapore has a small, highly developed parliamentary democracy with a president who serves as the chief of state and a prime minister who is the head of the government. Tourist facilities are modern and widely available.

This is an Asian country unique in many ways. Wary of Western personal freedoms (viewed as the seat of all Western problems), the Singaporean government has stepped in to regulate every facet of its citizens' lives. With an emphasis on hard work, thrift, patriotism, and obedience, the government has created one of the most graft-free countries in Asia—employees will vigorously resist bribes. Because the tenets put forth by the government also happens to follow the teachings of Confucius, these have been readily accepted by most Singaporeans.

Speaking the Lingo

You'll find three different races (Chinese, Malay and Indian) living and working together, making Singapore a true melting pot of different cultures, languages, and religions. The national language is Malay, and the official languages are Chinese, Malay, English, and Tamil. English is understood and widely used in commerce, business, and day-to-day life. Street signs, roads, maps, and hotel names are all in English.

While your colleagues may speak English, it may not be the same "English" that you recognize. This linguistic variance is often filled with unusual inflections, syntax, and grammar. Most Singaporeans (of whatever race) use *Singlish,* a blend of English with the dialects of Cantonese, Hokkien, and Malay. Certain shorthand phrases of English have also worked their way into the mainstream dialect.

Global Guide

Don't let the climate stop you from going, however—most buildings are air conditioned, and the Singapore natives have tried to make everything as comfortable as they can. When it does rain, it's usually only briefly.

Don't be surprised if you also hear phrases that may sound a bit pushy, if not downright aggressive: "Do you want to sign this contract, or not?" In fact, it's not aggression at all. In Chinese, it's polite to offer your conversation partner both options in any sentence—and when Chinese is translated into English, that dual-option choice is often included. This means you'll often hear "or not" tacked on to the end of the sentence: "Are you hungry, or not?"

Tip of the Hat

There's no official religion in Singapore, and its cosmopolitan population worships in a wide variety of ways. The Malays are primarily Muslim; Indians are either Hindu or Muslim; the Chinese may be Buddhist, Confucianists, Taoist, or Christian (or several at the same time).

Holiday List

Ancient festivals and customs are celebrated enthusiastically in Singapore, and traditional holidays in many different religions are important. Holidays, which are based on Gregorian and ethnic or religious calendars, include:

Jan. 1: New Year's Day.

Varies: Chinese New Year.

Varies: Hari Raya Puasa (Muslim Feast of Fast-Breaking).

Varies: Hari Raya Haji (Muslim Feast of Sacrifice).

Spring: Easter holidays.

May 1: Labor Day.

Varies: Vesak Day (Birthday of Buddha).

Aug. 9: National Day.

Varies: Deepavali (Hindu: Festival of Lights).

Dec. 25: Christmas.

Be On Time

Your colleagues in Singapore expect you to be punctual for meetings and dinners. If you make them wait, they'll interpret this as an insult.

Try to schedule your appointments at least two weeks ahead of time, and once you've scheduled one, try not to break it.

Business hours are generally Monday through Friday from 9 A.M. to 5 P.M., and Saturday from 9 A.M. to 1 P.M. However, flextime has arrived in Singapore, so don't be surprised if many businesses stagger their work hours so that employees arrive anywhere from 7:30 A.M. until 9:30 A.M.

Shopping hours are usually 10 A.M. to 9:30 P.M. daily, although some shops stay open as late as 10 P.M. and some offer Sunday hours.

Banker's hours are traditionally from 9:30 A.M. to 3 P.M. Monday through Friday, and 9:30 A.M. to 11:30 A.M. on Saturdays.

Singapore is 13 hours ahead of Eastern Standard Time. Therefore, if it's 8 A.M. in New York City, it's 9 P.M. in Singapore (which, by the way, does not observe Daylight Saving Time).

Slow and Mellow

Conducting business in Singapore is relatively easy, but it moves at its own pace—slow and mellow. You'll have to be patient here. If you're trying to get something done, expect to take twice as long as you think it should.

Tip of the Hat

The island has an excellent communications and transportation infrastructure, and Western business services are readily available. Because most people speak English, language seldom acts as a barrier.

If you want to do well here, brush up on your manners, as politeness is the single most important quality to getting ahead in Singapore. This politeness can make things confusing, however, because if a Singaporean wants to say no, he can't—it's impolite. If you hear "yes" in Singapore, it may truly mean yes, but it also may mean "maybe" or "I can't bear saying no." A "yes" that is masquerading as "no" will usually be accompanied by a lack of enthusiasm, so pay attention and try to read the signals when you're negotiating.

In Western culture, speaking with pride about accomplishments indicates you have a healthy self-esteem. "I worked really hard on that brief; I'm sure we'll win the case" is not seen as bragging in the West. In Singapore, however, these attitudes are offensive. Talking about how hard you worked and that you're sure it will pay off is seen as bragging and showing a lack of modesty. In Singapore, downplay your talents and try to act in a humble, reserved way. It's fine to be competent, a Singaporean believes, but you don't need to advertise that competence to the world. If a Singaporean says, "Well, I finished that brief, but it's not very good," it could well be one of the best briefs the court has ever seen.

If you can establish a personal relationship with your colleagues, you'll be much farther ahead. Your Singapore colleagues believe they're doing business with you, not your company. Therefore, if you're replaced by someone, the new guy will have to start in all over to set up a good relationship. Hard work is revered in Singapore, and the person who works hard and long will be respected. Achievement is prized, while any sort of aggressive behavior is frowned upon.

Don't Lose Face

"Face" is the measure of your own innate quality, your status, and your character. But it's more than individual pride—it also affects the entire group. "Losing face" is a profound embarrassment—much more so than a blow to an individual's pride—because if one person loses face, the whole group loses face.

Losing face is a big concern in this Asian country, and one of the easiest ways to do so is to openly disagree with someone else. So how do you communicate criticism?

Discreetly and delicately. Hint at your disappointment; don't take out an ad in *The New York Times*. Never blast a colleague in public, and speak in general terms if you have something to complain about: "Some people aren't refilling the coffee pot when they've used all the coffee" is better than saying, "Jim, you slob! You used up the coffee and didn't fill it back up!"

Brief and Businesslike

Normally, when greeting someone in Singapore, you should not peer directly into the person's eyes (it's a sign of disrespect, especially if the person is older). Instead, look away or down at the ground.

In general, these days it's appropriate for people of the same sex to give a brief handshake when meeting. If people of the opposite sex are meeting, the woman should make the first move to offer her hand. More traditionally, the greeting in Singapore depended on which culture you're saying hello to. Because there are three major ethnic groups in Singapore, it follows that there have been three primary greeting traditions. Most young people in Singapore are comfortable shaking hands (although be prepared for a fairly limp, lengthy shake with both hands). Women from the U.S. (or Westernized Singaporeans) may shake hands with men and women, but a Singapore man will probably wait to shake hands to see what a woman does. If a woman doesn't want to shake hands, a brief "hello" head nod is acceptable.

Faux Pas

Women may shake hands in Singapore, but not too often or you'll risk being labeled as promiscuous.

Traditionally, Chinese men said hello by bowing, but lately the Western custom of shaking hands has become more popular. You may find a combination of shaking and bowing. Chinese Singaporeans have no problem in shaking hands with a woman, unlike other ethnic Singaporeans.

Because most Malays are Muslim (who do not touch the opposite sex), you should not offer to shake hands with a Malay of the opposite sex. However, if the Malay sticks out a hand, it's okay to shake it.

In lieu of shaking, a Malay may perform the *salaam* with a person of the same sex. In this gesture, you stretch out a hand (or both), touch the other person's hand(s), and then place your hands) over your heart. (A *salaam* may be performed between people of opposite sex if there is a scarf to prevent skin-to-skin contact.)

Many Indian Singaporeans are Hindu, who also avoid touching the opposite sex (although they aren't as rigid about it as Muslims). Indians tend to avoid contact between the opposite sex, but men make shake hands with men and women with women. Instead, the traditional Indian greeting is the *namaste*, in which you bow slightly while pressing the palms of your hands together as if praying. The namaste may be used by a Western businesswoman greeting an Indian Singaporean.

Here's My Card

Business cards are vital in Singapore, and because most business people here are Chinese, it's a good idea to have your card printed in Chinese on one side.

As in many Asian countries, the exchange of business cards is quite formal—almost like a tea ceremony:

➤ After being introduced, offer a card to each person present.

➤ Present the card with both hands, print side facing the recipient.

➤ The recipient receives the card with both hands.

➤ The recipient studies the card for a few moments.

➤ The recipient carefully puts the card in a pocket.

By Any Other Name

It's not surprising that in a place with four separate cultures, names can get tricky. The naming pattern differs between cultures.

Chinese names begin with a family name, followed by one or two personal names. Therefore, Zhu Peng Wu would be called Mr. Zhu. His wife would not normally use the family name "Zhu" but instead keep her maiden name. Therefore, if Mr. Zhu married Jia Chin Chu, she would not be Mrs. Zhu, but Madam Jia.

It's hard to know what the score is with Singapore Indians, who have adopted several traditions. In the past, Indians did not have last names, but today some have adopted a surname that they pass on from one generation to the next. More typically, an Indian man will begin his name with the first initial of his father's name, followed by his personal name. So "R. Chinder" would be "Chinder, son of Ravi." Indian women's names follow the same pattern.

Faux Pas

Never put a business card in your back pocket. This is where you sit, and the Singaporeans won't want their cards abused in this way. (And don't write on it, either.)

Malays, on the other hand, don't have family names. Malays, who are Muslim, are known by their given name plus "son of" (*bin*) "father's name." A Malay woman is called by her given name plus "daughter of" (*binti*) plus the father's name. If Khali binti Saud is married, you'd call her "Mrs. Khali." (If they're very Western, some Malays may drop the "bin" or "binti.")

If you're totally confused by now, it's probably best just to ask a Singaporean what he or she would care to be called. Go ahead and suggest what your colleagues may call you, too.

254

Hands Off

Keep your hands to yourself in Singapore—and that includes you married folks out there. Any contact between the sexes (even legally married men and women) is not acceptable here. That means no hugging or kissing, and no holding hands. On the other hand, feel free to hold hands with someone of the same sex. Men can even get away with walking around with their arms entwined—no one will think a thing of it.

Faux Pas

Don't smoke in Singapore. Most areas are nonsmoking, including public buildings and air-conditioned restaurants. Smokers are pretty much restricted to outdoor coffee shops.

As in many other countries, the left hand is considered unclean by Muslims and Hindus. While you're in Singapore, eat only with your right hand (you lefties will just have to suffer), and don't touch anything or anyone with your left hand if it's at all possible. If you're paying for something, hold out your right hand for the change. If somebody gives you a gift, accept it with the right hand (although if it's a big gift, you may take it in both hands).

No playing footsie under the table—the feet are considered unclean, so you shouldn't touch or move anything with your feet. Don't show the soles of your feet, either. This means you shouldn't cross your legs with your ankle draped across your knee (your sole will be clearly visible this way). This also means no propping your feet up on a desk or ottoman. If anyone else has a clear view of your soles, you're doing it wrong.

It's hard to know just where to stand in Singapore, as there are so many different cultures here. Optimum personal bubble dimensions differ from one culture to the next—so go for a middle range, and stand between two to three feet apart.

Lingo Rules

A smile may be your umbrella, but it can also mask a wide range of emotions in Singapore, covering embarrassment, shyness, unhappiness, or loss of face. A laughing Singaporean may not really think anything is funny.

If the others around the conference table suddenly erupt in giggles in the middle of a tricky negotiation, it's most likely just nerves.

Don't lose your cool. If you get in a dispute with a merchant or are having problems at your hotel, speak quietly and remain polite, but be firm. (If you lose your temper, you've "lost face," and you won't be taken seriously.)

If you're engaged in polite chitchat, you'll want to avoid discussing:

➤ Religion.

➤ Politics.

➤ Sex.

255

➤ Criticism of the food.

➤ Criticism of the bureaucracy.

➤ Problems in Singapore.

➤ Personal matters (affections, personal relationships, feelings, love, and emotions).

➤ Jokes about sex.

Instead, chat about your plans for the future, travel in Singapore or elsewhere, business success (not your own success, which would be considered bragging), art, music, compliments to Singapore, and food. (Compliment local cooking, and don't complain.)

Global Guide

If you hear a sudden intake of air through the teeth around the conference table, look sharp—it's the Singapore way of saying there's a problem.

Don't be shocked if your Singapore colleague looks at you intently over his desk and says: "Why aren't you married?" It's not unusual for Singaporeans to ask extremely personal questions. Don't feel you have to answer them—simply smile and note that such things aren't usually discussed in your culture.

If you're giving a speech, try to avoid too much humor; jokes aren't usually used to open a speech. You can aim for some levity later on in the talk, but don't use any sexual innuendo.

Don't Point

Watch your hand gestures, as well—don't point at a person or beckon with the fingers, as it's considered very rude. (You can point at an animal, but that's the extent of it, and pointing with two fingers is also rude to Indians.) If you feel you just have to gesture at someone, use your entire right hand with the palm out. Or if you just have to point with something, you can use your right thumb if you make sure to curl down the rest of the fingers on that hand.

If you want someone to approach you, beckon them with hand out, palm down, and scoop your fingers. (Wagging the finger the way you'd do in the United States is rude in Singapore.)

If you're in a business meeting and your suggested proposal is met by a side-to-side toss of the head, relax! They're not saying "no"—it's the Singaporean way of indicating "yes."

Other gestures to avoid:

➤ Don't slap the palm of the hand with your fist (it's an obscenity).

➤ Don't touch anyone's head.

➤ Don't stand with hands on your hips.

➤ Don't make a fist with the thumb and little finger extended (it's an insult).

Seen, Not Heard

Roles for men and women are very stringently separate here, although the vestiges of the idea of equality between the sexes is beginning to take hold. Still, men hold positions of authority and dominance in social situations.

Sartorially Speaking

You'll find that Singapore business people tend to dress more casually because of the heat—be prepared for hot, steamy weather! This is the tropics, after all, only 85 miles north of the Equator. In such a cosmopolitan and multicultural city, "diversity" is the ticket. It's acceptable to wear outfits common to any of the four main cultural groups at almost any time of the day, almost anywhere, and for whatever occasion.

For non-office wear, choose light summer clothing (especially natural fibers). Go for a "smart casual" look and you'll do fine, which means shirts (long- or short-sleeved, but not tee shirts), trousers (not jeans), and shoes (not athletic shoes). Many men find that open-necked *batik* shirts work well. You can wear jeans, but not shorts, for casual attire.

Business people seldom wear suits because of the heat; most wear casual clothes, including dark trousers, light long- or short-sleeved shirt, and tie (no jacket required). Many businessmen also jettison the tie.

Light-colored, skirts and long-sleeved blouses, or lightweight suits, are acceptable. Business women can get away without wearing stockings except for the most formal offices. Don't be surprised to notice that Singapore businesswomen fashions are more frilly than you'll find in the U.S.

It's a good idea to start out conservatively; go ahead and wear a jacket and tie until you see what the others are wearing; you can always remove them.

Tip of the Hat

Because there are Muslims and Hindus in Singapore, women should try to wear blouses that at least cover the upper arms. Keep your skirts to the knee or longer.

Just Say No!

Because Singapore is so proud of being honest and upright, there are strict rules here against graft. This means that most likely, no government worker will accept a gift, however well-intentioned you are when you offer it. Instead, to avoid the appearance of graft, you may give a gift to a group (either the entire office, or the company as a whole). Good "group gift" choices include educational materials or anything that can be seen and used by many people for a long time. You'd give a gift like this at the final banquet celebrating the closing of a deal, for example. Alternatively, you could give a small, personal gift of remembrance to every member of the office or company (typically, place the small item discreetly beside each plate at a formal banquet). Never give expensive items.

You may, of course, give a gift to a friend. But to make sure your gift isn't interpreted as a bribe, make sure you're really friends before you go around offering packages.

Global Guide

Small gifts you might consider include: items with a company logo, pens and pencils, cap with the name of your city or company, sweets, or cakes.

When you give a gift, don't be surprised when the person thanks you warmly and sets the gift aside. Gifts are not unwrapped in front of the giver, in case the gift is inappropriate and a loss of face would ensue. Moreover, unwrapping a gift right away is an indication of greed in Singapore. If someone gives you a gift, accept it gracefully but wait until you're alone before you tear into it.

If you give a gift to a Chinese person in Singapore, don't be surprised when they decline it. It's the Chinese way to refuse a gift three times (so as to avoid looking greedy).

Gifts to avoid in Singapore include:

➤ Handkerchiefs (they symbolize death, sadness, and crying).

➤ Knives, scissors, or cutting items (they suggest severing relationships).

➤ Stork or crane.

➤ Straw sandals.

➤ Anything in the color of white, blue, or black (associated with death).

➤ Pork or alcohol, pigskin or perfumes containing alcohol (against the beliefs of Muslims and Malays).

➤ Toy dogs or pictures of dogs to Malays (dogs are considered unclean).

➤ Frangipani flower (among Indians, these are used only for funerals).

➤ An even amount of money to an Indian (it's the opposite of the Chinese tradition—only give an odd amount to an Indian, such as US $11).

➤ Leather products to a Hindu (cows are sacred).

Let Me Entertain You

If anyone invites you to a social occasion, accept right away. It's important to establish a social relationship if you want to do business in Singapore. If you get a written invitation, respond in writing. If you're sending an invitation, use red or pink paper (not white or blue, which is associated with sadness).

Don't miss the religious temples, including Hindu, Muslim, Taoist, and Buddhist. But don't enter without first checking to see if you should take off your shoes and always ask for permission before taking photographs.

However, if you're going to be doing business with the government, don't invite government workers out on social occasions. Bribery laws are so strict that government officials will likely decline lest they give the appearance of being on the take.

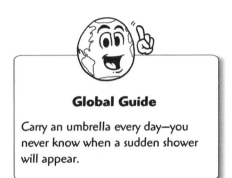

Global Guide

Carry an umbrella every day—you never know when a sudden shower will appear.

Visiting at Home

If you're visiting a Singaporean home for dinner, don't bring food as a hostess gift unless you've been told to bring a particular item. Bringing food this way normally implies that you don't think your hosts will be capable of providing a good enough meal. Instead, choose candy or a fruit basket to send afterwards. If you send flowers, make sure you send an even number (odd numbers of flowers is unlucky).

Food is tremendously important in Singapore, and any important happenings revolve around eating. In fact, a traditional greeting in Chinese can be literally translated as, "Have you eaten?"

When you get to Singapore, you'll probably be invited to business breakfasts, business lunches, and business dinners, not to mention business cocktails and banquets. If you're visiting with your spouse and you are invited to a business meal, it's okay to bring your partner along for dinner, but not for a business lunch. If you make a mistake and bring your spouse along to a business meal, no business will be discussed.

When you attend a business function, remember that you represent not just yourself, but your entire company. If you're seen as an honorable person, your company will be considered to be honorable, too.

Traditionally, Singaporeans take two-hour lunches (from noon until 2 P.M.); more recently, bosses have tried to persuade employees to limit this to

Faux Pas

Don't leave your chopsticks sticking straight up and down in your rice bowl, as they suggest incense sticks, which are associated with death.

one hour. You'll still find plenty of hangers-on to the old way, however. And since Friday is a Holy Day for Muslims, the faithful who work on Fridays take a two-hour lunch break.

Get adventurous and try some unusual dishes at one of the food courts. Everything is labeled in English, so you'll know what you're eating.

Tipping

Tipping is taboo in Singapore, which is seen as a form of "imperialism"—almost a bribe (there's that word again!). Singaporeans don't believe they need to be bribed into giving good service. Do not tip:

➤ Office clerks.

➤ Employees of private clubs.

➤ Airport employees.

➤ Government employees.

Hotels and most restaurants usually add a service fee to the bill, which is then shared by all the employees. Room service or messenger service personnel may be tipped from 50 cents to about US $2. In a restaurant, if no tip has been added, you may leave a tip of between 10 percent and 15 percent (but it's not required).

The Least You Need to Know

➤ There are three primary ethnic cultures in Singapore: Chinese, Malay, and Indian.

➤ Politeness, hard work, and restraint are prized.

➤ The Singapore government enforces a range of strict laws in almost every aspect of life.

➤ Singapore is one of the least corrupt Asian nations; strict rules against bribery are in force.

➤ Expect very hot, humid, wet weather here and dress accordingly.

➤ Any public contact between the sexes (even between married people) is not acceptable.

➤ Business cards are vital in Singapore.

Chapter 23

Japan

In This Chapter

➤ Learn how to adjust your body language to appropriate levels

➤ Discover the best way to negotiate in Japan

➤ Know the proper way to handle business cards

➤ Understand how to handle a visit to a Japanese home

➤ Find out the ins and outs of giving gifts

➤ Learn how to meet and greet the Japanese

Japan (or Nihon/Nippon) has a stable, highly developed parliamentary democracy with a modern economy; tourist facilities are widely available. An ancient land (the current emperor's dynasty stretches all the way back to 660 B.C.), Japan has always resisted any influence outside its own boundaries.

The etiquette and rules in Japan are many and complex: to succeed in busiiness here you really need to watch your cultural behavior. Read on for the details.

Japan is an island country lying off the east coast of Asia, historically closed to outside interests, influences, and control. It's separated from China by the East China Sea, and from the Soviet Union and South and North Korea to the west by the Sea of Japan.

While Japan has a very strong democracy, the constitution still provides for an Emperor, whose position is largely symbolic. The prime minister is the head of government, who is elected by the National Diet (Japan's parliament).

Japanese, Please

The official language of Japan is Japanese, an enormously complex tongue spoken nowhere else in the world. (While there are two major dialects, "Tokyo Japanese" is understood everywhere in the country.) The language, which is spoken without stress or emphasis on any words or syllables, can be expressed in at least four different degrees of politeness. (Japanese women usually use one of the more deferential forms.)

Japanese is an extremely complex language with lots of specialized forms of address; the decision on which form to use isn't made lightly. This is why a Japanese person may spend a lot of time asking detailed and very personal questions—your job title, responsibilities, number of employees you manage—all designed to identify your status. The Japanese need this information so they know which of the forms to use when speaking to you.

Say What?

Shinto literally means "the way of the gods," echoing the belief that minor deities are everywhere in nature.

Faux Pas

Don't lump the Asian countries together; there are profound differences between Japan, China, Korea, Malaysia, and others.

Shinto and Confucianism

Religion in Japan is often down-played, and the Japanese themselves might tell you they are not religious at all. Instead, many Japanese follow the philosophies of Confucianism and Shintoism. It's also possible to follow the teaching of Confucius or Shinto doctrine and still be Buddhist or Christian.

Shinto, which is found only in Japan, is deeply connected to Japanese tradition; for many years, Shintoism maintained that the Japanese Emperor was a God. After the end of World War II, Shinto was dismantled as Japan's state belief system; today, Japan has no official religion.

Shinto maintains the importance of the Japan homeland, which reinforces the idea that Japan comes first; foreign businessmen often find this disconcerting.

The largest traditional religion in Japan is Buddhism, practiced by 38 percent of the people (many more participate in Buddhist ceremonies occasionally). Many Japanese tend to perform Shinto ceremonies at birth and when getting married, and Buddhist ones at death. The Japanese are very tolerant of other religions; about 22 percent of the Japanese worship other faiths (about 4 percent are Christian).

It's Vacation

The Japanese like their holidays (where else would you find an "Adult's Day" *and* a "Respect for the Aged Day?"). Note that when a national holiday ends up on a Sunday, the next day is also considered to be a holiday. In addition, many Japanese companies and offices usually close down during the New Year season (Dec. 28-Jan. 3), during "golden week" (April 29-May 5) and during the O-Bon Festival (Aug. 12-15). This is a popular time for the Japanese to visit their ancestors' graveyards. For a list of other holidays, read on:

Jan. 1: New Year's Day.

Jan. 15: Adult's Day.

Feb. 11: National Foundation Day.

late March: Vernal Equinox Day.

April 29: Greenery Day.

May 3: Constitution Memorial Day.

May 4: Official Holiday.

May 5: Children's Day.

Sept. 15: Respect for the Aged Day.

Sept. (late): Autumnal Equinox Day.

Oct. 10: Health Sports Day.

Nov. 2: Culture Day.

Nov. 23: Labor Thanksgiving Day.

Dec. 23: Emperor's Birthday.

Don't Ever Be Late

The Japanese, in general, don't understand the phrase "fashionably late." Nothing is more in fashion in the Land of the Rising Sun than getting to an appointment on time—or, better yet, even earlier.

Take Your Time

Most businesses are open from 9 A.M. to 5 P.M. Monday through Friday. Many companies also stay open half a day on Saturdays (from 9 A.M. to noon), although a few companies recently have dropped the half-day on Saturday. Japanese worker bees are very industrious, however; they toil for 42.9 hours a week, without any overtime pay.

The entire country of Japan is 14 hours ahead of Eastern Standard Time. This means that if it's 9 A.M. in New York City, it will be 11 P.M. in Japan. So, if you want to reach a business counterpart at 9 A.M. in Japan, you'll need to call at 7 P.M. EST.

Just as Japanese philosophy believes there needs to be space to fully appreciate a thing of beauty, there also needs to be time in which to think before acting or relying. When you're in Japan, you need to discard your Western ideas about time (and the lack of it!) at the border.

When you ask a Japanese executive a question, expect to wait (sometimes a long time) for him or her to answer. If you know you'll be presenting information at a conference, send data via e-mail or fax several weeks ahead of time to allow the Japanese to digest it thoroughly.

Keep Smiling

No matter what happens in Japan, keep smiling. While you're smiling, remember that in Japan a smile can indicate genuine pleasure—or it can be a cover for unhappiness.

Global Guide

Work is serious business in Japan, so don't go tacking up silly Seinfeld jokes around the water cooler. Don't expect lots of funny patter during presentations, and don't offer your own, either.

Sometimes the Japanese smile when they are upset as a method of self-control.

Outright laughter or giggling may not mean you're a hit with your hosts; it may mean that you have embarrassed, confused, or shocked your audience.

Also remember the importance of the group in Japan, and don't expect praise for your own contributions. By the same token, try to avoid singling out one specific Japanese worker for commendation. One reason the group is so important may be because Japan is one of the most crowded places on earth. Moreover, very few foreigners live in Japan; more than 99 percent of the population were born in Japan.

Bowing: They Wrote the Book

In Japan, watch your protocol when you are faced with the responsibility of introducing two people. The process works like this: When introducing a younger man to an older man, the younger man's name is mentioned before the older man's. However, when a woman is introduced to a man, the woman's name is mentioned first. Likewise, a more senior level person's name is said first: "Mr. Yamada (older or more senior), may I introduce Mr. Smith (younger or less senior). Mr. Smith, this is Mr. Yamada."

Most Americans are aware that the Japanese traditionally bow upon saying hello or goodbye—but it's a two-way street. The Japanese don't live in a cultural vacuum; they are just as aware of our custom of shaking hands. Therefore, don't be surprised if someone sticks out a hand for you to shake. If this happens, don't look surprised—be gracious and shake back. Some Japanese prefer to shake hands.

Shaking hands is usually acceptable in business circles, unless you are dealing with a Japanese woman. While the handshake may very well be limp, this isn't an indication that the person is a wimp; the strength of the handshake in this country is not linked to the forcefulness of the person's character.

Still, the traditional (indeed, stereotypical) bow is still alive today and well in Japan. However, you would be well-advised to stay clear of trying to duplicate the Japanese bow and risk doing it incorrectly. A formal traditional Japanese bow is not expected from U.S. citizens. If you do feel so inclined, a simple slight bow from the waist will be appreciated. When in doubt—bow. For a primer on the traditional Japanese bowing technique, read on:

➤ Put your feet together.

➤ Flatten your palms on your thighs.

➤ When you're bowing, don't crane your neck around to see if anyone else is watching. Keep your eyes downcast.

➤ Bend from the waist.

➤ The more respect you want to show, the deeper your bow should be.

What's In a Name?

Don't use first names with your Japanese business colleagues, and don't suggest that they call you by your first name. In Japan, use the last name together with the word *"san,"* which stands for "Mr." or "Ms."

You'd address a colleague not as "Mr. Yakimoto," but rather as "Yakimoto-san."

If you're in a room with other Japanese, don't be rattled if a sudden silence descends on the room. Silence in Japan is not something to be filled in with idle chatter; it's not uncomfortable for them and is considered to be sometimes beneficial.

The Business of Meishi

The exchange of *meishi* (my-she) (business cards) is another one of those rituals that you need to get just right in Japan—and of course, there are definite rules here. Start out on the right foot by making sure to include as much information as you can on your card, including any professional organizations to which you belong. Next, be sure to have the same information printed in Japanese on the back of your card.

Global Guide

Present your business card with the thumb and index fingers of both hands, with the Japanese side facing the other person so he or she can read it with out making any changes to the card's position. Receive a Japanese business card with the thumb and index fingers of both hands. If a Japanese person bows to you, pay attention! The depth of the other person's bow to you is an indication of that person's assessment of your status. You should bow back at exactly the same depth (unless the person is of a superior status).

Say What?

You may hear the title *"sensei"* in Japan. It means "teacher" and its used as a title of honor for teachers, elders, artists, politicians, and anybody else in a respected position.

When you meet someone in Japan, don't just toss your card over in a devil-may-care fashion. Here's the drill:

➤ Bow (or shake hands, depending on how conservative your colleague is).

➤ Present your card with the thumb and index fingers of both hands, with the Japanese side facing the other person so he or she can read it right away.

➤ When accepting the other person's card, again, use both hands (thumbs and index fingers), examine it for a few seconds (right away), and try to commit it to memory.

➤ If you can't quite pronounce the name, don't be afraid to ask for help. It's better than getting the name wrong the next time you say it!

➤ Make sure you understand the other person's title. If you do understand it, make some comment.

➤ When you receive someone else's card, treat it like a valued memento, not like a piece of used scratch paper. Don't crumble it up or stuff it in your back pocket and never write on the back of the card—especially in front of the other person.

➤ Place the business card on the table—and keep it there for the length of the entire meeting. It's considered rude in Japan to ignore meishi.

Keep Your Distance

Don't be surprised at how far away the Japanese will stand from you when they're talking to you. Japanese people keep a much further distance from others when talking than North Americans are used to.

No matter how happy you are to see someone, don't slap the back of a Japanese person; in fact, don't touch another Japanese at all. While you're at it, stay away from touching the opposite sex in public—it's frowned upon in Japan.

When talking with Japanese people, don't be surprised if they won't meet your gaze. It's impolite to maintain direct eye contact in this country.

Global Guide

Some gestures that are common in the United States don't have any meaning in Japan, such as shrugging the shoulders or winking.

Finger Play

In Japan, the slightest gesture can carry meaning, so you'll want to keep yourself on a very tight rein here. Don't wave your hands, make big, expansive gestures, make any sort of unusual facial grimace, or be dramatic in any way. In the U.S., we can be so used to making dramatic gestures that we don't realize the messages we're sending to the Japanese, who can be startled by these expressions and gestures. If you do wave your hand in front of your face with the palm facing left, it means "no."

When you're traveling in Japan, there are some gestures you should just avoid either because they are impolite or because they may be understood:

➤ Don't point. (Instead, wave your hand with the palm up at the object.)

➤ Don't make the "okay" sign with the thumb and forefinger (it means "money" in Japan).

➤ Don't beckon someone to "come here" with a crook of your finger. Instead, beckon with the palm down.

➤ Don't blow your nose in public. If you must blow your nose, use a disposable tissue.

Just as there are some gestures and behavior that won't go over well, you can get away with other behaviors that might be frowned on elsewhere. If you want to spit in public in Japan, go right ahead. Likewise, feel free to snort or sniffle.

Japan has not historically been a country open to the equality of women, but equality for men and women is much more evident among younger Japanese. Nevertheless, male superiority and dominance is still widely accepted throughout the country.

Faux Pas

It's a dreadful mistake to blow your nose in a cotton hankie and then tuck it back in your pocket. If you must blow your nose in Japan, use a disposable tissue (discreetly, please!) and then toss it at the first opportunity.

Kimono or Suit?

By now you've probably got the message: Life is formal and conservative in Japan, so it's not surprising that business attire is likewise fairly straight-laced. Don't wear casual clothes here on business, and never wrap your kimono right over left. That's reserved for corpses; instead, wrap your kimono left over right.

Other clothes tips to keep in mind:

➤ Women should not wear pants for business affairs.

➤ Unless you want to stand heads above your Japanese colleagues for some power-mad reasons of your own, avoid wearing high heels unless you're extremely tiny.

➤ Don't wear wrinkly, dirty clothes.

➤ Avoid hard-to-lace up shoes. You'll be removing them often, so choose slip-ons to save time.

While you may feel free to clomp around in shoes in Western-style office buildings and restaurants, you'll be expected to take off your shoes when entering private homes as well as traditional Japanese restaurants, temples, and many tourist sites. Make sure your stockings are clean!

Talk Is Soft

Because the Japanese are generally a soft-spoken people, quiet tones are appreciated. You may like to use a booming tone to dominate business meetings back home in the U.S., but you'll gain more points here by modulating your voice.

Pauses—even very long ones—are not unusual in Japan, and don't make the Japanese uncomfortable.

Global Guide

When speaking English for your interpreters, speak slowly and avoid difficult-to-translate American slang.

Accentuate the Negative

Remember that a Japanese person will answer "yes" to a question phrased in the negative. In other words, if you say, "Doesn't this product line work very well?" a Japanese executive will say "yes" if it's not. In the United States, the executive would say, "No, it doesn't."

Taboo Subjects

In general conversation, avoid asking your Japanese colleague about age or salary. Likewise, steer clear of talk about religion, politics, or how much that person paid to buy anything. Instead, talk about eating: where to dine, what kinds of food you prefer, who serves the best sushi. The Japanese talk about dining the same way the English talk about the weather.

Artful Negotiation

Eastern and Western cultures have very different methods of negotiating, discussing ideas and arriving at conclusions. It's important to realize that in Japan, negotiations will begin at the top executive level and proceed downward.

In the U.S., we are accustomed to bluntly coming out with our point and then tacking on supporting details until we feel like we've convinced the other fellow. In Japan, however, things are much more discreet. It's more typical to begin on a side issue and work your way up to your main point very carefully. When listening to a Japanese colleague presenting an idea or a plan, you'll need to be patient and wait for the primary ideas to appear.

In general, the Japanese tend to rely more on feelings than on facts.

The purpose for a meeting in Japan is not for everybody to get together and share information. The Japanese already know all the details before they get there; instead, meetings are for reaching agreement. While there may be some sort of agenda, don't be surprised if everybody ignores it. Japanese workers consider that an agenda may get in the way of the building of consensus, and rigidly trying to stick to a prearranged agenda is not a good idea here. The Japanese prefer to think that you have all the time in the world to discuss the issues with them and come to agreements.

When it comes to negotiating in Japan, it pays to listen to the Eastern culture. If you want to make your point, do so in a positive, supportive, and persuasive manner. Now is not the time to pound your fist on your colleague's desk to drive home a point. Don't pile on the pressure, and don't be confrontational. Issuing ultimatums may make you feel good, but it won't get the job done here.

Connections are extremely helpful when you want to grease the works in Japan—but choose someone who isn't in either the Japanese company or in yours. Make sure that the person you select as an intermediary isn't of a lower status than the person with whom he or she will have to communicate. If you can't find a helpful and effective intermediary, make a personal call. Letter writing isn't the way to get things done in Japan, and may even be ignored completely.

Faux Pas

Don't use a Western lawyer for your business dealings in Japan; use a Japanese attorney. This sends an important message of cooperation.

Even after the ink has dried on your contract, don't figure that there's no going back and changing anything. In Japan, contracts aren't thought of as totally final; either of you can always renegotiate.

Gifts Are Essential

Giving a gift is absolutely essential among Japanese businesses. There are several times a year when gift-giving goes on: July 15 (the middle of the year) and at the end of the year, which the Japanese recognize on Jan. 1. You're also expected to pony up on any first business meeting.

Not surprisingly in a country that elevated serving tea to high art, it's not just the gift, but the ceremony of the whole exchange that's important, and the whole area of gift-giving can be fraught with peril if you mess up.

In the U.S., we believe that it's the thought that counts—but in Japan things can get much more complicated. For starters, if you give someone a present in Japan, that person will feel that he or she must reciprocate with something of equal value—so unless you don't care about the other fella's purse strings, it's a good idea not to be extravagant. There may be no way to tell whether your gift will be something small or almost priceless—you just never know. It can be hard to figure out, so it's a good idea if you let your Japanese coworkers present their gifts first, and then buy something along a similar vein.

Not Another Ginsu Knife ...

When in Japan, don't figure that you can impress your Japanese hosts with a fancy Nikon or other Japanese-brand item; gifts from well-known foreign manufacturers are a better choice. Other well-accepted sorts of gifts include:

➤ Imported liquor.

➤ Electronic toys (if your colleague has children).

➤ Anything from a well-known company.

There are certain presents that would not be appreciated in Japan, no matter what. For instance, a knife is not something that would go over big in the relationship-building department, as giving one symbolizes the severing of a friendship.

Wrapping Savvy

You've also got to worry about the wrapping the present comes in. (We told you this wouldn't be simple!) The rules for gift-wrapping are complicated and actually could fill a book just to go into it all. First of all, it's extremely important to wrap your gifts beautifully (rice paper is a good choice). Many gift-wrapping materials that would seem perfectly fine in the U.S. could strike the wrong chord here. (For example, a gift wrapped in black-and-white paper might be considered chic and elegant in the U.S., but would cause offense in Japan.)

Tip of the Hat

If you're in doubt about what's okay when gift-wrapping (and you should be!), simply ask your hotel's concierge, who can usually get the job done for you (or at least tell you how to do it without causing major offense).

Hostess Gifts

While it's rare to be invited to a Japanese home, if an invitation is extended, you'll need to bring along a small gift of appreciation for your hostess. Cake, candy, or flowers are all good choices—as long as you don't choose white flowers, which are linked to death. While you're at it, make sure that you don't present an even number of anything—and especially avoid the number four. No matter how illogical it may seem, avoid giving four of anything.

On the Town

People in Japan love to entertain, and you will almost assuredly be invited out for various business entertainments—but don't expect to be invited to anyone's home. This is almost never done.

Instead, you'll probably be taken from bars to restaurants, and perhaps to a "hostess bar" (business women should steer clear of these). If your hosts should ask you where you might like to go and you're tired of the traditional bar scene, acceptable alternatives could include a karaoke bar or a visit to see some Sumo wrestling.

And if you're having trouble tying that *obi,* you'll be happy to know that despite the fact that the Japanese are extremely polite, prompt and conservative, it's acceptable to be late for social occasions.

Turnabout Is Fair Play

No matter how insistent your Japanese hosts may be that you are the guest and should not possibly be expected to fork over any yen, eventually you should invite them out for an evening. It's a good idea to choose a Western-style restaurant for this meal. (Besides, you may be tired of all that sushi by now.)

At a Japanese Home

If your hosts should happen to invite you home, feel free to act thrilled—this is very unusual and a great honor. You'll bring a hostess gift (see above)—and don't worry if you're late. That's acceptable.

When you arrive, don't just bang on the door and schlep right inside wearing your Doc Martens. One way to ensure you don't offend is to take off your shoes immediately upon entering the door. Face your host as you remove them, and after you have done so, neatly arrange your shoes with the toes pointing toward the outdoors. That signifies that your shoes are ready for your departure when the evening is over.

Once your shoes are off, you'll be given a pair of slippers. You'll wear these from the door to the living room, where you'll slip out of the slippers and pad around in your stocking feet.

Should you need to go to the bathroom, remember to put your slippers back on until you arrive at the bathroom door, where you take them off and put on your "toilet slippers." Don't forget to change back again into your "living room" slippers once you leave the bathroom.

After all that slipper on-ing and off-ing, you'll probably be happy to be seated and begin the meal. Expect to be seated at a low table with the family. If you are, don't sit on your haunches here—either sit cross-legged or move your legs to one side. Those of you who find this uncomfortable may be given a back rest by the family.

Don't expect an early evening, or a quick meal. Dining in a Japanese home is an elaborate affair, and it won't usually end until about 11 P.M. If you're the guest of honor (and you may well be),

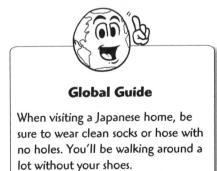

Global Guide

When visiting a Japanese home, be sure to wear clean socks or hose with no holes. You'll be walking around a lot without your shoes.

you'll be seated directly in front of the *tokonoma,* an elevated alcove that usually contains a scroll hanging on the wall and an ornament or flower arrangement on the floor.

Miso to Nuts

When it comes to their food, the Japanese are very serious indeed—not just about the taste, but about the way it's presented.

Of course, when in Japan, you will be expected to eat with chopsticks. It's not that hard to manage, if you watch the Japanese at work. Remember that you should never point with your chopsticks at another person, just as you wouldn't point your finger at anyone. When you're not using your chopsticks, you may line them up neatly on the chopstick rest.

If you want a refill for your soup bowl or teacup, hold the bowl or cup with both hands as it's being filled. In fact, when accepting anything—a plate of food, a present, a business card—use two hands.

Dinner Is Served

At dinner, wait for your host to ask you to sit before you do so. Get ready to get up, though, if an older person or someone of higher rank than your host enters the room.

The prime example of this concentration on the details is *"kaiseki,"* the aesthetic arrangement of "fixed price" meals of many dishes (expect to pay up to 20,000 Japanese yen for this).

Allow your host to order for you (it's a lot easier, anyway). Traditional foods that you may find on a Japanese menu include:

➤ *Fugu (Foo-gu):* A delicacy of blowfish (toxic unless skillfully prepared by certified chefs).

➤ *Okonomiyaki (Oh-kon-ah-me-yak-ee):* A pancake containing meat, fish or vegetables.

➤ *Sukiyaki (Soo-kee-ah-kee):* Thinly sliced beef prepared tableside.

➤ *Sushi (Soo-she):* Raw fish, seafood, or vegetables wrapped in seaweed and served on rice.

➤ *Yakitori (Yak-oh-tory):* Skewered chicken slices grilled over charcoal.

When the food arrives, eat with great enthusiasm, and be effusive in your gratitude afterwards.

Down the Hatch!

At the beginning of dinner, expect your host to make the toast for the meal.

If you're over 20 in Japan, you're legally entitled to drink alcohol. You'll find beer and whiskey in vending machines most places. But be aware that the Japanese take a dim view of drinking and driving—there are strict laws about this. Don't drink at all if you're going to be driving.

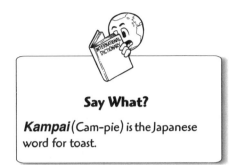

Say What?

Kampai (Cam-pie) is the Japanese word for toast.

Tips

You've probably had plenty to worry about what with handling chopsticks and trying to keep up with your Japanese hosts. At the end of the meal, at least you don't need to worry about trying to figure out what percentage to tip in Japan—it's not usually expected at all.

Likewise, you shouldn't tip in taxis, restaurants, or hotels. If you do offer a tip, don't be surprised when the tip-ee turns it down. You'll note a 10 percent to 15 percent service charge added to your hotel or restaurant bill—that's all the tip anyone expects.

The Least You Need to Know

➤ You'll get on well in Japan if you are polite, quiet spoken, and moderate in all your gestures and behavior.

➤ The group, not the individual, is all-important in Japan.

➤ Age equals rank in Japan.

➤ Be indirect when making suggestions, offering accusations, or criticisms.

➤ Gifts are essential among business associates, but the rules are complex.

➤ Negotiation begins at the top and proceeds downward.

Chapter 24

South Korea

In This Chapter

➤ Discover the importance of Confucian thought

➤ Get the details on rank and status in South Korea

➤ Learn about South Korea's attitude toward Japan

➤ Find out how South Koreans like to do business.

➤ Understand the negotiating style.

The only things most Americans know about South Korea come from old M*A*S*H reruns on TV. In fact, after the war years, the Republic of Korea has transformed itself from a poor agricultural land into a highly developed, stable, democratic republic. After great sacrifices, South Korea today boasts the world's eleventh-richest economy, although it now finds itself battling an economic crisis that is undermining its once unshakable sense of confidence and national identity.

The Land of the Morning Calm stands today on the world's stage, rooted in 5,000-year-old traditions while careening into the modern technological age. In any good-sized town, you'll find discos, karaoke bars, coffee shops, and stores selling designer label clothing, jostling cheek-by-jowl with traditional markets offering dried fish, ginseng, and *kimchi*.

South Korea, located in eastern Asia, is part of a peninsula 625 miles long and 150 miles wide. This country borders the Sea of Japan and the Yellow Sea. Slightly larger than Indiana, South Korea is made up of mostly hills and mountains, with wide coastal plains in the west and south. It's separated from its cantankerous northern neighbor, North Korea, by the Demilitarized Zone.

Global Guide

Occasional typhoons bring high winds and floods, and low–level seismic activity is common in the southwest.

South Korea is often included on East Asian itineraries, but even as a lone destination, it offers more than enough to fill a two-week stay. The best times to visit are from September to October and April to May because of the fairly mild spring and fall weather and little rain. Day temperatures will be in the 60s to 70s, with nights in the 50s (cooler in the mountains). You'll need a sweater in the evenings. June through August is the hot and rainy monsoon season, with highs in the 80s to 90s and lows in the 60s to 70s. Go only for skiing from December through February, when it's very cold.

Who's In Charge?

The Korean legal system combines elements of continental European civil law systems, Anglo-American law, and Chinese classical thought. The president is chief of state; head of government is the prime minister. A state council is appointed by the president, on the prime minister's recommendation.

The country's obsession with tranquility may arise from its perilous location surrounded by powerful neighbors. The nation of Korea was founded on a peninsula attached to mainland China in A.D. 668, where it flourished undisturbed through a series of dynasties until the twentieth century. When the conquering armies of Japan arrived, they annexed and occupied Korea, treating it as a colony until the end of World War II.

After the war, the U.S. and the Soviets agreed to divide overseeing responsibilities for Korea following the 38th parallel line; the U.S. took responsibility for overseeing South Korea, and the Soviets were given control north of the line. However, trouble arose; when the United Nations scheduled elections, the south refused to participate unless the north let U.N. observers supervise the process. The north refused and held unsupervised elections, which were won by a Soviet-backed leader. Tensions rose as North Korea began to import heavy artillery from the U.S.S.R. In 1950, the North attacked the South and easily took control of Seoul.

The U.S. led a U.N. force to counter the attack, pushing the North Koreans back into their territory so far north that China sent millions of Chinese volunteers into Korea to rebuff the invasion. For most of the three-year fight, the enemies pushed each other back and forth across the 38th parallel, until a cease fire agreement was established along the 38th parallel. However, no real peace treaty has ever been signed, although a nonaggression pact was finally hammered out in December 1991.

Korean Spoken Here

Korean is the official language, but English is widely taught in junior high and high school. For this reason, translators aren't always necessary during negotiations in the cities. Because most business people in South Korea do speak English, you may have your written materials printed in English. Still, Koreans do appreciate your interest in their language. *"An-yang-ha-say-yo"* means "hello," and *"Gam-sa-ham-ni-da"* means "thank you."

However, don't expect to find anyone outside of Seoul who speaks more than a few words of English, and English is still rarely spoken among the older generation, even in the cities.

Everywhere you will notice the respect with which Koreans treat their elders—even in language, where the fundamental principles of the Korean language are based on the many verb endings that indicate how much respect a particular person should have.

Say What?

Mudang means fortune teller. South Koreans consult fortune tellers for many reasons, including business deals. All it takes for a business deal to fall through is for a mudang to give it a negative report.

Religion

There is no official, state religion in South Korea, but most Koreans are either Christian (49 percent) or Buddhist (47 percent). You'll also find followers of Chondogyo (Religion of the Heavenly Way) and other folk religions.

Most Koreans—whatever their stated beliefs—also practice *shamanism* (a belief in spirits, ancestor worship, and the importance of fortune telling). Most also follow the philosophy of Confucius.

Life Is a Holiday

If you're going to South Korea for business, it's a good idea to make room reservations far in advance—especially for the last weeks in April and most of October. It's also a good idea to confirm your hotel reservation (and any special requests you have) by fax.

Here are some major holidays you'll need to note:

Jan. 1 and 2: New Year Holidays.

January or February: Lunar New Year.

March 1: Independence Movement Day (Independence from Japan).

April 5: Arbor Day.

May 5: Children's Day.

May 14: Buddha's Birthday.

June 6: Memorial Day.

July 17: Constitution Day.

August 15: Independence Day.

late Sept.-early Oct.: Chusok-Korean (Thanksgiving Holidays).

Oct. 3: National Foundation Day.

Dec. 25: Christmas.

Tip of the Hat

June through August is a bad time to visit because from mid-July to mid-August, the entire country is also on vacation. Try to avoid scheduling business trips or appointments from mid-July to mid-August, in early October, and at Christmas.

Don't Be Late

Don't be late for prearranged meetings and events. Korean business people expect you to be punctual, although they may be either a half-hour early or late. Remember to be on time for social events as well.

Open at Nine

Typical business hours run from 9 A.M. to 5 P.M. Monday through Friday, and from 9 A.M. to 1 P.M. on Saturday.

Banks will be open from 10 A.M. to 4:30 p.m. Monday through Friday, and from 9 A.M. to 1 P.M. on Saturday. (Remember that in the winter, banks open and close a half hour earlier.)

Government offices are open from 9 A.M. through 5 P.M. Monday through Friday and from 9 A.M. through noon on Saturday.

South Korea is 14 hours ahead of Eastern Standard time, so when it's 9 A.M. in New York city, it's 11 P.M. in South Korea.

Let's Call a Meeting!

You'll find that South Koreans often prefer to do business one-on-one, as opposed to the Japanese, who prefer to do everything in groups. Because your lone Korean business contact will have to represent your interests to the entire company, choose that contact wisely. If you want to schedule a meeting, the best times are usually from 10 A.M. to 11 A.M. and from 2 P.M. to 3 P.M.

At your first meeting, don't open your briefcase and immediately start flinging out files. Take the time to sit and get to know your Korean counterparts. Remember that while South Korea may seem to be as modern and sophisticated as New York or Paris, traditional values are still cherished here (especially among older Koreans). No matter how you feel, try to remain respectful and restrained until you notice your hosts begin to thaw; hang onto your cloak of formality as long as the others do.

Expect to be served tea at the start, and don't decline, no matter how you feel about tea.

Joking of any sort is frowned upon in meetings conducted in the Land of the Morning Calm. There is a time and place for yuks, but negotiation sessions are not one of them. Lighthearted comments will be taken in the wrong way.

Faux Pas

Don't incorporate triangles into your business presentations. Triangles are considered a "bad omen" in this superstitious country.

Business Pace

Things may seem modern in South Korea, but the pace is decidedly slower. It's not laziness, but a respect for tranquility. It's also a negotiation stance; South Koreans have learned that dragging their feet can exhaust the competition. Don't start complaining about your deadlines, and expect to make several trips to Korea before you clinch a deal.

Talk Is Cheap

While South Koreans wrote the book on politeness, it shouldn't be too hard to find a good topic of conversation. You'll be on safe ground if you discuss the cultural heritage of Korea, the Olympics (or any other sort of sport), kites, and family health matters.

Guide the chitchat away from these rocky conversational waters:

➤ politics

➤ communism or socialism

➤ Japan

➤ your host's wife

While it's appropriate to hold a person's gaze while you're saying hello and shaking hands, you should not maintain eye contact for long periods of time during a conversation. People of equal status in South Korea hold each other's gaze for about half the time during a conversation. A lower-ranking person will avert his or her gaze most of the time.

Nix to Japan!

Never, ever forget that many Koreans still deeply resent Japan for the many years Japan held Korea as a virtual colony. This Colonial period still evokes intense feelings in most Koreans, which often translates into a negative reaction to all things Japanese. Visiting business people should show respect toward Korea and never compare Korea negatively with Japan.

Everyday Life

Remember that everyone in South Korea has a rank (based on Confucian philosophy), and everybody knows his or her place. The ranking goes like this:

➤ Sons defer to fathers.

➤ Employees defer to the boss.

➤ Wives defer to husbands.

➤ Younger siblings defer to older siblings.

➤ Single women defer to married women (the link to a man establishes a woman's rank in society).

Global Guide

Even twins have a special ranking in South Korea! Younger twins must defer to older twins, even if the difference is a matter of minutes.

As you walk around South Korea, be aware that in many of the street markets, you may encounter things that are disturbing to Western sensibilities (especially the sight of freshly slaughtered dogs hanging on hooks). Don't take pictures of crosswalks, airports, harbors, military facilities, underground shopping areas, or anything where a "No Photographs" sign is seen.

Don't leave your camera, candy bars, or anything else that's heat-sensitive on the floor if you're staying in traditional housing during the fall, winter, or early spring. Koreans heat their buildings with pipes that lie beneath the floor boards.

Take a Bow

This is Asia, so don't be surprised to see Korean men greet each other with a gentle bow (and sometimes a handshake). Eye contact is maintained during this greeting. If your colleague really respects you, he'll support his right forearm with his left hand as he's shaking.

You can tell who's who, rankwise, by the person who bows the lowest and starts off the greeting. However, the most senior person will be the first to offer a hand to shake. Because older people are revered in South Korea, always approach and speak to an older person first.

Women rarely shake hands here, and it's not a good idea for a Western man to reach out and grab a Korean woman's hand. Western women would have to wait until the cows come home for Korean men to shake their hands. If you're a woman and you want to shake, reach out and grab the Korean's hand.

Let Me Introduce You

If you're at a business meeting or a social gathering, don't go barging up to the first group you meet and introduce yourself. Wait to be introduced (remember, South Korean is formal!). If there's someone at the party you're dying to meet, use an intermediary to present you.

Who's on First?

South Koreans have three names: the first is the family name, followed by the generational name, and ending with the given name. Confused? It may help to remember that the family names tend to be only one syllable (such as Sung), whereas generational names tend to be two syllables.

In a Korean family, all siblings would have the same last name and a common given name—the only way to tell them apart is by the third (given) name. The most common last names are Kim, Park, and Lee.

If you're writing a letter, begin by addressing the person: "To My Respected Mr. Sung Kim" (not just Mr. Sung).

Despite the conservative treatment toward women, married Korean women keep their maiden names. However, if you don't know a woman's maiden name, it's okay to call her "Madame" followed by her husband's family name.

Faux Pas

Never write the name of a Korean in red ink. Korean Buddhists only use red ink to write a Korean's name when the person is dead.

Card Play

Business cards are hot commodities in South Korea; it's a way for your hosts to find out not only your name and address, but your title and (hence) your rank. It's a good idea to present your business card to your South Korean contacts before asking for theirs. Here's the drill:

➤ Present your card with both hands, with the Korean language side facing toward the recipient.

➤ Nod politely (this nodding of the head is especially important if you're meeting with senior representatives).

➤ If the person responds by handing you a business card, nod your head to indicate your thanks for the opportunity to meet them.

> ➤ Glance at it briefly (it's impolite to look at it for too long).

> ➤ Now put it away.

Never present or receive a business card with the left hand—it's disrespectful.

Chinese characters (which Koreans usually can understand) are considered to be more sophisticated, so if you're traveling to South Korea and China, have your business cards printed in Chinese on one side.

Body Rules

Remember that South Koreans are fairly reticent and conservative. It's okay to hold hands with a person of the same sex, but don't go draping your arm over anybody's shoulder and avoid physical contact of any kind with older people or anyone of the opposite sex.

Women can cross their legs, but men should keep their feet flat on the floor (especially at formal business meetings).

You'll find that personal space in South Korea is at a premium, as this country is one of the most crowded on earth. (If you thought things were tightly packed in India or Japan, you're in for a surprise! It's even more crowded here.)

As a result, you'll find that South Koreans stand much closer to each other (and to you) that you might be accustomed to. If you're walking down the street, be prepared to be bumped, shoved, and jostled without hearing an apology. South Koreans reason that because they didn't mean to shove you, they don't need to apologize.

If you find something's funny, go ahead and laugh and don't worry about covering up your mouth while you do it, as Korean women do. At the same time, if you notice a chorus of giggles at your business meeting, it may not necessarily mean they think you're the next best thing to Jay Leno. It could be that they're embarrassed or they think they've lost face, and they're expressing that discomfort by laughter.

Mind Your Manners

If you want to catch the attention of a waiter across the room, don't leap up and wave your hands over your head. Instead, extend your arm palm downward, and wiggle your fingers up and down. Never beckon toward someone by crooking a finger toward yourself.

There are a host of gestures you'll need to avoid when visiting South Korea, including:

> ➤ When you're visiting the Freedom Pavilion, don't wave at, point to, or attempt to communicate in any way with North Korean border guards.

> ➤ Don't yawn with your mouth open.

> ➤ Don't touch anyone or anything with your feet (they're considered unclean in South Korea).

➤ If you've got to blow your nose, do so in private. Hawking into your hanky in public will offend a Korean's sensibilities.

➤ Don't use a toothpick in public; it's rude.

➤ Don't maintain continuous eye contact; you'll be perceived as too aggressive or hostile.

Tradition Rules

Although Korean attitudes are very slowly changing, women's lib has yet to arrive on South Korean shores. For example, in one very forward-thinking Korean company that employs 200,000 people, only four out of its 2,000 executives are women. Most working women—even those with advanced degrees—are traditionally employed only as secretaries, assembly workers, or teachers. (Remember, only a few generations ago women were kept in total seclusion in South Korea, much the way they are today in some parts of the Middle East.)

The country is profoundly influenced by Confucian philosophy, which assigns a ranking to everyone based on gender and age. Because Confucius believed that women were inferior to men, South Korea is dominated by men.

If you see a South Korean woman opening the door for a man, don't leap to the conclusion that the country is a hotbed of equality. In fact, women are a couple of rungs lower on the social status scale, and what you're really seeing is a woman deferring to a man's higher status.

However, this tradition doesn't apply to Western business people. Still, women may be surprised when asked personal questions regarding your age or your marital status. This may be rude and illegal in the U.S., but it's okay in status-conscious South Korea.

Global Guide

Because it is unlikely to find many South Korean women in business, it's wise to tell South Koreans ahead of time if women will be part of your company's team.

Stow the Flash

Don't try a casual or flashy approach in the way you dress here. Koreans appreciate executives who present themselves in standard, low-key yet formal business attire. They probably won't take you seriously unless you do, no matter what your profession happens to be.

Women should avoid tight skirts, as you may well be hunkering down on the floor in both homes and restaurants.

When business is over for the day, you'll still want to remember you're in a formal, conservative country. Women should avoid see-through blouses and slit-up-the-thigh

Faux Pas

Don't wear jeans or sandals when visiting Panmunjom. Unkempt or shaggy hair is also forbidden.

dresses in favor of modest, classic clothes. Revealing clothing is considered—well, rude in South Korea.

If you bring your kids along, they can get away with shorts, but all of you should avoid the colors of yellow or pink.

Remember to kick off your shoes before entering private homes, temples, or even your own hotel room if you're staying in a traditional hotel. In fact, it's not a bad idea to wear loafers your entire stay. You'll spend a lot less time unlacing!

Driving a Bargain

When you go to South Korea, you'll have to be on your negotiating toes, where subtlety and flair are appreciated. Be flexible and willing to adjust and you'll do much better here. Some Koreans have been known to nix a deal simply because they didn't like the Westerner's negotiating style. South Koreans are typically more independent than most of their Asian neighbors and tend to be more individualistic. While very straightforward, they also can be defensive.

Whenever you must deal with South Koreans on a business level, keep in mind the pervasive beliefs in Confucianism, which places the group above the individual. If you were negotiating in the United States, you might think, "What is in my best interest?"—but in South Korea, your colleagues are probably thinking, "What's the best interest of the group, and how can I maintain harmony among us?" If you want to close a deal, emphasize the benefits to the group (either to the company or the country—Koreans are extremely patriotic).

In South Korea, personal relationships are always more important than business contacts, so take the time to try to establish a connection with your hosts. This is why "cold calls" don't work in this country—the introduction is everything! If they don't know you, they aren't that interested in doing business with you.

Strictly Business

Remember that life is extremely conservative here, and there's a strong work ethic. You won't find the South Koreans slouching around the water cooler discussing the Korean equivalent of the latest episode of *Friends*.

Age Before Beauty

While age is always important in Asia, age and rank are especially revered in South Korea. Koreans tend to line up by order of rank and importance. If you're a lowly peon on the company totem pole, don't charge first into a meeting room in South Korea; instead, let the most senior member of your group enter a room first, followed by the next most seniored person.

Sign on the Dotted Line

In these litigious times, U.S. business experts value contracts as a way of specifying every single detail of a business relationship. Koreans, however, think of a contract more as a sort of general guideline that broadly defines the negotiated details but that leaves room for flexibility and interpretation. Realizing the differing attitudes, the Korean government has tried to come up with some "model" contracts that take both stances into consideration.

Give and Take

If you are given a gift while visiting, don't make a big deal out of it. Accept the gift graciously with both hands, and offer a simple thank you. Never open the present in front of the giver. That could cause major embarrassment.

If you're doing the giving, don't be surprised at an initial show of reluctance—that's just Korean politeness. Politely insist, and you'll find your hosts will accept the present. Typically, it's customary to give a gift of about the same value when one is given to you. Keep that in mind, therefore, when shopping.

Home Sweet Home

It's highly unlikely that you'll be invited home to meet the family—entertaining is rarely done at home. However, if you do wangle an invitation, consider it an honor and accept promptly. It's a nice gesture to bring along a hostess gift. Some acceptable choices include:

➤ Crafts or books from your home town.

➤ Chocolates.

➤ High-quality tea (no generic brands from the Piggly-Wiggly!).

➤ Impersonal gifts with your company logo (as long as they weren't made in Korean or Japan).

However, never give a gift of alcohol to a South Korean woman (but it's okay for men).

When you get to the home, remove your shoes and place them with the heels toward the dwelling. Once inside, remember that it may be perfectly acceptable to ask for a "house tour" back home in Sandusky, but don't start nosing around a private home in South Korea. Don't expect your hostess to show you around her house, and don't peek into other rooms by yourself on the way to the bathroom, either. It's considered rude.

When the visit is over, thank your host politely and then follow it up with a nice, brief note of thanks. It's a nice touch if you then invite your host to a meal later on.

On the Town

If you're in South Korea on business, you'll almost assuredly be taken out for drinks at a local bar. But there are other fun things to do here.

Try to attend a cultural event: Ask at your hotel what's playing at the Korean Classical Music Institute or the Sejong Cultural Center in Seoul. Among the traditional types of music are:

➤ *A-ak:* Confucian ritual music.

➤ *Tang-ak:* Chinese court ceremonial music.

➤ *Hyang-ak:* Local court ceremonial music.

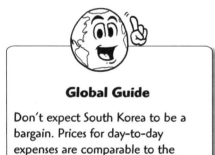

Global Guide

Don't expect South Korea to be a bargain. Prices for day-to-day expenses are comparable to the West.

Sightseeing is also fun. If you visit a temple, take off your shoes before entering (place them with the toes facing away from the building). When it's time to go, don't sit with your back to the temple to pull your shoes back on.

Sports are big in South Korea. Try to attend a demonstration of *tae kwon do,* the martial art that originated in Korea, or check out *sirum,* a Korean wrestling match. It's quite different from Western-style wrestling. Brush up your table tennis skills so you can play this sport everywhere.

Man Too to Nuts

It's common to schedule business dinners, or to grab a quick business lunch at a local eatery—but don't expect to discuss your company over Pop Tarts and coffee. Business breakfasts haven't caught on yet in South Korea. If you want to meet the local residents, spend some time in a *tabang* (tah-bahng) (coffee shop).

If you do go out en masse with your Korean counterparts, you'll either pay for everybody or you'll be the guest—there's no such thing as Dutch treat when dining with a Korean. The rule is that the one who does the inviting does the paying. (However, it's also polite for the younger person to pay for the older person, so expect some old-fashioned haggling over whose treat it will be.)

Be prepared to use chopsticks—forks will be hard to come by outside of Seoul. (Porcelain spoons are used for soup.) When you're finished the meal, place your chopsticks on the table (or a chopstick rest, if there is one). Whatever you do, don't stack them across the top of your bowl—it's considered to be bad luck. Even worse is to leave them sticking into the bowl of rice; it's in very bad taste. (That's how you make an offering to an ancestor.)

When your partner passes food to you (and don't be horrified if what you see coming your way resembles chicken's feet), take some, and then pass the food on with your right hand supported by your left.

If you notice that your table mate's bowls or tea cups are empty, go ahead and fill them up. It's polite tableside manners. They'll reciprocate. However, unless you want to find yourself drinking out of your table mate's cup, don't drink all of the liquid out of your cup. Once it's empty, your host may fill it back up and then trade cups with you.

Some table manners don'ts:

➤ Don't help yourself with your fingers.

➤ Don't take food directly from the serving plate and pop it into your mouth, no matter how delicious it looks. Place it on your plate first before you eat.

➤ Don't eat fruit with your fingers (eat slices with your chopsticks).

➤ Don't put bones or shells in your plate or bowl (they go on the table or on a spare plate).

➤ No matter what your mother said, don't clean your plate. If you do, this indicates you're still starving and your host didn't fill you up. (If your host offers more food, refuse, even if you really want more. Wait for two offers before accepting seconds.)

➤ Don't refuse to sing after your meal if everyone at your table breaks into song.

Faux Pas

Don't tip (the service charge is generally included in the bill), but do give a slight bow and say thank you.

Dinner In Korea

Dinner is the largest meal of the day in South Korea, usually between 6 P.M. and 8 P.M. In South Korea, don't be surprised if you find yourself sitting on the floor during the meal. Men should cross their legs while sitting on a cushion, or they may sit with their legs to the side. Women always sit with their legs to the side—never straight out under the table.

Be cautious if what you're eating is covered with bits of green peppers. Some of the peppers are so hot they make jalapeños seem like cucumbers!

Here's Mud In Your Eye

Expect to be entertained when you travel to South Korea—Koreans base their business relationships on personal ones—and you can expect to engage in some social drinking of *Soju* (so-jew) (Korean alcohol) or beer at a bar (*"no-ray-bang"*) where you'll drink and sing along to a karaoke machine. Since most of these karaoke machines also have songs in English, be prepared to sing at least one song to impress your hosts. If you're invited, it's considered impolite to refuse (but don't bring your wife). Also note that there are also "room salons" where Korean women serve food and drink to patrons.

If you don't drink alcohol, it's usually better to indulge in a white lie and say you can't drink because of a medical problem. Choosing not to drink is something the average Korean may not understand.

If you do indulge—or overindulge—don't make rash or wild promises. Even if you're dead drunk, you'll be held accountable for all comments and promises you made while lying under the table.

The Least You Need to Know

➤ Rank and status are all-important, with the elderly and men holding all the cards.

➤ Because of their former status as a Japanese colony, South Koreans have intense negative feelings toward anything related to Japan.

➤ South Koreans tend to be formal and conservative, placing more value on personal relationships than on business connections.

➤ The group (either company or country) always comes before the individual.

➤ South Koreans prefer to do business one-on-one.

➤ The pace is slower here; it's a sign of tranquility.

Chapter 25

Australia and New Zealand

In This Chapter

➤ Discover how New Zealand and Australia differ

➤ Understand the impact and treatment of native populations

➤ Learn the tricks of negotiation "Down Under"

➤ Find out the importance of punctuality

➤ Learn about the importance (or lack) of class

Every country where the inhabitants speak English seems like home, but don't forget you're really in another part of the world. What's important to understand is that these two countries aren't just carbon copies of former British colonies. In fact, one of the quickest ways to alienate an Aussie or a Kiwi is to confuse one country with the other; New Zealanders in particular, as inhabitants of the smaller country, strive to establish a separate identity apart from their giant neighbor. Read on to discover the special cultural expectations of this part of the globe.

Both Australia and New Zealand offer stunning physical beauty with lots of interesting things to do. One important thing to remember if you're planning a trip Down Under: The seasons are the opposite of those in the Northern Hemisphere; when it's summer in the United States, it's winter in Australia and New Zealand.

Aussies

Australia has lots of "titles" under its belt:

➤ the world's smallest continent

➤ the sixth-largest country

➤ the world's largest island (approximately 3 million square miles)

➤ the only country that is also a continent

Nestling between the Indian Ocean and the South Pacific Ocean, the Australian climate swings from arid to temperate in the south and east to tropical in the north. A tropical, invigorating sea breeze known as "the Doctor" blows along the west coast in the summer. While most of its countryside is barren desert, Australia has a wide range of environments, including tropical rain forests in its northern regions, temperate forests along the east coast, and even a few snowy mountains spotting the Great Dividing Range. Off the northeast coast is the world's largest coral reef, which runs for more than 1,200 miles.

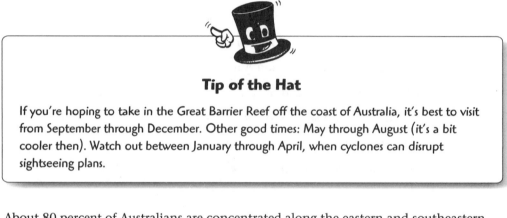

Tip of the Hat

If you're hoping to take in the Great Barrier Reef off the coast of Australia, it's best to visit from September through December. Other good times: May through August (it's a bit cooler then). Watch out between January through April, when cyclones can disrupt sightseeing plans.

About 80 percent of Australians are concentrated along the eastern and southeastern coasts. Australia has a prosperous Western-style capitalist economy, rich in natural resources. Although much of Australia's vast, desolate center still seems like an untamed frontier, there are plenty of places in the country where you can find that sophisticated urban experience.

Global Guide

Try some adventures Kiwi-style: Hurl yourself off cliffs or bridges tethered to the top by bungee cords, rocket down narrow river caverns on jet boats, or crawl into a Velcro suit and try to stick yourself to a wall.

Kiwis

About the size of Colorado, New Zealand has a temperate climate with sharp regional contrasts. It consists of two large islands (called, logically enough, "North Island" and "South Island") as well as numerous small islands found in the South Pacific Ocean southeast of Australia. North Island has more people, probably because of its warmer, more temperate climate. Bundle up to visit South Island, which is colder—but also more spectacular, with fjords, soaring glaciers, and hundreds of streams and lakes. New Zealand is predominately mountainous with some large coastal plains for diversion.

In the Driver's Seat

New Zealand and Australia both have highly developed, stable parliamentary democracies that recognize the British monarch as sovereign. Both countries enjoy a modern economy with plenty of good tourist facilities. How different can two countries be that share a monarch and a language? You'd be surprised!

First of all, there are profound psychological differences based on their historical origins: Australia's European population came to the island not on a tourist visa, but dragging balls and chains—Australia started out in the 1700s as a British penal colony. New Zealand, on the other hand, was never used as a prison.

There are other differences. New Zealand has adamantly refused to become involved with nuclear weaponry, and is adamant about declaring itself a nuclear free zone. New Zealand prohibits ships from entering its ports if they're carrying nuclear arms. Since the U.S. won't confirm which of its ships have these arms, New Zealand had to ban all U.S. military ships. This stance resulted in the suspension of the Australia/New Zealand/United States mutual defense treaty.

Finally, the two countries have treated their native populations in very different ways. In New Zealand, the Maoris (pronounced MAU-rees) still occupy a substantial amount of the country's good land. Maori words have infiltrated the English language, and about 10 percent of New Zealanders are Maori. Australia has been far less accommodating to its indigenous population, where only about 1.5 percent of Aussies are Aborigines.

In both countries, the chief of state is Queen Elizabeth II of the United Kingdom (she's represented on the island by a governor general). The head of government is a prime minister, with an Executive Council appointed by the governor general on the recommendation of the prime minister.

Tip of the Hat

There are no high-level elections, as the queen is a hereditary monarch and the governor general is appointed by the queen.

New Zealand

New Zealand was originally settled in the 1300s by the Maoris, who called the land *Aotearoa* (Land of the Long White Cloud). Oral Maori history recounts how 10 great canoes arrived from an island near Tahiti to populate New Zealand, where the Maoris proceeded to peacefully go about their business for the next 500 years, untouched by the outside world. Wearing spectacular zigzag tattoos, they made war among

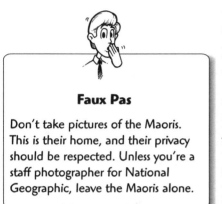

Faux Pas

Don't take pictures of the Maoris. This is their home, and their privacy should be respected. Unless you're a staff photographer for National Geographic, leave the Maoris alone.

themselves and either enslaved or ate anyone who got out of line.

It was only a matter of time before someone happened along and put an end to this halcyon lifestyle, and in 1642, someone did. Dutch explorer Abel van Tasman sighted the land but sailed away without bothering to stick his flag into the ground; subsequently, Captain James Cook claimed the islands 130 years later for the British throne.

Still, it wasn't until the 1830s that white settlers arrived, just in time to start trouble among the Maoris. For the next 10 years, they squabbled until a conditional peace was established, followed by another bloodier war in the 1860s. Once that war ended, the two cultures have worked together with a laissez faire attitude that persists to this day.

Since 1984, the government has accomplished major economic restructuring, moving an agrarian economy toward a more industrialized, free market economy that can compete globally. This dynamic growth has boosted real incomes, broadened and deepened the technological capabilities of the industrial sector, and contained inflation.

Australia

It's hard to believe that just 200 years ago, the only way you could get someone to go to Australia was to sentence him to a prison term at the penal colony there. Today, the country has become a popular tourist mecca drawing millions of tourists a year—and with the Summer Olympic Games to be held in Sydney in the year 2000, the crowds will only get bigger.

But in the early years of overseas exploration, Europeans were curious about what mysteries lay unexplored in that large blank space in the corner of European naviga-tors' maps marked *Terra Australis Incognita* ("Unknown Southern Land"). It wasn't until 1770 that Captain Cook reached the southeast coast, stuck the Union Jack into the sand, and claimed the land he called New South Wales for England. He then sailed 2,500 miles along its shores, charting the coast and barrier reef.

While he was floating along, however, he couldn't help but notice the dark-skinned nomadic hunters and gatherers living along its shores. The distant ancestors of these people had begun their migration into the land as early as 75,000 years earlier.

It took England 17 years to figure out what to do with this country, but eventually they began sending convicts from overflowing British prisons to the penal colony at Botany Bay. Soon other convict colonies began springing up like mushrooms after a spring rain, and English jurists were only too happy to transport more convicts from crowded British prisons. Eventually, free settlers followed, exploring and domesticating the land.

For a hundred years, Australia was the end of the line for the world's transportation and communication lines. Its isolation, together with its history as a penal colony, instilled a special frontier spirit and independent attitude that persists today in the heart of every Aussie.

Where's Your Didgeredoo?

While the official language of both countries is English, Maori is also spoken in New Zealand. Don't be surprised if the Australian version of English leaves you mystified. Australians use slang liberally.

Religion

Most Kiwis do not declare a religion (33 percent); the rest are Anglican (24 percent), followed by Presbyterian (18 percent), Roman Catholic (15 percent), Methodist (5 percent), Baptist (2 percent), and other Protestant (3 percent).

Most Aussies are evenly split between the Anglican (26.1 percent) and Roman Catholic (26 percent) religions; Christians (24.3 percent) and non-Christians (11 percent) define the rest of the population.

When to Visit

The best months for visiting Down Under are October and April, although September through May is pleasant in most parts of the country. December and January are the hottest months, while July and August the coldest.

If you're planning a business trip, remember that Christmas and Easter may be especially busy and many executives will be on vacation. Read on for other important holidays:

> **Jan. 1:** New Year's Day.
>
> **Jan. 26:** Australia Day.
>
> **April 25:** ANZAC Day.
>
> **June 13:** Queen's Birthday.
>
> **Dec. 26:** Boxing Day.
>
> **Dec. 31:** New Year's Eve.

Just for Fun

If you're in pursuit of more leisurely activities, the best way to soothe the soul is to go on a hike, which the Kiwis call "tramping." As a bonus, it's a good way to meet the Kiwis and to soak up the amazing beauty of the place.

While you're tramping about Down Under, don't reach out and touch a koala as you go. The adorable, sleepy-looking creatures, which look so adorably sweet clinging to their eucalyptus branches, are not fond of being petted. Many zoos have ended the practice of allowing visitors to handle the animals.

Punctuality Plus

Prior to making the long trip to Australia for work purposes, take the time to get to know your contacts Down Under by fax or e-mail. The electronic age is alive and well in this part of the world. Remember that Aussies don't drop in and they won't appreciate it if you do—be sure to call ahead for appointments first.

Never arrive late for a business appointment while visiting New Zealand and Australia; indeed, even being punctual may not be good enough. You'll rate points if you get to your meetings a five or ten minutes early.

Yes, We're Open

Banks are open weekdays from 9 A.M. through 4:30 P.M., but trading in foreign currencies stops at 3 P.M. Shops are generally open from Monday through Thursday from 9 A.M. to 5:30 P.M., Friday from 9 A.M. to 9 P.M., and Saturday from 9 A.M. to noon. Sunday trading is becoming more common.

Time Zones

It may be just an island, but giant Australia takes up three time zones all by itself.

Western Australia—This time zone includes Perth. It's the farthest away from the United States, and it's 13 hours ahead of Eastern Standard Time. (Singapore and Hong Kong share this time zone.) So if it's 6 A.M. in New York, it's 9 P.M. in Perth.

Northern Territories—The Northern Territories (including Darwin) and South Australia time zone is the middle section of Australia. It's 14 and a half hours ahead of Eastern Standard Time.

Eastern Australia—This time zone is the closest to the United States, and is 15 hours ahead of Eastern Standard Time. It includes:

➤ New South Wales.

➤ Sydney.

➤ The capital territory of Canberra.

➤ Victoria (including Melbourne).

➤ Tasmania (including Hobart).

➤ Queensland (including Brisbane).

And that's not all. When you travel to Australia from the Americas, you cross over the International Date Line. When flying west (United States to Australia), you lose a day; when you fly eastward (Australia to the U.S.), you gain a day.

The entire country of Australia practices Daylight Savings Time except for Queensland and Western Australia (these regions stay on Standard Time all year).

Informality Rules!

Informality rules in all aspects of life in Australia, even while riding in a taxi or limo. If you are going somewhere without a companion to chat with, don't sit in the back seat, but climb in the front, next to the driver. That's what natives do, because Aussies don't want to look as if they're putting on airs.

Nonresidents will find that Australian and New Zealand are democratic—the banker is no more important than the taxi driver and everyone strives to be "just an ordinary bloke." If someone acts in a cocky or overbearing way, in typical know-it-all fashion, the Aussies and Kiwis will quickly indicate their disapproval.

Global Guide

Because the seasons are opposite, when the U.S. is on Daylight Savings Time, Australia is on Standard Time, and vice versa.

Howdy, Mate!

Far more relaxed than their British cousins, Aussies and Kiwis have no problem with foreigners who introduce themselves in social situations.

Handshakes, used when greeting and leaving, are firm and accompanied by eye contact. "How do you do?" is common in formal settings. "Hello" or "G'day" is fine for friends in Australia. Women often give a kiss on the cheek.

Say What?

You'll hear the term *mate* in Australia; it's used by both men and women, and you'll hear it more often than you'll hear "sir." It refers to anyone of your own gender.

Of the two countries, New Zealanders have the reputation as being a bit more reticent. On first meeting, you'll probably consider a New Zealander to be a bit reserved. Don't hold back. Instead, take it upon yourself to break the ice. If you're friendly and open, the typical New Zealander you've just come to know will probably respond. Once a relationship is established, New Zealanders quickly progress to a first name basis.

No matter what movies you may have seen or books you've read, if you meet a Maori business person, don't worry about whether or not to rub noses. Maori business people share similar customs to other New Zealanders.

Titles

At first meeting, address both New Zealanders and Australians by their title or Mr., Mrs., Miss, and their surname. However, both Aussies and Kiwis are quick to switch to a first name basis.

If you have a slew of academic or professional titles, don't trot them out—especially in Australia, and especially if you're trying to impress someone. It's almost impossible to impress the Aussies, and if you did manage it—chances are they would never admit it to you anyway.

Moreover, Australians are proud of their "classless" society, and will be impressed by personal characteristics long before they will be impressed by initials after your name. In fact, the quickest way to get teased is to boast about your titles and qualifications.

Where's Your Card?

If you bring your business card along, it's perfectly acceptable to hand it over during an introduction—but don't get hurt if your colleague doesn't flip one over to you. Many Australians don't use business cards. This could be in part a holdover from their profound dislike of bragging and boasting; a business card can look like a way of trying to impress.

Let's Get Matey

In Australia, when men are among their "mates," they avoid being too physically demonstrative. Unless you want to make your hosts uncomfortable, you should avoid this, too.

New Zealanders are far more restrained and more like their British cousins than are Australians; expansive behavior of any kind (even while gulping down a few pints) is frowned upon.

Faux Pas

Don't litter while on Australian turf, even if the garbage is biodegradable. Cleanliness is important to the people there, and they frown on unsanitary habits such as throwing an apple core into the street.

If you get the urge to make a gesture that you'd hesitate to perform in front of your mother-in-law back home, odds are it won't be well-received in New Zealand and Australia, either. Try to avoid:

➤ Winking (man to woman): It's considered in-appropriate.

➤ The "thumbs up" gesture (hitchhiking or "okay" in the U.S.): It's rude.

➤ Chewing gum in public in New Zealand: It's rude.

➤ Using a toothpick in public in New Zealand: Again, this is considered rude!

➤ "V for Victory" with palm inward: In New Zealand, this gesture is obscene.

Get a Suit

Pack a professional yet comfortable business wardrobe for your trip to Australia in styles that are similar to what's worn in the United States. In general, business clothes are slightly more formal than in the United States, although casual wear is the same. (In Australia, women don't wear pants as often as they do in the United States.)

Men can't go wrong with a dark suit and tie; businesswomen should wear a dress, or a skirt and a blouse with a jacket. If in doubt about what to wear to a certain event, ask your Australian counterpart to offer some appropriate suggestions.

In Australia, be prepared for rapidly changing weather. The wisest approach is to wear layered outfits; you'll appreciate being able to remove or put on a jacket. Also take along a light raincoat and umbrella.

Global Guide

Don't be surprised by what the Australians wear (or don't wear) on the beaches. Lady Jane is the nude beach in Sydney.

Top restaurants in both countries may require a jacket and tie. In autumn, a light wool sweater and/or a jacket will suffice for evenings, but winter demands a heavier coat—a raincoat with a zip-out wool lining is ideal. Comfortable walking shoes are a must.

Can We Talk?

Topics of conversation appropriate for a casual discussion with a Kiwi or an Aussie include:

➤ International politics.

➤ Weather.

➤ Team sports—rugby or soccer (they call it football).

➤ Hunting, sailing, and fishing.

Stay away from discussions about:

➤ Racial strife.

➤ Labor disputes (Australia).

➤ Religion.

➤ Kangaroo population control (Australia).

➤ Nuclear arms.

➤ Treatment of Maoris (New Zealand) or Aborigines (Australia).

Never, ever talk about New Zealand and Australia as if they were the same place; they're very different destinations. Don't praise one country to a resident of the other.

In both countries, residents love a good, spirited conversation and enjoy hearing others' opinions. Go right ahead and debate (without getting personal or ugly) and you'll be respected for your convictions. Both Kiwis and Aussies are vocal about politics; someone without apparent beliefs or convictions loses credibility and respect.

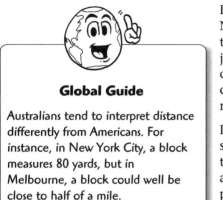

Global Guide

Australians tend to interpret distance differently from Americans. For instance, in New York City, a block measures 80 yards, but in Melbourne, a block could well be close to half of a mile.

Don't worry about going deaf when you're talking to a New Zealand business contact. Chances are you'll need to keep asking that person to repeat what he or she has just said. New Zealanders are known for speaking in quiet tones, especially in public places. Talking loudly is considered in bad taste here, where things are much more genteel than in boisterous Australia.

In Australia, it's usually acceptable to strike up a conversation with a stranger. So, don't hesitate to ask directions from a person on the street or to find out more about the culture by chatting with a native in a local pub. The latter is the local gathering place for many professionals after a long day's work.

Getting Down to Business

Australians put new spin on the word "casual." Even in business, acting laid back is the byword and being friendly is a prerequisite for negotiating in the land Down Under.

Indeed, no matter how high the stakes, many Australians stress the need for leisure activity during the negotiation process. Taking a holiday with an Australian may be the best way to break the ice. And while most people see status and money as the key motivating factors for working hard, it's the lure of leisure time during the weekend and on holidays that inspires many Australians to focus on strenuous work during week days.

However, just because business turns into a casual transaction, don't underestimate the Australian business acumen. Although the country's population is small (some 17 million), for the most part, expect both well-educated and very competitive individuals.

What's important to understand about Australia is that high-pressure tactics and lots of bluster and hype won't go over well here. Australians prefer honesty and directness. If you put on an exciting dog-and-pony show for your Aussie colleagues, they may feel the need to pierce all that hyperbole with some caustic humor.

Tip of the Hat

Seek out sporting clubs (motor, rugby, or soccer) that allow nonmembers to sign in. You can enjoy an inexpensive, high-quality lunch or dinner and entertainment on the weekends.

Teasing, in fact, is something Aussies love to do. If you get teased, grin and bear it. By all means, never get angry or hurt. If you can laugh it off—or even better, tease back—you'll go much farther here.

New Zealanders value their egalitarian society. Emphasize honesty and forthrightness in negotiations. Avoid hype and ostentation.

Home Sweet Home

Don't expect an instant invitation to an Aussie's house—they'll want to take their time before they get to know you well enough to invite you over for some shrimp on the barbie.

It's just the opposite in New Zealand, however, where the Kiwis love to drag folks back home for a bite—New Zealanders love to entertain. Although your New Zealand host will not expect you to bring along a token of appreciation, it's always nice to take something. Most likely, a box of chocolates or bottle of whiskey will be appreciated.

In the unlikely event you do get invited to an Australian home, you may want to give a small gift of flowers, wine, or crafts from back home. Avoid ostentation.

Soup to Nuts

Your first meeting with an Australian or New Zealander will probably take place in the office. After than, you may meet over a meal at restaurant or hotel. Typically, a lunch appointment is for getting business done; if you're invited out for dinner, most likely spouses will be included and it will be more of a social engagement.

If you're the meat-and-potatoes sort of person, you'll be thrilled with your trip Down Under. Meat is eaten at almost every meal here, although as a rule, Aussies and Kiwis are extremely health conscious and love to exercise. Vegetarianism, however, has not yet made it big here, perhaps because a large part of the economy is concerned with raising meat for food.

Popular foods in Australia include toad in a hole (beef or chicken casserole) and Vegemite, a yeast spread that Aussies love the way Yanks crave peanut butter in the U.S. (Caution: Start with a small taste; it's not exactly like peanut butter!)

Tea Time

Don't get confused about "tea" down under: Afternoon tea is served between 3 P.M. and 4 P.M., and plain "tea" is what you might think of as "dinner"—the meal served between 6 P.M. and 8 P.M. At lunch, a few dollars will buy you anything from fish and chips to nachos, and noodles.

International influences have transformed the Australia and New Zealand dining scene from a "roast of the day" mentality to a cosmopolitan mix of European and Eastern fare, and top class seafood restaurants. Remember you're on an island here, so don't hesitate to go for local seafood—feast on Bluff oysters, New Zealand mussels, scallops, and crayfish (clawless lobster). You'll also find lots of great Indian, Chinese, and Southeast Asian eateries, as well as taverns and fine restaurants.

While you're chowin' down, don't expect lots of conversation during the meal. Eating is serious business Down Under, and silence reins until after you've eaten. Then the fun begins!

Check Out the Pub

Go ahead and check out the pubs, especially in smaller towns, if you want a real slice of Aussie life (you'll likely see poker machines adjacent to bars or eating areas). Even where good restaurants are expensive, you can usually get a good, cheap pub lunch or snack at a milk bar or coffee shop. While you're in there, try some local beers.

Faux Pas

Remember, in an Australian pub, each person is responsible for buying a round of drinks. Never miss your turn to "shout for a round" or you'll be branded as an Ugly American.

Tipping

Tipping is not widely practiced in New Zealand. Only in the better city restaurants will you be expected to show your appreciation for good service with a 10 percent tip. This is true even for cabbies; unless you've expected the driver to tote huge mountains of luggage, don't be shocked if your taxi driver refuses your tip. A porter will be happy if given about 25 cents for each piece of luggage carried. Still, the tipping policy is changing (especially in touristy areas). Everyone you'll meet seems to have a different opinion on the subject, so use your own judgment.

The Least You Need to Know

➤ Australia and New Zealand are very different countries—don't mix them up!

➤ Australia started out as a penal colony, but New Zealand did not—the differences are still obvious today.

➤ Both countries are fairly informal, but New Zealand is more conservative of the two.

➤ While still honoring the Queen of the UK as their sovereign, the two countries are not as conservative as their mother country.

➤ Don't boast and brag Down Under if you don't want to offend.

➤ In Austrailia, it's okay to start a conversation with a stranger.

Part 5
The Middle East

One of the most important things to understand when you're traipsing around the globe is the role that religion plays in many countries—but especially in the Middle East. The influence that Islam has in the culture of the Middle East—especially in the conduct of women—is pervasive. (If you don't believe that, try wearing a thong bikini on the street in Saudi Arabia and see what happens.)

The less your destination resembles the United States, the more you need to bone up on the cultural expectations before you get there. This is especially true if you're visiting those Islamic countries that are quite willing to throw you in the clink for eating a Ho-Ho in public during Ramadan, for example. Ignorance of these cultural/religious taboos is not an excuse here—so read on to find out exactly what you can, and can't, get away with. And bon voyage!

Chapter 26

India

In This Chapter

➤ Understand the Indian's attitudes toward public behavior

➤ Discover the correct way to use Indian titles

➤ Learn how India's caste system still influences the country

➤ Find out the rules for gift giving in India

➤ Discover the many rules regarding sacred and unclean parts of the body

---

India has an economically developing democratic republic. Tourist facilities varying in degree of comfort and amenities are widely available in the major population centers and main tourist areas. The different cultures, regions, and religions of this vast country prevent blanket generalizations, as what is culturally accepted in a poor Hindu peasant family might be very different from what would be expected with a wealthy upper class Muslim group.

India is a part of southern Asia, bordering the Arabian Sea and the Bay of Bengal between Burma and Pakistan. About twice the size of Alaska, its upland plain (the Deccan Plateau) lies in the south, with a flat to rolling plain along the Ganges deserts in the west and the Himalayas in the north. The climate varies from tropical monsoons in the south to temperate in the north.

India has a federal republic, winning independence from the United Kingdom on August 15, 1947. The chief of state is the president; the head of government is the prime minister. A Council of Ministers is appointed by the president on the recommendation of the prime minister. The parliament (or *Sansad*) consists of the Council of States and the People's Assembly.

Global Guide

The English language is widely spoken in India, and has become a unifying force in India. It's the most important language for national, political, and commercial communication.

India's economy encompasses traditional village farming, modern agriculture, handicrafts, a wide range of modern industries, and a multitude of support services. Production, trade, and investment reforms since 1991 have provided new opportunities for Indian businesspersons and an estimated 300 million middle class consumers. While New Delhi has attracted foreign investment and revived confidence in India's economic prospects since 1991, economic policy changes haven't yet produced many more jobs or reduced the risk that international financial strains will re-emerge within the next few years. Nearly 40 percent of the Indian population remains too poor to afford an adequate diet.

Tower of Babel

There are 14 major languages in India, each spoken by a million or more Indians, with more than 300 minor languages and dialects. Most of the time, Indians can't understand each other's language.

Hindi is the national language and primary tongue of 30 percent of the people; other languages include Bengali, Telugu, Marathi, Tamil, Urdu, Gujarati, Malayalam, Kannada, Oriya, Punjabi, Assamese, Kashmiri, Sindhi, and Sanskrit. Hindustani is a popular variant of Hindu/Urdu, and is spoken widely throughout northern India.

Although English is widely used throughout the vast Asian country, you are bound to run into a language barrier at some point on your Indian visit. Remember, patience is a virtue, so smile and try to express your thoughts slowly and clearly. Your good natured communications attempts will be appreciated. Still, you can conduct business in English, and you don't need to have your written materials translated.

Religious Faith

India is a mass mixture of cultures, religions, and castes. Most of the Indian people are Hindu (80 percent), followed by Muslim (14 percent), Christian (2.4 percent), Sikh (2 percent), Buddhist (0.7 percent), and Jains (0.5 percent).

Hinduism is unique among religions in that it did not begin with a particular founder; rather, the religion evolved from Indian mythology. As a result, there are many variants of Hinduism and no single authoritative text (such as the Koran or The Bible). The religion teaches belief in reincarnation and karma, and has many different gods. To escape the cycle of reincarnation, Hindus most stop committing either bad or good deeds—which requires a sort of nonintervention with humanity. Cows are considered sacred by many Hindus, who therefore don't eat beef or wear leather.

The next most common religion is Islam, which requires surrender to the will of Allah. Pork and alcohol are prohibited to Muslims. Because most of the Indian population does not eat beef or pork, or drink alcohol, it's not surprising that the Indian diet primarily includes chicken, lamb, and vegetables.

About 2 percent of Indians are Sikhs, a religion that includes parts of both Hinduism and Islam. While Sikhs belief in reincarnation, they don't recognize caste differences and they reject nonintervention in the world.

Faux Pas

Don't take the picture of an Indian without asking permission first. Many people in this country are deeply offended by a stranger capturing their image on film.

Holiday in India

If you want to visit India during its best weather, bypass the heat and monsoon seasons by arriving sometime between October and March.

Note that businesses may shut down over religious holidays; the dates for many of these will change year-by-year. When a holiday falls on a weekend, businesses will typically close the Friday before or the Monday after the weekend holiday. Here is a list of common holidays:

Jan. 26: Republic Day.

Feb.-March: Mahashivratri.

Varies: Idu'l Fitr.

March-April: Good Friday.

March-April: Ramnavami.

May-June: Buddha Purnima.

Varies: Muharram.

Varies: Bakrid (Idu'l Zuha).

Aug. 15: Independence Day.

Aug.-Sept.: Janmashtami.

Oct.-Nov.: Dussehra.

Oct.-Nov.: Diwali.

Nov. 25: Guru Nanak's Birthday.

Dec. 25: Christmas.

Expect Tardiness

When you go to India, your country's reputation precedes you—you'll be expected to be prompt. But because punctuality is ignored in India, your hosts and colleagues may be very late (and sometimes they may not show up at all).

When you're planning a trip to India, write for an appointment two months before you arrive. (Remember that mail to and from India can be slow, and the unreliable India phone service makes faxes questionable, too.) Business executives prefer to schedule late morning or early afternoon appointments; aim for between 11 A.M. and 4 P.M.

Business hours typically run from 9:30 A.M. through 5 P.M., Monday through Friday. Banks are open from 10 A.M. to 2 P.M. Monday through Friday, and from 10 A.M. through noon on Saturdays. Government offices are open from 10 A.M. through 5 P.M. Monday through Saturday (except that these offices close the second Saturday each month).

India is 10 and one-half hours ahead of Eastern Standard Time. This means that if it's noon in New York City, it's 10:30 P.M. in India.

Greetings

A handshake is the common greeting between two men in India, but the *"namaste"* is a traditional greeting used instead of shaking hands. The namaste is done by holding your hands together at the chin (it looks as if you're praying). Then, you nod or give a short bow while saying the word "namaste" (*nah-mahs-tay*), which can stand for either "hello" or "goodbye."

In large cities, Indian men and Westernized Indian women will shake hands with foreign men. If you're a Western woman, you should not stick out your hand to initiate handshaking with an Indian man. Keep in mind, however, that India is full of conflicting castes and religions with specific rules about personal interactions.

Remember that most Indians are Hindu, and Hindus avoid contact between men and women. This means that it's okay for men to shake hands with men, and women with women, but only Westernized Indian men will offer to shake hands with a woman.

Likewise, there is no contact between Muslim men and women. In fact, if you would be so rash as to rush up and grab a religious Muslim man, he would be required to ritually cleanse himself before he could pray again. Because of this, women shouldn't offer to shake hands with any Muslim man. (If he's Westernized, he may offer to shake your hand; in this situation, that's perfectly okay.)

Titles

Indians love a good title, so if your colleague has one (such as professor or doctor), use it. Don't call anyone by his or her first name unless you're invited to do so—instead, use Mr., Mrs., or Miss.

Hindu surnames represent another complex situation. Traditionally, Hindus don't have surnames; a Hindu man uses the initial of his father's first name, followed by his own personal name. For example, R. Chinder is really "Chinder, son of R." Legally, both names would be written out with a "s/o" to stand for "son of"—you would write "Chinder s/o Ravi." You would call him "Mr. Chinder," however. (Remember, too, that long Indian names are often shortened.)

Hindu women follow the same pattern, with the father's initial followed by a first name. Legally, the name is written with the "d/o" to stand for "daughter of." When an Indian woman marries, she stops using her father's initial and instead follows her personal name with her husband's name. This, if V. Kamala marries our R. Chinder, she would then be known as "Mrs. Kamala Chinder."

On the other hand, some Indians use the Western style surnames, and Christians may have biblical surnames. Muslim names are usually derived from Arabic. Typically, you would call a Muslim by a given name plus the word *bin* ("son of") plus the father's name. Thus, Anwar bin Ali is "Anwar, son of Ali" and you would address him as "Mr. Anwar," not "Mr. Ali."

A Muslim woman is known by her given name plus *binti* ("daughter of"), plus the father's name. If she marries, she is known as "Mrs." plus her given name. So Ana binti Anwar would become Mrs. Ana when she marries.

Indian Sikhs always have a given name plus the word *Singh* (men) and *Kaur* (women). You'd address an Indian Sikh named Ravi Singh by a title and first name; you would say Mr. Ravi, not "Mr. Singh."

Say What?

Haji is the title for a Muslim male who has completed the pilgrimage to Mecca. A woman who has made the pilgrimage is addressed as *Hajjah*.

Not Everyone Is Equal

India still maintains a rigid system of inequality, with a deeply ingrained sense of differences between castes. Male chauvinism is quite common and women don't have very many privileges. The origins of the caste system are lost in the mists of antiquity, but it has existed for thousands of years. While the government has outlawed discrimination on the basis of caste, it still plays a significant role in politics and business.

There are only four traditional castes, but these are broken down into thousands of subcastes. The highest caste is the *Brahmin*. The hierarchy of the Indian caste system parallels the structure of the human body: The high castes work with their heads, and low castes work with their bodies.

If an office manager needs a file sitting on a shelf behind his desk, he'll push a buzzer and summon in a lower caste peon from the outer office to get the file for him rather than turn around and grab the file himself. This is not laziness—it's a strict adherence to the principle of the caste system.

The *Rg Veda* calls the lowest caste "two-footed cattle." To this day, the work that this lowest caste performs is the same work that would be done by animals in other countries.

Watch Your Body

In India, the left hand is typically used to clean up after finishing restroom visits. Even if you're left-handed, you should always use your right hand to accept and pass food while dining at an Indian table. Likewise, use your left hand when you give money to an Indian.

But that's not the only part of your body that is suspect in this country; your feet are also considered unclean. Be extra careful not to step on anyone's toes or bump feet under the table. However, if you accidentally do, be sure to say you are sorry.

While you're at it, you should never touch an Indian's head, either. Many Indians believe that the head is the seat of the soul, so you should not even touch the hair of a child.

Be cautious not to invade an Indian's personal space. When talking to someone, an arm's length away is considered the proper distance. If your conversation partner steps back even further, don't worry about your breath, just give them some room by edging backward a little more. Generally speaking, Hindus tend to stand about three feet apart (or farther).

By now, it should come as no shock that PDAs (public displays of affection) are not popular in India. Don't touch (except for shaking hands), hug, or kiss in any greeting.

"Yes" Means "No"

When in India, think "mirror image" when it comes to gestures. What we may mean to signify "yes" will be interpreted as "no" in India, and vice versa. Indians will show agreement by shaking the head from side to side; to show disagreement, an Indian will nod the head up and down, or toss the head up and back.

If you want to express remorse or honesty, simply grasp your ear in earnest à la Carol Burnett. Your Indian friend will get the message from that simple gesture.

Tip of the Hat

Ears are considered to be sacred appendages, which is why you grasp your ear to show sincerity. It's also why you should avoid pulling someone else's ears or boxing their ears.

Avoid these gestures:

➤ Don't stand with arms crossed (it's interpreted as an angry gesture).

➤ Don't point with your finger (it's rude).

➤ Never whistle (it's impolite).

➤ Don't pull anyone's ears (the head is the seat of the soul).

➤ Never point your feet at someone else (feet are unclean).

➤ Don't wink at someone else (it may be misinterpreted as an insult or a sexual proposition).

➤ Don't beckon with palm up and wagging a finger (it's an insult).

Suit Up

Men should wear a suit and tie (but when it gets hot—and it will—you can take off the jacket). Business women should choose a conservative dress or pantsuit.

Shorts are only acceptable when you're jogging; short sleeved shirts and long trousers are otherwise preferred for casual attire. Women must keep their upper arms, chest, back, and legs covered always. If a woman jogs, you've still got to jog in long pants.

Faux Pas

If you're going to be visiting a temple, remember that leather goods (such as purses and belts) may offend Hindus.

Saris: Not for Everyone

While technically any woman can wear a *sari,* Indian women privately complain that most Western women look awful in these unique Indian dresses. Walking gracefully in a sari can be difficult, and there are little-known "insider" rules for the correct place-ment of the loose end of the material that drapes over the shoulder.

Indian women take great pride in their saris, and can spend quite a lot of money for different ones for different occasions. If you dig up a bargain basement sari, keep it to yourself. It won't matter anyway, as any Indian woman can tell at a glance just how much you spent for your sari.

Punjabi Suit

If you look tubby in a sari, or you just don't feel comfortable in one, you have another Indian option: the *Punjabi* suit of loose pants and long over-blouse. These are usually sold as a set; the pants can be either loose and flowing, or tight from the knee down and bunching over the ankles.

Safari Suit

Men find the safari suit comfortable for most official occasions during the hot season— it's a short-sleeved shirt jacket with matching pants. In northern parts of the country during the winter, you can break out the traditional business suit and tie. In Bombay during the monsoon season, a shirt with a tie is perfectly acceptable.

Gifts Are Good

Gifts are an important part of doing business in India—but don't unwrap the present in front of the giver. If someone gives you a wrapped present, set it aside until the person leaves. Then, you can tear into it.

When it's your turn, choose your gift carefully. If you know that the recipient does indeed drink alcohol, then a nice gift would be a bottle of imported whiskey (buy it at the airport or at a duty free shop to avoid the 27 percent Indian sales tax).

The following are not-so-good ideas:

➤ any sort of leather goods as a gift, in case the recipient is a Hindu (remember the sacred cow)

➤ any gift with pictures of dogs, or stuffed dogs, to an Indian Muslim (dogs are considered to be unclean)

➤ a gift of money in an even number—give an odd amount (US $11 instead of US $10, for instance)

Once you've selected a gift, wrap it up carefully—but don't use black or white paper. These colors are considered to be unlucky. Good choices in wrapping paper colors are green, red, and yellow.

If you are given a garland to hang around your neck when you arrive at a function, don't leave it on for more than a couple of seconds. The polite thing to do is to immediately take it off and carry it the rest of the evening. This action indicates humility, a virtue important in the Indian culture.

Tip of the Hat

If you invite an Indian colleague somewhere and he says, "I'll try to come," it most likely means he can't make it. In the Indian culture, saying, "No" would seem too harsh, so Indians respond instead with vague non-responses so as not to hurt your feelings.

Home Entertainment

Not too long ago, bringing a hostess gift when you were invited to an Indian home would have been insulting—as if you were commenting that your hosts could not afford fruits or chocolates. However, hostess gifts are accepted today. If you're invited to an Indian business contact's home for dinner, bring a fruit basket or a box of chocolates as a token of appreciation. Flowers are another good choice, but don't choose frangipani blossoms (they are associated with funerals). You'll also score some points with the kids by bringing a small gift for each of the family's children.

Alcohol can be a terrific gift, if you know that the family drinks alcohol. Otherwise, avoid it. Some people like to ask ahead of time what they can bring, if they know they are going to be staying with an Indian family. Acceptable items that may be hard to find in India include:

➤ Good knives.

➤ Computer disks.

➤ Chocolate.

➤ Disposable razors.

➤ Household goods (such as plastic containers with tight lids).

➤ Perfume.

➤ Toiletries.

Faux Pas

Poverty and personal affairs are off-limits topics in India. Instead, if you need to make small talk, bring up Indian traditions and traveling to other countries.

Remember to arrive between 15 to 30 minutes late to a meal at a private home.

If you're staying in a home with servants, it's a nice touch to leave a tip for them as well, if they've done some extra work for you. Always check with the host first, and let them help figure out how much money might be appropriate. (If you give too much, your host might not appreciate the precedent!)

If It's Bombay, It's Casual

Different parts of the country have a different sort of "style," requiring different kinds of attitudes. Bombay leans toward a relaxed, informal style, with casual chic dress. If your dress is considered okay by Western standards, you'll be fine in Bombay.

Official parties are more common in New Delhi, where strict protocol is the rule. This capital of India is where you'll find the politicos and diplomats, for whom "keeping up appearances" is like breathing. In New Delhi, when the food comes out it signals the end of the party—you're expected to eat and then leave. Since this may occur quite late, it's a good idea to eat and drink something before you get to the party.

Southern Madras tends to be a bit more quiet than her northern neighbors, more conservative than Bombay. Because people in Madras seem to go to bed earlier than those in the north, parties don't last as long here.

A Little Baksheesh (Tip)

When it comes to tipping in India, the more often you do it, the more things will get done. In fact, tipping isn't really considered to be a reward for good service—it's almost looked on more like a necessary bribe to get things rolling. You'll be surprised how quickly a little *baksheesh* (bribe) will grease the works and open closed doors.

Pillau to Nuts

If you want to entertain your Indian colleagues, go for a business lunch instead of a dinner. It's perfectly okay for businesswomen to entertain an Indian colleague—but don't be surprised if he makes a grab for the check.

While generalizations are very difficult to make when it comes to dining in India, one thing is pretty much accepted everywhere—don't ever eat or pass food with your left hand. Here's a tip to help you remember this rule: Keep your left hand in your lap during meals, and you won't be tempted to break this taboo.

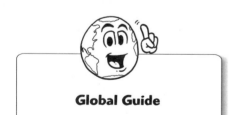

Global Guide

Wash your hands before and after any meal. Hindus may expect you to wash out your mouth as part of the bargain.

Never offer anyone else food from your bowl (not even your spouse) as it's considered to be "unclean" as soon as it hits your bowl. At the same time, keep your mitts off any communal dish; if you touch serving dishes, the rest of the Indians at the table won't.

Don't thank your hosts at the end of the meal; an Indian will consider that an insult, as if the "thank you" is a form of payment. Instead, offer to return the favor of inviting the person out to another dinner.

Don't be surprised if eating utensils aren't used among friends. Indians consider that eating is a sensual, tactile pleasure. Utensils just get in the way.

Breaking Your Fast

For breakfast, expect to find *dosai* and *idli* and other *"tiffin"* (snack) foods. They're also considered tea time or snack foods and can usually be ordered at a restaurant at any time.

Tip of the Hat

Yogurt is an essential ingredient in any Indian meal, often served at the end of a meal to cool the palate (which is probably on fire; Indian food is SPICY!). It may be brought to the table plain or flavored, or mixed with raw vegetables.

Lunch

A *thali* (tali) meal is complete in itself and can include a sweet (which Indians often taste or eat first). The thali meal is presented on a rimmed metal tray, on which all the food is served on a plate, with rice or bread placed in the middle and an assortment of side dishes arranged around the side. Each meal should contain foods that offer the six "critical essences"—sweet, sour, salty, pungent, astringent, and bitter. This meal is primarily vegetarian and is especially popular in southern India, although there are regional varieties. Thali is available only at lunch and dinner.

Dinner Is Served

Tandoori food (food baked in a special container) is a typical choice for dinner. In a tandoori restaurant, go for a meal with several people so that you can order several kinds of bread, several kinds of meat (with and without gravy), one or two vegetable dishes, and a vegetable-and-yogurt salad (*raita*). Everyone shares, and order the breads as you need them so they come hot to the table.

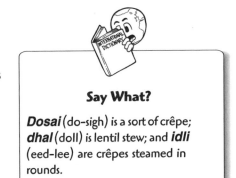

Say What?

Dosai (do-sigh) is a sort of crêpe; *dhal* (doll) is lentil stew; and *idli* (eed-lee) are crêpes steamed in rounds.

The Least You Need to Know

➤ While technically outlawed, the caste system still affects daily life in India.

➤ Public displays of affection are frowned upon.

➤ Tipping is the way to get things done in India.

➤ You'll be able to get by speaking English in India, which enjoys "associate" status in this country.

➤ India's vast mixture of religions and cultures create many physical and cultural taboos.

➤ Gifts are an important part of doing business in India.

Chapter 27

Saudi Arabia

In This Chapter

➤ Learn the taboos of Saudi Arabian Islamic practices

➤ Discover the best and worst times to visit the country

➤ Find out how Western business women should dress

➤ Learn the best ways to open a business relationship

➤ Discover the details of Islamic practice

For a country that welcomes Muslim pilgrims so warmly (some two million Muslims flock to Mecca and Medina each year), Saudi Arabia can be an inhospitable place to just about everybody else—especially Western women, who have an enormously difficult time adjusting to the conservative attitudes. In the struggle to maintain the fragile balance between modernization and fundamentalism, Saudi Arabia tries to absorb technology from the West without being contaminated by its cultural influence. Consequently, much of the country is hidden behind walls and veils, at once mysterious and mystifying.

Saudi Arabia continues to be a country apart, shadowed by religious taboos, visa restrictions, and a lack of interest in developing Western-style tourism. Travelers who do make it inside the country find a seemingly modern nation with a way of life that dates to the seventh century.

Saudi Arabia is part of the Middle East, bordering the Persian Gulf and the Red Sea. Slightly more than one fifth the size of the U.S., about half the country (an area the size of France) is taken up by the "Empty Quarter," the largest sand desert in the world. The center and north of Saudi Arabia is mostly gravel plain.

Oil was discovered in the 1930s and has formed the basis for the nation's current high standard of living. Though the Saudi economy was slowed by the price reductions that began in the late 1980s, the country is economically sound.

Al-Saud Is King

Saudi Arabia has a monarchy ruled by a king chosen from and by members of the Al-Saud Family. At the moment, the Custodian of the Two Holy Mosques (King Fahd Bin Abdul Aziz) serves as both the Head of State and the Prime Minister, and is assisted by an appointed Council of Ministers.

All Saudi Arabians have the right to march right into the palace with a direct petition to the monarch, the regional governors, or other government officials. These petitions are most often received during the regular public audiences. The king rules through royal decrees issued in conjunction with the Council of Ministers, and with advice from the Consultative Council.

Islamic law is the basis of the authority of the monarchy and underlies the country's conservative customs and social practices.

Tip of the Hat

While Saudi Arabia has a modern and well- developed infrastructure with a wide range of facilities for travelers, the country does not issue visas for tourism.

The Best Time to Visit

The best time to visit Saudi Arabia is between April and May and October to November, when day temperatures are generally moderate and nights are cool. During December through March, the day temperatures are fine, although it can be very cold in the mountain areas. Summers can be extremely hot (up to 130° F in the shade in some areas) and surprisingly humid (because of the sea), or very dry because of inland winds. Sandstorms can blow up almost anywhere in the country, some lasting up to four days.

Arabic Spoken Here

Arabic is the official language—and it's much more complex than you might at first think. Cairene Arabic is the oral dialect most folks understand throughout the Arabic world. Classical (also called Modern Standard) Arabic is the language of the *Qur'an* (the Koran, which is the Islamic book of holy writings), and also of most textbooks for learning written Arabic.

Citizens who have been educated abroad also speak English.

Islam Only

Islam is the official religion of Saudi Arabia—indeed, it's the only religion. Public observance of any other religion is forbidden, and non-Muslim religious services are illegal. Public display of non-Islamic religious articles (such as crosses or Bibles) isn't permitted. Travel to Mecca and Medina, the cities where the two Holy Mosques of Islam are located, is forbidden to non-Muslims.

A monotheistic religion, Islam's holy book is the Qur'an, and Friday is its Sabbath day. Five times daily, Muslims are called to prayer from the minarets of mosques that dot the countryside.

Because two of Islam's holiest sites are in Saudi Arabia, the country considers itself the birthplace of the religion. Islam is a total way of life for the Saudis, affecting not just family but the entire social structure of the country. The idea of separation of church and state is foreign to Saudi Arabians—their religion permeates every corner of their existence.

Islam derives from the same monotheistic roots as Judaism and Christianity, and Muslims generally regard Christians and Jews with respect (in Islam, Jesus is regarded as one of the Prophets of Allah, and Jews and Christians are considered fellow "People of the Book"). Mohammed was the last Prophet, and it was to him that Allah dictated the Koran. The Koran is Saudi Arabia's constitution, and *Shari'ah* (Islamic law) is the foundation of the Saudi legal system.

The Saudi form of Islam is conservative and fundamentalist, based on an eighteenth-century revivalist movement that has a great effect on Saudi society—especially on the position of women, who don't go out without being totally muffled up in black robes (*abaya*) and masks. However, this way of life is being threatened by modernization and rapid development.

At prayer times, shops close and Muslim men have to go the nearest mosque for prayers. (This happens four times a day: mid-day, afternoon, sunset, and evening.)

In a country profoundly influenced by its religion, it's not surprising that there are many taboos. Read the following tips if you want to avoid harassment and possible jail terms:

➤ Don't try to convert a Muslim to your religion—proselytizing is illegal.

Global Guide

During the quarterly daily prayers, non-Muslims and women wait outside the shops for the duration of a prayer, between one half to three quarters of an hour.

➤ Don't ever walk in front of anyone while they're praying.

➤ Don't expect to be able to go into any mosque if you are not a Muslim.

Say "Cheese!"

You may see a lot to photograph while you're visiting—but don't photograph royalty, women, airports, ports, and industrial or military facilities. It's also best to request permission before photographing mosques. Photographs that depict poverty or squalor are discouraged by the government, and "excessive" use of a camera in populated areas may also attract unfavorable attention.

Small Change

Saudi businesses are happy to accept major credit cards (Visa, Master Card, and American Express), ATM cards, phone cards, and traveler's checks. An ATM card is a good idea for convenient access to cash, your bank account in and outside the country, and for use in shops where credit cards aren't accepted.

Tip of the Hat

Take a reserve of small-denomination U.S. dollars and avoid using the old-style U.S. $100 bills (counterfeits are so common that many banks no longer accept these bills).

Haggling

In Saudi Arabia, the price of almost anything is negotiable (to a point). In Bedouin markets, you can haggle incessantly, but elsewhere it's a two-step process: You ask for a discount, you get a counter offer. You can either take it or leave it. If you don't bargain with merchants in the markets, it's considered an insult.

Traveler's Checks

Cashing travelers' checks can be a real pain; many banks and moneychangers either won't take them, or they will only exchange the type they sell, or they'll only cash checks for account holders. Always carry your original purchase receipt with you, as the few places that do cash checks will require it.

If you're changing cash, moneychangers will give you a slightly better rate than banks. To avoid additional exchange rate charges, it's a good idea to take traveler's checks in Saudi riyal, U.S. dollars, or British pounds.

Islamic Holidays

Saudi Arabia's only holidays are Islamic, and if you're heading to Saudi Arabia on business, schedule your trip so that it doesn't coincide with *Ramadan* (the exact dates vary from year to year). During this religious holiday, it's extremely difficult to find people in their offices. Tourist sites also close early during this time.

Ramadan

As in all Muslim countries, the month of Ramadan is a very important holiday. Ramadan is the month of the Prophet's first revelations, and during this month, Muslims fast between dawn and dusk. (If you're a non-Muslim, you don't have to fast, but it's thoughtful if you avoid eating in public out on the streets.) At the end of Ramadan comes *eid el-Fitr* (the End of Fast-Breaking), when the fasting is over.

Islamic Calendar

Remember that the Islamic calendar consists of 28-day lunar months, so an Islamic year is 354 days long; this means that holidays will be on different days every year. Muslim holidays depend on actual lunar observations.

The Islamic calendar began in A.H. 1 (in the "year of the Hejira") (Hej-ear-ah—when the prophet Mohammed went to Medina), which marked the year that the Prophet Mohammed moved from Mecca to Medina to evade religious persecution. A.H. 1 is the same as A.D. 622 of the Gregorian calendar. In the Islamic calendar's 30-year cycle, 11 years are leap years. In non-leap years, the 12 months starting with the New Year have alternating 30 or 29 days.

Jan. 1: New Year's Day.

Varies: Ramadan Bairam.

Varies: Islamic New Year.

February: Jinadriyah National Festival of folklore and Culture (the only non-religious festival).

March: Eid al-Adah (the other big feast of the year marking the time when Muslims should make the pilgrimage to Mecca).

July 23: National Day.

It doesn't matter if you're a Methodist, a Moonie, or a Marxist, if you're visiting Saudi Arabia during Ramadan, it's mandatory that you follow the rules of this religious holiday; if you're caught smoking, drinking, or eating in public during this period, you can be sent to prison until the end of Ramadan.

Ramadan ends with a huge feast, Eid al-Fitr, during which everyone prays together, visits friends, gives presents, and stuffs themselves silly. In 1999, Ramadan is in December.

Try to avoid visiting during the extended religious holidays of Ramadan, El Fitr, the hajj (the pilgrimage to Mecca), and al-Adha (the feast days at the end of the Hajj). Many places will be closed, and it's hard to get much accomplished.

Slow Down...

Life in Saudi Arabia drifts along at a slower pace than the West. While most Arabians will be late, you should be on time. In fact, it's standard Arab practice to keep you waiting, so it's a good idea not to cram too many appointments into one day. No matter how annoying it is to be on time and then have to wait for all your Saudi colleagues to show up, continue to be punctual to meetings.

Friday is the Muslim holy day (the work week runs Saturday through Wednesday). Government offices are open from 7:30 A.M. to 2:30 P.M., Saturday to Wednesday. Business offices are usually open from 8 A.M. to noon, and from 3 P.M. to 6 P.M. Saturday to Thursday. Shops differ, but most stay open until 10 P.M. and many are open on Friday evenings, too. Most restaurants stay open until 11 P.M. Banks are open from 8 A.M. until noon, and from 5 P.M. to 8 P.M.—but bank branches in airports, as well as shops, work around the clock.

Global Guide

An appointment is rarely private. Expect your visit to be delayed and interrupted by phone calls, other visitors, etc.

Global Guide

Offer refreshments, such as coffee and tea (even if you're staying in a hotel).

Saudi Arabia is eight hours ahead of Eastern Standard Time, which means that if it's noon in New York City, it's 8 P.M. in Saudi Arabia.

Doing Business the Saudi Way

Don't rush right into business. Saudis like to establish a relationship of mutual trust first. When you sit down to a business meeting, prepare for a long-term affair. Time moves slower here, and the meeting will most likely start off with discussions about your health, the trip, and so on.

Saudis won't do business with someone they don't know, and they can't know you until they find out a bit about you—so sit back and schmooze. If you try to rush them through an agenda, you won't get very far and you may well irritate them enough that talks break down completely.

You must have a Saudi contact-sponsor, who will sound out the opinions of decision makers before you meet with them. Choose your contact wisely, as you can't change sponsors. Don't be surprised (or offended) if other businesspeople sit in on your meeting and take care of their business.

Greetings

There are several styles of greeting you may encounter, so it's best to wait to see how your colleague is going to greet you. Westernized Saudis (men, anyway) will shake hands with other men, so go ahead and shake hands with everyone (of the same sex) you meet.

Some Saudi men will shake hands with Western women because they understand this is not a cultural problem in the West. However, you won't find a Saudi woman in business, so odds are you won't have to worry about shaking hands with one. If you happen to notice a veiled woman with a Saudi man, she won't be introduced, so you don't need to worry about how to greet her.

More traditionally, a greeting between two men may be followed by a kiss on both cheeks; then your hand may be held for a while by the person you're meeting (don't pull it back until it's released).

If an acquaintance takes your hand as you walk, don't pull away—he's just being friendly.

Titles

If you've ever tried to manage to work your way through an Arabic name, you know how confusing it can be. To make things easy, just ask your colleague to give you names of everybody in English. Find out what their full names are if you think you'll need to be contacting them by letter.

Use titles with last names. King Fahd bin Abdul-Aziz al Saud's title is King—his given name is Fahd. "Bin Abdul-Aziz" has a patronymic meaning of "son of Abdul-Aziz," and "Al-Saud" is the name of the royal family, meaning "House of Saud." Occasionally, you may find an extra "bin" in the name—this happens if the person's grandfather was famous; the grandfather's name might be added in there, too.

The title *"Sheikh"* (pronounce it "shake," not "sheek") does not necessarily indicate membership in the Saudi royal family; it's simply a title used by an important leader who knows a lot of the Koran.

Take My Card—Please!

Everyone uses business cards in Saudi Arabia—you'll be expected to exchange cards with everyone you meet at a business get-together. Business cards should be printed in English on one side, and in Arabic on the other.

Move In Close

Expect to talk to Saudi Arabians at a much closer proximity than you're used to doing comfortably. Expect to be touched (by a Saudi of the same sex, anyway) quite a bit during a conversation. Don't back up, shift nervously, or drop your eyes. If you're walking down the street and a Saudi reaches for your hand, don't pull away or run shrieking into the night. Men often walk hand-in-hand in Egypt. It's a sign of friendship.

It's always permissible to smile, make eye contact, and reach out and touch someone—as long as you're in a same-sex group. While the Saudis like to be physical, that doesn't extend to the opposite sex. In fact, you should never display sexual affection (and that means something as innocent as kissing, holding hands, or hugging) in public—even with your spouse. In general, Western men should not speak to a Saudi woman to whom they have not been introduced (unless it's an unavoidable business situation).

The Hands Have It

As in many parts of the world, the left hand is considered to be unclean, so you should use the right hand for everything (especially eating and making gestures). You can, however, use both hands at the same time if one isn't strong enough.

Do not:

➤ Point at another person (it's rude).

➤ Show the bottom of your foot to an Arab (feet are unclean).

➤ Cross your legs (shows the sole of your foot).

➤ Make the "thumbs up" gesture (rude).

Gender Gap

The Saudi Embassy in Washington, D.C. advises women traveling to Saudi Arabia to dress conservatively—wear ankle-length dresses with long sleeves and don't wear trousers in public.

In many areas of Saudi Arabia, particularly Riyadh and the central part of the Kingdom, women are pressured to wear a full-length black covering known as an "abaya" (ah-bye-ah) and to cover their heads. Most women in these areas, therefore, wear the abaya and carry a headscarf to avoid harassment. Women who appear to be of Arab or Asian origin, especially those presumed to be Muslims, face a greater risk of harassment.

Adult men and women may not mingle in public, unless they are family or close relatives; you may have to produce proof that you're married or related. Women who are arrested for socializing with a man who is not a relative may be charged with prostitution.

No matter how much you're craving that Big Mac, if you don't have a close male relative with you, you might not be served at some restaurants (particularly fast food outlets). In addition, many restaurants no longer have a "family section" in which women are permitted to eat. These restrictions are not always posted, and in some cases women violating this policy have been arrested.

Say What?

Mutawwa'iin are religious police who travel with uniformed police in Saudi Arabia to make sure conservative standards of conduct are observed.

Women are not allowed to drive vehicles nor ride bicycles on public roads. In public, dancing, music, and movies are forbidden. Pornography, which is very broadly defined by Saudi authorities, is strictly forbidden. Homosexual activity is considered to be a criminal offense and those convicted may be sentenced to lashing and/or a prison sentence, or death.

Religious Police

The norms for public behavior in Saudi Arabia are extremely conservative, and religious police are charged with enforcing these standards. Mutawwa'iin (religious police), accompanied by uniformed police, have police powers to ensure that conservative standards of conduct are observed. In the course of their duty, the Saudi religious police have harassed, accosted, or arrested U.S. citizens for improper dress or other infractions (such as drinking alcohol). They've hassled women who are associating with a non-relative male.

While most incidents have resulted only in inconvenience or embarrassment, the potential exists for physical harm or deportation. U.S. citizens who are involved in an incident with the Mutawwa'iin should report the incident to the U.S. Embassy in Riyadh or the U.S. Consulates General in Jeddah or Dhahran.

Global Guide

The strict dress code for women is not implemented inside Western residential and beach compounds.

Dress for Success

While foreign women are not required to wear the traditional full-length abaya (black cloak) over their clothing, dress very modestly if you're a woman (keep elbows and knees covered in loose-fitting clothing). Women should wear a knee-length tunic/dress over slacks and a scarf on their heads. Women should also avoid extreme makeup in the presence of Saudi men. Saudis say that the idea behind all these recommendations is not to sexually attract men's attention.

In some towns, even modestly dressed Western women will be treated with disrespect, or can be chastised by the religious police for immodest behavior. Follow these tips:

➤ Men should not wear shorts or open shirts in public.

➤ Don't wear shoes when walking on carpets.

➤ Wear a coat and tie when first meeting a Saudi business associate.

➤ Try wearing a head wrap for the desert—it provides better protection against sun and sand than a hat and it can't be blown off your head by the wind.

➤ Men may wear either a Saudi dress or their normal western dress.

➤ It worked for Sampson, but long hair for men is not recommended.

Saudi Arabian dress is strongly symbolic, representing the people's ties to the land, to the past, and to Islam. The predominantly loose, flowing garments reflect the practicalities of life in a desert country as well as Islam's emphasis on keeping what you've got covered up.

Tip of the Hat

If you remove your shoes, place them with soles together to avoid pointing the sole at anyone.

Traditionally, men usually wear an ankle-length shirt woven from wool or cotton (known as a *thawb*), with a *ghutra* (a large square of cotton held in place by a cord coil) worn on the head. For those rare days when it gets a bit chilly, Saudi men chuck a camel-hair cloak (*bisht*) over the top.

Women's clothes are decorated with tribal motifs, coins, sequins, metallic thread, and appliques. Unfortunately, only their family gets to see them in all their glory, as Saudi women must wear a black cloak and veil (*abaya*) when they leave the house, to protect their modesty.

Watch Your Language

Be sensitive about what you say regarding politics, economics, and law—they are based on principles written in the Koran, and criticizing the book is akin to criticizing the word of God. Be careful not to insult the personal or family honor of people you meet.

Gifts Are Good

It is acceptable to give a gift in Saudi (as long as you give and receive gifts with the right hand, and never the left). Since it's important for Muslims to always know where Mecca is (since that is the direction a Muslim must face during prayer), a beautiful compass makes a nice gift.

A small gift either promoting the company or representing your country will generally be well received. Take along a gift from your home country; it will always be appreciated by a Saudi. Under no circumstances give alcohol or any representation of women (photos, sculpture, etc.)—these are prohibited by Islamic law.

Compliment in a general sense ("You have a beautiful house") but avoid specifics ("What a nice suit!") or your host may feel obliged to give you what you admire. And you can't refuse a gift—it's offensive. Accept (and give) gifts with your right hand only.

On the Town

A man visiting a Saudi should not expect to meet his wife or adult daughter or sister. When he happens to meet a Saudi female, he should not look into her face or shake hands with her.

Don't assume wives are included in an invitation to a Saudi's home (if they're not specifically mentioned, they're not invited). If they are invited, they'll probably go into the women quarters and eat with the women of the household—separately from the men. A man shouldn't bring the hostess a gift or inquire about a host's wife if she's not present during the meal. If she's introduced, don't shake her hand unless she presents it.

If you do go visit in a Saudi home, you aren't expected to bring a "hostess gift" when you visit a Saudi home, however. Eat as much as you can if you're invited to a Saudi's house for a meal—it shows appreciation. Try to take a second helping. After that, it's okay to decline more (but be gracious).

If you're intent on having a major banquet, get a permit if you decide to have a dinner party for more than 15 people while in the country.

Addas to Nuts

Saudis love dining out. You'll find all kind of restaurants: American, Chinese, Egyptian, French, Filipino, Indian, Indonesian, Iranian, Italian, Japanese, Lebanese, Mexican, Mongolian, Moroccan, Turkish, Saudi, Thai, and Yemeni. You'll also find plenty of international fast food restaurants such as McDonalds, Burger King, Taco Bell, Kentucky Fried Chicken, Pizza Hut, and Wimpy—as well as local Saudi chains (Harvey, Lebanon Juices, and Fakeeh Al-Tazej).

Business entertaining is usually conducted in hotels or restaurants, and although the custom of eating with the right hand persists, it's more likely that knives and forks will be used.

Lunch

The main meal of the day is lunch, when everyone eats either meat on skewers or kebabs, served with soup and vegetables. Arabic cakes, cream desserts, and rice pudding are also popular. Don't be surprised by long lunch hours—you'll have plenty of time to eat all this food.

Faux Pas

Customs regarding smoking are the same as in Europe; non-smoking areas are indicated.

Faux Pas

During Ramadan, Muslims are not allowed to eat, smoke, or drink during the day, and it is illegal for a foreign visitor to do so in public.

Dinner Is Served

In larger cities you'll find a wide variety of international cuisine (including fast food). Local dishes are often strongly flavored and spicy. At every meal, you'll find pita bread—and you'll likely find at least some of the following: rice, lentils, chick peas (hummus), and cracked wheat (bulgur). The most common meats are lamb and chicken; beef is uncommon, and pork is forbidden under Islamic law.

Say What?

Mezzeh (mez-ah) is the Arab equivalent of hors d'oeuvres. Messeh may include up to 40 dishes.

Arabic unleavened bread (*khobz*) (koobs) is eaten with almost everything; other staples include grilled chicken, *felafel* (fel-ah-fell) (deep-fried chickpea balls), *shwarma* (shwarm-ah) (spit-cooked sliced lamb), and *fuul* (fool) (a paste of fava beans, garlic, and lemon). Traditional coffee houses (where everyone drinks tea) used to be everywhere, but they're being displaced by cafes.

Alcohol and pork are prohibited, and eating is done with the right hand only.

Raise a Glass

Don't expect to find alcoholic beverages anywhere in the country; they're illegal, although this doesn't mean they don't exist. However, there are no bars, and there are severe penalties for infringement. It's important to note that this "no drinking" rule applies to everybody, no matter what religion you are. Arabic coffee and fruit drinks are popular alternatives, and alcohol-free beers and cocktails are served in hotel bars.

Tipping

The practice of tipping is becoming much more common; waiters, hotel porters, and taxi drivers should be given 10 percent. While tips are not generally expected in Saudi restaurants because service charges are included, this money does not go to the (poorly paid) waiters—so you might want to consider adding a few riyal to your bill. Otherwise, tipping is not necessary, as service is included in the bill.

The Least You Need to Know

➤ The Saudi form of Islam is conservative and fundamentalist.

➤ While outwardly modern, Saudi Arabia maintains an ancient conservative outlook.

➤ The pace of business is much slower here, and a Saudi will want to know you before getting down to business.

➤ Failure to bargain with merchants is an insult.

➤ Saudis like to establish a relationship before going into business.

➤ Dress—especially for women—must be conservative.

Chapter 28

Egypt

In This Chapter

➤ Learn the basics of Islam, the primary religion of Egypt

➤ Discover the proper way to interact with Egyptians of the same and opposite sex

➤ Find out the details on cultural taboos

➤ Understand the rules of business dress

➤ Learn the place of women in Egypt

There is great disparity between rich and poor in Egypt, with little likelihood of upward social mobility. Egypt has the largest Arab population in the world; it therefore considers itself to be the leading Arab nation.

Slightly more than three times the size of New Mexico, Egypt sits at the top of northern Africa, bordering the Mediterranean Sea between Libya and the Gaza Strip. A land of stark beauty and ancient history, Egypt can be a minefield of cultural taboos to the unsuspecting.

Basically a vast desert plateau interrupted by the Nile valley, its climate is (not surprisingly) hot—dry in the summer and moderate in winter. It's a violent land, with periodic droughts, frequent earthquakes, flash floods, landslides, dust and sandstorms, and occasional volcanic activity.

Who's In Charge?

The president is chief of state, and the prime minister is head of government. At the end of the 1980s, Egypt faced problems of low productivity and poor economic management compounded by rising population, inflation, and massive urban overcrowding.

In the face of these pressures, Egypt tried to stabilize its economy in 1991 by enacting reform measures, which were fairly successful. As Egypt moves toward a more decentralized, market-oriented economy, the economic reforms and new investment opportunities have prompted increasing foreign investment.

While in Islam, all believers are equal; in actuality, however, Egypt is dominated by a very small, elite upper class.

Speaking the Lingo

Arabic is the official language in Egypt, with 11 different dialects. Cairene Arabic is the spoken dialect most folks understand in Egypt and throughout the Arabic world.

Saudi, or Upper Egyptian Arabic, is the second most common dialect in Egypt. Spoken Egyptian Arabic is differentiated from Arabic spoken in other parts of the world by some consonant sounds and local slang phrases.

Classical (also called Modern Standard) Arabic is the language of the *Qur'an* (the Koran, which is the Islamic book of holy writings), and also of most textbooks for learning written Arabic.

Coptic is a "dead" language still used in the liturgy of the Coptic Christian Church and English and French are widely understood by educated Egyptians.

Islam Is King

The official religion of Egypt is Islam (99 percent) and most of the rest are Coptic Christians. While the Coptics got to Egypt first, they aren't well represented in business or the Egyptian government, and feel that most Muslims discriminate against them.

The Islamic religion is of enormous importance in Egypt—it's a total way of life affecting not just family, but the entire social structure of the country. The idea of separation of church and state is foreign to Egyptians, for whom their religion permeates every corner of their existence.

Egyptians are almost entirely Eastern Hamitic stock (Egyptians, Bedouins, and Berbers) with about 1 percent Greek, Nubian, Armenian, and other European (primarily Italian and French).

Life Is a Holiday

If you're heading to Egypt on business, schedule your trip so that it doesn't coincide with *Ramadan* (the exact dates vary from year to year). During this religious holiday, offices and tourist sites close early.

The Islamic calendar consists of 28-day lunar months, so an Islamic year is 354 days long; this means that holidays will be on different days every year. Muslim holidays depend on actual lunar observations.

Tip of the Hat

If you're doing business in Egypt, use two dates on all paperwork: the Western (Gregorian) calendar date, and the Arabic (*Hijrah*) date. Coptic Christians have a third calendar, but you don't need to include that date on your papers.

Ramadan

As in all Muslim countries, the month of Ramadan (the month of the Prophet's first revelations) is a very important holiday. During the month Muslims fast between dawn and dusk. (If you're a non-Muslim, you don't have to fast, but try to avoid eating in public.)

At the end of Ramadan comes *eid el-Fitr* (the End of Fasting)—when the fasting is over.

Islamic Calendar

The Islamic calendar began in A.H. 1 (in the "year of the Hejira"), which marked the year that the Prophet Mohammed moved from Mecca to Medina to evade religious persecution. A.D. 622 of the Gregorian calendar is A.H. 1 in Egypt.

It pays to know when national holidays will occur:

> **Jan. 1:** New Year's Day.
>
> **Varies:** Ramadan Bairam.
>
> **April 25:** Liberation of the Sinai Day.
>
> **May 1:** Labor Day.
>
> **Varies:** Islamic New Year.
>
> **July 23:** National Day.
>
> **Oct. 6:** Armed Forces Day (anniversary of the 1973 war).

Slow Down

Life in Egypt drifts along at a slower pace than in the West. While most Egyptians will be late, you should be on time. In fact, it's standard Arab practice to keep you waiting, so it's a good idea not to expect to have too many appointments in one day.

Friday is the holy day in Egypt, so no business goes on during Fridays. Typically, the work week runs from Saturday through Wednesday; most people take off Thursday and Friday. However, most retail stores close on Sunday, not Friday. Shops usually close from 4 to 7 P.M. during the *iftar* (when Muslims break the fast). During the Islamic holiday of Ramadan, hours for offices and business are often shortened.

In general, however, you'll find offices of multinational companies are open Sunday through Thursday from 9 A.M. to 5 P.M. Many Egyptian private businesses are open Saturday to Thursday from 8:30 A.M. or 9 A.M. to 4 P.M. Most shops and boutiques are open 10 A.M. to 9 P.M. in winter, and to 10 P.M. in summer (although large stores close for a long afternoon break throughout the year). The government hours are from 8 A.M. to 2 P.M., closing on either Thursday and Friday, or Friday and Saturday.

Egypt is seven hours ahead of Eastern Standard Time, so when it's noon in New York City, it will be 7 P.M. in Egypt.

Meet and Greet

The rules for greeting others in Egypt varies, depending on how Westernized the Egyptian is. You can expect that westernized Egyptians will shake hands with other men, and a few will shake hands with Western women.

A more traditional Egyptian will greet another man by grasping the other's right hand, putting the left hand on the other's right shoulder, and exchanging kisses on each cheek. Kisses may be exchanged between two men, or two women, but never between a man and a woman in public.

A traditional Arab may not introduce you to his wife; if he acts as if she's not standing there right by his side, you should likewise ignore her, no matter how hard it may seem.

A Rose by Any Other Name

The most common name you'll probably hear in Egypt is Mohamed (as a first name)—and first names are usually used with titles, whether that is Mr., Mrs., Madame, or Dr. (Jane Smith would be Dr. Jane or Mrs. Jane, not Dr. Smith or Mrs. Smith).

Don't be surprised if the person you thought of under one name is introduced to you the next time as someone else. Egyptians have many different names. For example, Mahmoud *Abu*-Atef means "Mahmoud, son of Atef."

Faux Pas

Don't reach out and grab an Egyptian man's hand to shake when you first meet. Western business women should wait to see if an Egyptian man offers his hand before making a move to shake hands.

Global Guide

Women don't change their names when they get married, so don't be surprised if someone is introduced to you as "Mrs. Fatima, Dr. Ahmed's wife."

Take a Card

Everyone uses business cards in Egypt—you'll be expected to exchange cards with everyone you meet at a business get—together. Business cards should be printed in English on one side, and Arabic on the other. It's quite common in Egypt to include the home number on a business card, so if you're having extras printed up, go ahead and have all your numbers included.

Body Talk

It's always okay to smile, make eye contact, and reach out and touch someone of the same sex. In general, Western men should not speak to an Egyptian woman to whom they have not been introduced unless it's unavoidable in business.

Up Close and Personal

Egyptians communicate from a much closer distance than you're used to doing comfortably. Expect to be touched (by an Egyptian of the same sex, anyway) during a conversation, so don't back up, shift nervously, or lower your eyes.

If you're walking down the street and an Egyptian drapes an arm around you, don't pull away. Men often walk hand-in-hand in Egypt. It means you're friends, nothing more.

The Eyes Have It

When you're in Egypt, an intense, penetrating stare is not a challenge but an indication of openness and honesty. On the street, however, this type of eye contact by a Western woman can pave the way for unwanted attention from Egyptian men.

Watch That Hand

As in many parts of the world, the left hand is considered to be unclean, so you should use the right hand for everything (especially eating and making gestures). You can, however, use both hands at the same time if one isn't strong enough.

It's considered rude to:

➤ Point at another person.

➤ Show the bottom of your foot to an Arab (feet are unclean).

➤ Cross your legs (reveals your sole).

➤ Make a "thumbs up" gesture.

Women vs. Men

About 10 percent of the Egyptian workers are women, many of them in both professional and service jobs. You'll find plenty of women secretaries and doctors, but not so many woman executives.

Dress Conservatively

You don't need to wear traditional Egyptian clothes when in Egypt (indeed, it may offend Egyptians to see you in native dress) but you must dress conservatively. No matter how hot it gets, you need to cover your entire body. Men should wear trousers and a long sleeved shirt buttoned to the collarbone, with a jacket and tie for business meetings. Men should not wear jewelry (especially necklaces).

Women should wear high necklines and long sleeves (at least covering the elbow), with hems between the ankle and the knee. Don't wear pants, pantsuits, or tight clothing. While your head doesn't have to be covered, it's a good idea to keep a scarf in your purse just in case.

While technically people should take off shoes when entering a private home, many Egyptians don't follow this rule, so watch your hosts and do what they do. However, shoes are removed when entering a mosque.

Tip of the Hat

When in doubt about what to wear, ask your host indirectly if it's appropriate. Ask, "What are you wearing?"

Talk Is Cheap

There are some things you can talk about in Egypt, and some things you can't, and the dividing line is pretty clear. Good topics of conversation include Egyptian achievements and sports. Favorite sports include soccer (you call it football), tennis, boxing, basketball, horse racing, and water sports.

It's considered rude or controversial to discuss:

➤ Israel.

➤ Women (not even your host's family, unless he brings up the topic first).

➤ U.S. cultural and economic influence.

➤ Islamic fundamentalists.

➤ France and Britain.

Humor

You'll be delighted at the Egyptian's wonderful sense of humor—they can be very self-deprecating. But no matter how much fun they seem to be having at poking at themselves, don't ever join in: Never tease or make fun of Egypt or the Egyptians.

Saving Face

Saving face is just as important in Egypt as it is in Japan. Protecting everyone's dignity is of enormous importance, and you may end up having to compromise just to protect someone else's pride.

Getting Down to Business

When you sit down to a business meeting in Egypt, prepare for a long-term go-around. Time moves slower here, and the meeting will most likely start off with discussions about your health, the trip, and so on. Egyptians won't do business with someone they don't know, and they can't know you until they find out a bit about you. So sit back and schmooze. If you try to rush them through an agenda, you won't get very far and you may well irritate them enough that talks break down completely.

You know the meeting is drawing to a close when the coffee urn comes trundling down the hall. That sweet smell you notice drifting under the door means that incense is being lit—another sign that the meeting is almost over.

The Giving Game

It is acceptable to give a gift in Egypt (as long as you give and receive gifts with the right hand, never the left). Because it's important for Muslims to always know where Mecca is (that is the direction a Muslim must face during prayer), a beautiful compass makes a nice gift.

Let Me Entertain You

If you're looking to go nightclubbing, check out the five-star hotels—that's where you'll find them. Dancing goes on in discos, but if you're looking to find a date, don't expect to find one here—many discos impose a rule allowing "couples only."

If you're invited home to meet the family, be prepared for a great celebration: The Egyptians love to entertain.

Be careful during the meal not to add any salt to the food. It's considered to be an insult. If you're served something you can't stand, don't refuse the

Global Guide

If you visit an Egyptian home, you should bring a hostess gift (chocolate or pastry is a good choice)—flowers may be acceptable, although they were once used only for funerals or weddings.

offering. Take some, and shuffle it around on your plate. Afterwards, be sure to leave a bit of food on the plate; it means you've eaten your fill.

Lentil Soup to Nuts

Egyptian food tends to be a mixture of Mediterranean cuisine, with some modifications to suit local palates. In most restaurants, major credit cards (Visa, MasterCard, and American Express) are accepted, but its best to call first to make sure. Reservations are not necessary unless otherwise noted.

Breakfast

You can expect to find some version of beans, bean cakes, eggs, pickles, omelets, onions, or cheese and bread on your breakfast table.

Lunch

Lunch is the main meal of the day, and comes somewhere between 2 p.m. and 5 p.m. The best Egyptian food is served in private homes, but there are many small restaurants offering local dishes. *Ful* (cooked, mashed fava beans) is a favorite, served with a pita-type bread called *aish baladee*.

Tamiyaa (you probably recognize it as "falafel") is popular as well, but if you're squeamish when it comes to trying new things—you'll find pizza Hut, Kentucky Fried Chicken, and McDonalds outlets located at strategic points throughout the city.

Dinner Time

The male guest of honor is usually seated to the right of the host, not at the opposite end of the table. Once you're seated, you may be surprised to find there aren't any eating utensils at your place.

Dinner is usually some variant of leftover lunch, featuring starch (usually rice and bread) with vegetables cooked with meat, chicken, or fish. Because most Egyptians are Muslim, it's a good idea to remember the dietary restrictions that are part of the Islamic faith: Alcohol and pork are forbidden.

Nix to Alcohol

Because Muslims are not permitted to drink alcohol, you may find it hard to locate hard liquor in Egypt. In fact, you will probably find it only at international hotels; most Egyptian restaurants serve only wine and beer.

Tipping

Wages in Egypt are very low, so tips are a vital part of the income of Egyptian workers (especially those who

Global Guide

In general, keep small denominations of cash available to tip people who may do you a service, such as a porter or doorman. A little goes a long way here, along with a smile and a "thank you."

do menial labor). This includes guards at ancient sites and monument watchers and keepers at mosques.

You may hear requests for *baksheesh* from people who have performed no service. "Baksheesh" does not mean tip—it means "a gift for the poor (alms)." These folks aren't asking for a tip; they're begging. It can be quite difficult to turn down a request for money, especially if the beggar is a ragged child. Look to your own conscience when it comes to doling out money in this way, but remember that if you do give some money to a begging child, be prepared to be surrounded by a crowd of Egyptians with their hands out if you do.

The Least You Need to Know

➤ Dress formally and conservatively in Egypt; women should not show too much skin or wear tight clothing.

➤ Touching between same-sex groups is fine; never touch a person of the opposite sex.

➤ Business meetings start slow and revolve around personal chitchat in the beginning as a way of getting to know you on a personal basis.

➤ Islam is the primary religion of most Egyptians, which governs their entire personal and work life.

➤ Because Muslims can't drink alcohol, it's difficult to find liquor to drink.

➤ Saving face is just as important in Egypt as Japan.

➤ You must dress conservatively in Egypt.

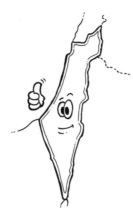

Chapter 29

Israel and the Palestinian Territories

In This Chapter

➤ Learn about the importance of the three major religions in Israel

➤ Discover the fine points of cultural etiquette for women

➤ Find out the differences in business between the U.S. and Israel

➤ Learn about the attitude toward punctuality

➤ Discover the rules of physical proximity

Israel is the "promised land" to Jews, the birthplace of Christ to Christians, and the place where Muhammad entered Paradise, so it's not surprising that this tiny country has profound emotional and spiritual effect on everybody. Some visitors are moved by the magnificent religious shrines, while others are impressed by the tenacity of a people who have made the desert bloom in the face of constant adversity. Israel is a land not so much of conflict as it is of cultures in search of dignity and a place to call home. Yet while Jews, Muslims, and Christians all hold Jerusalem sacred, at times it seems all three would rather see the city destroyed than share it with the others.

The city is divided into the mostly-Arab East Jerusalem, the rapidly expanding "new city" known as West Jerusalem, and the walled Old City, where most of the sights are found (and which is also divided into Armenian, Christian, Jewish, and Muslim quarters).

Smaller than New Jersey, Israel is bordered by the Mediterranean Sea to the west, Lebanon and Syria to the north, Jordan to the east, and Egypt to the south. The dominant geographic feature is the Rift Valley, which runs from Turkey through Israel;

this valley contains the Dead Sea, as well as the Jordan River and Lake Galilee. Israel doesn't get much rain (the Jordan is its only main river), and the only arable land is in the north.

The Dead Sea is Israel's main body of water—below sea level and as salty as a potato chip (in fact, it's the lowest place on earth). It's flanked by the Judean Desert, which turns into the Negev Desert further south.

Northern Israel is mountainous, with laurel forests and tumbling streams. A fifth of the country is covered with national parks (about 300 of them)——in fact, the Israelis are renowned for having made the desert bloom, as well as having reintroduced a number of species that had become locally extinct since Biblical times.

Tip of the Hat

For information on national parks and environmental issues, contact the Society for the Protection of Nature in Israel.

Country Basics

The state of Israel has a parliamentary democracy with a modern economy, and has occupied the West Bank, Gaza Strip, Golan Heights, and East Jerusalem since the 1967 war. As a result of negotiations between Israel and the Palestinians, an elected Palestinian authority now exercises jurisdiction in most of Gaza and most of the major cities of the West Bank. Palestinian Authority police are charged with keeping order in those areas.

Remember that areas of Israeli and Palestinian responsibilities and jurisdiction in the West Bank and Gaza are complex, and details on entry, customs requirements, and other matters in the West Bank and Gaza may change with a moment's notice.

Hebrew and Arabic

Hebrew and Arabic are the official languages of Israel, and English is the most common foreign language. In the past, Hebrew was not spoken by any Jewish population on a day-to-day basis; it was mostly used for religious reasons, much the way that Latin was used in the Roman Catholic church. With the founding of the state of Israel, however, Hebrew became a unifying force among the people and is now spoken throughout Israel. Other languages you may hear in Israel include French, Yiddish, and Russian.

Remember that while English is read from left to right and front to back, Hebrew is read from right to left and back to front. This means that what we consider to be the front of a publication is interpreted as the back to someone familiar with Hebrew. When producing written materials to take to Israel, remember that it's likely your audience is going to read the back of the material first. Design it appropriately.

Religion

Surprisingly, although the state of Israel was established to provide a homeland for Jews, there is no "official" state religion. Still, about 82 percent of the population are Jews; 14 percent are Muslim (mostly Sunni Muslim), and 2 percent are Christian; another 2 percent are various other smaller subgroups.

Most Palestinians are Sunni Muslims, but there are also Christian Palestinians and a small polulation of many different ethnic and religious groups. In Palestinian parts of the country, Muslim culture is more evident: You'll see fewer women out and about, and those you do see will be pretty much muffled in clothing.

About 1.6 percent of Israelis are Druze, a group of Arabs who keep their religious beliefs a secret (although it's known they worship Jethro, the father-in-law of Moses).

Until recently, Israel's culture has been predominantly religious, although that religion could be Jewish, Christian, or Muslim. You still get that rural summer-camp kibbutz sense, but Israel is rapidly transforming itself into a cosmopolitan consumer society. In fact, most Jewish Israelis lead pretty much of a secular life, although they still take part in occasional religious ceremonies. You'll still find orthodoxy alive and well here, however; in fact, orthodox factions are becoming stronger and louder. You can identify male orthodox (also called "Hasidic") Jews by their dark clothes, long beards, and curly sideburns.

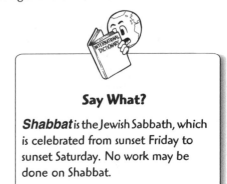

Who is a Jew? That depends, and the criteria seems to change. Israeli law allows any Jew to immigrate to Israel, and legal authorities are always wrestling with the fine points about exactly who qualifies. Sometimes, people who had professed to be Christian but whose parents were both Jewish have been denied citizenship in Israel, while many Soviets who claimed Jewish ancestry were accepted although they knew almost nothing about Judaism.

> **Say What?**
>
> **Shabbat** is the Jewish Sabbath, which is celebrated from sunset Friday to sunset Saturday. No work may be done on Shabbat.

Ashkenazi Jews

The Ashkenazi Jews came from Germany, Poland, and Russia (most Jews in the United States also came from this group). The native language of Ashkenazi Jews is Yiddish, although many also speak the language of their native country.

Sephardic Jews

Columbus set sail in the same year that the Sephardic Jews were thrown out of Spain and Portugal, moving throughout the Mediterranean (especially into the Middle East). Before the Zionist movement brought Jews from around the world to Israel, most Jews in Israel were Sephardic. As Israel fought to establish a homeland, most Sepharidc Jews (especially from Cairo and Baghdad) emigrated to Israel.

For many years, there were about the same number of Sephardim and Askhenazim Jews in Israel, but with the disintegration of the former U.S.S.R., the influx of Ashkenazi Jews tipped the scale in their favor, making them the dominant group. This has not always pleased the Sephardim.

Other Subgroups

Ethiopian and Yemeni Jews make up two smaller groups in Israel, and there has been some tension over their assimilation into the country and charges of racism brought against the government.

A Separate Calendar

You may know your calendar by heart, but Israel doesn't mark its days by the Gregorian calendar of the west. Instead, both Judaism and Islam use lunar calendars of 28 days, which means that a year only has 354 days and that holidays occur on different days according to the Gregorian calendar. Don't worry about coping with a lunar calendar, however; when it comes to "official business" with foreigners, most Israelis follow the Gregorian calendar.

It's probably no surprise that most of Israel's holidays and festivals are religious. It's important to know when to expect these holidays (especially Jewish holidays), because the country grinds to a halt during those times. It's usually a good idea to avoid major Jewish holidays, as the country fills up with pilgrims, everyone hikes prices, and it's almost impossible to travel between cities.

Faux Pas

When negotiating deadlines with an Israeli, remember that a delivery in a certain number of months may involve a month of 28 days, not 30.

Yom Kippur (the Day of Atonement), the holiest day in the Jewish calendar, falls in October. This holy day is marked with 25 hours of abstinence from just about everything, together with prayer, contemplation, and confession. The Feast of Passover celebrates the Jewish exodus from Egypt. Not all Jewish holidays center on abstinence, however; Purim (the celebration of Jewish resistance to assimilation) is a joyful celebration of survival.

As with all people who follow Islam, the month of Ramadan is a very important holiday to Muslims. Ramadan is the month of the Prophet's first revelations, and during this month, Muslims fast between dawn and dusk. (If you're a non-Muslim, you don't have to fast, but it's thoughtful if you avoid eating in public out on the streets.) At the end of Ramadan comes *eid el-Fitr* (the End of Fast-Breaking), when the fasting is over. Everyone prays together, visits friends, gives presents, and chows down—big time.

The following are holidays you need to know in this part of the world:

> **Varies:** Ramadan Bairam.
>
> **Varies:** Islamic New Year.
>
> **Spring:** Passover.
>
> **April 1:** Yom Ha'Atzma'ut (Independence Day).
>
> **late spring:** Shavuot (Pentecost).
>
> **Sept. (est.):** Rosh Hashanah (Jewish New Year).
>
> **Sept. (est.):** Yom Kippur (The Day of Atonement).
>
> **Sept.-Oct.:** Sukkot (Feast of Tabernacles).
>
> **Oct. (est.):** Simhat Torah (Celebration of the Law).
>
> **Late Nov.- mid Dec.:** Hanukkah (Festival of Lights).

Any time is a great time in Israel, because whatever time of year it is, some part of the country is pleasant. You can't really define the Israeli climate at any one point in time, however. For example, when you need your snow boots in Jerusalem, you can wear a bikini at the Dead Sea. As small as Israel is (you can drive its length in less than eight hours), the climate varies greatly from north to south. Generally speaking, however, Israel is temperate with two main seasons—winter and summer. Winter lasts from November to March, with quite severe weather (the north is very wet). Summer is hottest in those areas below sea level, although it can still get quite chilly in the desert areas.

One of the best times to go is during March and April, when the wildflowers are in bloom, and during September and October. The Negev Desert forms the southern two thirds of the country, and summer in the Negev can be too hot to enjoy (temperatures above 100° F).

Faux Pas

Don't smoke on the Shabbat (from sundown Friday to sundown Saturday).

Money Talks

You can bring as much foreign and local currency as you've got into Israel, so stuff those suitcases with money—you're going to need it! Israel is not cheap. On the other hand, you get what you pay for.

Expensive hotels and restaurants will be just as happy to take U.S. dollars as Israeli currency, and if you pay this way, you'll save yourself the 17 percent VAT (value added tax). Small shops, however, are not allowed to accept foreign currency—and if you're hobnobbing at the lower end of the economic pecking order, you'll need *shekels*. U.S. dollars are the easiest to exchange (you can do it anywhere), but traveler's checks, as well as hard currency from almost anywhere else in the world, will be widely accepted.

If you don't feel like toting around bushels of cash, don't worry—the credit card is popular in Israel (Israelis are renowned for living on credit), so you can use a credit card at most places. ATMs are ubiquitous, and most of them take international credit cards.

You Be Prompt

Because the population of Israel is so cosmopolitan, the attitude toward punctuality also varies widely. Typically, promptness is not a Middle Eastern custom, although if your colleagues are more Westernized, they may be more prompt. (Most Ashkenazi Jews are also more prompt.) All Israelis will expect you to be prompt, however.

Because the Jewish sabbath begins at sunset on Friday and ends on sunset on Saturday, no business is conducted on Shabbat. Instead, the work week runs from Sunday through Thursday.

Business hours vary from place to place, depending on the religion of the owner. You'll find most Jewish businesses closed on Fridays and Saturdays; Islamic-owned businesses will close all day on Fridays, and Christian businesses close on Sundays. (Palestinians may be either Christian or Moslem.)

Banking hours run from 8:30 A.M. to 2 P.M. Sunday through Thursday in commercial areas, although some are open late (until 7 P.M.); branch banks tend to split their hours, from 8:30 A.M. to 12:30 P.M. Sunday through Thursday, and then from 4 P.M. to 5:30 P.M. on Sundays, Tuesdays, and Thursdays. Many banks close at noon on Friday.

Keep in mind that Israel is seven hours ahead of Eastern Standard Time, which means that when it's noon in New York City, it's 7 P.M. in Israel.

Business of Confrontation

Business meetings begin slowly, with lots of personal chitchat. This is especially true if you're dealing with Arab Israelis, who won't want to do business with you until they know and like you.

Once the meeting gets going, however, things may heat up quickly; most Israelis have very confrontational negotiating styles, which may become very emotional. Don't hesitate to respond in the same way—it's expected. Once you seem to have hashed things out, however, don't expect an immediate decision; the pace of business is much slower in Israel than in the U.S.

Life in Israel is nothing if unpredictable, and living in the midst of ancient enemies has made fatalists of many in this part of the world. Don't expect Israeli's to embrace long-range plans, or to substitute short-term gain for eventual benefit. If you want to be successful in this part of the world, you've got to promise an immediate return on investment.

You'll know the business meeting is drawing to a close when the coffee cups come out. Arabs also may light incense at the end of a meeting—it doesn't mean they are going to start smoking funny cigarettes, it's just the end of the discussion.

Shalom!

Different cultures have different ways of greeting, but Israelis who do business internationally generally shake hands upon introduction. Because of the Orthodox Jewish prohibition against touching women, businesswomen should not offer to shake hands first (wait until you see if your colleague offers his hand). Orthodox Jews typically wear black clothing, and a *yarmulke* or hat.

The traditional Arab greeting between men is to clasp right hands, place left hands on the other's right shoulder, and exchange kisses on each cheek. (However, Arabs used to dealing with foreigners will probably just stick out a hand to shake.)

If your colleague doesn't introduce his wife, who seems to be hovering in the background like some sort of potted plant, don't dart around your colleague to address her. Traditional Arabs and Orthodox Jews typically don't include their wives in introductions.

Titles

Names can be confusing in Israel, as Israeli Jews may have come from just about anywhere else in the world. Typically, their names reflect this heritage. Usually, you can expect the name of a Jew or Arab to follow the U.S. style—first name first, surname last. Address Israeli Jews with both a title and a surname.

It's not easy to translate names from Arabic to other languages, so spelling of Arabic names may differ. This is why you'll see Colonel Muammar Qaddahafi's name also spelled "al-Qaddafi," "al-Qadhafi," "Qathafi," "Gaddafi," and so on. Because Arab last names may be very confusing, it's a good idea to just ask your Arabic colleague to write the name in English. Find out both of their full names for when you need to write them, and ask how they should be addressed in person.

Global Guide

It's correct to say **Shalom** for both "hello" and "goodbye."

Say What?

The Term **al** before the last name in Arabic means "son of" or "from the town of"; the term **abu** means "father of."

Take a Card

Because Orthodox Jews cannot touch any woman and can't accept anything directly handed to them by a woman, a woman should not hand her business card directly to an Orthodox Jew. Instead, place the card on a table within reach of the man.

Speak Up

Speak up with confidence in a straightforward way if you want to earn the respect of your Israeli counterpart. But if you start hearing "Tut, tut" in response to something you've said, don't get your britches in a twist—it's not a sign of disapproval. It just means that your Israeli contact doesn't agree with your conclusions or assumptions.

Feel free to discuss politics with both Arabs and Jews, but don't make jokes about it and don't be intentionally antagonistic—almost all Israelis have been personally touched by tragedy related to the conflict, and emotions are close to the surface.

Good topics of conversation in Israel include sports; avoid talking about how much foreign aid Israel receives, and never swear or use the word "God" to a Muslim.

Body Wars

Throughout the Middle East, the left hand is considered unclean (it's reserved for toiletry functions), so even lefties should not eat, touch, or gesture with the left hand. (If the right isn't strong enough to handle something, only then can your left hand pitch in.)

Feet are something else that Arabs find appalling—specifically, the soles of your feet. Never show the bottom of your foot to an Arab; one sure way to avoid this is to keep both feet on the ground. Don't cross your legs when you sit, and you won't have to worry about this.

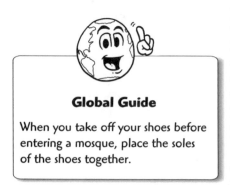

Global Guide

When you take off your shoes before entering a mosque, place the soles of the shoes together.

Expect physical contact in Israel, and don't back away when your fellow conversationalists move in close. Don't be surprised if you're touched often in the conversation (however, business women should not touch others in Israel as they chat). If you're walking down the street with an Israeli, don't be surprised if he reaches for your hand. Don't jerk away—this touch is a sign of acceptance and friendship in the Middle East. It won't be misinterpreted by others.

Shrugging the shoulders in response to something you've said is a sign of exasperation, especially if the Israeli holds his or her hands out with palms up.

Eyes Ahead

Maintain eye contact at all times when talking with an Israeli business contact—it will be interpreted as sincerity. If you start staring at your toes, your colleagues in Israel will think you're rude, disinterested, or that you don't agree with the status quo.

Use Your Hands

Go ahead and talk with your hands in Israel; energetic gestures are commonly used. However, don't point—it's rude (especially among Arabs). But watch out how you interpret gestures: Pointing a forefinger at the open palm of the other hand is a type of gesture meaning "it will never happen."

Our thumbs may be one thing that separates us from lower animals, but thumbs aren't something to flaunt in the Middle East. Any gesture that displays an extended thumb (such as that hitchhiker's thumbs-out attitude), is offensive.

We're All Equal

Israel is one country that prides itself on being an egalitarian culture, in which women are treated equally. The emphasis on equality of the sexes pervades the culture, even in the requirement of compulsory military training for both men and women, although there may be some inequality in some roles.

Unfortunately, this emphasis on equality does not mean that all races are treated without bias. Strong negative bias exists against Palestinians and Arabs, and even against some Jews from certain countries.

Suit to a Tee

Conservative dress is the norm here (despite the heat). Men should wear long trousers and a long-sleeved shirt; a jacket and tie are must-haves for business meetings. Keep your shirt buttoned up, although you may notice that many of your colleagues take off their ties when the meeting ends. (If they do so, you can, too.)

While there really aren't any "clothing laws" in Israel, all women should dress modestly (especially in conservative areas). Women who strut around in a thong bikini may draw wolf whistles in New York, but they'll hear hisses of disapproval from Orthodox Jews and traditional Muslims. Instead, think "Victorian"—wear garments with a high neckline and sleeves at least to the elbow, and keep those hemlines below the knee (ankle length is better). Tight and revealing is not acceptable, which is why pants or pantsuits aren't a good choice. A scarf may not be required, but it can come in handy. Take one along.

On the other hand, fitting in is all well and good but you should not adopt the dress of Israelis you're visiting. This means don't wear a yarmulke if you're not Jewish (unless you're inside a synagogue), or a turban if you're not Arab.

Take along some modest clothing for visiting religious shrines, and remember to take off your shoes when you enter a mosque. You probably won't need a tux unless you're planning on visiting on snapping up some hors d'oeuvres at a foreign embassy party.

To Give or Not To Give ...

Be sure that you don't give any gift to someone that would violate their religious beliefs. If you want to give food, make sure it's kosher if it's going to an Orthodox person. Ask if you're not sure.

If someone gives you a gift, remember to accept it with the right hand (not the left).

If you do visit a private home, it's a nice gesture if you bring a hostess gift of flowers or candy.

Tip of the Hat

Respect all posted rules. At times it seems that every place in Israel is sacred to some group.

Entertaining Style

When in Israel, do like the Israelis—strive to be fashionably late for a visit in an Israeli home. This doesn't mean you can stroll in three hours after the appointed hour, however; if you're going to be seriously detained (by more than half an hour), call and make polite excuses.

Global Guide

Leave a bit of food on your plate so that your hosts will understand you've eaten your fill.

Matzo to Nuts

Israeli eating habits are dictated to some extent by religious laws—Jews can't eat dairy and meat products together, nor can they eat certain birds or fish, and neither Muslims nor Jews can eat pork. In addition, observant Jews are not permitted to cook on the Sabbath, so for most of Saturday they will eat *cholent*, a heavy stew cooked on Friday night.

You'll find plenty of different kinds of food in Israel, which is truly a melting pot of immigrants—and all of them brought their own cuisine with them. Yemeni

Jewish food features flame-grilled meats, stuffed vegetables, and an astonishing array of offal; Eastern European Jewish food includes schnitzel, goulash, gefilte fish, and blintzes; Arab dishes include *felafel* (ground chickpeas flavored with spices and deep fried), *tahini* (sesame paste), *hummus* (chickpea and garlic paste), and flatbreads.

Food Taboos

Pork is prohibited to observing Jews, and strict Muslims don't drink alcohol or eat pork. Always eat with your right hand because the left is considered unclean.

Here's to You

Don't get rowdy or drunk in public while you are visiting Israel. Most Israelis won't be impressed by such boorish behavior. Indeed, religious laws forbid alcohol for Muslims and orthodox Jews, so coffee or tea (drunk Arab-style with mint, and so sweet it makes your teeth hurt) are the beverages of choice. Palestinians also make juices from tamarind, dates, and almonds.

Tipping

Tipping has arrived in Israel in a big way, and you'll be expected to dig deep and come up with at least 15 percent whether it's been earned or not. Before you begrudge parting with a few shekels, remember that hospitality workers are paid a pittance in Israel. Although there's a value-added tax on most goods, you should be able to get a refund if you can face up to the torturous bureaucratic red tape you need to cut through to get your money back.

The Least You Need to Know

➤ Israelis may be Jewish, Muslim, or Christian, with different ethnic cultural practices. Be sensitive to them all.

➤ Dress conservatively and modestly (especially if you're a woman).

➤ Expect the pace of business to be slow, but expect Israelis to favor short- over long-term gains.

➤ Shabbat is the Jewish Sabbath celebrated from sunset Friday to sunset Saturday.

➤ You can bring as much foreign currency as you want into Israel.

➤ Throughout the Middle East, the left hand is considered unclean.

Glossary

Al (pronounced *al* as in *Alan*) The term "al" before the last name in Arabic means "son of" or "from the town of."

Abu (pronounced *aboo* as in *A boot*) The term "abu" before the last name in Arabic means "father of."

Autostrades The Italian version of "superhighway" where high speeds are a must.

Baksheesh Arabic term with a meaning that falls somewhere between a tip and a bribe, used to grease the wheels when necessary to get things done.

Blat If you want to get something done in Russia, you've got to use *blat* (influence or connections): You give me some of your caviar and I'll give you some toast points.

Clotted cream A type of thickened unsweetened cream (also known as Devonshire cream) that looks much like whipped cream; this is usually served with scones (with teas) in the U.K.

Dhal (pronounced *doll* as in *doll*) A type of lentil stew made in India.

Dosai A sort of crepe in India.

Fan-dien Literally, "eating place"; this is the Chinese word for "hotel."

Flemings Flemish-speaking Belgians whose language is a dialect of Dutch. The 5.5 million Flemings live primarily in the north and west areas of Belgium.

Hagwon The South Korean for "private language school."

Haji The title for a Muslim male who has completed the pilgrimage to Mecca. A woman who has made the pilgrimage is addressed as *Haijah*.

Heuriger The German word for "wine garden," a place in Germany to find a tasty bargain meal where you can sample new wines and food specialties.

Hong bao A money gift traditionally given in a red envelope to Chinese children and service people during the Chinese New Year. The money is usually given in even number of crisp new bills.

Ghost Month   The period when ghosts from Hell walk the earth in Taiwan, and no one travels, swims, gets married or moves. Instead, everyone visits Taoist temples.

Hygge   The Danish word for "cozy and snug" used to indicate a special Danish get-together at home with friends.

Idli   Crepes steamed in rounds.

Il secondo   The Italian phrase for "the main course."

Jam karet   The Indonesian term meaning "rubber time" that refers to the Indonesia lack of concern about the ticking clock.

Kampai   The Japanese word for toast.

Khamsin   A hot, driving windstorm that arrives in the Egyptian spring.

Les bises   The French word for the "double kiss" used between friends in social situations.

Magyar   The Hungarian word for the language of Hungary—Hungarian.

Mate   An Australian term used by both men and women that's heard more often than you'll hear "sir" or "ma'am." It refers to anyone of your own gender.

Meltemia   The breeze that keeps the Greek summer bearable.

Mezedopolio   A restaurant in Greek that serves locally produced wine or beer and appetizers, open only during the day.

Mezzeh   The Arab equivalent of hors d'oeuvres. Messeh may include up to 40 dishes.

Mudang   An Eastern fortune teller. South Koreans consult fortune tellers for many reasons, including business deals. All it takes for a business deal to fall through is for a *mudang* to give it a negative report.

Mutawwa'iin   Religious police who travel with uniformed police in Saudi Arabia to make sure conservative standards of conduct are observed.

Ouzeri   A Greek restaurant serving appetizers and ouzo, an anise-flavored liqueur.

Ponte   Literally, this is the Portuguese word for "bridge," but it's used to refer to a "long weekend." If a national holiday falls on a Tuesday or Thursday, many businesses will call for a "ponte" and also close on the Monday or Friday in between.

Public schools   In Britain, "public" schools are what Americans would call a "private school" (and vice versa).

Quebecois   The name for French-speaking Canadians who live in the province of Quebec, Canada.

Raita   A vegetable-yogurt type of salad in India.

Selamat   The Indonesia word for "peace" that traditionally follows any greeting.

Sensei A Japanese word that means "teacher" and is used as a title of honor for teachers, elders, artists, politicians, and anybody else in a respected position.

Shabbat The Jewish Sabbath, which is celebrated from sunset Friday to sunset Saturday. No work may be done on Shabbat.

Shinto Literally, "the way of the gods," the belief that minor deities are everywhere in nature.

Tapas A type of Spanish appetizer usually served at bars called *tabernas, bars, mesones,* or *cafes.*

Walloons French–speaking Belgians who live in the south and east areas of Belgium; there are about 3 million Walloons in Belgium.

Further Reading

Axtell, Roger E., *Gestures: The Do's and Taboos of Body Language around the World* (John Wiley & Sons, Inc., 1991).

Cofer, Judith Ortiz, "Don't Misread My Signals," (Glamour, 1992).

Cooper, Robert, *Culture Shock! Thailand* (Graphic Arts Center Publishing Co., 1990).

Craig, JoAnn Meriwether, *Culture Shock: Singapore* (Graphic Arts Center Publishing Co., 1996).

Crocetti, Gina L., *Culture Shock: United Arab Emirates* (Graphic Arts Center Publishing Co., 1996).

Draine, Cathie and Barbara Hall, *Culture Shock: Indonesia* (Graphic Arts Center Publishing Co., 1996).

Dresser, Norine, *Multicultural Manners: New Rules of Etiquette for a Changing Society* (John Wiley & Sons, 1996).

Eu–Wong, Shirley, *Culture Shock: Switzerland* (Graphic Arts Center Publishing Co., 1996).

Evans, David J.J., *Cadogen Guide: Portugal* (Cadogen, 1998).

Kolanad, Gitanjali, *Culture Shock! India* (Graphic Arts Center Publishing Co., 1998).

McGinnis, Christopher J., *The Unofficial Business Traveler's Pocket Guide: 165 Tips Even the Best Travelers May Not Know* (McGraw-Hill, 1998).

Morrison, Terri; and Wayne A. Conaway and Joseph J. Douress, *Dun & Bradstreet's Guide to Doing Business Around the World* (Prentice Hall, 1997).

Morrison, Terri; and Wayne A. Conaway and Joseph J. Douress, *Kiss, Bow or Shake Hands: How to Do Business in 60 Countries* (Adams Media Corp., 1994).

Morrison, Terri and Wayne A. Conaway, *The International Traveler's Guide to Doing Business in Latin America* (Macmillan, 1997).

Nollen, Tim, *Culture Shock! Czech Republic* (Graphic Arts Center Publishing Co., 1997).

Pybus, Victoria and Susan Dunne, *Live and Work in Scandinavia* (Vacation Work, 1995).

Rabe, Monica, *Culture Shock! A Practical Guide to Living and Working Abroad* (Graphic Arts Center Publishing Co., 1997).

Richardson, Paul E., *Russia Survival Guide* (7th ed.)(Russian Information Services, Inc., 1996).

Sinclair, Kevin and Iris Wong Po-Yee, *Culture Shock: China* (Graphic Arts Center Publishing Co., 1995).

Taylor, Sally Adamson, *Culture Shock! France* (Graphic Arts Center Publishing Co., 1997).

Visser, Margaret, *The Rituals of Dinner* (Grove Weidenfeld, 1991).

Wilson, Susan L., *Culture Shock! Egypt* (Graphic Arts Center Publishing Co., 1998).

Embassies

Before traveling to another country, you can find lots of information that you need by contacting that country's embassy in Washington, D.C. Once abroad, assistance for U.S. citizens is as close as the nearest U.S. embassy.

In the international phone numbers listed below, the number in brackets ([]) is the country code.

Argentina

The Embassy of the Argentine Republic
1600 New Hampshire Avenue, NW
Washington, D.C. 20009
Tel: (202) 939-6400
Fax: (202) 332-6400

The Embassy of the United States
4300 Avenida Columbia
1425 Buenos Aires
APO AA 34034
Tel: [54] (1) 777-4533/4534
Fax: [54] (1) 775-4205

Australia

Embassy of Australia
1601 Massachusetts Avenue, NW
Washington, D.C. 20036
Tel: (202) 797-3000
Fax: (202) 797-3168

U.S. Embassy
Moonah Place
Canberra
A.C.T. 2600

Mailing address:
APO AP 96549
Tel: [61] (6) 270-5000
Fax: [61] (6) 270-5970

Austria

Embassy of Austria
Gartenbaupromenade 2
4th Floor
A-1010 Vienna
[43] (1) 313-39 (1:00 p.m.–4:00 p.m.)

Azerbaijan

Azerbaijan Embassy
Prospekt Azadlig 83
370007 Baku
Hotel Intourist
Baku
(9) (9412) 98-03-35/36/37

Belarus

Embassy of Belarus
46 Ulitsa Starovilenskaya
Minsk, Belarus
(7) (0172) 31-50-00

Belgium

Embassy of the Kingdom of Belgium
3330 Garfield Street, NW
Washington, D.C. 20008
(202) 333-6900
(202) 333-3079 (fax)
U.S. Embassy
25 Boulevard du Regent
B-1000
Brussels

Mailing address:
APO AE 09724
[32] (2) 508-2111
[32] (2) 511-2725 (fax)

Bolivia

Embassy of Bolivia
Banco Popular Del Peru Building
Corner of Calles Mercado and Colon
P.O. Box 425
La Paz
(591) (2) 369798

Brazil

The Embassy of the Federative Republic of
Brazil
3006 Massachusetts Avenue, NW
Washington, D.C. 20008
Tel: (202) 745-2700
Fax: (202) 745-2827

U.S. Embassy
Avenida das Nacoes
Lote 3
Brasilia
Mailing address:
APO AA Miami, 34040, Unit 3500
Tel: [55] (61) 321-7272
Fax: [52] (61) 225-9136

Canada

Embassy of Canada
501 Pennsylvania Avenue, NW
Washington, D.C. 20001
Tel: (202) 682-1740
Fax: (202) 682-7726

U.S. Embassy
100 Wellington Street
Ottawa, Ontario K1P 5T1

Mailing address:
P.O. Box 5000
Ogdensburg, NY 13669
Tel: (613) 238-5335
Fax: (613) 233-5720

Chile

Embassy of the Republic of Chile
1732 Massachusetts Avenue, NW
Washington, D.C. 20036
Tel: (202) 785-1746
Fax: (202) 887-5579

U.S. Embassy
Codina Building
1343 Agustinas
Santiago

Mailing address:
APO AA 34033
[56] (2) 232-2600
[56] (2) 330-3710

China

Embassy of the People's Republic of China
2300 Connecticut Avenue, NW
Washington, D.C. 20008
(202) 328-2500 or 2520

U.S. Embassy
Xiu Shui Bei Jie 3
Beijing, PRC or
100600, PSC 461, Box 50
Beijing, China
[86] (1) 532-3831

Colombia

Embassy of the Republic of Colombia
2118 Le Roy Place, NW
Washington D.C. 20008
(202) 387-8338

The Embassy of the United States
Calle 38
No. 8-61
Bogota, Colombia
[57] (1) 320-1300

Costa Rica

Embassy of the Republic of Costa Rica
2114 S Street, NW
Washington D.C. 20008
(202) 234-2945
U.S. Embassy
APO AA 34020
Apdo 920-1200
Pavas, San Jose
[506] 20-39-39

Croatia

U.S. Embassy
Andrije Hebranga 2
10000
Zagreb
[385] (1) 445-5500

Czech Republic

Embassy of the Czech Republic
3900 Spring of Freedom Street, NW
Washington, D.C. 20008
(202) 363-6315

Embassy of the Slovak Republic
2201 Wisconsin Avenue, NW
Suite 380
Washington, D.C. 20007
(202) 965-5160

U.S. Embassy Czech Republic
Trziste 15
118 01 Prague 1

Mailing Address:
Unit 1330
APO AE 09213-5630
[42] (2) 2451-0847

U.S. Embassy Slovak Republic
Hviezdoslavovo Namestie 4
81102 Bratislava
[42] (2) 330-861, 333-338

Denmark

Embassy of the Kingdom of Denmark
3200 Whitehaven Street, NW
Washington D.C. 20008
(202) 234-4300
U.S. Embassy
Dag Hammarskjolds Alle 24
2100 Copenhagen O

or

APO AE 09716
[45] (31) 42-31-44

357

Egypt

Embassy of the Arab Republic of Egypt
3521 International Court, NW
Washington, D.C. 20008
(202) 895-5400

U.S. Embassy
8 Kamal El-Din Salah Street
Garden City, Cairo, Egypt
U.S. Mailing Address:
APO AE 09839
[20] (2) 355-8368

Finland

Embassy of Finland
3301 Massachusetts Ave., NW
Washington, DC 20008
(202) 298-5800

American Embassy
Itainen Puistotie 14B
00140
Helsinki

France

Embassy of France
4101 Reservoir Road, NW
Washington, D.C. 20007
(202) 944-6000
U.S. Embassy
2 Avenue Gabriel
75382 Paris Cedex 08
Paris, France

Mailing Address:
APO AE 09777
[33] (1) 42-96-12-02

Germany

Embassy of the Federal Republic of Germany
4645 Reservoir Road, NW
Washington, D.C. 20007
(202) 298-4000

U.S. Embassy
Deichmanns Avenue
53179 Bonn 2
Bonn, Germany
[49] (228) 3392063

Greece

Embassy of Greece
2221 Massachusetts Ave., NW
Washington, DC 20008
202-939-5800

American Embassy
91 Vassilissis Sophias Ave.
101 60 Athens
(30-1) 721-2951

Hungary

Embassy of the Republic of Hungary
3910 Shoemaker Street, NW
Washington, DC 20008

U.S. Embassy
Szabadsàg tèr 12, H-1054
Budapest
Tel: 267-4400
Fax: 269-9326

Hong Kong

Department of State
Country Desk Official
Office of Chinese and Mongolian Affairs
Rm 4318
Washington, DC 20520
202-647-6802

American Consulate General
Hong Kong
26 Garden Road, Hong Kong
Tel: 852-2523-9011
Fax: 852-2845-1598

Iceland

Embassy of Iceland
1156 15th St. NW
Washington, DC 20005
202-322-3040

American Embassy Reykajavik
Laufasvegur 21, 101 Reykjavik
562-9100

India

Embassy of the Republic of India
2107 Massachusetts Avenue, NW
Washington, D.C. 20008
(202) 939-7000

U.S. Embassy
Shanti Path
Chanakyapuri 110021
New Delhi
[91] (11) 600651

Indonesia

Embassy of Indonesia
2020 Massachusetts Avenue, NW
Washington, D.C. 20036
(202) 775-5200

The Embassy of the United States
Medan Merdeka Selatan 5, Box 1
Jakarta, Indonesia (APO AP 96520)
[62] (21) 360-360

Ireland

Embassy of Ireland
2234 Massachusetts Avenue, NW
Washington, D.C. 20008
(202) 462-3939

U.S. Embassy
42 Elgin Road, Ballsbridge
Dublin, Ireland
[353] (1) 79-37-33

Israel

Embassy of the State of Israel
3514 International Drive NW
Washington D.C. 20008
(202) 364-5500; (202) 364-5590

U.S. Embassy
71 Hayarkon Street
PSC 98, Box 100
Tel Aviv 63903
APO AE 09830
[972] (3) 663449

Italy

The Embassy of the Republic of Italy
1601 Fuller Street, NW
Washington, D.C. 20009
(202) 328-5500

U.S. Embassy
Via Veneto 119/A
Rome, Italy or
Box 100 APO AE 09624
[39] (6) 46741

Japan

Embassy of Japan
2520 Massachusetts Avenue, NW
Washington D.C. 20008
(202) 939-6700

U.S. Embassy
Akasaka 1-chome
Minato-ku (107)
Tokyo

Mailing Address:
Unit 45004, Box 258
APO AP 96337-0001
[81] (3) 3224-5000

Luxembourg

Embassy of Luxembourg
2200 Massachusetts Avenue, NW
Washington, DC 20008
202-265-4171

U.S. Embassy
22 Blvd. Emmanuel-Servais
2535 Luxembourg
40123

Malaysia

Embassy of Malaysia
2401 Massachusetts Avenue, NW
Washington D.C. 20008
(202) 328-2700

U.S. Embassy
376 Jalan Tun Razak
50400 Kuala Lumpur
[60] (3) 248-9011

Mexico

Embassy of Mexico
1911 Pennsylvania Avenue, NW
Washington, D.C. 20006
(202) 728-1600

U.S. Embassy
Paseo de la Reforma 305
Colonia Cuauhtemoc
06500 Mexico D.F.

Mailing address:
P.O. Box 3087
Laredo, TX 78044-3087
[52] (5) 211-0042

The Netherlands

Embassy of the Kingdom of the Netherlands
4200 Linnean Avenue, NW
Washington D.C. 20008
(202) 244-5300

U.S. Embassy
The Hague
Lange Voorhout 102
2514 EJ The Hague, Netherlands
PSC 71, Box 1000
APO AE 09715
[31] (70) 310-9209

New Zealand

Embassy of New Zealand
37 Observatory Circle
Washington, DC 20008
202-667-5227

U.S. Consulate General
General Building
29 Shortland Street
Auckland

Norway

Royal Embassy of Norway
2720 34th St.
Washington, DC 20008

United States Embassy
Drammensveien 18
0244 Oslo
22-44-8550

Peru

Embassy of Peru
1700 Massachusetts Avenue, NW
Washington, D.C. 20036
(202) 833-9860

U.S. Embassy
Corners of Avenidas Inca Gareilaso de
la Vega and Espana
Lima, Peru
[51] (14) 338-000

The Philippines

Embassy of the Republic of the Philippines
1600 Massachusetts Avenue, NW
Washington, D.C. 20036
(202) 467-9300

U.S. Embassy
1201 Roxas Boulevard
Ermita Manila 1000
APO AP 96440
[63] (2) 521-7116

Poland

Embassy of the Republic of Poland
2640 16th Street, NW
Washington, D.C. 20009
(202) 234-3800

U.S. Embassy
AmEmbassy Warsaw
Aleje Ujazdowskie 29/31
Box 5010 Unit 1340
[48] (2) 628-3041

Russia

Embassy of the Russian Federation
250 Wisconsin Avenue, NW
Washington, D.C. 20007
(202) 628-7551

U.S. Embassy
Novinskiy Bulvar
19/23
Moscow

Mailing Address:
APO AE 09721
Moscow
[7] (095) 252-2451

Saudi Arabia

The Embassy of the Kingdom of Saudi
Arabia
601 New Hampshire Avenue, NW
Washington D.C. 20037
(202) 342-3800

U.S. Embassy
Collector Road M
Riyadh Diplomatic Quarter

Saudi Mailing Address:
P.O. Box 94309
Riyadh, 11693
[966] (01) 488-3800

Singapore

Embassy of the Republic of Singapore
3501 International Place, NW
Washington, D.C. 20008
(202) 537-3100

U.S. Embassy
30 Hill Street
Singapore 0617
[65] 338-0251

South Africa

Embassy of the Republic of South Africa
3051 Massachusetts Avenue, NW
Washington D.C. 20008
(202) 232-4400

U.S. Embassy
225 Pretorius Street
Arcadia 0083
P.O. Box 9536
Pretoria, SA
[21] (12) 342-2244

South Korea

Embassy of the Republic of Korea (South)
2450 Massachusetts Avenue, NW
Washington D.C. 20008
(202) 939-5600

U.S. Embassy
82 Sejong-Ro
Chongro-Ku
Seoul

Mailing Address:
AMEMB, Unit 15550
APO AP 96205-0001
[82] (2) 397-4114

Spain

Embassy of the Kingdom of Spain
2375 Pennsylvania Avenue, NW
Washington D.C. 20037
(202) 452-0100

U.S. Embassy
Serrano 75
28006 Madrid
Spain

Mailing address:
APO AE 09642
[34] (1) 577-4000

Sweden

Embassy of the Kingdom of Sweden
1501 M Street, NW
Washington, D.C. 20005
(202) 467-2600

U.S. Embassy
Strandvagen 101
S-115 89 Stockholm
[46] (8) 783-5300

Switzerland

The Embassy of Switzerland
2900 Cathedral Avenue, NW
Washington D.C. 20008
(202) 745-7900

U.S. Embassy
Jubilaeumstrasse 93
3005 Berne Switzerland
[41] (31) 437-011

Thailand

Embassy of the Kingdom of Thailand
1024 Wisconsin Avenue, NW
Suite 103
Washington, D.C. 20007

U.S. Embassy
95 Wireless Road
Bangkok

Mailing Address:
APO AP 96546
[66] (2) 252-5040

Turkey

Embassy of the Republic of Turkey
1714 Massachusetts Avenue, NW
Washington D.C. 20036
(202) 659-8200

U.S. Embassy
110 Ataturk Boulevard
Ankara
PSC 93, Box 5000

Mailing Address:
APO AE 09823

United Kingdom

Embassy of the United Kingdom of Great
Britain and Northern Ireland
3100 Massachusetts Avenue, NW
Washington D.C. 20008
(202) 462-1340

U.S. Embassy
24/31 Grosvenor Square
W.1A 1AE
London, England
[44] (71) 499-9000

Venezuela

Embassy of the Republic of
Venezuela
1099 30th Street, NW
Washington, D.C. 20007
(202) 342-2214
U.S. Embassy

Avenida Francisco de Miranda and
Avenida Principal de la Floresta
P.O. Box 62291, Caracas 1060A
[58] (2) 285-2222

Index

A

accepting compliments, 38-39
accomodations (hotels), 13-14
addressing
    ambassadors, 30
    cabinet officers, 30
    heads of state, 30
    royalty, *see* royalty, addressing
alcohol, *see* dining out
ambassadors, addressing, 30
appointments, making
    Germany, 102
    Latin America, 64-65
    Russia, 201
Ashkenazi Jews (Israel), 339
ATM cards (Saudi Arabia), 318
attire, *see* clothing
attitudes (Taiwan), 217-218
Australia, 289-290
    clothing, 296-297
    dining out, 299-300
        pubs, 300
        tea time, 299-300
    discussion topics, 297-298
    government, 291-293
    greetings, 295-296
    history of, 292-293
    holidays, 293
    languages, 293
    negotiations, 298-299
    punctuality, 294
        business hours, 294
        time zones, 294
    religions, 293
    times to visit, 293
    visiting homes, 299
avoiding crime, *see* crime

B

banking (Scandinavia), 177
banquets (China), 235
baronet and wife, addressing, 28
barons and baronesses,
  addressing, 27-28

Belgium, 75-77
    business cards, 79
    business hours, 78
    clothing, 81
    dining out, 82-83
        toasting, 83
    discussion topics, 81
    gestures, 80
    giving gifts, 81-82
    government, 76-77
    greetings, 79-80
        names, 80
    holidays, 77-78
    languages, 77
    negotiations, 81
    privacy, 79
    punctuality, 78
    religions, 77
    time zones, 78-79
    visiting homes, 82
    women, 80-81
    work weeks, 78
bilingual business cards, 5
body language
    Canada, 49
    Eastern Bloc, 192
    Egypt, 331
    France
        eye contact, 91
        smiling, 91
    Israel, 344-345
    Japan, 264
        bowing, 264-266
    Korea, 282
    Portugal, 125
    Scandinavia, 181-182
    Spain (eye contact), 136
    Switzerland, 147
bowing (Japan), 264-266
Brazil (languages), 64
breakfast, *see* dining out
burping, 33
business cards, *see* greetings
business hours
    Australia and New
      Zealand, 294
    Belgium, 78
    Canada, 47

China, 228
Egypt, 329-330
France, 88
Germany, 102
Greece, 167-168
Indonesia and Malaysia,
  240-241
Israel, 342
Italy, 112-113
Japan, 263-264
Korea, 278
Mexico, 56
Portugal, 124-125
Russia, 201
Saudi Arabia, 320
Scandinavia, 179
Singapore, 251
Spain, 133-135
Switzerland, 144-145
Taiwan, 214-215
United Kingdom, 153-154
business relationships, *see*
  negotiations
business transactions (Saudi
  Arabia), 318

C

cabinet officers, addressing, 30
calendars, *see* holidays
Canada, 43-46
    body language, 49
    clothing, 50
    dining out, 51-52
    French-Canadians, 45-46
    gestures, 49-50
    gift-giving, 50-51
    government, 44-45
    greetings, 48-49
    holidays, 46-47
    languages, 46
    negotiations, 50
    punctuality, 47-48
        business hours, 47
    religion, 46
    size of country, 44
    time zones, 47-48

car rentals (avoiding crime), 16
cash, *see* currency
caste systems (India), 307-308
China, 223
    business relatonships, 230-231
    clothing, 232-233
    dining out, 234-236
    economy, 225
    entertainment, 234
    gender gaps, 232
    geography, 224
    gestures, 232
    giving gifts, 233
    government, 224-225
    greetings, 229-230
    holidays, 228
    Hong Kong, relationship
      with, 225
    languages, 226-227
    personal space, 231
    punctuality, 228-229
        business hours, 228
        time zones, 228-229
    religions, 227-228
    speaking softly, 231-232
    times to visit, 224
    traveling there, 226
    weather, 224
    women, treatment of, 232
chivalry (Latin America), 69
chopsticks (Taiwan), 220
class systems
    Greece, 169
    India, 307-308
    Spain, 133-135
cleaning your plate, 33
clothing, 37
    Australia, 296-297
    Belgium, 81
    Canada, 50
    China, 232-233
    Eastern Bloc, 193-194
    Egypt, 332
    France, 92-93
    Germany, 105
    Greece, 169-170
    India, 309-310
        punjabi suits, 310
        safari suits, 310
        saris, 309-310
    Indonesia, 245-246
    Israel, 345-346
    Italy, 116
    Japan, 267
    Korea, 283-284
    Latin America, 69
    Malaysia, 245-246
    Mexico, 59
    New Zealand, 296-297

Portugal, 126
Russia, 203
Saudi Arabia, 323-324
Scandinavia, 182-183
Singapore, 257
Spain, 137
styles of dress, 9
Switzerland, 148
Taiwan, 218
United Kingdom, 156
Cold War (Russia), 203-204
colors (gift-giving taboos), 34
comfort zones, *see* personal space
communication
    accentuating the negative
      (Japan), 268
    avoiding slang, 4
    body language, *see* body
      language
    business letters (Germany),
      106
    compliments, accepting, 38-39
    discussion topics, *see*
      discussion topics
    gestures, *see* gestures
    greetings, *see* greetings
    languages, *see* languages
    learning languages, 4-5
    negotiations, *see* negotiations
    saving face (Egypt), 333
    saying no, 38
    silence, 4
    smiling, 39
    speaking clearly (Germany),
      105-106
    speaking softly
        Indonesia and
          Malaysia, 244
        Japan, 268
compliments, accepting, 38-39
Consular Information Sheets, 13
contact lenses, 12
conversation, *see* discussion topics
courtesy (Latin America), 69
credit cards, losing, 11
crime, avoiding, 15-17
    car rentals, 16
    drugs, 16-17
    getting arrested, 19-20
    in the workplace, 18
    terrorists, 18-19
    trains, 15-16
currency, exchanging, 10
    Israel, 341-342
    Taiwan, 219
Customs (U.S.), 12
Czech Republic, *see* Eastern Bloc

D

Denmark, *see* Scandinavia
dim sum, 220
dining out
    Australia, 299-300
    Belgium, 82-83
    Canada, 51-52
    China, 234-236
    Eastern Bloc, 195-196
    Egypt, 334-335
    France, 95-98
    Germany, 108
    Greece, 171-173
    India, 312-314
    Indonesia, 247
    Israel, 346-347
    Italy, 118-120
    Japan, 272-273
    Korea, 286-288
    Latin America, 71
    Malaysia, 247
    Mexico, 61-62
    New Zealand, 299-300
    Portugal, 128-130
    Russia, 205-207
    Saudi Arabia, 325-326
    Scandinavia, 186-188
    Singapore (tipping), 260
    Spain, 138-140
    Switzerland, 149-150
    Taiwan, 220-222
    United Kingdom, 158-161
dinner, *see* dining out
direct eye contact, 5, 39
discussion topics
    Australia, 297-298
    Belgium, 81
    Eastern Bloc, 194
    Egypt, 332-333
    France, 89, 93-94
    Greece, 170
    Israel, 344
    Italy, 115
    Japan (taboos), 268
    New Zealand, 297-298
    Portugal, 126
    Russia, 202
    Scandinavia, 183
    Singapore, 255-256
    Spain, 135-136
    Switzerland, 147-148
doctors
    finding, 15
    medical instructions, 11-12
dowagers, addressing, 29
dressing, 9

driver's licenses, 11
drugs (avoiding crime), 16-17
dukes and duchesses, addressing, 22-23
   daughters of a Duke, 24
   sons of a Duke, 23-24

E

earls and countesses, addressing, 25
   sons and daughters of an earl, 25-26
Eastern Bloc, 189-190
   body language, 192
   clothing, 193-194
   dining out, 195-196
      alcohol, 196
      dinner, 195
      lunch, 195
      tipping, 196
   discussion topics, 194
   giving gifts, 194
   greetings, 192
   holidays, 191
   languages, 190-191
   negotiations, 193
   punctuality, 191-192
   religions, 191
   visiting homes, 195
   women, 193
eating out, *see* dining out
economies
   China, 225
   Russia, 198-199
Egypt, 327
   body language, 331
   business hours, 329-330
   business relationships, 333
   clothing, 332
   dining out, 334-335
   eye contact, 331
   gestures, 331
   giving gifts, 333
   government, 327-328
   greetings, 330-331
      business cards, 331
      names, 330
   holidays, 328-329
      Ramadan, 329
   humor, 333
   languages, 328
   religion, 328
   saving face, 333
   topics of discussion, 332-333
   women, treatment of, 331
elderly people, respecting, 8
embassies, 355-363

England, *see* United Kingdom
entertainment, *see* dining out
equality, *see* women, treatment of
esquires, addressing, 29
exchanging currency, *see* currency
expensive gifts (taboos), 35-36
eye contact, 5, 39
   Egypt, 331
   France, 91
   Israel, 345
   Spain, 136

F

face, saving, 7
   China, 231
   Egypt, 333
   saying no, 38
   Singapore, 252-253
   Taiwan, 215-216
feng shui, 223
finding doctors, 15
flowers
   as gifts, 6
   gift-giving (taboos), 34-35
   Mexico, 61
formalities, 9
France, 85
   body language
      eye contact, 91
      smiling, 91
   business hours, 88
   clothing, 92-93
      business, 93
   dining out, 95-98
   discussion topics, 93-94
   gestures, 91-92
   giving gifts (hostess gifts), 95
   government, 86
   greetings, 90-91
   holidays, 87-88
   languages, 86
   privacy, 89
   punctuality, 88-89
   religions, 87
   visiting homes, 94-95
      hostess gifts, 95
   women, 92
French-Canadians, 45-46

G

gender gaps, *see* women, treatment of
Germany, 99
   business hours, 102
   business letters, 106

   clothing, 105
   dining out, 108
   entertainment, 107
   geography, 100
   gestures, 104-105
   giving gifts, 107
   government, 99-101
   greetings, 102-104
   holidays, 101
   jokes and humor, 106
   languages, 100
   making appointments, 102
   negotiations, 106
   personal space, 104
   punctuality, 101-102
   religions, 101
   speaking clearly, 105-106
   time zones, 102
   women, treatment of, 105
gestures, 7
   Belgium, 80
   Canada, 49-50
   China, 232
   Eastern bloc, 192
   Egypt, 331
   France, 91-92
   Germany, 104-105
   India, 308-309
   Israel, 345
   Italy, 113
   Japan, 266-267
   Korea, 282-283
   Latin America, 68-69
   Portugal, 125
   Russia, 202
   Saudi Arabia, 322
   Scandinavia, 181-182
   Singapore, 256
   United Kingdom, 155
getting arrested, 19-20
gift-giving
   Belgium, 81-82
   Canada, 50-51
   China, 233
   Eastern Bloc, 194
   Egypt, 333
   France (hostess gifts), 95
   Germany, 107
   Greece, 170-171
   India, 310-312
   Indonesia, 246
   Israel, 346
   Italy, 117
   Japan, 269-270
   Latin America, 70
   Malaysia, 246
   Mexico, 60-61
   Portugal, 127
   Russia, 204
   Saudi Arabia, 324

Singapore, 257-258
Spain, 137
Switzerland, 148
taboos, 33-36
Taiwan, 218-219
United Kingdom, 158
glasses, 12
government
    Australia, 291-293
    Belgium, 76-77
    Canada, 44-45
    China, 224-225
    Egypt, 327-328
    France, 86
    Germany, 99-101
    Greece, 165
    Hong Kong, 212
    India, 303
    Indonesia, 238
    Israel, 338
    Italy, 110
    Japan, 261
    Korea, 276
    Malaysia, 238
    Mexico, 54
    New Zealand, 291-293
    Portugal, 122
    Saudi Arabia, 316
    Scandinavia, 176-177
    Singapore, 249-250
    Switzerland, 142
    Taiwan, 212
    United Kingdom, 152
Greece, 163-164
    business relationships, 170
    class systems, 169
    clothing, 169-170
    dining out, 171-173
    discussion topics, 170
    entertainment, 171
    geography, 164-165
    giving gifts, 170-171
    government, 165
    greetings, 168-169
    holidays, 166-167
    languages, 166
    punctuality, 167-168
    religion, 166
greetings
    Australia, 295-296
    Belgium, 79-80
    Canada, 48-49
    China, 229-230
    Eastern Bloc, 192
    Egypt, 330-331
    France, 90-91
    Germany, 102-104
    Greece, 168-169
    handshakes vs. kisses, 5

India, 306-307
Indonesia, 242-244
Israel, 343-344
Italy, 114
Japan, 264-266
Korea, 280-282
Latin America, 67-68
Malaysia, 242-244
Mexico, 58
New Zealand, 295-296
Portugal, 125
Russia, 201-202
Saudi Arabia, 321
Scandinavia, 180-181
Singapore, 253
Spain, 134-135
Switzerland, 145-146
Taiwan, 216-217
United Kingdom, 154

H

haggling (Saudi Arabia), 318
hands, unclean (Saudi Arabia), 322
handshakes, 5
    India, 306
heads of state, addressing, 30
Hebrew, 338
holidays
    Australia, 293
    Belgium, 77-78
    Canada, 46-47
    China, 228
    Eastern Bloc, 191
    Egypt, 328-329
        Ramadan, 329
    France, 87-88
    Germany, 101
    Greece, 166-167
    Hong Kong, 213-214
    India, 305
    Indonesia, 239
    Israel, 340-341
    Italy, 111-112
    Japan, 262-263
    Korea, 277-278
    Latin America, 64
    Malaysia, 239
    Mexico, 55
    New Zealand, 293
    Portugal, 123-124
    Russia, 200
    Saudi Arabia, 319-320
        Ramadan, 319
    Scandinavia, 179-180
    Singapore, 251

Spain, 133-135
Switzerland, 144
Taiwan, 213-214
United Kingdom, 153
holy day taboos (food and drink), 32
Hong Kong, *see* China
Hong Kong, *see* Taiwan
honor, saving face, 7
hostess gifts
    France, 95
    Japan, 270
hosting international visitors (serving food and drink), 31-33
    cleaning your plate, 33
    holy day taboos, 32
    refusing multiple times, 33
    slurping and burping, 33
hotels, 13-14
hugs (Latin America), 68
humor, 8
    Egypt, 333
    Germany, 106
    United Kingdom, 157
Hungary, *see* Eastern Bloc

I

Iceland, *see* Scandinavia
India, 303-304
    caste systems, 307-308
    clothing, 309-310
        punjabi suits, 310
        safari suits, 310
        saris, 309-310
    gestures, 308-309
    gift-giving, 312
    government, 303
    greetings, 306-307
        titles, 307
    holidays, 305
    languages, 304
    personal space, 308
    punctuality, 305-306
    religions, 304-305
    tipping, 312
Indonesia, 237
    clothing, 245-246
    dining out, 247
    giving gifts, 246
    government, 238
    greetings, 242-244
    holidays, 239
    languages, 238
    negotiations, 241-242
    punctuality, 240-241
    religions, 238-239

speaking softly, 244
taboos, 245
women, treatment of, 245
international health insurance, 12
international visitors, hosting
  (serving food and drink), 31-33
  cleaning your plate, 33
  holy day taboos, 32
  refusing multiple times, 33
  slurping and burping, 33
invading personal space, *see*
  personal space
Ireland, *see* United Kingdom
Islam (Saudi Arabia), 317-318
Israel, 337
  body language, 344-345
  business hours, 342
  business relationships, 342-343
  clothing, 345-346
  currency, 341-342
  dining out, 346-347
  discussion topics, 344
  eye contact, 345
  gestures, 345
  giving gifts, 346
  government, 338
  greetings, 343-344
    business cards, 344
    titles, 343
  holidays, 340-341
  languages, 338-339
  personal space, 344
  punctuality, 342
  religion, 339-340
    Ashkenazi Jews, 339
    Sephardic Jews, 340
  women, 345
Italy, 109-120
  clothing, 116
  dining out, 118-120
  discussion topics, 115
  entertainment, 118
  geography, 109-110
  gestures, 113
  giving gifts, 117
  government, 110
  greetings, 114
  holidays, 111-112
  languages, 111
  negotiations, 116
  personal space, 113
  punctuality, 112-113
  religions, 111-112
  visiting homes, 117
  women, 115
itineraries, 11

J

Japan
  accentuating the negative, 268
  body language, 264
    bowing, 264-266
  business hours, 263-264
  clothing, 267
  dining out, 272-273
  discussion topics (taboos), 268
  entertainment, 270-272
  geography, 261
  gestures, 266-267
  giving gifts, 269-270
  government, 261
  greetings, bowing, 264-266
  holidays, 262-263
  languages, 262
  negotiations, 268-269
  personal space, 266
  punctuality, 263
  religions, 262
  speaking softly, 268
  visiting homes, 270-272
Jewish holidays, 340
jokes, 8
  Germany, 106
  United Kingdom, 157

K

karoke bars (China), 235
kings (Saudi Arabia), 316
kissing as greetings, 5
knights and wife, addressing,
  28-29
Korea, *see* South Korea

L

languages
  Australia, 293
  avoiding silence, 4
  Belgium, 77
  Canada, 46
  China, 226-227
  Eastern Bloc, 190-191
  Egypt, 328
  France, 86
  Germany, 100
  Greece, 166
  Hong Kong, 213
  India, 304
  Indonesia, 238

  Israel, 338-339
  Italy, 111
  Japan, 262
  Korea, 276-277
  Latin America, 64
  learning phrases, 4-5
  Malaysia, 238
  Mexico, 54
  New Zealand, 293
  Portugal, 122-123
  Russia, 199
  Saudi Arabia, 316-317
  Scandinavia, 177-178
  Singapore, 250
  Spain, 132
  Switzerland, 142-143
  Taiwan, 213
  United Kingdom, 152
Latin America, 63
  business relationships, 66-67
    business cards, 68
  chivalry, 69
  dining out, 71
  gestures, 68-69
  gift-giving, 70
  greetings, 67-68
    hugs, 68
    titles, 67-68
  holidays, 64
  languages, 64
  punctuality, 64-65
    making appointments,
      64-65
line-waiting, 37-38
lodging (hotels), 13-14
lunch, *see* dining out

M

making appointments
  Germany, 102
  Latin America, 64-65
  Russia, 201
Malaysia, 237
  clothing, 245-246
  dining out, 247
  giving gifts, 246
  government, 238
  greetings, 242-244
  holidays, 239
  languages, 238
  negotiations, 241-242
  punctuality, 240-241
  religions, 238-239
  speaking softly, 244
  taboos, 245
  women, treatment of, 245

manners, *see* table manners
marquess/marchioness,
  addressing, 24-25
    sons and daughters of a
    marquess, 25
medical instructions, 11-12
meishi (Japan), 265-266
Mexico, 53
  business hours, 56
  clothing, 59
  dining out, 61-62
  entertainment, 61
  gift-giving, 60-61
  government, 54
  greetings, 58
  holidays, 55
  languages, 54
  negotiations, 60
  personal relationships, 57-58
  personal space, 58
  punctuality, 56
  religion, 55
  social status, 56-57
  tactfulness, 60
  womens' roles, 59
money, *see* currency
music (Portugal), 128

N

names, *see* titles
national anthems, 8
negotiations
  Australia, 298-299
  Belgium, 81
  Canada, 50
  China, 230-231
  Eastern Bloc, 193
  Germany, 106
  Indonesia, 241-242
  Italy, 116
  Japan, 268-269
  Korea, 284
  Malaysia, 241-242
  Mexico, 60
  New Zealand, 298-299
  Portugal, 127
  Scandinavia, 184-185
  Singapore, 251
  Switzerland, 146-147
  United Kingdom, 157
New Zealand, 290
  clothing, 296-297
  dining out, 299-300
    pubs, 300
    tea time, 299-300
    tipping, 300

discussion topics, 297-298
government, 291-293
greetings, 295-296
history of, 291-292
holidays, 293
languages, 293
negotiations, 298-299
punctuality, 294
  business hours, 294
  time zones, 294
religions, 293
times to visit, 293
visiting homes, 299
Northern Ireland, *see* United
Kingdom
Norway, *see* Scandinavia

O-P

officials, *see* government
older people, respecting, 8

packing, 12
passports, 10
personal space, 7, 36-37
  China, 231
  Egypt, 331
  Germany, 104
  India, 308
  Israel, 344
  Italy, 113
  Japan, 266
  Mexico, 58
  Russia, 202
  Saudi Arabia, 321-322
  Singapore, 255
  Taiwan, 217
  United Kingdom, 155
photographs, taking
  (Saudi Arabia), 318
pinching women (Italy), 115
Poland, *see* Eastern Bloc
Portugal, 121
  body language, 125
  clothing, 126
  dining out, 128-130
  discussion topics, 126
  geography, 121-122
  giving gifts, 127
  government, 122
  greetings, 125
  holidays, 123-124
  languages, 122-123
  music, 128
  negotiations, 127
  punctuality, 124-125
  religions, 123
  visiting homes, 128
  women, 126

prescriptions, 12
prince consorts, addressing, 22
princes and princesses,
  addressing, 22
privacy
  Belgium, 79
  France, 89
pubs
  Australia and New
    Zealand, 300
  hours (United Kingdom), 153
punctuality, 9, 36
  Australia, 294
  Belgium, 78
  Canada, 47-48
  China, 228-229
  Eastern Bloc, 191-192
  France, 88-89
  Germany, 101-102
  Greece, 167-168
  Hong Kong, 214
  India, 305-306
  Indonesia, 240-241
  Israel, 342
  Italy, 112-113
  Japan, 263
  Korea, 278-280
  Latin America, 64-65
    making appointments,
    64-65
  Malaysia, 240-241
  Mexico, 56
  New Zealand, 29
  Portugal, 124-125
  Russia, 200-201
  Scandinavia, 179
  Singapore, 251
  Switzerland, 144
  Taiwan, 214
  United Kingdom, 153-154
punjabi suits (India), 310
purchasing items, *see* business
  transactions

R

Ramadan
  Egypt, 329
  Saudi Arabia, 319
religions
  Australia, 293
  Belgium, 77
  Canada, 46
  China, 227-228
  Eastern Bloc, 191
  Egypt, 328
  France, 87
  Germany, 101
  Greece, 166

Hong Kong, 213
India, 304-305
Indonesia, 238-239
Israel, 339-340
    Ashkenazi Jews, 339
    Sephardic Jews, 340
Italy, 111-112
Japan, 262
Korea, 277
Malaysia, 238-239
Mexico, 55
New Zealand, 293
Portugal, 123
Russia, 200
Saudi Arabia, 317-318
    religious police, 323
Scandinavia, 178
Spain, 133-135
Switzerland, 143
Taiwan, 213
United Kingdom, 153
respect, 8
royalty, addressing, 21-29
    baronet and wife, 28
    barons and baronesses, 27-28
    daughters of a Duke, 24
    dowagers, 29
    dukes and duchesses, 22-23
    earls and countesses, 25
    esquires, 29
    knights and wife, 28-29
    marquess/marchioness, 24-25
    prince consorts, 22
    princes and princesses, 22
    sons and daughters of a
      marquess, 25
    sons and daughters of a
      viscount, 26-27
    sons and daughters of an earl,
      25-26
    sons of a Duke, 23-24
    United Kingdom, 155
    viscounts and viscountesses,
      26
Russia, 197
    clothing, 203
    Cold War, 203-204
    dining out, 205-208
    discussion topics, 202
    economy, 198-199
    entertainment, 205
    geography, 197-199
    giving gifts, 204
    greetings, 201-202
    holidays, 200
    languages, 199
    personal space, 202
    punctuality, 200-201
    religions, 200
    visiting homes, 204
    women, 202-203

S

safari suits (India), 310
safety (hotel), 13-14
sarcasm, 8
saris (India), 309-310
Saudi Arabia, 315-316
    best times to visit, 316
    business hours, 320
    business relationships, 320
    buying things, 318
    clothing, 323-324
    dining out, 325-326
    gestures, 322
    gift-giving, 324
    government, 316
    greetings, 321
    holidays, 319-320
    language, 316-317
    personal space, 321-322
    religion, 317-318
      religious police, 323
    taking photographs, 318
    visiting homes, 325
    women, 322-323
saunas (Scandinavia), 185
saving face, 7
    China, 231
    Egypt, 333-334
    saying no, 38
    Singapore, 252
    Taiwan, 215-216
saying no, 38
Scandinavia
    banking, 177
    body language, 181-182
    business hours, 179
    clothing, 182-183
    dining out, 186-188
      tea time, 186
      tipping, 187
      toasting (Skoal!), 187
    discussion topics, 183
    geography, 176-177
    government, 176-177
    greetings, 180-181
    holidays, 179-180
    languages, 177-178
    negotiations, 184-185
    punctuality, 179
    religions, 178
    visiting homes, 185
    weather, 177
    women, 182
Scotland, *see* United Kingdom
security, *see* crime, avoiding
Sephardic Jews (Israel), 340
siestas, 133
silence, embracing, 4

Singapore
    clothing, 257
    dining out, tipping, 260
    discussion topics, 255-256
    entertainment, 259
    geography, 249
    gestures, 256
    giving gifts, 257-258
      taboos, 258
    government, 249-250
    greetings, 253-254
    holidays, 251
    languages, 250
    negotiations, 251
    personal space, 255
    punctuality, 251
    saving face, 252
    visiting homes, 259-260
    women, 257
slang, avoiding, 4
slurping, 33
smiling, 39
    France, 91
    Japan, 264
smoking, 10
social classes (India), 307-308
social status (Mexico), 56-57
socializing (Mexico), 61
South Korea, 275
    body language, 282
    business relationships, 284-285
    clothing, 283-284
    dining out, 286-288
    entertainment, 286
    family rankings, 280
    gestures, 282-283
    government, 276
    greetings, 280-282
    holidays, 277-278
    languages, 276-277
    negotiations, 284
    punctuality, 278-280
      business hours, 278
    religions, 277
    visiting homes, 285
    women, treatment of, 283
Spain, 131
    body language (eye
      contact), 136
    business hours, 133-134
    business relationships, 134
    class systems, 133
    clothing, 137
    dining out, 138-140
      tapas time, 139
      tipping, 140
    discussion topics, 135-136
    geography, 131-132
    giving gifts, 137
    greetings, 134-135

holidays, 133
languages, 132
religions, 133
visiting homes, 137
women, treatment of, 136
speaking
English in foreign countries
(avoiding slang), 4
learning languages, 4-5
speaking clearly (Germany),
105-106
speaking softly
China, 231-232
Indonesia, 244
Japan, 268
Malaysia, 244
standing in line, 37-38
Sweden, *see* Scandinavia
Switzerland
body language, 147
business hours, 144-145
clothing, 148
dining out, 149-150
discussion topics, 147-148
entertainment, 148-149
geography, 141-142
giving gifts, 148
government, 142
greetings, 145-146
holidays, 144
languages, 142-143
negotiations, 146-147
posture, 147
punctuality, 144
religions, 143
visiting homes, 149
women, treatment of, 146

T

table manners, *see* dining out
taboos
clothing, 37
discussion topics
Egypt, 332-333
France, 89
food and drink, 32
Israel, 347
gift-giving
Belgium, 82
colors, 34
expense, 35
flowers, 34
India, 310
wine and liquor, 35
wrapping, 35
Indonesia, 245

Malaysia, 245
taking photographs
(Saudi Arabia), 318
Taiwan, 211
attitudes, 217-218
business hours, 214-215
business relationships, 215
saving face, 215-216
clothing, 218
dining out, 220-222
entertainment, 219
exchanging currency, 219
giving gifts, 218-219
governments, 212
greetings, 216-217
holidays, 213-214
languages, 213
personal space, 217
punctuality, 214
religions, 213
times to visit, 212
tapas time (Spain), 139
tea houses (Taiwan), 222
tea time
Australia and New Zealand,
299-300
Scandinavia, 186
United Kingdom, 159-160
telling jokes, 8
terrorists, 18-19
thieves, avoiding, 13
time zones
Australia and New
Zealand, 294
Belgium, 78-79
Canada, 47-48
China, 228-229
Germany, 102
timeliness, *see* punctuality
tipping, *see* dining out
titles, *see* greetings
toasting, *see* dining out
topics of discussion, *see* discussion
topics
trains (avoiding crime), 15-16
traveler's checks (Saudi Arabia),
318

U

U.S. Customs, 12
unclean hands (Saudi Arabia), 322
United Kingdom, 151
addressing royalty, 155
business relationships, 154
clothing, 156
dining out, 158-161
entertainment, 158

gender gaps, 156
geography, 151-152
gestures, 155
giving gifts, 158
government, 152
greetings, 154
holidays, 153
jokes and humor, 157
languages, 152
negotiations, 157
personal space, 155
punctuality, 153-154
religions, 153
women, 156

V

vacations, *see* holidays
vaccine records, 12
viscounts and viscountesses,
addressing, 26
sons and daughters of a
viscount, 26-27
visas, 10
visiting homes, *see* gift-giving
vodka (Russia), 207-208

W

waiters (France), 95
women, treatment of
Belgium, 80-81
China, 232
Eastern Bloc, 193
Egypt, 331
France, 92
Germany, 105
Indonesia, 245
Israel, 345
Italy, 115
Korea, 283
Malaysia, 245
Mexican, 59
Portugal, 126
Russia, 202-203
Saudi Arabia, 322-323
Scandinavia, 182
Singapore, 257
Spain, 136
Switzerland, 146
United Kingdom, 156
wrapping gifts, 6
Japan, 270
taboos, 35